VOLUME 611

MAY 2007

THE ANNALS

of The American Academy of Political
and Social Science

PHYLLIS KANISS, *Executive Editor*

The Politics of Consumption/
The Consumption of Politics

Special Editors of this Volume

DHAVAN V. SHAH
LEWIS FRIEDLAND
DOUGLAS M. McLEOD
University of Wisconsin–Madison

MICHELLE R. NELSON
University of Illinois at Urbana-Champaign

SAGE Publications
Los Angeles • London • New Delhi • Singapore

The American Academy of Political and Social Science

3814 Walnut Street, Fels Institute of Government, University of Pennsylvania,
Philadelphia, PA 19104-6197; (215) 746-6500; (215) 573-3003 (fax); www.aapss.org

Origin and Purpose. The Academy was organized December 14, 1889, to promote the progress of political and social science, especially through publications and meetings. The Academy does not take sides in controverted questions, but seeks to gather and present reliable information to assist the public in forming an intelligent and accurate judgment.

Meetings. The Academy occasionally holds a meeting in the spring extending over two days.

Publications. THE ANNALS of The American Academy of Political and Social Science is the bimonthly publication of the Academy. Each issue contains articles on some prominent social or political problem, written at the invitation of the editors. Also, monographs are published from time to time, numbers of which are distributed to pertinent professional organizations. These volumes constitute important reference works on the topics with which they deal, and they are extensively cited by authorities throughout the United States and abroad. The papers presented at the meetings of the Academy are included in THE ANNALS.

Membership. Each member of the Academy receives THE ANNALS and may attend the meetings of the Academy. Membership is open only to individuals. Annual dues: $84.00 for the regular paperbound edition (clothbound, $121.00). Members may also purchase single issues of THE ANNALS for $17.00 each (clothbound, $26.00). Student memberships are available for $53.00.

Subscriptions. THE ANNALS of The American Academy of Political and Social Science (ISSN 0002-7162) (J295) is published six times annually—in January, March, May, July, September, and November—by Sage Publications, 2455 Teller Road, Thousand Oaks, CA 91320. Telephone: (800) 818-SAGE (7243) and (805) 499-9774; Fax/Order line: (805) 499-0871; e-mail: journals@sagepub.com. Copyright © 2007 by The American Academy of Political and Social Science. Institutions may subscribe to THE ANNALS at the annual rate: $612.00 (clothbound, $692.00). Single issues of THE ANNALS may be obtained by individuals who are not members of the Academy for $34.00 each (clothbound, $47.00). Single issues of THE ANNALS have proven to be excellent supplementary texts for classroom use. Direct inquiries regarding adoptions to THE ANNALS c/o Sage Publications (address below). Periodicals postage paid at Thousand Oaks, California, and at additional mailing offices.

All correspondence concerning membership in the Academy, dues renewals, inquiries about membership status, and/or purchase of single issues of THE ANNALS should be sent to THE ANNALS c/o Sage Publications, 2455 Teller Road, Thousand Oaks, CA 91320.Telephone: (800) 818-SAGE (7243) and (805) 499-9774; Fax/Order line: (805) 499-0871; e-mail: journals@sagepub.com. *Please note that orders under $30 must be prepaid.* Sage affiliates in London and India will assist institutional subscribers abroad with regard to orders, claims, and inquiries for both subscriptions and single issues.

Printed on acid-free paper

THE ANNALS

Editorial Office: 3814 Walnut Street, Fels Institute for Government, University of Pennsylvania, Philadelphia, PA 19104-6197.

For information about membership* (individuals only) and subscriptions (institutions), address:
Sage Publications
2455 Teller Road
Thousand Oaks, CA 91320

For Sage Publications: Joseph Riser and Esmeralda Hernandez

From India and South Asia, write to:
SAGE PUBLICATIONS INDIA Pvt Ltd
B-42 Panchsheel Enclave, P.O. Box 4109
New Delhi 110 017
INDIA

From Europe, the Middle East, and Africa, write to:
SAGE PUBLICATIONS LTD
1 Oliver's Yard, 55 City Road
London EC1Y 1SP
UNITED KINGDOM

*Please note that members of the Academy receive THE ANNALS with their membership.
International Standard Serial Number ISSN 0002-7162
International Standard Book Number ISBN 978-1-4129-5935-3 (Vol. 611, 2007) paper
International Standard Book Number ISBN 978-1-4129-5934-6 (Vol. 611, 2007) cloth
Manufactured in the United States of America. First printing, May 2007.

The articles appearing in *The Annals* are abstracted or indexed in Academic Abstracts, Academic Search, America: History and Life, Asia Pacific Database, Book Review Index,CABAbstracts Database, Central Asia: Abstracts &Index, Communication Abstracts, Corporate ResourceNET, Criminal Justice Abstracts, Current Citations Express, Current Contents: Social & Behavioral Sciences, Documentation in Public Administration, e-JEL, EconLit, Expanded Academic Index, Guide to Social Science & Religion in Periodical Literature, Health Business FullTEXT, HealthSTAR FullTEXT, Historical Abstracts, International Bibliography of the Social Sciences, International Political Science Abstracts, ISI Basic Social Sciences Index, Journal of Economic Literature on CD, LEXIS-NEXIS, MasterFILE FullTEXT, Middle East: Abstracts&Index, North Africa: Abstracts&Index, PAIS International, Periodical Abstracts, Political Science Abstracts, Psychological Abstracts, PsycINFO, Sage Public Administration Abstracts, Scopus, Social Science Source, Social Sciences Citation Index, Social Sciences Index Full Text, Social Services Abstracts, SocialWork Abstracts, Sociological Abstracts, Southeast Asia: Abstracts& Index, Standard Periodical Directory (SPD), TOPICsearch, Wilson OmniFileV, and Wilson Social Sciences Index/Abstracts, and are available on microfilm from ProQuest, Ann Arbor, Michigan.

Information about membership rates, institutional subscriptions, and back issue prices may be found on the facing page.

Advertising. Current rates and specifications may be obtained by writing to The Annals Advertising and Promotion Manager at the Thousand Oaks office (address above).

Claims. Claims for undelivered copies must be made no later than six months following month of publication. The publisher will supply missing copies when losses have been sustained in transit and when the reserve stock will permit.

Change of Address. Six weeks' advance notice must be given when notifying of change of address to ensure proper identification. Please specify name of journal. POSTMASTER: Send address changes to The Annals of The American Academy of Political and Social Science, c/o Sage Publications, 2455 Teller Road, Thousand Oaks, CA 91320.

THE ANNALS

OF THE AMERICAN ACADEMY OF POLITICAL AND SOCIAL SCIENCE

Volume 611   May 2007

IN THIS ISSUE:

The Politics of Consumption/The Consumption of Politics

Special Editors: DHAVAN V. SHAH
LEWIS FRIEDLAND
DOUGLAS M. MCLEOD
MICHELLE R. NELSON

FORTHCOMING

Religious Pluralism and Civil Society
Special Editor: WADE CLARK ROOF
Volume 612, July 2007

Social Entrepreneurship for Women and Minorities
Special Editors: TIMOTHY BATES, WILLIAM JACKSON III,
and JAMES H. JOHNSON Jr.
Volume 613, September 2007

INTRODUCTION

The Politics of
Consumption/
The
Consumption
of Politics

By
DHAVAN V. SHAH,
DOUGLAS M. McLEOD,
LEWIS FRIEDLAND,
and
MICHELLE R. NELSON

As consumer culture pervades the social life of citizens in America and Europe, it becomes increasingly important to clarify the relationship between consumption and citizenship. With this in mind, faculty and students at the University of Wisconsin organized a conference titled "The Politics of Consumption/The Consumption of Politics." Held in October 2006, the meeting provided a forum for leading scholars to discuss the interplay of markets, media, politics, and the citizen-consumer. Revised and expanded versions of the papers they presented are collected in this volume with the goal of advancing this emerging area of inquiry. It is our hope that the essays and research papers we have collected here help define the next wave of theory building and research inquiry on the intersections of consumer culture, civic culture, and mass culture.

Keywords: citizen-consumers; competitive consumption; civic engagement; lifestyle politics; materialism; political branding; socially conscious consumption; taste cultures

Nearly a half century before Thorstein Veblen published *The Theory of the Leisure Class* (1899/1994), his now-classic refutation of neoclassical notions of consumption as utility maximization, another writer was critiquing American society's materialistic values. Henry David Thoreau's call to "simplify, simplify" in *Walden* (1854/1995), his chronicle of more than two years of austere living on the shores of Walden Pond, still resonates with contemporary readers struggling to find ways to exist in ecological and social harmony. Thoreau's prescient question—"What is the use of a house if you haven't got a tolerable planet to put it on?"—demands concerted attention in the political and environmental climate of the early twenty-first century.

Likewise, Veblen's (1899/1994) assertions, echoed and expanded by Bourdieu (1979/1984), that consumers' preferences are determined socially, a consequence not of need but of individuals' positions in social hierarchies, continue

DOI: 10.1177/0002716207299647

to serve as a touchstone for academics troubled by the advancement of consumer society. Part of this apprehension lies in the belief that consumers no longer just imitate the consumption patterns of those situated a rung or two above them in status but also imitate those at the top of the social ladder (Schor 1998). People work too hard and spend too much in the pursuit of products and lifestyles that always remain beyond reach.

Although this perspective has been criticized for underestimating how often consumption patterns emanate from lower levels of social hierarchies and over-estimating the importance of class in determining the social positioning of taste, such critiques seem to miss the broader argument being advanced by critics of contemporary consumption, who assert that people are misled by an overly mate-rialistic mass culture, mainly in the form of commercialized mass media, to focus on the superficial and synthetic. The resulting consumer culture emphasizes acquisitiveness and individualism at the expense of civic-mindedness. The result, they argue, is the decline of civil society in favor of consumer society.

This position is not without controversy. Others scholars argue that civic cul-ture and consumer culture are not antithetical; instead, they may be inherently inseparable. As Schudson (1981) contended, "Not only are people's individual needs defined socially, but their individual needs include a need for social con-nection which is sometimes expressed materially." This is most obvious in the political consumerism associated with "lifestyle politics" that has come to func-tion as a form of civic participation for many people (Bennett 1998; Schudson 1999). This view asserts that a sizable amount of consumption has become so steeped in the concerns of citizenship that "it is no longer possible to cut the deck neatly between citizenship and civic duty, on one side, and consumption and self interest, on the other" (Scammell 2000).

This is illustrated by the rise of socially conscious consumers—environmentalists, antiglobalists, fair trade and sweatshop activists, freecyclers, and downshifters—who purchase (or "buycott") products in ways that demonstrate public-spiritedness and global expansiveness (Stolle, Hooghe, and Micheletti 2005). Resounding some of Thoreau's appeals, these forms of political consumerism weave together various threads of personal consciousness and political advocacy: the fear of ecological degradation, the rejection of materialism and the market, the protection of children and the disadvantaged, and the inherent integrity of human beings.

Such socially conscious consumption has become as much a badge of belonging as the status conscious consumption critiqued by Veblen and others. Indeed, the same cultural capital that structures status consumption also may shape patterns of political consumerism and civic engagement, with the social identity reflected in particular forms of consumption also creating access to networks of opportunity and participation (Keum et al. 2004). Accordingly, collective iden-tity may be fashioned and maintained through brand subcultures (e.g., iPod, Jeep, Patagonia), lifestyle consumption (e.g., wine tastings, biker bars, fair trade cafes), and gift giving (Belk 1988; Thompson 2000). It remains to be seen whether these consumer alignments are beneficial for civil society in the long term, as traditional forms of participation require concerted revitalization in response to their apparent decline.

Of course, consumption and politics intersect in other ways as well. The state and corporations jointly shape the course of consumer regulation and protection efforts and often make decisions that advance commercial interests over public concerns. Political campaigns are now grounded in marketing principles, with branding of political candidates and issues, targeted political advertising, staged media events, and market segmentation strategies all commonplace. Even social movements and corporations have politicized consumption by structuring action and initiatives around products and services through buycotts, cause-related marketing, logo politics, and online consumer activism (Cohen 2003; Hilton 2003; Scammell 2000).

Political campaigns are now grounded in marketing principles, with branding of political candidates and issues, targeted political advertising, staged media events, and market segmentation strategies all commonplace.

It is with these issues in mind that faculty and students at the University of Wisconsin organized an international conference titled "The Politics of Consumption/The Consumption of Politics."[1] Held October 19-21, 2006, the meeting provided a forum for the participants, leading scholars from Europe and North America, to discuss the intersection of consumption, citizenship, media, and marketing. We shared the papers collected in this volume, exchanging perspectives on research and theory that substantially advance this emerging area of inquiry. It is our hope that the essays and research papers we have collected here help define the next wave of research on the intersections of consumer culture, civic culture, and mass culture.

Themes and Structure

The conference drew together a number of central themes that were used to structure this volume. These themes revolve around the shifting conception of the consumer and consumption and its alignment with the changing nature and meaning of citizenship; the relations between consumers, citizens, and the state; consumer and citizen responses to the market; the branding of politicians and social movements; and political consumerism as a form of activism. Taken together, these essays not only point out the main issues, but also the tensions that will mark the next wave of research on the politics of consumption.

The core theme, which runs from the opening to the concluding article, concerns consumerism and its discontents. Schor opens this volume (after having closed the conference) by resurrecting the valuable contributions of major consumer critics—Veblen, Adorno, Horkheimer, Marcuse, Galbraith, and Baudrillard—which in recent years have been supplanted by micro-level approaches to the problems of consumerism. She argues that the emergence of problems associated with globalization, environmental degradation, and excessive consumption necessitate a reconsideration of critical macro-level approaches to understanding modern consumer society. Schor reviews and critiques each of these classic contributions and then isolates their contemporary relevance for a rebirth of macro-level social inquiry. Yet Schor also calls for a "revalorizing" of consumption, a shift toward recognition of its potential value to community life instead of its unthinking denigration as a scourge on social relations.

This theme is further advanced by Friedland, Shah, Lee, Rademacher, Atkinson, and Hove, who analyze the field of cultural consumption in the contemporary United States, drawing on the methods of correspondence analysis employed by Bourdieu (1979/1984). We observe many parallels between 1960s French society and millennial U.S. society in terms of the determinants of taste within the field structure observed by Bourdieu yet also find that the composition of cultural capital in America differs in some important respects. Most notably, we discover that more refined and nurturing consumer practices align with news consumption and civic engagement, with this communal orientation at odds with, and potentially losing ground to, patterns of cultural consumption stressing coarseness, excess, and an individual orientation. The domination of individual over communal concerns in the United States reveals a more gendered and ideological positioning of taste cultures than in 1960s France, with this macro-social perspective providing insights about some of the shifts Schor highlights.

Other scholars point to the increasing penetration of consumption into the heart of the state and political process, emphasizing the centrality of government in the politics of consumption and the tensions between conceptions of the public as citizen-consumers. Livingstone and Lunt examine how the United Kingdom's Office of Communications has affected media regulation. Central to this analysis is an implicit shift in the conception of the regulatory beneficiary from citizen to consumer. By analyzing the political discourse of the Office of Communications, as well as information gathered from interviews with key players and focus groups with members of the public, the authors reveal the impact of changing conceptions of citizens/consumers and the potential to privilege the interests of powerful stakeholders.

Hilton further explores the shape of civil society, regulatory systems, and citizen/consumer rights. Operating in a different register, he considers how consumption itself, particularly consumer protection regimes, became a political project that was central to the post–World War II state. Hilton engages in a comparative historical analysis of consumer protection initiatives that emerged in the East and the West during the latter half of the twentieth century. His survey covers the unique constellations of protection activities that developed to maintain consumer confidence and economic vitality, which included government policy, citizen initiatives, and consumer media. In the process, Hilton illuminates a broader landscape of consumer protection that has transcended national boundaries to provide numerous consumer benefits; however, this optimism is tempered by a corresponding shift in the conceptions of consumer protection as focused on consumer choice, which disadvantages less affluent citizens.

Cohen demonstrates how consumption regimes reshape urban space itself, with large-scale planning projects linked to urban renewal systematically organized around the process of suburbanization and the attempt to preserve the viability of the downtown. Cohen's historical analysis reminds us that the investigation of consumption and civic engagement occurs within local contexts. She compares the power granted to department stores in the retail and urban development of New Haven and Boston in the post-WWII era. She shows how the interplay of politicians, policy makers, and national retailers, with little consideration of diverse audiences and local business offerings, led to the downfall of department stores and revitalization efforts. In doing this, she calls into question the public subsidy of private corporations without consideration of the consequences for civic spaces and corporate civic responsibility.

This question of the place of consumption in shaping everyday meaning is at the heart of the articles presented by Arnould, Thompson, and Belk. Arnould argues that given that market-mediated consumer culture is a dominant social fact of our age, moral denunciations of consumption have played themselves out in ritualized forms. New practices of citizenship will have to navigate the market, not operate in opposition to it. After considering the meaning and potential for consumer agency as well as the assumptions behind anticonsumerist ideologies, Arnould forcefully argues that consumer escape is not possible—or even desirable. He invokes market cases involving microbreweries and the Fair Trade movement to argue that political action is possible within consumption practices and existing market structures.

Thompson takes a different view, understanding the economy of consumption as "carnivalesque," following Bakhtin, and arguing for muckraking scholarship that criticizes the actual functioning of the market system. He contends that most political critiques of consumption are moralistic, a thematic point he shares with Schudson, below. Unlike Schudson, however, he traces this moralistic turn to the nineteenth-century fusion of Calvinism and patriarchy. In its place, he calls on scholars to critically analyze the constitutive networks and material consequences of market systems with the goal of mobilizing citizen-consumers. These activist-consumers could then combat the problems plaguing specific facets of consumer culture.

Belk approaches problematic aspects of contemporary consumer culture from another angle. He points to the emergence of a sharing economy within consumption as an alternative to both the market and the gift economy. The potential of sharing as an alternative form of distributing resources has a long and personal history. He notes that while sharing is routinely practiced within the family unit, its potential is largely unrecognized as a community resource, citing the recent emergence of car sharing as an example of the potential of sharing. The Internet has reinvigorated public interest in the concept of sharing by introducing file sharing, open-source code, bulletin boards, shareware, Web logs, online gaming, Wikipedia, and other distributed practices. However, he argues that the intellectual property rights movement threatens to erode the altruistic spirit of this public space with one that promotes self-interest.

Nelson, Rademacher, and Paek explore the underpinnings of sharing and civic identity through a case study of consumers in a second-order, online consumption community: Freecycle.org. Results show that these individuals hold downshifting attitudes (favor less work and less consumption). Yet the downshifting does not necessarily mean increased civic engagement in a traditional sense. Rather, political and civic engagement for this group included political consumption and digital forms of political participation. We contend that the time displacement theory—that less time working and shopping means more civic engagement—is too simplified to account for the interplay between contemporary consumption and participation.

Social movements and issue publics have rediscovered consumption as a focal agenda setter. Micheletti and Stolle explore the antisweatshop movement as an agent of social change. The authors trace the history of sweatshops and the movement that has evolved to oppose them. They identify four types of movement actors (i.e., unions, antisweatshop activist groups, international humanitarian organizations, and Internet spin doctors) and review the nature of their persuasive strategies and tactics. This is followed by an explication of the roles that consumers play in this dynamics of sweatshop issues. The article culminates in an assessment of the effectiveness of the movement. Micheletti and Stolle demonstrate how the antisweatshop movement has become a global advocacy network, growing in scope, density, and sophistication, and using the Internet as its primary organizational mode, another emergent theme.

At the same time, politics itself is increasingly subject to the practices of branding, as demonstrated by Scammell. She begins by providing an overview of the branding concept, and then demonstrates how the branding orientation has been integrated into the political arena by tracing the re-branding of Tony Blair prior to the 2005 U.K. general election. That is, insights from market research were used to create message strategies that reframed the images of Blair and the Labour Party. She argues that the Blair case exemplifies a fundamental shift in the marketing of candidates away from a mass media model (i.e., using mass media and advertising to set the political agenda) to a consumer model (i.e., conceptualizing citizens as consumers, using market research to understand them, and a broader array of brand communication, including personal and interactive channels, to persuade them).

Bennett and Lagos extend this argument, as well as issues raised by Micheletti and Stolle, to demonstrate how younger activists are increasingly moving away from governance altogether in the attempt to create nongovernmental regulatory regimes via the Web, and how, in particular, the focus on branding and "logo logic" gives both form and structure to these efforts. They examine the use of "logo campaigns" by political activist groups, a practice that attaches critical political messages to popular consumer brands (i.e., Nike or Starbucks) to draw attention to larger political, economic, or environmental issues (i.e., sweatshop labor or environmental degradation). They identify the role of logo campaigns in building consumer awareness, holding the brand hostage, sustaining long-term campaigns, fostering political relationships, and contributing to nongovernmental regulation. However, potential impediments to logo campaigns include the proliferation of uncoordinated messages and activist groups, and the limits of applying such campaigns beyond certain high-profile brands.

Expanding on the centrality of online communications for the politics of consumption and the consumption of politics, DeVreese charts how the shift to the Net itself has become a primary source of political information for younger cohorts and in the process demonstrates that the very forms of consuming politics are changing. His study of the Internet habits of young people in the Netherlands shows that time spent online is not antithetical to political participation. In fact, most of the online activities, including those unrelated to media or politics, were positively related to political participation. Furthermore, by examining a wide range of possible indicators of participation, DeVreese suggests that traditional notions of civic and political engagement should be expanded to include active and passive forms of engagement. More refined views of civic engagement and online activities offer a hopeful presentation of youth civic engagement.

This shifting nature of civic and political participation is again taken up by Shah, McLeod, Kim, Lee, Gotlieb, Ho, and Brevik. We theorize a communication mediation model of political consumerism (i.e., consumer behaviors that are shaped by a desire to express and support political and ethical perspectives), which we then test using original panel survey data. These panel data allow us to test cross-section and panel models of individual difference and aggregate change based on demographics, dispositional factors, communication variables, and consumption orientations. Our analyses reveal a generally consistent pattern across the static and change models: conventional and online news consumption encourages political talk and certain consumption orientations, which in turn lead to political consumption. The relative consistency of the results across models indicates that both conventional and online news use contribute to political consumerism indirectly through their influence on mediating factors.

The final article by Schudson advances themes that he has developed over many years and that he synthesized for the opening address of the conference. It provides a strong counterpoint to the civic republicanism at the core of U.S. political discourse that has long viewed consumption as opposed to citizenship. Schudson argues against the moralistic view of participation in the marketplace as an inferior form of activity to participation in politics. Challenging the perspective that consumption lacks virtue in its own right, or that it displaces civic life, Schudson concludes that critics who make invidious distinctions between the roles of citizens and consumers are misguided. He notes that both political and consumer behavior can be motivated by either enhancing the public good or satisfying egocentric needs. Consumption can be altruistic (e.g., gift giving), political (e.g., boycotts and buycotts) and democratic (e.g., the "egalitarian ambience" of McDonald's). Conversely, civic and political activity may serve to advance personal desires or to enhance the egotistical joy of victory. Through this argument, Schudson attempts to restore perspective to conceptions of citizenship and consumption, adding this unique perspective to the other contentions and conclusions that populate this volume.

[B]oth political and consumer behavior can be motivated by either enhancing the public good or satisfying egocentric needs.

Controversies and Opportunities

From these articles we can synthesize a numbers of noteworthy controversies and opportunities toward which future theory, research, and interpretation on the politics of consumption should be directed. We purposefully sketch these sites of contestation in very broad terms, for each domain holds considerable space to determine the specific parameters of the scope of study. Nonetheless, this delineation is a call for concerted attention around these issues and the continued development of this interdisciplinary terrain:

1. *The consumer critique: Didactic and moralistic.* What do we still have to learn from consumer critiques as scholars concerned with the politics of consumption and the consumption of politics? How do these critiques inform and suggest avenues for action regarding the challenges of the current political and environmental climate? Are elements of this critique moralistic and do they demand rethinking? What is the value of complicating the consumer/citizen contrast?
2. *The power to create change: The citizen and the state.* What is the role of the state and corporate interests in the politics of consumption? Should we focus our scholarly attention and activist agendas on the state-corporation over the citizen-consumer given the centrality and power of the former? How can citizen-consumers and social movements influence nation-states and corporations?
3. *A hyphenated public: Consumers, citizens, or citizen-consumers.* What are the promise and perils of a hyphenated conception of the public as a group of citizen-consumers? Do politicians and the state increasingly view citizens as consumers and approach them in this manner? Can citizens ever escape the market and would this even be a desirable

end? Is there hope for a commons, where sharing is the norm rather than the exception? How can citizens exercise their power through consumption?

4. *The marketing of politics: Candidates and social movements.* How has branding come to dominate the public face of political candidates and political parties, as well as the formation of issue publics? How have other marketing principles been applied to political campaigning? Is political branding a tool for legitimate democratic change or simply another way to dupe the consumer?

5. *The nature of civic participation: Thick versus thin engagement.* Do political consumerism and logo politics represent new forms of civic participation? Are these forms of participation displacing conventional modes of participation? Are they comparatively thin forms of political participation, or equally robust for sustained democratic engagement? How is the Internet changing the notion of the coordinated civic action? Is this sort of action individual and erratic or collective and coordinated?

As consumer culture pervades the social life of citizens in America and Europe, it becomes increasingly important to clarify the relationship between consumption and citizenship. This means looking beyond lifestyle politics and socially conscious consumption to consider other ways in which consumption has become politicized. This may involve deeper exploration of the connections between taste cultures and certain political ideologies, with particular attention to how social networks formed around brand communities and civic life overlap and mutually constrain one another. At the same time, the relationship between media consumption and competitive consumption deserves greater attention, especially whether the overspent consumer and the strains posed by contemporary consumerism can be linked to patterns of media use. It may be that digital media provide a way to counter these effects. These new modes of Internet youth may be central to the formation of youth culture and foster new modes of belonging, particularly in terms of how cultures of music and style shape identity. Clearly, these types of explorations must attend to the power of state and corporate institutions and consider differences across cultural contexts in an era of globalism. There is much to do to understand the deeper connections among communication, consumption, and citizenship.

Note

1. The faculty organizers of the conference wish to recognize the enormous contributions of the students, past and present, involved in the Consumer Culture and Civic Participation (CCCP) working group. These students were critical in imagining and managing the event. In particular, we thank Lucy Atkinson, Sun-Young Lee, and Mark Rademacher for their dedicated efforts in planning the conference. Tom Hove deserves special recognition for his efforts in administering the preparation of the articles presented in this volume. Hilde Breivik, Melissa Gotlieb, Shirley Ho, Eunkyung Kim, Nam-Jin Lee, and Muzammil Hussain were also instrumental in conference planning and execution. This volume would not exist without their efforts.

The staff in the School of Journalism and Mass Communication also merit recognition for their support of this effort. We especially thank Corinne Ahrens, Susan Brandscheid, Janet Buechner, Brian Deith, Daron Nealis, and Erica Salkin for their assistance, ideas, and initiative. Support for this conference and research initiative was also provided by the Department of Communication Arts, Department of Marketing, Department of Political Science, Center for Communication and Democracy, Center for European Studies, Center for German and European Studies, Center for International Business

Education and Research, Center for Politics, Center for World Affairs and the Global Economy (WAGE), and the Global Studies Program. Major support was provided by the Walter J. Clara Charlotte Damm Fund of the Journal Foundation.

References

Belk, Russell W. 1988. Possessions and the extended self. *Journal of Consumer Research* 15 (2): 139-68.

Bennett, W. Lance. 1998. The uncivic culture: Communication, identity, and the rise of lifestyle politics. Ithiel de Sola Pool Lecture, American Political Science Association. *PS: Political Science and Politics* 31 (December): 41-61.

Bourdieu, Pierre. 1979/1984. *Distinction: A social critique of the judgment of taste*. Cambridge, MA: Harvard University Press.

Cohen, Lizabeth. 2003. *A consumers' republic: The politics of mass consumption in postwar America*. New York: Knopf.

Hilton, M. 2003. *Consumerism in twentieth-century Britain: The search for a historical movement*. Cambridge: Cambridge University Press.

Keum, H., N. Devanathan, S. Deshpande, M. R. Nelson, and D. V. Shah. 2004. The citizen-consumer: Media effects at the intersection of consumer and civic culture. *Political Communication* 21 (3): 369-91.

Scammell, M. 2000. The Internet and civic engagement: The age of the citizen consumer. *Political Communication* 17:351-55.

Schor, Juliet B. 1998. *The overspent American*. New York: Basic Books.

Schudson, Michael. 1981. Criticizing the critics of advertising. *Media, Culture and Society* 3:3-12.

———. 1999. Delectable materialism: Second thoughts on consumer culture. In *Consumer society in American history: A reader*, ed. Lawrence Glickman. Ithaca, NY: Cornell University Press.

Stolle, D., M. Hooghe, and M. Micheletti. 2005. Politics in the supermarket: Political consumerism as a form of political participation. *International Political Science Review* 26 (3): 245-69.

Thompson, C. J. 2000. A new Puritanism? In *Do Americans shop too much?* ed. J. Schor, 69-74. Boston: Beacon.

Thoreau, H. D. 1854/1995. *Walden, or, life in the woods*. New York: Dover.

Veblen, Thorstein. 1899/1994. *The theory of the leisure class*. New York: Penguin.

In Defense of Consumer Critique: Revisiting the Consumption Debates of the Twentieth Century

By
JULIET B. SCHOR

In the past twenty-five years, the literature on consumption has gained analytic power by positioning itself against the consumer critics of the twentieth century (Veblen, Adorno and Horkheimer, Galbraith, Baudrillard), arguing that these accounts were totalizing, theorized consumers as too passive, and simplified motives. The literature moved to micro-level, interpretive studies that are often depoliticized and lack a critical approach to the subject matter. The author argues that developments such as the emergence of a global production system, ecological degradation, and new findings on well-being warrant a reengagement with the critical tradition and macro-level critiques. This article considers three traditions—Veblenian accounts of status seeking, the Frankfurt School, and Galbraith and the economic approach to consumer demand—arguing that the flaws of these models are not necessarily fatal and that the debate about producer versus consumer sovereignty should be revisited in light of the changing political power of transnational corporations.

Keywords: consumption; consumer critic; Veblen; Galbraith; Frankfurt School; producer and consumer sovereignty; status seeking

In the past twenty-five years, there has been a flowering of literature on consumption across a wide range of disciplines. Scholars in history, anthropology, cultural studies, English and other literatures, sociology, geography, and marketing (among others) have studied consumption from a large number of angles, with a multiplicity of research methods and perspectives (for reviews, see Slater 1997; Miller 1995; Arnould and Thompson 2005). These contributions have enormously enhanced scholars' understandings of the emergence and growth

Juliet B. Schor is a professor of sociology at Boston College. An economist by training, she is the author of The Overworked American, The Overspent American, *and most recently* Born to Buy. *She is also a cofounder and board member of the Center for a New American Dream, an NGO committed to transforming U.S. consumption patterns.*

NOTE: The author would like to thank Margaret Ford for research assistance.

DOI: 10.1177/0002716206299145

of consumer society; how consumers experience their consumption activities and goods, subcultures, consumer agency, and meanings; the role of consumption in the constitution of social inequalities such as gender, race, and class; the connections between consumption, nationalism, and empire; the nature of retailing; spatial dimensions of consumption; and many more dimensions of consumption.

Before the emergence of this new field of consumption studies, the theoretical starting points for work on consumption were typically a handful of consumer critics stretching back almost a century—Veblen, Adorno and Horkheimer, Galbraith, Baudrillard, and Marcuse among others. The new literatures gained analytic power and forcefulness in part by differentiating themselves from these earlier perspectives, in what was undoubtedly a productive positioning. Among the objections to the critical accounts were that they were overly totalized; that they failed to give the consumer sufficient credit for acting intentionally and with consequence; that they portrayed too unitary a consumer marketplace; and that they were elitist, indeed reactionary, in their privileging of high rather than popular culture.

These are important objections. However, I will argue that their legacy has become constraining by ruling out more sophisticated and less problematic versions of the critics' arguments and by putting macro-level or systemic critiques of consumer culture off limits. In the process, the field has ended up with a certain depoliticization and difficulty examining consumption critically. Interpretive accounts, while important, have their own limitations, including the tendency to accept consumers' own accounts of themselves without a critical or more complex and macroscopic lens.

This development has become especially problematic in the contemporary United States, as the ecological impacts of domestic consumption patterns have become devastating, as the rising consumer norms associated with a middle-class lifestyle are increasingly difficult for households to attain, and as the psychological evidence questioning the contributions of consumption to well-being becomes more compelling (Layard 2005; Kasser 2002; Schor 1998, 2005; Easterlin 1973, 1995).

In this article, I will consider three major traditions of consumer critique and the debates about them (for a study of the consumer critique literature, see Horowitz 2004; see also Slater 1997; Schudson 1991). First, there is the line of argument begun by Veblen with *The Theory of the Leisure Class* (1899/1994) (and extended by Duesenberry 1949; Hirsch 1976; Frank 1985; Schor 1998; and Heffetz 2006). Pierre Bourdieu (1979/1984) is a related but more sociological treatment. Second, there is the tradition begun by Theodor Adorno and Max Horkheimer. Finally, there is the tradition of Galbraith (1958), Packard (1957), Friedan (1964), and Ewen (1988).

My larger point is to show that the flaws of these models are not necessarily fatal and to try and stimulate new work that builds on some of their insights. Furthermore, I attempt to clarify some of the features of the models and to show that they may be more compatible with recent formulations (such as rational, or "agentic," consumers) than may be generally assumed. Finally, I argue that the debate about producer versus consumer sovereignty should be revisited in light of the changing political power of transnational corporations.

Veblen and Models of Status Consumption

The Theory of the Leisure Class (Veblen 1899/1994) is a biting analysis of the spending patterns of the rich and *nouveau riches* in the late nineteenth century. The basics of Veblen's account have been reproduced in later treatments, including formal analytic models. The core of the approach is a hierarchical social structure driven by a competitive status competition in which position is determined by wealth. Publicly visible consumption is the mechanism by which wealth is validated in the competition, or "game." The need for public display, or visibility, is caused by the possibility of what contemporary theorists call moral hazard, that is, the incentive to lie or behave unethically, which in this case is the exaggeration of wealth. Visibility is in many (but not all) ways an efficient, that is, low-cost and accurate mechanism for transmitting information. The need to commit real resources eliminates pretenders and provides a readily assessable status claim. Visibility is central to the model and provides much of its analytic power as well as a host of falsifiable hypotheses. The emphasis on visibility also signals that this is a model, not of all consumption spending, but of the relationship between visible consumption, and not only nonvisible expenditures, but also alternatives to private consumption (such as public consumption, savings, and leisure time). This is a point that has perhaps not been as clear in the literature as it should be.

Let me briefly note some of the features of the model that are relevant for the later critiques. Dynamically, the model uses a "trickle-down" mechanism in which status goods are first adopted by the wealthy, whose spending patterns are eventually mimicked by households further down the wealth distribution. As incomes rise, high-status luxuries become lower-status necessities and new luxuries develop (see also Simmel [1957] for this model applied to fashion). A second feature of the model is that individuals are highly intentional status maximizers. They are fully informed, in command of their desires, and operate in a well-organized social environment of shared assumptions and values. Consumption is neither individually expressive nor nonrational. (This is similar to conventional economic theories of the rational consumer and to some postmodern accounts of consumption.) However, in contrast to those approaches, Veblenian consumers have a pure social orientation. Consumption is carried out for its social value, rather than for intrinsic product benefits or personally inscribed meanings. In that sense, it is akin to anthropological accounts that stress the role of consumption in the construction and reproduction of culture (Douglas and Isherwood 1978) or sociological accounts that emphasize symbolic meanings (Baudrillard 2001). Like some of these culturalist accounts, Veblen's theory relies on a commonly recognized set of consensual status symbols. However, in contrast to most culturalist accounts, in which consumption is a satisfying and welfare-enhancing activity, Veblenian consumers are frustrated because all status is positional and Prisoner's Dilemmas abound. (Absolute increases in spending only yield social value when they improve relative position; when increases in standard of living are general, they are like being on a treadmill, merely keeping people from falling behind.)

The Backlash against Veblen

For much of the twentieth century, class-based status-driven models were the dominant approach to consumption, especially within U.S. sociology (Lynd and Lynd 1929; also see Schor [1998, chap. 3] for a discussion of this literature). Visible consumption display was thought to be more important in the United States than Europe because birth-based status claims were weaker and there was more upward mobility. Most of the research in this tradition was heavily materialist and studied purchasing patterns rather than qualitative data on consumers' intentions or their interpretations of goods. (The literature called these concepts the "coding" and "de-coding" of consumption symbols.) In the 1970s, this weakness was exposed, and critics argued that (1) consumers did not actually know which goods were more expensive, and (2) the proliferation of consumer goods had eroded the homogeneity of the status system (Felson 1976, 1978). Later, cultural studies accounts of media consumption emphasized an active viewer making her or his own meanings, undaunted by the symbolic meanings intended by producers or any hegemonic structure (such as a price-driven ranking). More generally, research in both sociology and other fields shifted from a critical to an interpretive framework that relied far more on consumers' own interpretations of their actions and what consumption means to them. By contrast, in status-driven systems, consumers may not be willing to discuss their motives with researchers. Evidence of status seeking is largely behavioral.

Status models fell into widespread disfavor and denunciation of Veblen became almost ritual. In his influential *The Romantic Ethic and the Spirit of Modern Consumerism* (1987) and elsewhere, Colin Campbell claimed that the Veblenian approach was not empirically supported and failed to sufficiently account for the importance of novelty in "modern" consumer societies. As an alternative, he argued that consumers were driven by an endless cycle of day-dreaming-purchase-and-disappointment. Interestingly, in view of the subsequent discrediting of the "consumer as dupe" model, scholars failed to notice that Campbell's consumers are trapped in an unsatisfying and costly purchasing cycle (see also McCracken 1988; Campbell 1994).

Postmodern consumer theory also rejected Veblen. Although social differentiation was an essential principle for foundational postmodern consumer theorists such as Baudrillard, as the characterization of postmodernity as an era of fragmentation, pastiche, and *bricolage* developed, it became less compatible with the single-minded, consistent, purposive Veblenian status seeker (Jameson 1984; Featherstone 1991; Firat and Venkatesh 1995). (See Negrin [1999] for a discussion of postmodern fashion theory.) The "postmodern" consumer is a playful and adventurous individual, putting on and taking off roles like costumes from her or his eclectic closet, shunning conventional (upscale) status aspiration. As Holt (2000) has argued, the "good life" is no longer a matter of acquiring a well-defined set of consensual status symbols but is a project of individual self-creation. Studies of subcultures also rejected the trickle-down model on the basis of a growing tendency for consumer innovation to come from the social margins, as trends in fashion, music, art, and language were originating among poor inner-city youths, rather than the wealthy.

The "postmodern" consumer is a
playful and adventurous individual, putting
on and taking off roles like costumes from
her or his eclectic closet, shunning
conventional (upscale) status aspiration.

In the midst of this ferment, Bourdieu's *Distinction* (French edition 1979, English 1984) affirmed the principle of class patterning of consumption, but it expanded on the standard status model by adding "cultural capital" as a second component of status. *Distinction's* unmistakable Veblenian roots may account for some of the negative reception the book received in the United States. An interesting although limited debate ensued, in which key tenets of the class/consumption approach were explored, such as whether taste and consumer choice follow class patterns in the United States or whether consensual status symbols still exist (Lamont and Lareau 1988; Halle 1993; Holt 1997, 2002). The dominant view continues to be that this is an outmoded theory of limited usefulness in explaining consumer behavior. (Tellingly, two Veblenian accounts of the past decade—my *Overspent American* [Schor 1998] and Robert Frank's *Luxury Fever* [1999]—were written by economists, rather than sociologists.)

Are Status Models Still Useful?

The critics of Veblen have rightly identified key shortcomings and limitations of both his theory and status models more generally. For example, the universe of goods is far more complex and less unidimensional than the model suggests, and the informational demands on consumers to keep up with the array of goods are substantial and increasing. (On the other hand, the Internet has made information cheap and accessible, and there appears to be an increasing preoccupation with consumption, perhaps partly because the informational demands are so high.)

Critics are also correct about the reversal of the flow of cultural and consumption innovation and an increase in the speed of diffusion, although this is not a fundamental critique. (The diffusion path does not have to be linear; it just needs a significant downward-sloping segment.) The point about the project of self-creation in consumer society is also undoubtedly right, but it does not require that that process occurs in a vacuum with respect to social inequality and status. One of the questions the literature has not sufficiently explored is the extent to which the project of the self is driven by individual traits or whether it is heavily influenced by class and other group positionality and constrained by economic resources. As an oft-heard quip puts it, Why is it that those people who are attempting to construct themselves as differentiated individuals are wearing the same logos, buying the same Crate & Barrel couches, and watching the same television programs? The status model is compatible with a certain, although not unlimited, degree of individuation, as long as differentiation is matched by consumers' ability to decode consumption styles and choices. Furthermore, the postmodern point about fragmentation can be accommodated by reformulating the balance between local and global status competitions. (Here global is not used literally, but in relation to the overall society [see Frank 1985].) While Harley-Davidson riders, Star Trek fans, or club-goers may reject the global status game, they do exhibit strong local status hierarchies (Schouten and McAlexander 1996; Jenkins 1992; Thornton 1996).

It is regrettable that the literature largely failed to test the model against data in part because the interpretive turn led away from falsifiable behavioral analyses. Some economists have conducted empirical tests of status seeking and found strong support for its existence in purchasing patterns (Brown 1994; Chao and Schor 1998; Heffetz 2006). Other evidence, such as the growing role of brands, the increase in brand value, and the growth of luxury brands support the ongoing importance of status consumption. However, the literature seemed intent on going in another direction.

Partly, this was due to a view that society has become more mobile and less unequal, which in turn has led to a collapse of consensual status symbols, and the distinction between "high" and "low" culture (Twitchell 1999; Lipovetsky 1994). The idea is that consumption has become more "democratic" and "egalitarian" because society has become more democratic and egalitarian. However, the data reveal just the opposite. Socioeconomic mobility (across income groups) has declined markedly (Bowles, Gintis, and Groves 2005). The distributions of income and wealth have grown far more unequal in the past twenty-five years, along a number of dimensions. The proportion of income and wealth going to the top 20 percent (relative to the bottom 80 percent) has risen significantly. The proportion going to the top 5 percent and the top 1 percent relative to the bottom 95 percent and 99 percent has also increased dramatically. Within every quintile, both income and wealth have also become less equally distributed (Wolff 2002; Mishel, Bernstein, and Allegretto 2004).

These trends in the distributions of economic resources were mirrored in consumption patterns. Beginning in the 1980s, luxury goods markets expanded dramatically, with both upscaling of goods and services and product innovation at the high end (Frank 1999). As the corporate financial scandals of the early twenty-first century came to light, so too did the consumption excesses associated with this public looting. Curiously, consumption studies, which were busy rejecting the models that make sense of this behavior, had little to say about these developments. Perhaps they had thrown out the proverbial Veblenian baby with the bathwater.

Adorno and Horkheimer and the Frankfurt School Critique

Within the humanities, the Frankfurt school has been the most influential of the consumer critiques. In their classic article, Adorno and Horkheimer (1944/1972) outlined a pessimistic view of the "culture industries" (for which read "consumer culture") in which consumers are trapped in a "circle of manipulation and retroactive need" (p. 121). Drawing on Marxian formulations of the alienation of workers in capitalism, Adorno and Horkheimer theorized the sphere of culture as being driven by imperatives from the production side. Indeed, theirs is a functionalist analysis in which life outside the factory (the sphere of leisure) is an "afterlife," structured by a dehumanized workplace. The requirements of profit making lead to cultural production that is formulaic, soothing, and banal, but that maximizes audience size. Art loses its revolutionary potential, instead acting like a drug that lulls the worker into passivity outside the factory and makes it possible for him (this is a very male vision) to return the next day to the mindless work on offer. Capitalist production creates capitalist culture and a passive citizenry, in which cultural consumption is used to reproduce an exploitative economic system.

Not surprisingly, critics have taken issue with much of this account. One problem is that it is a so-called totalized and functionalist vision without contradiction or possibility for resistance. The realm of consumption is structured to reproduce the realm of production. Even the contradictions of a more conventional Marxist account are absent because culture undermines the development of revolutionary consciousness that would otherwise occur in the course of alienated production. Thus, the model cannot account for the fact that consumer resistance is always present in the marketplace. Furthermore, while functionalist accounts are not always incorrect, they often are, in part because they fail to specify the mechanisms by which the hypothesized functional relationship is reproduced. In this case, there is no reliable microeconomic (i.e., enterprise level) explanation for why culture producers act to ensure workplace docility for industrial manufacturers. (The argument that a common ownership structure across the two sectors is evolving is a weak one, and with the exception of General Electric's holdings in the culture sphere, it has not been historically validated.)

On the other hand, the inclusion of both the production and consumption side in the analysis is a major methodological strength, a point that has not been sufficiently recognized. Analyses that look only at production or consumption are always partial and risk either incompleteness or getting it "wrong." This point is worth remembering in light of some of the literature on the relation between production and consumption that emerged in the early days of "consumption studies." The move, prompted by feminist, postmodern, and interpretive traditions, to revalorize consumption analytically and symbolically from its degradation in the Marxist and culturally conservative traditions is essential for the field. But the line of argument that inverts the relationship, arguing that consumption has somehow become "dominant" and that production is now merely an appendage to a consumption-driven system, is as wrongheaded in its own way as the production-centric analyses of Marxism. (For examples of the consumption-dominant line of argument, see Baudrillard [2001] and Firat and Venkatesh [1995]. For an insightful study that analyzes both sides of the market, see Schneider [1994].) It is a theoretical overreaction that has undermined a more analytically powerful approach.

Analyses that look only at production or consumption are always partial and risk either incompleteness or getting it "wrong."

A second criticism is that the approach is elitist in its denigration of popular culture. I will bracket this point and return to it in the next section in my discussion of Galbraith. Let me turn instead to a related topic, which is the debate about "dupes versus agents," a long-standing preoccupation of the literature in which Adorno and Horkheimer figure prominently.

Agents versus Dupes and the Micro-Macro Relation

This debate has been widely discussed in the literature, (so I will not belabor it here). The hapless, manipulated consumers in Adorno and Horkheimer's (1944/1972) dystopic formulation gave way to a view of consumers as motivated, discerning, even demanding, in their relationship to producers of cultural texts, products, and advertising. Beginning with the contributions of the Birmingham School on subcultures, and continuing with studies of fan cultures, brand communities, and many other consumer activities, research on consumers over the past twenty-five years has painted a very different picture of an active, or, as the literature terms it, "agentic," consumer (Hall 1980; Jenkins 1992; de Certeau 1984; Fiske 1989; Davis 1995). Whether it is Trekkies rewriting the scripts of their favorite episodes, cosmetic-surgically altered women with feminist sensibilities, or off-road vehicle enthusiasts, the literature describes a consumer experience in which participants emphasize choice, control, and even power. In marketing circles, the failure of the New Coke became the canonical example of this view.

It is worth asking how representative these accounts are—I suspect the consumer does not feel as empowered at the bank, phone company, and auto dealer as in her or his Manilow fan club or reading group—but my larger point is that this literature is a fairly good account of an important realm of consumer activity. There is little question that consuming is a, if not "the," realm of agency in contemporary society. In the simplistic formulation of agents versus dupes, the agentic view is clearly preferable. After all, it is hard to do good social science from the assumption that people are idiots. (On the other hand, it is also important not to overstate the case for the agentic consumer. For every hip indy music connoisseur, there is most likely a bleached-blond, Coach-carrying, North Face–jacketed college student with a Tiffany heart bracelet around her wrist who is inarticulate about her consumer choices.)

But the agents versus dupes framing has been a theoretical cul-de-sac. The strong agency view results in an inability to analyze producers' power or the relation between individual choice and predictable market outcomes. Furthermore, it often conflates the micro and macro levels of analysis—the individual consumer and the market (or economic structure)—and insists on an isomorphism between them. That isomorphism exists in neoclassical economics, although I suspect most consumption scholars do not accept that model's strong conclusions. It was probably also a feature of the period that Adorno and Horkheimer (1944/1972) were writing in. As Douglas Holt (2002) has argued, in the 1940s and 1950s advertisers wielded enormous cultural authority, and we might say that consumers willingly ceded their "agency" to them.

[T]he agents versus dupes framing has been a theoretical cul-de-sac.

However, for every era, this micro-macro identity needs to be established or refuted, and not assumed, and some of the most productive analyses of contemporary consumer society are those that make those analytic linkages. Bourdieu's (1979/1984) *habitus* is one mechanism that reconciles agentic consumers with a high level of determinacy in outcomes. Far from being duped, Bourdieu's individuals are savvy strategic actors (i.e., agents), yet they reproduce determinate and predictable class-based consumption outcomes. Partly, they are operating on the basis of motives that have become subconscious, and partly they are rational actors in a system that is characterized by considerable social irrationality. Of course, in Bourdieu's account producers are almost incidental, but this need not be so. One can reconstruct his analysis in such a way that the market (i.e., producers) plays a large role in generating meanings and driving the pattern of tastes.

An even stronger formulation of this point is that agency (or more properly sub-jectivity) is increasingly constructed *by* producers, rather than being deployed against them. Nike is an example of an enterprise whose success might be inter-preted as stemming from the mobilization of a type of consumer agency that is actualized through the purchase of Nike products. This is a twist on a point made by Slater (1997) Holt (2002), and others, which is that in the contemporary period, consuming has become the privileged form (or site) of identity construction. If we accept the view that individual agency is now central to the operation of consumer society (in contrast to an earlier era in which there was more overt social confor-mity), it is the companies who figure out how to successfully sell agency to con-sumers that thrive. In this formulation, subjectivity does not exist prior to the market (à la neoclassical economics) but is a product of it. This does not make sub-jectivity "false" as in earlier critiques, but it does imply that subjectivity is con-strained and market driven. After all, only certain forms of subjectivity are profitable. So while consumers have gained one kind of power (market innovations begin with them), they have lost the power to reject consumption as a way of life. (Baudrillard 2001; Holt 2002). They are trained from the earliest ages to be con-sumers (Schor 2004), and it becomes nearly impossible to construct identity out-side the consumer marketplace. As has been frequently noted, even those who choose to live as anticonsumers cannot escape the fact that theirs has become an advertised and marketed lifestyle, with magazines, courses, clothes, and accou-trements to promote simplicity and a rejection of consumerism.

John Kenneth Galbraith and *The Affluent Society*

If Veblen and the Frankfurt School were each dominant in sociology and the humanities, respectively, *The Affluent Society* (Galbraith 1958) was the most influential popular discussion of consumption in the post-WWII era. It was an instant and long-lived best seller, and its intellectual legacy helped define the "counterculture." (After all, the culture that was being "countered" was con-sumer culture.) (See Horowitz [2004, 102-8] on the impact of *The Affluent Society*.) *The Affluent Society* makes three major claims about consumption—that producers create consumer desire, that the consumption–well-being link is weak, and that the structural pressures to increase private consumption drive out public goods. Like the other two critiques, Galbraith's views have been widely discredited in the scholarly literature.

First, Galbraith takes aim at the standard economic assumption that consumer desires (or preferences) are determined outside the market and that what firms do is respond to those preferences. Galbraith reverses the model, arguing that the system has elevated production to a "paramount position" and desire (or preferences) is the adaptive variable. Second, once affluence has been achieved, consumers no longer have urgent or intrinsic needs, the satisfaction of which yields significant increases in human well-being. Instead, firms turn to sales and marketing to create the "craving for more elegant automobiles, more exotic food, more erotic clothing, more elaborate entertainment—indeed for the entire modern range of sensuous, edifying and lethal desires" (Galbraith 1958/1998, 115). And of course, they are responsible for those "bigger and better tailfins" which the critics made so much of. Finally, the system is no longer in "social balance" because the emphasis on private consumption crowds out public goods.

The rejection of Galbraith must be seen partly in its historical context. Holt (2002) has argued that the Frankfurt view lost favor partly because marketers responded to the backlash against them in the late 1950s and 1960s by becoming culturally less authoritative and more responsive (see also Frank 1997). Something analogous happened with Galbraith. As the neoliberal economic regime that began in the 1980s developed, ideologies of consumers' independence and intelligence became deeply naturalized. Furthermore, marketing and advertising has become so successful that the need for producers to "create" wants came to seem like a quaint early-twentieth-century idea. With mall parking lots filled to capacity, credit card debt soaring, and consumers trampling each other in holiday shopping stampedes, it is hardly surprising that biological determinist arguments of insatiable desire became dominant (see Twitchell [1999] for an influential version). The delegitimation of modern liberalism, paternalist state policy, and Keynesian economics (with its passive workers), plus the right-wing celebration of the individual, combined to further undercut the consumer critics.

At the same time, however, a growing body of empirical literature provides support for one of Galbraith's central tenets, namely, the weakness in affluent societies of the link between consumption and well-being. This comes from both cross-sectional studies in psychology, which show inverse correlations and in some cases causal relations between materialism and a large number of measures of human functionings and well-being (see Kasser [2002] and, on children, Schor [2004, chap. 8]), and from time series data that reveal that in the wealthy countries of the global North, the substantial rise in consumption of the post-WWII period has been accompanied by *no* increase in subjective well-being at all (Layard 2005). Furthermore, in the United States the de-linking of income and social well-being indicators is a powerful challenge to the prevailing notion that consumption promotes human well-being. The now substantial empirical findings on well-being, materialism, and income have not yet been well integrated into the consumption literature, but they should be.

Elitism and the Content of Consumers' Choices

Like the Frankfurt School, Galbraith has been criticized for viewing consumers as passive and manipulated. He has also been attacked as a hypocrite and an elitist, a charge that is leveled at many consumer critics. Galbraith's singular status as an academic celebrity exposed his personal consumption habits—ski trips to Gstaad and summers in Vermont appear in the attacks on him (Lebergott 1993; Twitchell 1999). But it is worth noting that for all the ink that has been spilled on Galbraith's famous tailfins, the book has relatively little discussion of particular consumer choices and far more about volume of consumption.

The tendency to make the conversation personal is worth noting for a moment. Moral philosophers are not attacked in print for adulterous behavior or ungenerous actions toward colleagues. Economists are not exposed as frauds for accepting tenure and removing themselves from the vicissitudes of the "free" market they believe in so passionately (for other people). Yet personal consumption habits are fair game. It is a curious double standard.

[V]irtually all consumption goods and practices have social meanings and effects. They should therefore be as much fair game for analysis and critique as any other social phenomena.

The charge of elitism is more important. The disdain for popular culture and tastes is certainly a feature of much consumer critique, and it is not surprising that scholars have become reluctant to make critical analyses of consumer choices. This reproduces the liberal position embodied in economics and political theory that consumer choices are not discussable, as noted by Stigler and Becker (1977) in their classic article "De Gustibus Non Est Disputandum." One might have expected that the widely noted erosion of the high/low divide in culture would have opened up space to discuss particular consumer choices, but it seems not to have.

Curiously, there seems to be far more willingness to do so when those choices reveal strategic intentions to reproduce dominant race and gender positions, rather than class. In the antebellum period, white consumers shifted from purchasing colored items to a preference for "white goods" such as white linens, white gravestones, white household decorations, and white clothing, as a way of differentiating themselves from slaves and other people of color (Heneghan 2003). Few scholars would find it illegitimate to critique this consumption for its role in expressing and reproducing the system of racial domination. But critics who analyze goods whose primary purpose is to express exclusiveness and high social position are criticized for questioning people's choices.

The general point is the well-known one that virtually all consumption goods and practices have social meanings and effects. They should therefore be as much fair game for analysis and critique as any other social phenomena. But liberal ideology cordons off this particular sphere as purely private, or asocial, and therefore not a legitimate subject for analysis, and such a view has permeated much of the consumption studies literature. This may be a personally comfortable position, especially for academics, whose high cultural capital puts them in a vulnerable position. But its democratic veneer is thin, and analytically untenable. It has also become a de facto defense of the consumption status quo.

Producer versus Consumer Sovereignty Redux

So where does the discussion of market sovereignty leave us? Are we closer to the now-conventional wisdom that consumers rule, either through their considerable power to reject products they do not like, or through their growing role in the production of cultural innovation and ultimately not only products but marketing messages as well? Or is the growing corporate power that is widely acknowledged in other spheres, such as the state and the university, also relevant in consumer markets, in ways that are not identical to what Galbraith (1958) argued, but closely related? Having succeeded spectacularly well in ensuring growing demand for goods, perhaps the transnational companies that dominate consumer markets have redirected their attention to consolidating control over the environment in which they operate. This has entailed the capture of state policy and the undoing of decades of regulation and consumer protection, as well as the creation of international institutions and treaties such as the WTO, which privilege corporate profitability above democratic control, labor rights, or environmental protections. Their approach to the youngest consumers (Schor 2004) is another variant of this strategy, for ultimately the attempt is to control the very formation and development of consumers' preferences. These are empirical and debatable questions. For my part, the view that corporations have grown more rather than less powerful is the more compelling one. And in that light, it is striking that this growing power has been accompanied by the dominance of an ideology that posits the reverse—that the consumer is king and the corporation is at his or her mercy.

I also wonder whether Adorno and Horkheimer (1944/1972) merit a rereading in the post-9/11 U.S. context, with the militarization of everyday consumption (camouflage fashion, flyovers at sporting events, and Hollywood movies glamorizing the military), the linking of patriotism with spending, and the growing climate of political and cultural repression. After all, what they were ultimately concerned about was the growth of a totalitarian society, anchored by a conformist consumer culture. While that vision may not have seemed particularly credible in the mid-1980s, when the new consumption studies began, it looks more insightful from the perspective of 2006.

Finally, I want to note that my argument in this article is not that a return to the critical traditions of the early twentieth century is a sufficient basis for articulating a compelling challenge to contemporary consumer culture. That, after all, is a reactive move. But it is a necessary first step to recovering a tradition of engaged, critical scholarship at the macro level. From here the task is to construct a truly twenty-first-century approach, a new, critical paradigm that engages the ways in which consumption has grown and radically transformed notions of individuality, community, and social relations. I look forward to collaboration—with the authors of this volume, other consumption scholars, and those in the emerging consumer activism sector—to make that new paradigm a reality.

References

Adorno, Theodor, and Max Horkheimer. 1944/1972. The culture industry: Enlightenment as mass deception. In *Dialectic of enlightenment*. New York: Herder and Herder.

Arnould, Eric J., and Craig J. Thompson. 2005. Reflections: Consumer culture theory (CCT): Twenty years of research. *Journal of Consumer Research* 31 (4): 868-82.

Baudrillard, Jean. 2001. *Selected writings*, expanded ed., ed. Mark Poster. Stanford, CA: Stanford University Press.

Bourdieu, Pierre. 1979/1984. *Distinction: A social critique of the judgment of taste*. Cambridge, MA: Harvard University Press.

Bowles, Samuel, Herbert Gintis, and Melissa Osborne Groves. 2005. *Unequal chances*. Princeton, NJ: Princeton University Press.

Brown, Clair. 1994. *The standard of living*. Cambridge, UK: Blackwell.

Campbell, Colin. 1987. The romantic ethic and the spirit of modern consumerism. Oxford, UK: Basil Blackwell.

———. 1994. Conspicuous confusion: A critique of Veblen's theory of conspicuous consumption. *Sociological Theory* 12 (2): 34-47.

Chao, Angela, and Juliet Schor. 1998. Empirical tests of status consumption. *Journal of Economic Psychology* 19 (1): 107-31.

Davis, Kathy. 1995. *Re-shaping the female body*. New York: Routledge.

de Certeau, Michael. 1984. *The practice of everyday life*. Berkeley: University of California Press.

Douglas, Mary, and Baron Isherwood. 1978. *The world of goods: Towards an anthropology of goods*. London: Allen Lane.

Duesenberry, James S. 1949. *Income, saving and the theory of consumer behavior*. Cambridge, MA: Harvard University Press.

Easterlin, Richard A. 1973. Does money buy happiness? *The Public Interest* 30 (Winter): 3-10.

———. 1995. Will raising the incomes of all increase the happiness of all? *Journal of Economic Behavior and Organization* 27:35-47.

Ewen, Stuart. 1988. All consuming images: The politics of style in contemporary culture. New York: Basic Books.

Featherstone, Mike. 1991. *Consumer culture and postmodernism*. Thousand Oaks, CA: Sage.

Felson, Marcus. 1976. The differentiation of material life styles: 1925-1976. *Social Indicators Research* 3:397-421.

———. 1978. Invidious distinctions among cars, clothes, and suburbs. *Public Opinion Quarterly* 42 (Spring): 397-421.

Firat, Fuat, and Alladi Venkatesh. 1995. Liberatory postmodernism and the re-enchantment of consumption. *Journal of Consumer Research* 22:239-67.

Fiske, John. 1989. *Reading the popular*. London: Routledge.

Frank, Robert H. 1985. *Choosing the right pond: Human behavior and the quest for status*. New York: Oxford University Press.

———. 1999. *Luxury fever*. New York: Free Press.

Frank, Thomas. 1997. *The conquest of cool*. Chicago: University of Chicago Press.

Friedan, Betty, 1964. *The feminine mystique*. New York: Dell.

Galbraith, John Kenneth. 1958. *The affluent society.* Boston: Houghton Mifflin.
———. 1958/1998. *The affluent society.* Fortieth anniversary ed. New York: Houghton Mifflin.
Hall, Stuart. 1980. Encoding/decoding. In *Culture, media, language,* ed. Stuart Hall, Dorothy Hobson, Andrew Lowe, and Paul Willis. London: Hutchinson.
Halle, David. 1993. *Inside culture: Art and class in the American home.* Chicago: University of Chicago Press.
Heffetz, Ori. 2006. *Conspicuous consumption and the visibility of consumer expenditures.* http://forum .johnson.cornell.edu/faculty/heffetz/papers/conspicuous.pdf.
Heneghan, Bridget T. 2003. Whitewashing America: Material culture and race in the antebellum imagination. Oxford: University of Mississippi Press.
Hirsch, Fred. 1976. *The social limits to growth.* Cambridge, MA: Harvard University Press.
Holt, Douglas. 1997. Distinction in America: Recovering Bourdieu's theory of tastes from its critics. *Poetics* 24:326-50.
———. 2000. Postmodern markets. In *Do Americans shop too much?* ed. Juliet Schor. Boston: Beacon.
———. 2002. Why do brands matter? A dialectical theory of consumer culture and branding. *Journal of Consumer Research* 29 (1): 70-90.
Horowitz, Daniel. 2004. *The anxieties of affluence: Critiques of American consumer culture.* Amherst: University of Massachusetts Press.
Jameson, Fredric. 1984. Postmodernism, or the cultural logic of late capitalism. *New Left Review* 146:59-92.
Jenkins, Henry. 1992. Textual poachers: Television fans and participatory culture. New York: Routledge.
Kasser, Tim. 2002. *The high price of materialism.* Cambridge, MA: MIT Press.
Lamont, Michele, and Annette Lareau. 1988. Cultural capital: Allusions, gaps, and glissandos in recent theoretical developments. *Sociological Theory* 6 (2): 153-68.
Layard, Richard, 2005. *Happiness: Lessons from a new science.* New York: Penguin.
Lebergott, Stanley. 1993. *Pursuing happiness.* Princeton, NJ: Princeton University Press.
Lipovetsky, Giles. 1994. *The empire of fashion.* Princeton, NJ: Princeton University Press.
Lynd, Robert S., and Helen Merrell Lynd. 1929. *Middletown.* New York: Harcourt, Brace, and Company.
McCracken, Grant. 1998. Consumer goods, gender construction, and a rehabilitated trickle down theory. In *Culture and consumption.* Bloomington: University of Indiana Press.
Miller, Daniel, ed. 1995. *Acknowledging consumption.* New York: Routledge.
Mishel, Lawrence, Jared Bernstein, and Sylvia Allegretto. 2004. *The state of working America 2003-04.* Washington, DC: Economic Policy Institute.
Negrin, Llewellyn. 1999. The self as image: A critical appraisal of post-modern theories of fashion. *Theory, Culture and Society* 16 (3): 99-118.
Packard, Vance. 1957. *The hidden persuaders.* New York: David McKay.
Schneider, Jane. 1994. In and out of polyester: Desire, disdain, and global fiber competitions. *Anthropology Today* 10 (4): 2-10.
Schor, Juliet B. 1998. *The overspent American.* New York: Basic Books.
———. 2004. *Born to buy.* New York: Scribner.
———. 2005. Sustainable consumption and worktime reduction. *Review of Industrial Ecology* 9 (1): 37-50.
Schouten, John, and James McAlexander. 1996. Subcultures of consumption: An ethnography of new bikers. *Journal of Consumer Research* 22 (June): 43-61.
Schudson, Michael. 1991. Delectable materialism: Were the critics of consumer culture wrong all along? *The American Prospect* 2 (Spring): 26-35.
Simmel, Georg. 1957. On fashion. *American Journal of Sociology* 62:54-58.
Slater, Don. 1997. *Consumer culture and modernity.* Cambridge, UK: Polity.
Stigler, George J., and Gary S. Becker. 1977. De Gustibus Non Est Disputandum. *American Economic Review* 67 (2): 76-90.
Thornton, Sarah. 1996. *Club cultures: Music media and subcultural capital.* Middletown, CT: Wesleyan University Press.
Twitchell, James. 1999. *Lead us into temptation.* New York: Columbia University Press.
Veblen, Thorstein. 1899/1994. *The theory of the leisure class.* New York: Penguin.
Wolff, Edward. 2002. *Top heavy.* New York: New Press.

Capital, Consumption, Communication, and Citizenship: The Social Positioning of Taste and Civic Culture in the United States

In this article, the authors analyze the field of cultural consumption in the United States. Using the 2000 DDB Lifestyle Study, they examine a cross-section of Americans in terms of their occupational categories, media usage, consumption practices, social behaviors, and indicators of civic and political engagement. In doing so, the authors find many parallels to the determinants of taste, cultural discrimination, and choice within the field structure observed by Bourdieu in 1960s French society. However, there are also some notable differences in terms of the composition of cultural capital consistent with the concept of omnivorousness. The distribution of positions is largely defined by patterns of taste that discriminate between refinement, moderation, nurturance, and a communal orientation, on one side, and coarseness, excess, aggressiveness, and an individual orientation, on the other. Historical and national differences partly account for this variation, but a major role may be played by the increasing formation of identities around media and consumption, leading to a more gendered and ideological positioning of taste cultures in the U.S context.

Keywords: Bourdieu; correspondence analysis; high culture; cultural capital; middlebrow; omnivore; political participation; popular culture

By
LEWIS FRIEDLAND,
DHAVAN V. SHAH,
NAM-JIN LEE,
MARK A. RADEMACHER,
LUCY ATKINSON,
and
THOMAS HOVE

Pierre Bourdieu's *Distinction* (1979/1984) has earned wide influence for its path-breaking and elaborate analysis of the economy of cultural goods: the social conditions for their production, consumption, and valuation. Correspondingly, it defines the different modes of taste that assign these goods their value as "cultural capital." Treating "culture" in the anthropological rather than the normative sense, Bourdieu analyzes the phenomena of taste at elite, middlebrow, and popular levels of cultural consumption. He covers such areas of taste as food, sport, fashion, manners, home décor, art, music, and literature. In all these fields of cultural production, cultural goods circulate as a form of power or capital, as markers of distinction among classes and class fractions.

DOI: 10.1177/0002716206298694

Bourdieu's great innovation was to connect the production, consumption, and valuation of cultural capital with the social practices of establishing hierarchies, maintaining distances, and legitimating differences between dominant and dominated groups. Since taste plays such an important part in these social practices, Bourdieu (1979/1984) argues that its logic needs to be examined sociologically and placed within a history of struggles between the dominant and the dominated. "Taste classifies," he declares, "and it classifies the classifier. Social subjects, classified by their classifications, distinguish themselves by the distinctions they make" (p. 6). From this starting point, *Distinction* outlines a complex program for a science of cultural consumption. In pursuing this program, Bourdieu's explicit polemical goal was to demystify and expose the social misrecognitions that the Kantian tradition of aesthetic judgment helped rationalize. But many scholars have adapted Bourdieu's insights about the social meanings and uses of

---

Lewis Friedland is a professor in the School of Journalism and Mass Communication and the Department of Sociology at the University of Wisconsin–Madison. He is author, with Carmen Sirianni, of Civic Innovation in America: Community Empowerment, Public Policy *and the* Movement for Civic Renewal *(University of California Press) along with many other articles and books. His research focuses on the sociology of communication in the public sphere and civil society, as well as community media ecologies.*

Dhavan V. Shah is Maier-Bascom Professor in the School of Journalism and Mass Communication and the Department of Political Science at the University of Wisconsin–Madison. His recent research focuses on (1) the capacity of interpersonal and mass communication, particularly the Internet, to encourage engagement in civic life and (2) the influence of news framing on social judgment. He is author of nearly sixty articles and chapters and recently received the Krieghbaum Under-40 Award for early career contributions to the field.

Nam-Jin Lee is a doctoral student in the School of Journalism and Mass Communication at the University of Wisconsin–Madison. His main research areas include media framing, public deliberation, and public opinion. He is particularly interested in how democratic deliberation works as a process rooted in cognitive and communicative activities and on how the quality and quantity of mediated political communication and of political talk facilitate or constrain this process.

Mark A. Rademacher is a doctoral student in the School of Journalism and Mass Communication at the University of Wisconsin–Madison. His research focuses on the influence of media, consumption, and peer culture in late-adolescent identity development and maintenance.

Lucy Atkinson is a doctoral student in the School of Journalism and Mass Communication at the University of Wisconsin–Madison. She is interested in how individuals construct and negotiate political and social meanings through nontraditional means, such as consumption behaviors, and the role of mass media in this process. She is also interested in how news presentations influence audiences' perceptions, learning, and engagement.

Thomas Hove is a doctoral candidate in the School of Journalism and Mass Communication at the University of Wisconsin–Madison. He holds a Ph.D. in English from the University of Illinois at Urbana-Champaign. Currently he is writing a dissertation on Habermas's recent work and its relevance to communication research.

NOTE: The authors, who all contributed equally to this article, would like to thank DDB-Chicago for access to the Life Style Study and Marty Horn and Chris Callahan, in particular, for making these data available and sharing methodological details. Findings and conclusions in this manuscript are those of the authors and do not necessarily reflect the views of DDB-Chicago.

cultural goods for a variety of other purposes (see Holt 1997a, 1997b, 1998; Lamont and Lareau 1988).

Here, we take Bourdieu's concept of the field of consumption and apply it to the United States in 2000. Using the 2000 DDB Lifestyle Study, we analyze a cross section of Americans ($N = 3,122$) in terms of the associations among occupational categories, media usage, consumption practices, social behaviors, and indicators of civic and political engagement. In doing so, we are reproducing the field of consumption in a different national and historical context. Bourdieu's research, conducted in the late 1960s, was situated in a France that had a relatively stable class structure and a stratified system of institutions that reproduced cultural taste. The United States in 2000 differs not only in its class and cultural structure. It also lies at the other side of a historical shift in which consumption is less clearly the outcome of the intersection of class and culture but rather actively shapes it. Moreover, media consumption in the form of television, radio, magazines, newspapers, and the Internet has become an increasingly important marker of cultural consumption in this context. To test whether and how the concept of the field of consumption might apply in the United States, we have attempted to reproduce parts of the analysis of *Distinction* with the following two goals: first, to visualize the field of consumption in the United States and analyze whether the categories of Bourdieu's analysis of the field apply, even generally; and second, to expand and examine the patterns of the field of consumption in the social space in the United States that include media consumption as central to cultural consumption and taste.

One of the most useful outgrowths of Bourdieu's research on cultural consumption is his model for mapping what he calls "social space." He proposes this model as a challenge to the "substantialist" social-scientific habit of assigning a "mechanical and direct relation" between social classes, on one hand, and cultural goods, practices, and consumption patterns, on the other. Substantialist thinking "is inclined to treat the activities and preferences specific to certain individuals or groups in a society at a certain moment as if they were substantial properties, inscribed once and for all in a sort of biological or cultural *essence*" (Bourdieu 1994/1998, 3-4). As an alternative, he constructs a "relational" model of the social logic of taste judgments. This relational model considers any given activity or preference as "nothing other than *difference*, a gap, a distinctive feature, in short, a relational property existing only in and through its relation with other properties" (Bourdieu 1994/1998, 6).

From Bourdieu's relational perspective, class distinctions exist only as features of social space. Social space itself consists of the relative status positions people perceive themselves to occupy, along with their perceptions of the positions that other people occupy. It is always with reference to these perceived relations in social space that people acquire and judge cultural tastes. These relations are informed by complex rules of judgment, and these rules correspond with the contours of social space. Although Bourdieu sometimes organizes social space in three dimensions (1994/1998, 15), he usually organizes it in just two: "Agents are . . . distributed, in the first dimension, according to the overall volume of the capital they possess and, in the second dimension, according to the composition of their capital"

(2001, 231). On the Y-axis of social space, low quantities of capital are at the bottom and high quantities are at the top. Where Bourdieu's mapping becomes more complex is on the X-axis, which marks relative proportions, or composition, of economic versus cultural capital. On the left side of the X-axis, social classes, activities, goods, and professions have relatively higher degrees of cultural capital and lower degrees of economic capital. On the right side, they have relatively lower degrees of cultural capital and higher degrees of economic capital.

This map of social space is somewhat complicated, but it is useful for two complementary reasons. On one hand, it suggests the ineluctable dynamism and relativity of taste judgments. But on the other hand, it proposes ways to ground those judgments in concrete social relations. Our use of the map is designed to understand how Americans are arrayed in a space defined by these two central axes of economic and cultural capital, and whether the result is sensible. As noted, Bourdieu's maps have a clear logic. We wondered whether a similar logic would emerge here, and if not, how it would be different.

Operationalization. We treat cultural capital primarily as "an indicator and a basis of class position," and as a set of tastes that can be "mobilized for social selection." To do this, we make one central assumption: The products and the media people consume signal their cultural status. In Bourdieu's sociology, this assumption is an outcome of a long process of the formation of cultural capital for each class fraction, embodied in a habitus, a system of "dispositions" that "functions at every moment as a *matrix of perceptions, appreciations, and actions* and makes possible the achievement of infinitely diversified tasks" (Bourdieu 1977, 82-83). The habitus is a "kind of theoretical deus ex machina by means of which Bourdieu relates objective structure and individual activity. . . . It is similar but not reducible to class subculture" (DiMaggio 1979, 1464). In other words, the system of coordinates on which the field depends itself requires both cultural capital and a group habitus that is relatively fixed.

[W]e make one central assumption:
The products and the media people consume
signal their cultural status.

Bourdieu himself has recognized that a sociology of taste grounded in the strong state, hierarchical aesthetic and educational culture, and historically rigid class structure of France in the postwar period do not transpose easily to the United States. For a consumption practice or object to count as a signal of cultural capital, it needs "to be defined as a high status cultural signal by a relatively large group of people" (Lamont and Lareau 1988, 155-56). Here, we begin to encounter important differences between France and the United States. In the France of the late 1960s, certain high-cultural markers allow us to distinguish among classes. In Bourdieu's terms,

> Thus nothing more rigorously distinguishes the different classes than the disposition objectively demanded by the legitimate consumption of legitimate works, the aptitude for taking a specifically aesthetic point of view on objects already constituted aesthetically . . . and the even rarer capacity to constitute aesthetically objects that are ordinary or even "common" . . . or to apply the principles of a "pure" aesthetic in the most everyday choices of everyday life, in cooking, dress, or decoration, for example. (Bourdieu 1979/1984, 40)

In other words, the ability to distinguish objects according to their aesthetic value and thereby distinguish oneself from others is a primary marker of cultural capital. A major problem in applying this understanding to the United States is the now-long-standing controversy over whether and how a high culture can effectively set criteria of legitimate consumption.

Several scholars (Gans 1999, 1973/1999; Guillory 1995; Levine 1988; Rubin 1992) argue that America has never had a tradition of high culture analogous to that of countries like Germany and France. A typical member of a European elite might be assumed to have strong, fluent familiarity with nationally representative figures of high culture. But in America, there is no widely held expectation that elites will share a common knowledge of a select set of high cultural figures whose work cannot be understood without costly and laborious prerequisites (Bourdieu calls them "entry tickets") of intellectual training and aesthetic refinement.

The correspondingly strong link between elite social status and a high-cultural tradition has been disputed in America. Distinctively American forms of art and literature did not arise until the antebellum period of the nineteenth century (e.g., see Matthiessen 1941). By that time, international trends in the professionalization and popularization of art were well under way. In addition, America's elites increasingly comprised a technical professional class that did not have the traditions, training, or leisure to acquire high levels of cultural capital (Rubin 1992). As a result of these historical conditions and their legacy, the highest forms of culture in America are generally at best "middlebrow." Simply put, middlebrow culture refers to the phenomenon of gaining access to high culture only after it has first been mediated by mass culture. Guillory's (1995) canonical example of the middlebrow is the American Public Broadcasting System. A more salient recent equivalent would be Oprah's Book Club. What makes high culture middlebrow in America is that the mode of experiencing it is initially filtered through, and therefore made significant by, the mass media. This mediated status conferral also points to the central role of media and mass culture in the valuation of taste and fixing of class distinctions.

Analyzing arts participation in the U.S from 1982 to 2002, DiMaggio and Mukhtar (2004) observed that while there has not been a dramatic "meltdown" in the value of the arts as cultural capital, audiences for the arts have undergone a long-term attrition, particularly among younger cohorts (even after controlling for large overall increases in education). However, they find that declines for middlebrow activities (craft fairs, musical theater, historical sites) are greater than for high arts, which suggests that all arts activities are facing increased competition for attention from many sources, including media. They also found increased attendance for art museums and jazz concerts, consistent with Peterson's influential "omnivore" theory.

Peterson posits a qualitative shift in the basis for marking elite status, "from snobbish exclusion to omnivorous appropriation" (Peterson and Kern 1996, 900). With Kern, he finds that high-status culture consumers (highbrows) are more omnivorous than others, seeking out both high and low forms of taste, and that they have become increasingly so over time, confirming earlier findings by DiMaggio (1987) and Lamont (1992). In a comprehensive review that surveyed the research arc from *Distinction* to comparative international research on omnivorousness, Peterson (2005) confirms the finding that omnivorousness has become increasingly dominant among elites. But he also considers recent research comparing highbrow and lowbrow omnivorousness. He traces the evolution of research across three stages. First, highbrow "snobs" were distinguished from omnivores; lowbrow "slobs" were conceived as univores. Second, the element of breadth was introduced, opening up the possibility of lowbrow omnivores. Third, lowbrow omnivorousness is understood as having been diffused into lower status levels, as found by Bryson (1996) in a comparison of lowbrow musical tastes. She found that lowbrow omnivores tend to *avoid* the most marked genres of country, heavy metal, and rap, suggesting complex patterns of omnivorous inclusion and exclusion. Furthermore, Peterson (2005) suggests that the focus on high cultural tastes has made it more difficult to measure ominvorousness across class positions, and he calls for greater attention to sports, magazines, beverages, hunting and fishing, and food, as well as church attendance, associations, and self-improvement groups (pp. 266-67).

With these issues in mind, we generated correspondence maps of the social positioning of taste in the United States. We did so with the goal of exploring the social stratification of taste culture and integrating media consumption and civic practices into this investigation of the U.S. context. Our central research question concerns the transitivity of both Bourdieu's general framework and his specific reading of the field of consumption to another historical and geographical context. Before we do so, we first provide relevant details about our data and analytic strategy. We then provide a general reading of the field structure before analyzing each quadrant in greater detail.

Data and Analytic Strategy

The data in this study were gathered in a 2000 DDB Needham mail survey conducted by Market Facts, using a stratified quota sampling procedure. To do this, Market Facts began with a large list of names and addresses acquired from commercial list brokers. A sample, counterbalanced along demographic characteristics to account for expected differences in response rates, was then drawn from a pool of approximately five hundred thousand individuals. Then, the final sample of approximately five thousand individuals is drawn annually to best approximate the distributions within the nine Census divisions of age, income, household size, and population density. This starting sample is then adjusted within a range of subcategories that include race, gender, and marital status to compensate for differences in return rates, with more surveys mailed to population categories that respond at lower rates. Although this panel may underrepresent transient populations, the very poor, the very rich, and certain minority groups, the data have been verified as an effective barometer of mainstream America (Shah, McLeod, and Yoon 2001). Indeed, these data have been shown to produce responses that are highly comparable to conventional probability sampling procedures (Putnam 2000).

This particular survey comprises 3,122 adult respondents with a response rate of 62.4 percent against the mailout to prerecruited panelists. These data contain a wide range of indicators of consumption patterns, media usage, social behaviors, civic practices, and political ideology, and other types of socially signifying actions. Rather than detailing all of these indicators, which space does not allow, we discuss the analytic strategy used to generate the correspondence analysis maps used to examine the field structure in the United States.

To do so, we used the method of multiple correspondence analysis (MCA) to explore and visualize the structure of social positions and its relationship with lifestyle choices, social behaviors, media usage, product consumption, and civic and political indicators in the United States. MCA, which is a multivariate version of simple correspondence analysis, seeks to summarize the interrelationships between the categories of three or more discrete variables with a small number (usually two or three) of underlying dimensions and to visualize these relationships in a low-dimensional correspondence map such that categories sharing similar distributions lie close together in the map (Benzecri 1992; Greenacre 1984). As in principal components analysis, the nature of the relationships between the categories can be examined by interpreting the principal axes with each dimension reflecting a defining property of the social space.

Following Bourdieu (1979/1984), we analyzed the 2000 DDB Lifestyle survey data in two phases. First, MCA was conducted only for the indicators of cultural and economic capital. Using those indicators as socioeconomical and cultural markers, this analysis seeks to construct a social-space plane with a two-dimensional structure. Second, after the space of social positions has been constructed and fixed, those variables associated with cultural taste and social practices, and with civic engagement and political ideology, were superimposed onto the existing social space. To project the variables of cultural taste and lifestyle onto the social space, we entered the socioeconomic and cultural markers as *active* points while entering the lifestyle variables as *supplementary* points in a new correspondence analysis. In this way, the supplementary points overlaid onto the social space display the relationships of those supplementary points with the principal axes while not contributing to the total variance and to the positions of the dimensions (Greenacre 1984, 1993). These supplementary points help us interpret the principal axes and enable us to examine how social positions related to cultural taste and consumption behaviors.

Correspondence Analysis

As the first stage of analysis, we ran a multiple correspondence analysis for occupation and the indicators of economic and cultural capital. A total of thirty-four variables and all nonmissing cases were considered in the analysis, mainly income, education, and occupational categories. The total inertia (variance) was .012, 70.2 percent of which was explained by the two most dominant dimensions (46.5 percent for the first dimension and 23.7 percent for the second dimension).[1] Since the subsequent dimensions explained a relatively small amount of variance (9.0 percent for the third and 5.4 percent for the fourth), we considered only the first two in the construction of social space.

Next, we added the supplementary points to further visualize the social stratification of taste and cultural consumption in this U.S. context. The correspondence maps yielded two overarching dimensions: volume of economic and cultural capital on the vertical and form of cultural capital on the horizontal (see Figure 1). On the vertical (Y) axis, the bottom end is marked by lower levels of income and education and the corresponding occupational categories, whereas the top end is marked by higher levels of income and education. College-educated, white-collar professionals who earn more than $50,000 a year populate this upper half of the volume of capital axis. They consume products and media in a manner reflective of their positions in the social space. That is, they consume goods more for their aesthetic or symbolic value than for their utilitarian benefit, while their news consumption tends to focus on informational media. In terms of civic behaviors, these are the individuals who most engage in civic and political life. Individuals who occupy blue-collar and service professions, make less than $50,000 a year, and prefer entertainment media populate the lower half of the volume axis. Their consumption choices are driven by the utilitarian and pragmatic concerns and tend to be disengaged from traditional means of civic participation.

In Bourdieu's analysis of French society in the 1960s, occupation was a distinguishing factor on the horizontal dimension. Individuals on the right side might be viewed as possessing lower levels of cultural capital but comparatively higher levels of economic capital. They are characterized as industrialists, small shopkeepers, business owners, and craftsmen. On the left side of Bourdieu's maps, we would see individuals with higher levels of cultural capital compared to their levels of economic capital. They might be thought of as the artistic producers, cultural intermediaries, educators, and social workers.

Although occupation is important in our mapping of the field, it is less of a factor in defining the field structure than are media preferences, consumption habits, and civic behaviors. To the degree that occupation is relevant, it is reflective of youth and physicality. For example, early career professionals, precision craft workers and operator/fabricators, jobs that are either dominated by younger workers or require considerable stamina, characterize the far right end of the X-axis. Similarly, media use, consumption habits, and civic behaviors mirror this individualistic and aggressive skew. In terms of media use, they favor entertainment content such as sitcoms, rock music, and lifestyle publications. Consumption habits, for example, center on buying lottery tickets, hard liquor, and personal technology. Individuals at this end are also less likely to join in civic activities than those on the left side of the map.

Although occupation is important . . . it is less of a factor in defining the field structure than are media preferences, consumption habits, and civic behaviors.

Occupation maps similarly on the left side of the map, though on this end it reflects a more mature and communal orientation. In particular, retired people and homemakers by choice dominate this side of the axis. In comparison to other areas of the map, this side is most strongly defined by media use, with a strong preference for news content or entertainment programming that focuses on dramatic situations, social relations, and family. Along with this preference for informational and dramatic media content, people on this end of the continuum show comparatively higher levels of civic participation, with the intensity and frequency of participation rising along this dimension.

Accordingly, we interpret the vertical (Y) axis as representing the volume of economic and cultural capital, consistent with Bourdieu, whereas the horizontal axis indicates the composition of capital. However, the composition of capital in millennial U.S. society does not mirror that observed by Bourdieu in 1960s French society. We interpret the horizontal axis as characterized by refinement, nurturance, and moderation (i.e., a communal orientation) on the left side and coarseness, excess, and aggressiveness (i.e., an individual orientation) on the right. Notably, these two axes jointly identify the quadrants defined by their intersection. To fully understand how occupation, media use, consumption, and civic and social practices define and situate distinct lifestyles in this social space, we move to an examination of each quadrant.[2]

FIGURE 1
CORRESPONDENCE MAP OF THE VOLUME AND COMPOSITION OF CAPITAL

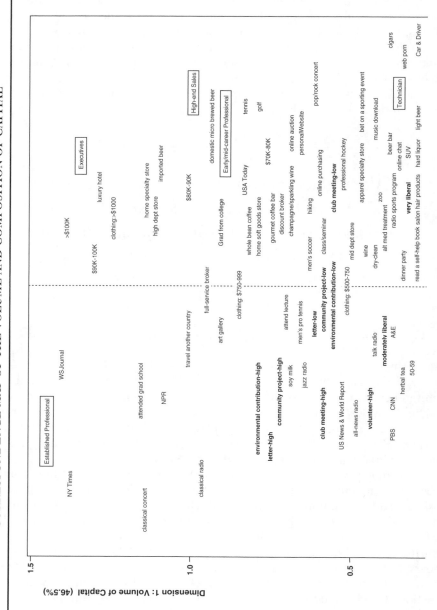

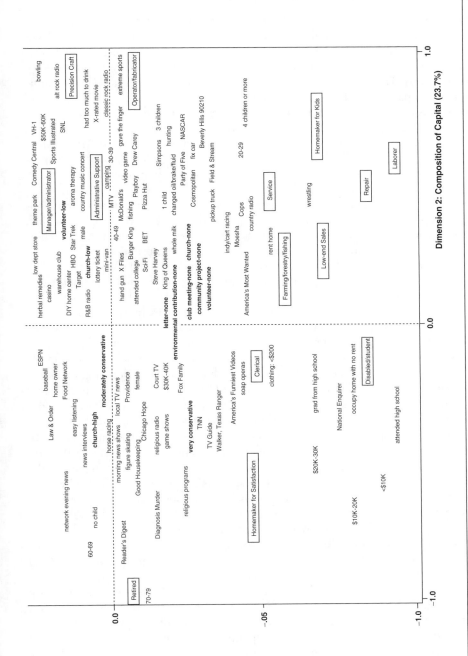

Dimension 2: Composition of Capital (23.7%)

Quadrant 1: High volume of capital–communal orientation (upper left)

This first quadrant is inhabited by middle- and upper-income, well-educated individuals with patterns of cultural consumption that correspond to an emphasis on cultural capital (see Figure 1). Their media use, consumption, and civic and social behaviors cluster around two visible groups, with the second composed of two subgroups. The top cluster possesses a high volume of cultural and economic capital. Occupationally, they are established professionals, such as doctors and lawyers. It is here that we find people who have attended graduate school and who make more than $100,000. In terms of media use, they rely predominantly on leading, prestige outlets for news and information, such as the *New York Times*, the *Wall Street Journal*, and National Public Radio. These media choices represent not so much a liberal leaning, but rather a reliance on the media of record. These are the outlets that set the agenda for other media in the areas of politics, finance, and culture. Their consumer behavior maps loosely onto Bourdieu's high-cultural-capital individuals. That is, individuals in this cluster prefer high art, such as classical music and classical concerts, to other forms of entertainment. Their high incomes also afford them the opportunity to travel internationally.

It is interesting to note that when it comes to our indicators of civic engagement, this top cluster of the quadrant is somewhat removed from the day-to-day civic practices such as volunteering and working on community projects. This is the privileged segment of American society that Republicans have effectively framed as defining the stereotypical, effete New York and California liberals, who personify the distance between cultural elites and "ordinary" Americans. Yet a liberal political ideology does not map cleanly onto this top cluster; instead, it corresponds more closely with those clustering in the lower end of this quadrant. Similarly, donating money to environmental causes and writing letters to the editor are linked to these established professionals; however, these activities, along with other civic practices, are also more closely associated with the second major cluster found in this quadrant.

In this second cluster, we find ideological moderates, both conservatives and liberals, although moderate liberals are pulled slightly more upwards along the volume axis, whereas moderate conservatives are drawn further leftward along the composition axis. These two positions bracket this second cluster. This cluster is also more varied in terms of its media use habits. Although our data lack the specific occupational markers, all other indicators point to this space in the field being occupied by white-collar service workers in social support occupations, such as professors, teachers, social workers, and civil servants. Individuals in this cluster favor broadcast news over print-based news, preferring to watch and listen rather than read. They choose news outlets such as CNN Headline News, network evening news, PBS, *U.S. News & World Report*, and talk radio. These news consumption habits share a clear trajectory with civic-life indicators. Exposure to information about current events and issues is associated with volunteering, contributing, community work, and letter writing. The occupants of this cluster are the foot soldiers of civil society, not only collecting information about their social and political environment but also working to support and improve their communities.

In terms of nonnews media use, this cluster straddles the fence between two domains that might be thought of as refined but not elite. At the right side of this cluster, higher on the volume of capital axis, we see a social life defined by more sophisticated activities, such as listening to jazz radio, going to art galleries, and attending lectures. At the left side of this cluster, along the composition axis, we see a preference for more conventional cultural pursuits, such as programming like *Law & Order*, the Food Network, and easy listening radio.

Quadrant 2: Low volume of capital–communal orientation (lower left)

Further down the left side of the map, we find a social cluster that represents a departure from Bourdieu's field of cultural consumption in France. Consistent with Bourdieu, here we find a social space dominated by somewhat older, less affluent, and less educated individuals. At the bottom of this quadrant are individuals who did not graduate from high school and who earn less than $10,000. In terms of occupations, these individuals are students, play support roles such as clerical workers, work within the home for personal satisfaction, or are retired.

The major departure is the centrality and force of religion in defining those relatively lower in volume of capital but compositionally higher in cultural than in economic capital. What is also striking is the structuring role of mass media in the U.S. case. This cluster is characterized by churchgoing individuals whose media use habits reflect a taste for moralistic content such as religious programs, traditionalist social dramas such as *Touched by an Angel* and *Walker, Texas Ranger*, and family-friendly fare such as *America's Funniest Home Videos* and the *Cosby Show*. In terms of news media use, individuals in this cluster favor softer, so-called infotainment programming, such as morning news shows and *Reader's Digest*. Branded consumption markers and civic engagement are less closely aligned with this cluster, though their church ties may provide them with badges of identity and opportunity for involvement. In line with this, we also see a strong relationship with a conservative political ideology.

Quadrant 3: High volume of capital–individual orientation (upper right)

The upper-right quadrant contains individuals who possess a relatively high volume of capital, but in contrast with the first quadrant, their composition of capital is more economic than cultural. Many of these behaviors reflect an orientation that can be interpreted as competitive, aggressive, and more individualistic. Despite these shared traits, occupying this quadrant are three distinct clusters that vary considerably from one another.

The cluster that occupies the uppermost space of this quadrant represents the economic power brokers of American society. Here we find individuals who have graduated from college, earn high incomes, and hold executive-level or upper midlevel corporate positions and high-end sales jobs. In comparison with previous clusters, media consumption does not appear to distinguish this cluster; the only defining media choice is reading *USA Today*, the newspaper of choice for America's "road warriors." Rather, what appears to define this cluster is their consumption of products. Clothing, fashion, and other luxury goods are important badges of their social and economic position. They frequent high-end and upper-middle-tier department stores, like Neiman-Marcus and Macy's, and lifestyle stores such as Crate & Barrel. Similarly, when they travel, this group prefers luxury hotels and activities such as snow skiing and tennis. In regard to civic participation, this cluster seems detached from conventional engagement in public life through volunteer or community participation.

Two distinct clusters occupy the lower half of this quadrant. The cluster in the lower-left position includes midlevel professionals such as managers and administrators. What truly defines this cluster is its product consumption and lifestyles. These individuals engage in consumption patterns that might be viewed as aspirational in nature (Schor 1998; Veblen 1899/1994), consumption that strives to mirror the practices of higher social strata. They are appearance minded, buy clothing at midtier department stores and specialty stores, get professional manicures and pedicures, and buy hair care products from salons. Yet they also express a certain orientation toward natural products and experiences with their use of alternative medical treatments such as acupuncture and with their enjoyment of activities such as hiking.

Civic engagement for this cluster is best defined as socially versus civically driven. Their engagement does not appear to seek political or social justice ends, but rather provides individuals with an opportunity to socialize with others. For example, this cluster visits gourmet coffee bars, hosts dinner parties, and occasionally volunteers or attends clubs and church. From an ideological standpoint, these people define themselves as moderately or very liberal, yet this ideological position does not inspire higher levels of engagement.

The third cluster in this quadrant is largely defined by the horizontal axis of the composition of capital. Although their volume of capital reflects a midlevel status, they emphasize the economic over the cultural in their taste patterns. Members of this cluster are employed in the technical support and precision crafts fields, careers that often require on-the-job training or more formalized apprenticeship programs. In overarching terms, their lifestyle can be defined as youthful, hypertechnological, and highly sexualized. This lifestyle is clearly reflected in their media use, with cultural consumption focused on outlets such as Comedy Central, *Sports Illustrated*, and classic and alternative rock. Moreover, this cluster actively uses the Internet for virtual gaming, downloading music, and adult content. They are also active producers of online content, maintaining Web sites and engaging in online chats.

This cluster's enjoyment of athletic events like hockey, sports betting, and heavy drinking reinforces the emphasis on the coarse and aggressive over the refined and temperate. It is not surprising, then, that this cluster is also defined by a lack of civic and political engagement in keeping with their highly individualistic and competitive cultural consumption practices.

Quadrant 4: Low volume of capital–individual orientation (lower right)

The lower-right quadrant represents a social space dominated by individuals with relatively lower volumes of capital, though they still emphasize the economic over the cultural. Cultural consumption within this quadrant is again defined by coarse, aggressive, and competitive forms. From a demographic perspective, this quadrant comprises individuals who attended but did not complete college; make less than $50,000 per year; and are employed in service industries, agriculture, forestry, or fishing, or are homemakers by necessity. Within this quadrant, two clusters, each with overlapping subclusters, distinguish themselves from each other in terms of their rural and urban lifestyle orientation.

The center of this quadrant contains a cluster of young, less affluent, urban families largely defined by their media consumption. Central to this cluster are family-oriented programs with primarily black and working-class casts such as *The Steve Harvey Show*, *King of Queens*, and *Moesha*, as well as African American lifestyle programming such as BET. Though this cluster might be interpreted as being dominated by the black middle class, it also likely contains other groups that populate large urban areas and more broadly represent the blue-collar, working, lower-middle class. Consumption variables are limited to dining at fast food restaurants like McDonald's, Burger King, and Taco Bell. Regretfully, this absence of consumption markers is likely a function of the lack of relative consumption indicators in this data that reflect the practices of those who populate this quadrant. Individuals with relatively low volumes of capital are not typically viewed as ideal consumers for a wide range of goods.

The second cluster within this quadrant represents a youthful, more exurban and rural population. Specifically this shift is visible in this cluster's media preferences. First, country music and *Field & Stream* magazine are defining features of this cluster. In addition, in contrast to the more family-oriented media consumed by the previous cluster, this cluster consumes more sexualized media such as *Playboy*. It may be that two overlapping clusters, one more rural and the other more urban, occupy this space. Yet what is interesting is the aspirational component of this type of consumption. Members of this cluster are limited by the volume of capital they possess to engage in the lifestyles depicted in *Cosmopolitan* or *Beverly Hills 90210*, yet appear to consume these media as a way of participating in upper-middle-class consumer culture.

Like the other cluster in this quadrant, our data limit the number of product consumption markers available for analysis. However, some interesting patterns do emerge that help define this cluster in rural and exurban terms, specifically, activities such as hunting, fishing, extreme sports, driving a pickup truck, and automotive maintenance. In regard to civic and political engagement, members of this cluster are the most disengaged, far removed from civic practices such as attending church, volunteering, or making environmental contributions. Politically, this quadrant is defined as middle-of-the-road. In short, due to their status position in society and their involvement in other activities, civic and political markers do not define these individuals.

Synthesis and Discussion

This preliminary mapping of the field of consumption in the United States has two primary goals. First, through this mapping, we hoped to compare our results with the general structure of the field of consumption found by Bourdieu (1979/1984). Second, we wanted to discover distinct properties of that field in the United States, in particular to understand whether the dual axes of volume and composition of capital remain determinant or whether some other principles may be at work in structuring the U.S. field. Although this first exploration does not answer these questions, it takes us a bit closer and provides an agenda for further exploration.

Before we attempt to synthesize these findings, we need to note some limits of our data. First, while the DDB Lifestyle Study is the most comprehensive data set on consumption patterns in the United States, it is a marketing study. We have already noted that it underrepresents the very rich and very poor. But more subtly, it may distort our analysis for the lower half of the field. It is skewed away from the lower ends of the mass market and toward those brands that can be sold to middle- and upper-middle-income consumers. Second, while Bourdieu began with a precise analysis of class, based on occupational and income categories, we had to reconstruct these categories from a general analysis to fit the broader available variables. While we believe we have attained construct validity for the variables used, there are gaps that themselves could contribute to the somewhat discontinuous structure of the field. We cannot be sure whether clusters represent real gaps in the field or missing gradations of occupational categories.

[T]he middlebrow in America confounds the presence of "high" culture.

Moving to the comparison with Bourdieu's (1979/1984) analysis of the field of cultural consumption in 1960s France, the upper left quadrants in both *Distinction* and our analysis appear similar in some respects. Bourdieu's space is marked by grades of intellectuals and service workers—teachers, social and medical workers, public sector executives, and intellectual and cultural workers. The U.S. quadrant also contains these groups, but it may be dominated by a larger class of professionals and knowledge workers, inclusive of the previous groups, but also shaped by legal and financial services and other highly educated fractions of the upper middle classes. We see a clear split between high-income members of this grouping, who appear to be higher cultural consumers, and a lower group that is among the most civically and politically active. Second, and closely related, this group appears to be stratified less by cultural capital in Bourdieu's sense than by clusters of media consumption. This may reflect a shift to a principle of stratification defined by volume of capital and media use.

One central difference is that the middlebrow in America confounds the presence of "high" culture. To be sure, aspects of the map of the social space of consumption found by Bourdieu appear in our own analysis (particularly the existence in the upper half of the map distinguished by a higher volume of cultural and economic capital). But in the United States, the meaning of the upper-left quadrant marked by a high volume of cultural capital is unclear. Our analysis shows that although traditional markers of "high" culture are here—for example, listening to classical music and attending art galleries—the space is less saturated with high-cultural markers and less stratified than France in the 1960s. Notably, some of the strongest markers of this social space are elite media, particularly newspapers of record such as the *New York Times*.

This finding is mirrored, to some extent, in the upper-right quadrant, high economic–lower cultural capital. This quadrant is the most isomorphic between the United States and France. In Bourdieu's (1979/1984) analysis, it is occupied by the wealthy, private sector executives, "engineers" (higher-level technical workers), and the traditional high-status "professions." We find analogous categories of the wealthy, college graduates, and midcareer professionals, but this space is much more densely populated, with multiple clusters defined by fine gradations of lifestyle and consumption. This, however, is where the specific commonalities break down.

The most prominent difference comes from our major finding of what we have labeled the communal/individual continuum that forms the horizontal axis. Although we set out to replicate the dimension of cultural capital used by Bourdieu as closely as possible, we are not sure that this horizontal dimension does, indeed, reflect cultural capital as understood by Bourdieu. Rather, we have found a dimension that seems to scale broadly along a communal to individual continuum, though this dimension also reflects contrasts between refinement and coarseness, between nurturing and competitive, and between genteel and aggressive.

A strong corollary is the importance of age cohort and gender in our mapping. Age and gender clearly structure the map to some extent. This structuring may point toward a larger, important analytical issue. Age and gender were largely omitted as structural principles of Bourdieu's (1979/1984) map of the field. For instance, age functions as a secondary effect of income through the life course in Bourdieu's analysis. In other words, those with a high volume of capital tend, by definition, to be older. Furthermore, the analysis in *Distinction* represents the distribution of occupations of male heads of households; women's occupations were entered in as secondary variables, when at all. We believe that the inclusion of women as equivalent to men in our analysis of these data, along with the use of age to help fix the social space, help to explain some of the differences we observe. America in 2000 and beyond is a more age-segregated society, and much of this segregation is a direct principle of lifestyle segmentation. Also, many more women have moved into the workforce in both American and French society since the 1960s.

Also worthy of note is the centrality of media consumption as a form of cultural consumption. The use of various newspapers, television programs, radio formats, and magazines was particularly relevant in marking individuals' social position, distinguishing them from others in the social space, while also providing aspirational reference points for consuming. The importance of digital media as a distinguishing feature is particularly pronounced among certain clusters, especially among the more youthful and aggressive set defined along the right side of the map, though print media and television also serve as key cultural markers. It is also notable that television consumption, especially of escapist fare such as sitcoms and reality shows, tends to cluster along the bottom half of the social space, whereas newspaper and magazine consumption tends to distinguish between those with higher and lower volumes of capital.

> *[T]here is a clear correspondence between civic behavior, political ideology, and the social positioning of taste cultures within the U.S. context.*

Finally, we find that there is a clear correspondence between civic behavior, political ideology, and the social positioning of taste cultures within the U.S. context. Civic life in our analysis does not follow a more or less linear distribution by age and income, as implied by both Putnam (2000) and Verba, Schlozman, and Brady (1995). Rather, we see strong clustering in the midlevels, around both the volume and composition axes. Furthermore, we see lifestyle-based subclusters of activity that themselves have distinct civic and political implications. More important, perhaps, we see a clear alignment between certain media consumption practices and certain civic activities with news consumption. Most interesting is the space just to the left of the volume axis that represents the engaged middle classes, running from moderately liberal to the moderately conservative. There seems to be some split between the church-attending, moderate conservatives on the lower end and the community-engaged, moderate liberals near the vertical axis. On the other, individual side of the social space, we see those who are more broadly disengaged from civic and political life, possibly due to a kind of liberalism that involves socializing and consumption, but relatively little formal civic engagement.

Clearly, this initial effort to map the field of cultural consumption in the United States provides a number of unique insights about consumer behavior, media use, civic practices, and their alignment with various demographic and occupational markers. What is needed is further analysis of the implications of the sort of social alignment and stratification that we observed here. Although the data do not allow us to make statements about the relationships among these factors over time, this is just the type of longitudinal analysis of the shifting nature of cultural capital that is so desperately needed to further illuminate the connections between citizenship, consumption, communication, community life, and the volume and composition of capital.

Notes

1. Multiple correspondence analysis (MCA) tends to inflate the total amount of variance of the points due to the inclusion of the cross-tabulation of each variable with itself in the analysis. We adjusted raw MCA results following a method suggested by Greenacre (1984, 1993).

2. Because of space limitations, we are unable to reproduce each quadrant of the field here. The full set of analyses, quadrant by quadrant, including details of the correspondence analysis, can be found at http://www.journalism.wisc.edu/cccp/research.php.

References

Benzecri, J. P. 1992. *Correspondence analysis handbook*. New York: Marcel Dekker.

Bourdieu, Pierre. 1977. *Outline of a theory of practice*. Cambridge: Cambridge University Press.

———. 1979/1984. *Distinction: A social critique of the judgment of taste*. Translated by R. Nice. Cambridge, MA: Harvard University Press.

———. 1994/1998. *Practical reason: On the theory of action*. Stanford, CA: Stanford University Press.

———. 2001. *Language and symbolic power*. Ed. J. B. Thompson. Trans. G. Raymond and M. Adamson. Cambridge, MA: Harvard University Press.

Bryson, Bethany. 1996. Anything but heavy metal: Symbolic exclusion and musical dislikes. *American Sociological Review* 61:884-99.

DiMaggio, Paul. 1979. Review essay on Pierre Bourdieu. *American Journal of Sociology* 84:1460-74.

———. 1987. Classification in art. *American Sociological Review* 52:440-55.

DiMaggio, Paul, and Toqir Mukhtar. 2004. Arts participation as cultural capital in the United States, 1982-2002: Do trends in participation augur decline? *Poetics* 32:169-94.

Gans, Herbert J. 1973/1999. *Popular culture & high culture*. Rev. and updated ed. New York: Basic Books.

———. 1999. *Making sense of America: Sociological analyses and essays*. Lanham, MD: Rowman & Littlefield.

Greenacre, Michael J. 1984. *Theory and applications of correspondence analysis*. San Diego, CA: Academic Press.

———. 1993. *Correspondence analysis in practice*. San Diego, CA: Academic Press.

Guillory, John. 1995. The ordeal of middlebrow culture. *Transition* 67:82-92.

Holt, Douglas B. 1997a. Distinction in America? Recovering Bourdieu's theory of tastes from its critics. *Poetics* 25:93-120.

———. 1997b. Poststructuralist lifestyle analysis: Conceptualizing the social patterning of consumption in postmodernity. *Journal of Consumer Research* 23:326-50.

———. 1998. Does cultural capital structure American consumption? *Journal of Consumer Research* 25:1-26.

Lamont, Michele. 1992. *Money, morals, and manners*. Chicago: University of Chicago Press.

Lamont, Michele, and Annette Lareau. 1988. Cultural capital: Allusions, gaps and glissandos in recent theoretical developments. *Sociological Theory* 6:153-68.

Levine, Lawrence W. 1988. *Highbrow/lowbrow: The emergence of cultural hierarchy in America*. Cambridge, MA: Harvard University Press.

Matthiessen, F. O. 1941. *American renaissance: Art and expression in the age of Emerson and Whitman*. New York: Oxford University Press.

Peterson, Richard A. 2005. Problems in comparative research: The example of omnivorousness. *Poetics* 33:257-82.

Peterson, Richard A., and Roger M. Kern. 1996. Changing highbrow taste: From snob to omnivore. *American Sociological Review* 61:900-907.

Putnam, Robert D. 2000. *Bowling alone: The collapse and revival of American community.* New York: Simon & Schuster.

Rubin, Joan S. 1992. *The Making of middlebrow culture.* Chapel Hill: University of North Carolina Press.

Schor, Juliet B. 1998. *The overspent American.* New York: Basic Books.

Shah, Dhavan V., Jack M. McLeod, and So-Hyang Yoon. 2001. Communication, context and community: An exploration of print, broadcast and Internet influences. *Communication Research* 28:464-506.

Veblen, Thorstein. 1899/1994. *The theory of the leisure class.* New York: Penguin.

Verba, Sidney, Kay L. Schlozman, and Henry Brady. 1995. *Voice and equality: Civic voluntarism in American Politics.* Cambridge, MA: Harvard University Press.

Representing Citizens and Consumers in Media and Communications Regulation

By
SONIA LIVINGSTONE
and
PETER LUNT

What do citizens need from the media, and how should this be regulated? Western democracies are witnessing a changing regulatory regime, from "command-and-control" government to discursive, multistakeholder governance. In the United Kingdom, the Office of Communications (Ofcom) is required to further the interests of citizens and consumers, which it does in part by aligning them as the citizen-consumer. What is meant by this term, and whether it captures the needs of citizens or subordinates them to those of consumers, has been contested by civil society groups as well as occasioning some soul-searching within the regulator. By triangulating a discursive analysis of the Communications Act 2003, key actor interviews with the regulator and civil society bodies, and focus groups among the public, the authors seek to understand how these terms ("citizen," "consumer," and "citizen-consumer") are used to promote stakeholder interests in the media and communications sector, not always to the benefit of citizens.

Keywords: citizen interests; consumer representation; media and communications regulation; civil society; public understanding of regulation

Introduction

Today our viewers and listeners are far more empowered. Digital television, the internet and increasingly broadband is putting more choice in the hands of the user. As a regulator, we will reflect that, welcome and encourage it. There can no longer be a place for a regulator . . . determining what people "ought" to have. (CEO, Office of Communications, as quoted in Carter 2003b)

The terms *citizen* and *consumer* have become widespread in contemporary political and public discourse. This article examines the relation between them through a telling case study: the United Kingdom's Office of Communications (Ofcom) is a new "superregulator" formed by converging five legacy regulators following the Communications Act 2003. Conceived as a powerful, sectorwide regulator that can respond flexibly to new challenges, Ofcom is developing

DOI: 10.1177/0002716206298710

a common approach to broadcasting, spectrum, and telecommunications in a manner that reflects broader changes in governance occurring internationally and across many sectors under New Capitalism (Chiapello and Fairclough 2002; Jessop 2002; Lunt and Livingstone forthcoming). The new-style regulation moves away from the previous hierarchical, "command-and-control" regime (Black, Lodge, and Thatcher 2005). Its "softer," "lighter touch," "joined-up" approach claims to democratize power by dispersing and devolving the role of the state, establishing accountable and transparent administration, and engaging multiple stakeholders, including civil society, in the process of governance. Regulation must, it is argued, make unified and strategic decisions for the whole market that reflect economic, technical, and social policy trends and balance the needs of the market with those of an "empowered" public.

Is "consumer" taking over from "citizen" in the communications sector, as suggested by the ubiquitous discourse of choice and empowerment?

For cultural critics, key questions arise regarding media and communications market developments, contents and services available to the public, mechanisms for representing the range and nature of public interests at stake, and, crucially, the regulatory underpinning for the information and communication requirements of a democratic society. To address these questions, critics must not only be clear about what citizens need and deserve from the media but also, we argue, they must engage

---

Sonia Livingstone is a professor in the Department of Media and Communications at the London School of Economics and Political Science. She has published widely on the subject of media audiences and, more recently, on children, young people, and the Internet. Recent books include Audiences and Publics *(edited, Intellect Press, 2005) and* The Handbook of New Media *(edited with Leah Lievrouw, Sage, 2006).*

Peter Lunt is a professor of media and communications at Brunel University. His main research interests are in consumption studies and audience research. He recently published a report for the United Kingdom's Office of Fair Trading, titled The Psychology of Consumer Detriment *(2005). Together with Sonia Livingstone, he is currently conducting a study of financial and communications regulation in the United Kingdom.*

NOTE: This article draws on a research project, The Public Understanding of Regimes of Risk Regulation (http://www.lse.ac.uk/collections/PURR/), funded by the Economic and Social Research Council (ESRC) as part of the "Social Contexts and Responses to Risk Network" (RES-336-25-0001) (http://www.kint.ac.uk/scarr/).

with the emerging regulatory framework. Our starting point is the unstable, indeed contested, relation between "citizens" and "consumers." Is "consumer" taking over from "citizen" in the communications sector, as suggested by the ubiquitous discourse of choice and empowerment? Does the "citizen" have a voice in regulatory debates, or is this subordinated to the market? To approach these questions, we begin with the story of the United Kingdom's Communications Act 2003.

The Communications Act 2003—A Tale of Two Terms

Central to the lively debate over media and communications regulation during the 1990s was a struggle over the position of the public (or "audience"; Livingstone 2005) in a converged market and a deregulatory regime prioritizing governance over government. Two distinct terms emerged as the discursive solution—"citizen" and "consumer," supposedly dividing the semantic terrain neatly between them, resolving ambiguities in the plethora of "listeners," "viewers," "users," and "customers" of the legacy regime. Yet once the act was passed, this solution almost immediately began to unravel, with boundary disputes demanding remedial action of various kinds on the part of the regulator and civil society (Livingstone, Lunt, and Miller forthcoming-a).

"The communications revolution has arrived," stated the Department for Trade and Industry and the Department for Culture, Media and Sport's (DTI/DCMS's) Communications White Paper (December 2000). This proposed "a new framework for communications regulation in the 21st century" (Foreword) whose central objectives (Executive Summary) were as follows:

> Protecting the interests of consumers in terms of choice, price, quality of service and value for money, in particular through promoting open and competitive markets; maintaining high quality of content, a wide range of programming and plurality of public expression; [and] [p]rotecting the interests of citizens by maintaining accepted community standards in content, balancing freedom of speech against the need to protect against potentially offensive or harmful material, and ensuring appropriate protection of fairness and privacy.

To achieve these objectives, the White Paper proposed the Office of Communications (Ofcom), including a quasi-independent Consumer Panel to further consumer interests and, within Ofcom, a Content Board to ensure citizen interests in relation to broadcast content.

Following a lively public consultation, the Draft Communications Bill (2002) marked a surprising linguistic shift, replacing the language of "consumer," "public," "community," and "citizen" with that of "customer" throughout. This apparently excluded the citizen interests expressed in the White Paper, signaling the intention to form Ofcom as primarily an economic regulator. A decisive intervention was made during prelegislative scrutiny of the bill, conducted by the Joint Select Committee for the House of Commons and House of Lords chaired by Lord Puttnam. After hearing a considerable body of evidence from diverse stakeholders (Harvey 2006; Redding 2005), the Report of the Joint Committee (2002, 103) argued that the draft bill downplayed consumer and citizen interests through portraying them as "customers" and argued instead for "the need for a broad understanding" of "consumer." Stressing the media's influence in shaping society, the report advocated two principal duties for Ofcom: to further the interests of citizens and to further the interests of consumers.

In its response, the government acknowledged the terminological confusion muddle impeding the passage of the bill by issuing a note (DTI/DCMS 2002) that explicated the government's rationale through, in effect, a mapping of discursive categories onto power relations among state, industry, and public. This proposed that the consumer interest should be understood in relation to economic goals while the citizen interest inheres in cultural goals, and that these in turn map onto the domain of telecommunications networks and services, on one hand, and broadcast content, on the other. Consumers are understood as individuals while citizens have collective status. The former interests would, it was proposed, be addressed by Ofcom's Consumer Panel (taking over the agenda of the legacy regulator, the Office of Telecommunications), while the latter would be addressed by Ofcom's Content Board (updating the role of legacy regulators such as the Independent Television Commission [ITC] and the Broadcasting Standards Commission [BSC]). Hence,

Consumer Interest	Citizen Interest
Economic focus	Cultural focus
Networks and services	Broadcast content
Individuals	Community
Consumer panel	Content board
Legacy regulator: Oftel	Legacy regulator: ITC, BSC

Nonetheless, in another surprising turn, Clause 3 of the November 2002 Communications Bill stated simply that the general duty of Ofcom would be "to further the interests of consumers in relevant markets, where appropriate by promoting competition." So, the "customer" of the draft bill became the "consumer," but there was no equivalent mention of citizens, notwithstanding the recommendation of the Joint Committee and the DTI/DCMS terminological note. As Jocelyn Hay (2002), chair of the civil society body, Voice of the Listener and Viewer, commented acidly, "The Bill simply re-iterates a now largely discredited faith that the 'market' and competition will provide choice and quality; it does NOT as experience shows."

Matters came to a head in June 2003 when the bill reached the Lords. Here Lord Puttnam proposed an amendment to Clause 3, reiterating the Joint Committee's proposal that Ofcom should further the interests of both citizens and consumers. There followed a heated debate over the meaning of these terms and over whether the bill should dictate how Ofcom should resolve conflict between these interests. Although citizen interests were defended—as a term with "a lengthy and distinguished pedigree" (Lord Bragg), as "fundamentally different from that of consumer" (Lord Peyton)—little light was thrown on the nature of the citizen interest in media and communications. Lord McIntosh, speaking for the government, sought to fend off dissent by asserting that consumer and citizen "are two sides of the same coin":

> It is not our intention—nor is it in the English language—to equate consumers with markets. The word that I have always used, in 50 years with the Labour Party, is that we have to be on the side of the "punters." I think everyone understands that. . . . "Consumers" is not a doppelganger for the wicked and self-seeking market, which some people in the Chamber seem to fear.

Lord Puttnam countered equally forcefully:

> My Lords, I do not wish to quibble with the Minister over words. However . . . [t]hey are quite different, both in law and as far as concerns Parliament.[1]

The subsequent vote defeated the government, and a few days later, the Communications Act 2003 was passed in July. Clause 3 states,

> 3(1) It shall be the principal duty of Ofcom, in carrying out their functions; (a) to further the interests of citizens in relation to communications matters; and (b) to further the interests of consumers in relevant markets, where appropriate by promoting competition.

Furthering the Interests of Citizens and Consumers—An Unfinished Tale

The discursive distinction between "citizens" and "consumers" emerged as the outcome of a protracted, public negotiation among multiple stakeholders. But what does it mean for regulatory practice (Black, Lodge, and Thatcher 2005)? Subsequent deliberations over terms have been led by Ofcom, following its launch in December 2003. Just days after the Lords' debate, Lord Currie (2003), Ofcom Chairman, noted with frustration,

> You may well have noticed that the careful balance established in the Communications Bill between the duties to citizens and those to consumers has been upset by a recent House of Lords amendment . . . that requires Ofcom to give paramountcy to the citizen in all matters concerning broadcasting and spectrum. . . . This late change . . . seems to us to be unfortunate.

Interestingly, Ofcom then defined its mission statement thus: "Ofcom exists to further the interests of citizen-consumers through a regulatory regime which, where appropriate, encourages competition" (see www.ofcom.org.uk). This differs from the actual terms of the act, conjoining "citizen" and "consumer" as the "citizen-consumer," and foregrounding competition as the primary instrument to further both sets of interests, not just the consumers'. Ofcom as an economic regulator is thus reasserted and, consequently, has been contested (e.g., Redding

2005). In practice, Ofcom's everyday discourse generally elides the two terms, speaking loosely of citizens-'n'-consumers and making little systematic distinction between them. As then-CEO Stephen Carter (2003a) commented,

> We are all of us both citizens and consumers. . . . To attempt to separate them or rank them would be both artificial and wrong. So it will be against that combined citizen-consumer interest that we will benchmark all our key decisions.

Similarly, Kip Meek, Senior Partner (Competition and Content), observed that "if it wasn't in the Act, citizen-consumer language might not—we might decide that wasn't terribly useful."[2] This may seem a pragmatic resolution of a tricky problem. However, we would argue to retain the distinction, supporting Lord Puttnam's view that "this is more than a matter of semantics" (Report of the Joint Committee 2002, 11). Jonathon Hardy from the Campaign for Press and Broadcasting Freedom described the inclusion of citizen interests in the Communications Act as "a slightly symbolic victory but important victory."[3] So, what is it a matter of, what kind of victory?

Interestingly, Ofcom does not speak with a single voice. Ed Richards (2003), then Ofcom's Senior Partner, Strategy and Market Developments, and now the new CEO, observed that "at the very heart of Ofcom is the duality of the citizen and the consumer." He contrasted the terms thus: the consumer interest centers on wants and individual choice. Under conditions of spectrum scarcity, market intervention was required to maximize the range and balance of content, but this requirement reduces in a digital age of abundance when consumer preferences will be expressed through viewing choices and broadcasting will become more like the publishing, film, and music industries, permitting regulation to recede. By contrast, the citizen interest centers on the long-term societal benefits of broadcasting in relation to democracy, culture, identity, and learning, all traditionally delivered through public service broadcasting and providing a continued justification for market intervention. Hence:

Consumer Interest	Citizen Interest
Wants	Needs
Individual	Society
Private benefits	Public benefits
Language of choice	Language of rights
Short-term focus	Long-term focus
Regulate against detriment	Regulate for public interest
Plan to roll back regulation	Continued regulation to correct market failure

Defining the Citizen Interest

Implicit in these negotiations are the multiple interests being advanced in a multistakeholder negotiation. Strikingly, the key terms of the act are interpreted both as identical (the citizen-consumer) and as opposed (citizen versus consumer). Just how Ofcom is to define the terms and, more fundamentally, reconcile the aims of maintaining a competitive market, meeting the needs of the public, and reflexively monitoring its own impact on both market and public sphere, was far from fixed by the act. Rather, this remains for the regulator to negotiate with its stakeholders. We now examine the views of three groups of stakeholders—the regulator, civil society, and the public.[4] Parliament is also a key stakeholder, but we have omitted this in part because its strategy is to devolve the role of the state to self-regulation and coregulation; the regulator's perception of Parliament's role does matter, however.

Strikingly, the key terms of the act are interpreted both as identical (the citizen-consumer) and as opposed (citizen versus consumer).

Through key actor interviews with senior figures at Ofcom and in civil society (twenty-five interviewees in all, conducted "on the record"; see Livingstone, Lunt, and Miller forthcoming-b), we identified considerable confusion regarding the definition of the citizen interest, the consumer interest being notably easier to grasp. Meek recognized the stakes are high, observing of the Communications Act,

> It was hard fought over because as with many of these things, it became a metaphor for . . . the soul of Ofcom was being fought over and . . . if you include the word citizen, QED Ofcom will not just be an economic regulator, it will look more broadly than that and that is what it was about.

The "soul of Ofcom," however, remains elusive. Ofcom's director of external relations, Tony Stoller, noted of the citizen/consumer distinction, "There are counters which are black and there are counters which are white, but most of the counters are shades of grey."[5] The director of communications, Matt Peacock, responsible for public relations, conflated the terms—"citizens/consumers, people basically, as I prefer to call them."[6] For the director of market research, Helen Normoyle, definitional ambiguity justifies setting them aside in Ofcom's research activities:

> It's a very tricky question. Because some issues are obviously consumer issues and some issues are obviously citizen issues but at the end of the day we're talking about people. So I, my personal preference is to cast the net wide and not to be too presumptive about what it is that we're talking about.[7]

Such questioning of the practicability of the citizen/consumer distinction is commonplace although, as here, often expressed as a "personal" view lest the speaker seem to evade the requirements of the act. For Ofcom, distinguishing citizen from consumer raises issues of representation. Stoller asks, "If you engage with consumers, do you engage separately with citizens?" His concern is partly with the task of identifying distinct consumer and citizen representatives, but more fundamentally with the question of who they really represent. He asks, "Do we get better advice from self-appointed, um—probably issue-driven—non-representative groups?" In short, the citizen interest might mean that people could and should represent themselves (by contrast with the consumer interest, which is, for Ofcom, appropriately and effectively measured through the tools of market research). Indeed, from a market research perspective, the citizens who speak up appear unrepresentative. Yet as an institution in the public sphere (Habermas 1997), Ofcom is accountable for which voices it includes and how they are weighed. For civil society bodies, these questions are equally critical. It is salutary to note that the civil society bodies we interviewed struggled to give an adequate account of their legitimacy among the constituency they represent, making them indeed vulnerable to the charge of being partisan or biased.

More surprisingly, perhaps, though clear about the importance of critiquing a reliance on economic regulation, civil society groups also struggle to define the citizen interest. Gary Herman of the Campaign for Press and Broadcasting Freedom commented, "I think it's horrible, the citizen/consumer opposition."[8] Allan Williams, senior policy adviser for communications at Which? (formerly, The Consumers' Association) also brushed aside the distinction as unworkable: "Well, they [Ofcom] talk about citizen-consumer, I mean, as much as we do—everyone fudges that." For civil society groups, the issue is less one of representation than one of communicative effectiveness. Williams explains,

> The risk is if you have just the language of citizens then you end up with, with a load of nebulous and quite high level public interest-type objectives rather than actually looking, are people getting the best deal in this market.[9]

An advocate requires a clear message to be effective, and the "nebulous" or "fuzzy" concerns of citizenship (perhaps as advanced by academics) can frustrate the civil society cause. Despite supporting a role for Ofcom in relation to citizen interests, Jocelyn Hay recognizes that

> it is much easier to regulate consumer issues which are basically economic issues and redress and fair representation and so on than citizenship issues which involve social, cultural, democratic issues which are far more difficult to quantify and measure.[10]

This reference to quantification is important: Ofcom is an evidence-based regulator, with a large research department, but issues that fit poorly within its market research ethos fit poorly within its purview. However, civil society bodies lack the resources to conduct alternative research. Hay continues, "We don't have the resources to do the research that is necessary in order to make it objective."

Williams agrees: "It's a capacity issue, you know, that there are lots of issues that we can deal with as a consumer organization and we try and prioritize." These accounts give primacy to "hard facts," acknowledging a high threshold to be passed if civil society voices are successfully to question the evidence-base of Ofcom's policy or to counter its individualized, segmented conception of the public (Freedman 2005). Capacity depends on money and time, but also on expertise. The challenge for civil society bodies lies in obtaining these resources without compromising their independence.

Paradoxically, the more open and transparent the regulator, the greater the problem of capacity for civil society. Ofcom, like other new regulators, is required to put considerable effort into a sustained engagement with diverse stakeholder interests across industry, the political sphere, consumer representatives, journalists, and the public. Thus, it publishes numerous reports, press releases, and consultations each year. In responding, civil society bodies are stretched, facing tough decisions about priorities, and worried about their funding base; meanwhile, the regulator is frustrated at the difficulty of obtaining sufficient representation from civil society. This is, again, more problematic for citizen than consumer interests, as the chairman of Ofcom's Consumer Panel, Colette Bowe, explains,

> The citizen issues are much harder because you have to find some other deliverers who you can forge an effective alliance with to deliver. Doesn't mean you're not still responsible for doing something, but it's harder and more complex, more diffuse.[11]

Emerging Directions

So, the citizen interest is difficult to define, requires the construction of diffuse stakeholder alliances, and is less amenable to quantitative research; this will surely undermine allocating resources to furthering the citizen interest. Such problems are compounded by the lack of direction and capacity in civil society, reducing the likelihood of externally driven change. As Deputy Chair Richard Hooper observed, "I think the good thing is that on the whole I don't think there are citizen groups out there who think that the citizen has been neglected."[12] Ofcom's secretary, Graham Howell, adds, "I'm not conscious of us being put under pressure by citizens' groups to suddenly bring citizenship up the agenda."[13] However, there is another—internal, organizational—motivation for change that is driving the regulator to reconsider the citizen interest, namely, Ofcom's anticipation of being externally evaluated in terms of its clarity of purpose, organizational efficiency, and accountability to Parliament. For Ofcom is "a creature of statute," as Robin Foster, Ofcom's Partner for Strategy and Market Developments, notes.[14] Colette Bowe adds,

> The scrutineer is the public, I mean literally, the scrutineer has to be Parliament, I think. Parliament acting on behalf of the pubic. . . . And, you know, interestingly in Ofcom's case, the word "citizen" is used in the legislation as well as "consumer," and I think it's for Parliament to hold Ofcom to account for how it's interpreting that remit.

Clearly, it is inconsistent to claim that both the citizen and consumer is an artificial and unworkable distinction and, simultaneously, that the terms refer to distinct issues that map neatly onto the remit of the Content Board and Consumer Panel, respectively. Moreover, it is becoming evident that the latter is not the case. Rather, the Consumer Panel is now broadening its purview to encompass citizen interests, for "there are consumer issues around broadcasting . . . like digital switch over," said Julie Myers (Policy Manager of the Consumer Panel),[15] and citizen issues in relation to telecommunications. Robin Foster described the relation between Ofcom's duties and its organizational structures as "a delicate balancing act," noting of the citizen interest that

> it was . . . largely talked about in terms of the media, the broadcasting side of Ofcom's activities, but in fact when you, the more you think about it, the more some aspects . . . of the issues which actually the Consumer Panel, so-called, is very interested in, are in many ways what I would describe as citizenship issues. They're about universal availability of telecom services around the country, they're about affordable access to, telephony services . . . for the less well off. They're about protecting the more vulnerable groups to make sure they have access to, uh, to communications. And all of those actually feel more like citizen rather than consumer issues.

Driving this is the idea of the citizen interest as social inclusion (Ofcom Consumer Panel 2005). Colette Bowe explains,

> We realized very quickly . . . that what we were talking about was not consumers. We were talking about citizens. We were talking about people who were perfectly capable in principle of going to the shop and buying the thing as a consumer, but actually might they be isolated from our society in a way that made it difficult to know that that was what they should be doing?

Indeed, Ofcom (2005, 39) announced a new work area for 2005-2006, namely, to "identify and articulate more clearly how the interests of citizens should be incorporated in Ofcom's decision-making process in a transparent and systematic way." Civil society bodies are now appraising the success of this endeavor. Pat Holland, of the Campaign for Press and Broadcasting Freedom, is cautiously optimistic:

> They are more open to arguments around . . . citizenship . . . they haven't exactly got as far as using the phrase like "positive regulation" or "enabling regulation," which are the sorts of phrase we would use, but I think there, there has been a definite opening to those ways of thinking.[16]

However, although this may presage an expanded conception of the citizen interest, a related trend (cf. above quotations from Foster and Bowe) narrows the notion of citizenship, associating it (paradoxically) with vulnerability. For, in the discourse of economic regulation, justifying regulatory intervention is more easily sustained on the grounds of vulnerability than on the grounds of public value. Several Ofcom figures recounted narratives of the vulnerable "citizen," at risk of social exclusion, this warranting a normative approach combining the ideology of social welfare with a neoliberal agenda. The paradox of the citizen-as-vulnerable is supported by Ofcom's market research perspective, for this constructs the "citizen" as a quantifiable but small segment of the population. For Helen Normoyle, citizens are the 10 to 20 percent who are vulnerable, lacking a voice to represent themselves directly and so usefully revealed through market research rather than collective action:

> So this is an instance where Ofcom or maybe the government or whoever would need to do something to intervene, to protect these citizens and to make sure that they don't get left behind, because the market by itself will not take care—it'll take care of the eighty percent or the ninety percent who are economically active or fit.

The Public's Perspective

And what are the public's views? We have seen how both the regulator and civil society speak for the public, so now we consider how the public envisions the role of regulation in their lives. We conducted sixteen focus group interviews during May 2006, with 114 people selected from diverse sociodemographic circumstances, asking them about public understanding of regulation broadly conceived, with communications as one area for focus.[17]

Their views, we suggest, are best captured by Billig et al.'s (1988) "dilemmatic" thinking, for they are neither apathetic and disengaged nor actively engaged and responsive to regulatory initiatives or consultations. Rather, they are ambivalent, expressing strongly felt but contrary views that, though aware of the contradictions, they seemed unable to resolve. Where we had feared puzzled responses or silence to our initial probe—"What do you think of when we say, 'rules and regulations'?"—instead we received an initial barrage of antiregulation views. Stories of stupid or unnecessary rules—in the workplace or school, getting a pension, or hiring a car—were plentiful. Hostility to the "nanny state" and tales of "red tape" impeding the application of common sense suggested a public supportive of the deregulation agenda: consumer choice, individual rights, liberalized markets. As a middle-class, midlife interviewee said, "Health and Safety at work—get the garlic and crosses out! It is ruining the industry, it's controlling this country I think. Ridiculous at times it gets." This theme was readily picked up— "They bring another rule out instead of thinking, well, we've already got enough rules, why don't we perhaps manage the ones that we actually have a little bit better?" One retired respondent concluded cynically, "The people that actually make the laws haven't a clue what they're doing."

Yet these views were qualified further into each discussion. Alternative stories emerged—of consumer failures, unprotected consumers, dangerous situations, and exploited individuals. Talking of finance contracts, one young person had learned the hard way that "they write these things and the consumer can fall foul of regulations designed to protect you by virtue of your own ability to understand it." Concerns for vulnerable groups (the young, elderly, and weak), pressured consumers (suffering lack of time or "information overload"), and irresponsible individuals (damaging the collective through their selfishness or thoughtlessness) all revealed limits to public support for deregulation and, indeed, a rather righteous support for consumer protection regulation. One retired person, recalling now-gone financial regulations, observed that "it's now just a market, and so what the government tries to do is to get banks to regulate themselves, to not lend too much to the wrong people." Another respondent concludes, "I don't think they [the banks] have any moral conscience at all." Regulation, on this view, should be guided by public values.

However, although the discussions covered many issues, those that directly influence people's health, work, finances, or family generated more attention than media and communications issues. On prompting, we obtained tentative statements about the importance of trustworthy news media, complaints about media panics, and concern over mobile phone tariffs; but overall, this was not an area of regulation that elicited strong views. Possibly, for risks that affect people as individual consumers (price, contract, choice, product information, etc.), the connection between regulation and daily life matters; for risks that affect people as citizens, as a collective, particularly in the long term, such connections are less compelling. Certainly, across the entire range of issues, and notwithstanding the strong views often expressed, few people described taking action regarding rules they considered unfair, regulations they wished changed, contracts they could not understand, risks they were worried about, or institutions meant to advise or support them (see also Couldry, Livingstone, and Markham forthcoming). In short, the public struggles to speak as a collective, being torn between its self-image as agentic and as vulnerable. It is also unclear how to articulate its responsibilities (especially compared with its rights), and it cannot readily find a point of focus for action—hence, exit without voice is a common response (Hirschman 1969).

Critical Alternatives

We suggest that contemporary debates over governance are shifting "the public" center stage. But how should society conceive of this public—as citizen, consumer, or in some other way? For critics, we suggest that the explicit contestation surrounding these terms offers an opening for intervention. Ofcom's critics—including the Consumer Panel, known informally as Ofcom's "critical friend"—argue that the regulator should encompass the "citizen interest" instead of broadening the notion of the "consumer interest," partly because to market liberals (notably, the media and communications industry), the consumer interest is and will continue to be interpreted narrowly in terms of price, choice, and value for money, thus legitimating an economic model of regulation. Arguments to broaden the consumer interest, instead of in favor of the citizen interest, could therefore become aligned with this narrow agenda, one that, as Needham (2003, 5) pointed out, replicates

> patterns of choice and power found in the private economy. The consumer is primarily self-regarding, forms preferences without reference to others, and acts through a series of instrumental, temporary bilateral relationships. Accountability is secured by competition and complaint, and power exercised through aggregate signalling.

How should critics frame the citizen interest in positive terms? Most academics concerned with the relation between the media and politics agree that access to information and communication resources are fundamental to informed citizenship and a prerequisite for democratic participation. Many worry that neoliberal economics and neoconservative politics have altered the balance of power in media and communications to the detriment of citizens, through increasing conglomeration in the political economy of media ownership, globalization and cultural imperialism, and the mainstreaming of a conservative media culture that marginalizes the expression of diverse or radical opinions. The outcome, it is held, is that the public is granted the rights of consumers (choice, price, etc.) but not of citizens.

The citizen interest . . . lies in determining what real choices are open to the public in seeking to meet their needs in a particular information and communication environment.

What is the alternative? Murdock and Golding (1989) focused on the distribution of communicative resources—notably, access to information and communication content and technologies, maximum diversity in content production, and mechanisms for feedback and to enable participation. Developing Scannell's (1989) advocacy of "communicative entitlements," Hamelink (2003, 1) gathered under the label "Communication Rights" those rights recognized by the United Nation's Universal Declaration of Human Rights that relate to information and communication to promote their visibility and implementation:

> Communication is a fundamental social process and the foundation of all social organization. . . . Communication rights are based on a vision of the free flow of information and ideas which is interactive, egalitarian and non-discriminatory and driven by human needs, rather than commercial or political interests. These rights represent people's claim to freedom, inclusiveness, diversity and participation in the communication process.

He argued that governments and civil society bodies must guarantee the conditions for freedom of expression, universality of access, diverse sources of information, diversity of ownership, and plurality of representation. Garnham (1999) developed Sen's analysis in terms of capability rather than either resources or rights, arguing that given considerably unequal starting points within any population, public policy should seek to equalize the set of alternatives genuinely open to people (i.e., their capabilities), recognizing that they may then choose to take these up or not. Access to, and the content of, the press, television, Internet, and so on should be evaluated, therefore, not in terms of what contents or services they provide but in terms of the possibilities they afford or impede. The citizen interest, in other words, lies in determining what real choices are open to them in seeking to meet their needs in a particular information and communication environment. Others have focused on practical efforts to translate the citizen interest into action. McChesney (e.g., McChesney and Nichols 2003) has been spearheading a media reform movement that supports such interventions as developing community radio and television, applying antimonopoly laws to the media, establishing formal study to determine fair media ownership regulations, reinvigorating public service broadcasting, and so forth. Pitched partly at the American context and partly at the global communications market, this represents one among several movements at local, national, and international levels that seek to challenge the consumer focus of the contemporary communications sector and its regulators. To the extent that national contexts vary, such movements must inevitably be tailored to specific regulatory regimes. But to the extent that the critical concerns are common, each can and should learn from the other, developing and sharing a discourse on—in the United Kingdom's terms, the citizen interest, but in other terms, communicative resources, rights, entitlements, and capabilities—to intervene in the process of media and communications governance more widely and wisely.

Notes

1. The above quotes are from the Report Stage of the Passing of the Bill, House of Lords, June 23, 2003; http://www.publications.parliament.uk/pa/ld200203/ldhansrd/vo030623/text/30623-04.htm (accessed June 25, 2005).

2. Interview with the first author, July 20, 2005.

3. Interview with the first author, July 21, 2005.

4. It is beyond our scope to explore the views of industry, though this absence—empirically the most difficult to rectify, being significantly outside the public record—inevitably undermines the completeness of our account.

5. Interview with the first author, August 10, 2005.

6. Interview with the first author, July 13, 2005.

7. Interview with the first author, June 27, 2005.

8. Interview with the first author, July 21, 2005.

9. Interview with the first author, March 4, 2005.

10. Interview with the first author, April 19, 2005.

11. Interview with the first author, September 28, 2005.

12. Interview with the first author, June 20, 2005.

13. Interview with the first author, June 9, 2005.

14. Interview with the first author, June 9, 2005.

15. Interview with the first author, June 28, 2005.

16. Interview with the first author, July 21, 2005.

17. They were half men and half women, half middle class and half working class, living in eight areas of the United Kingdom (urban, suburban, rural), and from four categories of life stage: young people in their first jobs, parents with young children, those in midlife, and the recently retired.

References

Billig, M., S. Condor, D. Edwards, M. Gane, D. J. Middleton, and A. R. Radley. 1988. *Ideological dilemmas*. London: Sage.

Black, J., M. Lodge, and M. Thatcher. 2005. *Regulatory innovation: A comparative analysis*. Cheltenham, UK: Edward Elgar.

Carter, S. 2003a. Speech: The Communications Act: Myths and realities. September 9. http://www.ofcom .org.uk/media/speeches/2003/10/carter_20031009.

———. 2003b. Speech to the Royal Television Society Cambridge convention. September 19. http://www.ofcom.org.uk/media/speeches/2003/09/carter_20030919 (accessed July 11, 2005).

Chiapello, E., and N. Fairclough. 2002. Understanding the new management ideology: A transdisciplinary contribution from critical discourse analysis and new sociology of capitalism. *Discourse & Society* 13 (2): 185-208.

Couldry, N., S. Livingstone, and T. Markham. Forthcoming. *Public connection? Media consumption and the presumption of attention*. Houndmills, UK: Palgrave.

Currie, D. 2003. Speech to the English National Forum Seminar. July 7. http://www.ofcom.org .uk/media/speeches/2003/07/currie_20030707 (accessed December 29, 2005).

Department of Trade and Industry/Department for Culture, Media and Sport (DTI/DCMS). 2002. Note on the meaning of "customer," "consumer," and "citizen," to the Joint Select Committee, Department of Trade and Industry and the Department For Culture, Media and Sport. http://www.parliament .the-stationery-office.co.uk/pa/jt200102/jtselect/jtcom/169/2070808.htm (accessed July 11, 2005).

Freedman, D. 2005. *How level is the playing field? An analysis of the UK media policy-making process*. A report on research into media policy-making in the UK. Swindon, UK: Economic and Social Research Council.

Garnham, N. 1999. Amartya Sen's "Capabilities" approach to the evaluation of welfare: Its application to communications. In *Communication, citizenship and social policy*, ed. A. Calabrase and J.-C. Burgelman. Boulder, CO: Rowman & Littlefield.

Habermas, J. 1997. *Between facts and norms*. Cambridge: Cambridge University Press.

Hamelink, C. 2003. Statement on communication rights. Presented to the World Forum on Communication Rights, December 11, 2005. http://www.communicationrights.org/statement_en.html (accessed December 29, 2005).

Harvey, S. 2006. Ofcom's first year and neo-liberalism's blind spot: Attacking the culture of production. *Screen* 47 (1): 91-105.

Hay, J. 2002. *The Communications Bill and the citizen*. http://www.vlv.org.uk/combill291202issues.html.

Hirschman, A. 1969. *Exit, voice and loyalty*. Cambridge, MA: Harvard University Press.

Jessop, B. 2002. *The future of the capitalist state*. Cambridge, UK: Polity.

Livingstone, S., ed. 2005. *Audiences and publics: When cultural engagement matters for the public sphere*. Bristol, UK: Intellect Press.

Livingstone, S., P. Lunt, and L. Miller. Forthcoming-a. Citizens and consumers: Discursive debates during and after the Communications Act 2003. *Media, Culture & Society*.

———. Forthcoming-b. Citizens, consumers and the citizen-consumer: Articulating the interests at stake in media and communications regulation. *Discourse and Communication*.

Lunt, P., and S. Livingstone. Forthcoming. Regulating markets in the interest of consumers? In *Governance, citizens, and consumers*, ed. M. Bevir and F. Trentmann. Basingstoke, UK: Palgrave Macmillan.

McChesney, R., and J. Nichols. 2003. Our media, not theirs: Building the U.S. media reform movement. *These Times Magazine*, April.

Murdock, G., and P. Golding. 1989. Information poverty and political inequality: Citizenship in the age of privatised communications. *Journal of Communication* 39 (3): 180-93.

Needham, C. 2003. *Citizen-consumers: New labour's marketplace democracy*. London: Catalyst Forum.

Office of Communications (Ofcom). 2005. *Annual plan, 2005/6*. April 12. www.ofcom.org.uk.

Office of Communications (Ofcom) Consumer Panel. 2005. *Annual report, 2004/5*. http://www .ofcomconsumerpanel.org.uk/englishannualreport2005_06.pdf (accessed July 17, 2005).

Redding, Don. 2005. On the cusp: Finding new visions for social gain from broadcasting. *Political Quarterly* 76 (Suppl. 1): 146-58.

The Report of the Joint Committee on the Draft Communications Bill. House of Commons and House of Lords. 2002, July 25. London: Her Majesty's Stationary Office.

Richards, E. 2003. Speech to the Royal Television Society dinner. December 4. http://www.ofcom .org.uk/media/speeches/2003/12/richards_20031204 (accessed September 2, 2005).

Scannell, P. 1989. Public service broadcasting and modern public life. *Media, Culture & Society* 11:135-66.

Consumers and the State since the Second World War

By
MATTHEW HILTON

In the twentieth century, consumption became a political project intimately bound up with the state. By the 1950s, governments across the world worked to promote a vision of consumer society based around access and participation—affluence for all—rather than choice and luxury for the few. This vision of consumerism was tied in with the geopolitics of the cold war but was also constitutive of other globalizing trends that connected not only Western Europe to North America but also both sides of the Iron Curtain as well as the global South and North. The article analyzes the development of, and compares the differences in, the various consumer protection regimes that emerged in the latter half of the century. It points to processes of convergence in consumer politics across the globe that saw the development of consumer political thinking in the Soviet bloc and the development of supranational protection regimes at the European level. In more recent decades, the politics of consumer society based upon access and the collective has been eclipsed by a politics that emphasizes choice and the individual. Such a change represents a profound shift in the relations between consumers, citizens, and governments.

Keywords: consumerism; consumer protection; regulation; citizenship

In the 1950s, a new consumer movement emerged based on the comparative testing of branded commodities and the promotion of a "best buy" in subscription-based magazines. Beginning in the United States in 1936 with the formation of the Consumers Union, organized consumerism spread to Europe in the period of

Matthew Hilton is a professor of social history at the University of Birmingham. He is the author of Smoking in British Popular Culture *(Manchester University Press, 2000) and* Consumerism in Twentieth-Century Britain *(Cambridge University Press, 2003). He has coedited* The Politics of Consumption *(Berg, 2001) and* Au nom du consommateur *(Decouvert, 2005) and has published widely in journals such as* Past and Present, The Historical Journal, Journal of Consumer Culture, Journal of Social History, Journal of Contemporary History, Voluntas, *and* Contemporary British History. *He is currently writing a history of global consumer politics since 1945.*

DOI: 10.1177/0002716206298532

postwar reconstruction and the emergence of the affluent society. Modeling themselves directly on their U.S. counterpart, several organizations were created in Europe in the 1950s. The activists associated with these groups liked to imagine themselves as the vanguard of a new consumer movement. In many cases they were, but if a global dimension is taken what becomes clear is that comparative testing constituted only one aspect of a broader politicization of consumption in the postwar period.

A whole range of organizations participated in a defense of the consumer in the decades following the 1940s. Elected politicians promised shoppers a better life just around the corner, constructing welfare regimes that guaranteed basic standards of living for all. State officials liaised with consumer experts in the media and in women's and housewives' organizations to develop informative labeling schemes. Business associations worked in conjunction with consumer representatives to develop quality certification marks. The cooperatives continued their campaigns against the abuses of the marketplace by trusts and cartels. And the trade unions continually sought regulatory solutions to some of the perceived inequities of capitalist development.

The significance of the 1950s as a key moment in consumer politics was the growth in interest in affluence as well as necessity. The advocates of the consumer society sought not only to protect the poor but the insecure rich as well. Consumer society was being held before citizens as the way forward for all. It is of no surprise, therefore, that seasoned campaigners against consumer injustices were revitalized in this period alongside the testing magazines of the new organized consumer movement. And it is also unsurprising that comparative testing did not enter an empty institutional arena. The renewed attention to the consumer was conducted through established frameworks of politics and economics, which meant that the consumer protection regimes emerging in the affluent society were incredibly diverse. For all the promotion of the free market promoted by the Marshall Plan, therefore, the new consumer society found itself open to question by a wide variety of consumer activists and prone to the different regulatory traditions and practices of each legally bounded nation.

This article sets out the full range of consumer politics operating in industrial capitalist societies after the Second World War. It captures the diversity of a consumer movement that states responded to—and helped construct—in a variety of ways. As the protection of consumers became a key political battlefield across the society being built in their name, different consumer protection regimes emerged. Many of these reflected the existing political economic framework of each state, and important comparisons can be made between certain ideal types: pluralist, corporatist, social democratic, individualist, and so on. But what is also apparent is the remarkable degree of convergence in consumer protection systems. States analyzed and copied the consumer protection measures of other states. They put forward best practices to serve as the benchmarks for different societies and economies. Particularly at the European level, they ultimately developed supranational consumer infrastructures, which overrode many of the particularities of nation-specific consumer measures.

This all suggests a response to the consumer interest far more complicated than either a direct reaction to the rise of comparative testing, a cheap political ploy by government ministers to maintain their popularity, or the imposition of an American-modeled market economy upon Europe and elsewhere. Instead, it suggests that consumer society was an amorphous entity in which many organizations had an interest. As the consumer became a universal category, it was inadequate to merely champion the rights of one consumer over another. Consumerism as a political project had to be seen as offering something to all consumers, rich and poor alike. The affluent society had to promise more choice for those who could afford it, but also more stuff for those who so far could not. In the consumer societies built after the war—and in the protection regimes established to look over them—a broad-ranging consumer politics aimed to bring everybody within its grasp. At this moment, consumption became an activity that was potentially democratic, universal, and open to all.

The emergence of organized consumerism in the 1950s owed its existence to several different trajectories of consumer organizing. When consumer representatives began to obtain a voice in state bureaucracies, governments cultivated the support and involvement of a whole variety of movements. The cooperative movement had a strong claim to being the oldest, most established, and most successful consumer organization over the previous century. Although weakened in many countries after the war, where it remained strong, as in Scandinavia, it could claim a prominent voice as the foremost representative of the consumer (Furlough and Strikwerda 1999; Theien 2006). But the trade unions and the labor movement more generally also played a prominent role in consumer advocacy, both before and after the war. Indeed, in Austria, the principal consumer testing organization owed its existence to the labor movement as the Austrian Trade Union and the syndicalist institution, the Chamber of Labour, created the Association for Consumer Information in 1961 (Thorelli and Thorelli 1974). Women's groups too built on decades of consumer protest: through organized consumer leagues protesting over labor conditions, through street protests against shortages in two wars, and in representing consumers in home economics councils, housing committees, and cost of living surveys. As economies were rebuilt in the 1940s, these women's groups dominated many consumer movements. In Japan, the politics of consumption was spearheaded by various federations of housewives' associations, while in Europe women's organizations assisted in the formation of new consumer initiatives and women journalists made consumer issues important public causes (Maclachlan 2002).

Twentieth-century governments have maintained a complex set of relationships with these organizations of the consumer. On one hand, grassroots consumer groups have existed independently of any state funding and have constituted pressure groups similar to other social movements. On the other hand, many have been sustained and nurtured by public finances and have been incorporated within—or emerged from—the institutions of the state. But what is clear is that consumer protection had become a state project, no matter that consumerism was often molded to fit existing national political economies. Unlike in previous centuries, when consumption could serve mainly as a theoretical and practical rallying point for economists and consumers, in the twentieth century, consumers were recognized as political entities to whom governments must respond: defending the consumer-citizen and working to protect his or her standard of living, while offering rewards in the future, became a typical populist manifesto of politicians of all persuasions.

Government intervention in consumer affairs began with the food and drug regulations of the late nineteenth century, followed by the curbs placed on trusts, cartels, and monopolies shortly afterwards, especially in the United States (Goodwin 1999; Nadel 1971). In two world wars, rationing and supply controls meant states were forced to listen to consumer concerns, and bureaucracies catering to consumer interests were established. The mobilization of the state around issues of consumption created opportunities for those who saw in the consumer a citizen around whom modern welfare regimes could be built. In the United States, for instance, liberals such as John Kenneth Galbraith and Lewis Mumford were attracted to institutions such as the Office of Price Administration because they saw in these state interventions a more social-democratic citizenship and one that satisfied their moral, protestant-inspired dilemmas over abundance as it urged frugality and "chastened consumption" in the present in order to enjoy indulgence in the future (Horowitz 2004). While many of these institutions were fiercely opposed, not least by big business, wartime state consumerism offered a "fair shares" politics of consumption that was attractive at the ballot box in the subsequent years of austerity and reconstruction (Zweiniger-Bargielowska 2000).

Following the Second World War, consumer society was championed as the bright future to which the ravaged economies must direct themselves. Through greater state spending on infrastructure, the expansion of credit facilities, the encouragement of home ownership in the new suburbs, and the creation of personal opportunities symbolized by the GI Bill (Serviceman's Readjustment Act) in 1944, all Americans were being invited to participate in the "consumers' republic" (Cohen 2003). Arguably, this model of an all-embracing consumer culture was exported through the Marshall Plan, but Roosevelt's "freedom from want" was mirrored in Beveridge's welfarism in Britain and in social democracy more generally in Europe (Donohue 2003). The sociologist Jean Fourastié elaborated upon a long-standing commitment to planning in French political economy, extolling the virtues of consumption as a civilizing process that would drag citizens from older modes of living to what he described the thirty years between 1945 and 1975 as: *les trente glorieuses* (Boulat 2005). In Germany, the social market economy espoused by the minister of economics, Ludwig Erhard, presented its own model of a future consumer society. He embraced an alliance with consumers in the rebuilding exercise, creating the Working Group for Consumers Unions in 1953, that drew on the existing expertise provided by the women's and cooperative movements. Riding the crest of the economic miracle, Erhard was able to claim no narrow vision of a consumer society; instead, he was able to announce "prosperity for all" (Landsman 2005).

This rhetorical construct of a future consumer society shared and participated in by everybody contrasts with a spirit of consumerism concerned solely with individual choice and acquisition. If *consumer democracy* as a term is perhaps only truly applicable to the United States, so all-pervasive was the idea that state policy, mass consumption, and universal standards of living were bound up with one another that the rhetoric crossed the Iron Curtain to the Soviet bloc. Even Stalin spoke of the need to pay attention to the production of consumer goods and, according to the most thoroughgoing study of twentieth-century consumer economies, the cold war became a "struggle over which system more effectively satisfied standards for the good life, with each spelling out, in opposition to the other, a definition of mass consumption suited to its resources and legacy of development" (de Grazia 2005, 344). The two competing cold war ideologies almost literally clashed in the kitchen at the Moscow Trade Fair in 1959. U.S. Vice President Richard Nixon and Soviet premier Nikita Khrushchev, walking around the model homes exhibited in the American display, engaged in a teasing dialogue about the relative merits of capitalism and communism in bringing more goods, better homes, and higher incomes to more and more people. Across both sides of the Iron Curtain, therefore, it seemed the expansion of consumption and the promotion of consumer society to everybody were defining features of the role of the modern state.

This rhetorical construct of a future consumer society shared and participated in by everybody contrasts with a spirit of consumerism concerned solely with individual choice and acquisition.

If standards of living were to be increased for everybody and the society of the consumer was to be brought to all, then it also stood to reason that politicians had to respond by offering shoppers some protection in this unknown age of affluence. The new regime of the shopper was not one where consumer sovereignty was to be the model for avoiding the perils of unwise purchasing. If consumers were to behave with confidence, providing the impetus for economic growth and making all the improvements in technology and productivity worthwhile, then they required assistance and support. They needed to be assured that their spending would result in greater utility for themselves and their families. They needed to know that in borrowing heavily to purchase a car, a house, and all the furniture to arrange inside the house, they would not lose everything if the house were found to be shoddily built, the car broke down on every trip, and the appliances bought for the home harmed those who switched them on. As firms grew in size and complexity, increasing the distance between the consumer and producer, citizens needed to know that constraints and curbs would be placed on businessmen's behavior; that capitalism would be kept in check; and that somehow, if not through the authority of choice but the authority of government, the market would still serve the interests for those it claimed to exist.

As affluence arrived, governments around the world attempted to develop regimes of consumer protection to provide consumers with the confidence to enter and participate in the market. While states responded in different ways, what must be emphasized above all is that from the 1960s and especially in the 1970s states did respond: it is with good reason that many consumer activists look back on these decades as the time when they achieved many of their greatest successes. The growth in consumer protection measures was simply incredible, sweeping aside many of the rudimentary consumer representative systems developed during the 1930s and 1940s and replacing almost entirely the now seemingly rudimentary regulations enacted at the end of the nineteenth century. In Germany, just 25 new laws were enacted relating to consumer protection from 1945 to 1970, but a further 338 were adopted by 1978. Similarly, in France, just 37 laws and ministerial decrees came into effect before 1970, a total that had grown to 94 by 1978 (Trumbull 2006a). In Britain, major laws relating to consumer safety, hire purchase, resale price maintenance, and trade descriptions appeared in the 1960s, followed by wider regulations on fair trading, credit, and unsolicited goods and services in the first half of the 1970s (Hilton 2003). In the United States, a flurry of consumer protection laws appeared in the late 1960s relating to the automobile industry, drug safety, meat quality, package labeling, credit reporting, product safety, and a whole host of other trade practices (Mayer 1989).

Moreover, these specific legislative remedies to market abuses were backed up with the creation of entire bureaucracies devoted to protecting the consumer. Across Europe and the United States, official institutions appeared that provided information to consumers about products, the operation of the market, and their rights within it. Various types of consumer councils emerged that drew on the grassroots consumer movement but that also utilized their own resources to represent consumers in various ministries that touched on consumer affairs. Some specifically dealt with consumer complaints, taking companies to court on behalf of individual shoppers or consumers as a whole in class action suits. Ombudsmen, trading standards officers, and weights and measures inspectorates were all expanded at national, regional, and local levels to watch over more disreputable manufacturers and traders. Standards institutes and official quality certification schemes were either controlled by the state or else heavily funded from the public purse. And codes of practice, regulatory watchdogs, and independent councils were established to monitor specific aspects of the market, such as advertising, financial services, and the utilities, whether supplied by nationalized industries, municipal authorities, or private corporations.

The most meaningful attempt at comparison so far has been carried out by a political scientist. Gunnar Trumbull has illustrated three broad models of consumer citizenship. First, an economic model of citizenship has regarded consumers as partners in the economy, such that the challenges facing them are the consequence of market failures and imperfections, be they information asymmetries or the inequities emerging from the abuse of monopolistic power. The solutions sought have therefore revolved around strengthening existing market mechanisms and ensuring the consumer can behave as predicted by economic theory. To some extent, this model has dominated consumer protection policies in countries such as Germany, Britain, Austria, and Japan. In the Scandinavian countries, however, a more "associational" model of citizenship has been pursued, whereby consumers have been regarded like other legitimate social interest groups. Rather than finding protections within the market, then, consumers have been given the right to participate in forums dealing with overall structural issues. Having made the assumption that consumers and producers share many interests, associational citizenship seeks to create mechanisms through which different interests can negotiate with one another on an equal footing. Finally, a model of political citizenship emphasizes the rights of consumers and recognizes their roles as sociopolitical actors. Since consumers are not solely economic beings, they ought to be protected from the risks and uncertainties with which only professionals are usually able to cope. To some extent, this was adopted in France and the United States and is dependent upon the existence of a highly mobilized and vociferous consumer movement to which governments are prepared to respond (Trumbull 2006b).

But if these models of citizenship serve as rough categories, they have also been tempered by the existing political and legal structures in which new consumer protection measures have had to be situated. While Trumbull (2006b) found consistency across the Scandinavian countries in their pursuit of an associational model of consumer citizenship, other consumer protection regimes have been influenced by existing policies that determine the role of the producer in the economy and the state. Within the economic model, therefore, Britain has largely sought more market-based solutions, while Germany and Austria have adopted more corporatist consumer-producer mechanisms. In Japan, the consumer has also had to fit in with a strong state and the existence of great producer political power at the center. Similarly, while France and the United States have regarded the consumer as a political entity, the United States has sought, as did Britain, market-based solutions to their grievances, while France, though sporadically and through much experimentation, has mobilized statist mechanisms to protect the consumer. The models of citizenship have just as often served as ideal types for the range of institutions and individuals seeking to speak for the consumer in any one location. This has resulted in much borrowing from one another and the existence of many consumer protection measures that seemingly typify the style of a more general regime identified in another country.

The Scandinavian experience has been most frequently invoked in discussions over consumer protection. The state moved early in its intervention into consumer affairs, incorporating the existing strands of the consumer movement into the official institutions of the state. For instance, in Denmark, the government

Home Economics Council was established as early as 1935. In many ways, these early state interventions have made the need for an independent consumer movement less apparent. In Sweden especially, the state has taken over many of the roles elsewhere performed by private groups. In 1951, the Institute for Informative Labelling was established, which has set out product standards that firms have adhered to, guaranteeing consumers information about the commodity and certain minimum levels of quality. In 1957, the Swedes also created the State Consumer Institute, which has undertaken the testing of goods. Sweden pioneered the use of the Consumer Ombudsman in 1971 (followed by Norway in 1973, Denmark in 1974, and Finland in 1978), which has mediated disputes between consumers and business, helping to develop binding agreements on trade associations over such matters as advertising standards and standard contract terms. And its Market Court has served to manage consumer legal cases brought by the Ombudsman on behalf of consumers. The availability of this legal tool has strengthened the power of the Ombudsman to an extent far greater than in similarly conceived systems elsewhere, although the availability of class action suits in countries such as the United States provides an alternative model for seeking redress for many consumers as a collective (Theien 2006; Thorelli and Thorelli 1974, 1977).

Sweden's associational system is mirrored in the more obviously corporatist systems of Austria and Germany. In the latter, the Alliance of Consumer Associations has negotiated with producers and other interests in a whole variety of committees and institutions across several government departments. Ostensibly, it operates on an equal footing with other economic interest groups, but in reality it has meant that consumer protection in Germany has become geared toward more technical issues, seeking to work with manufacturers to ensure that problems with products are resolved before they enter the market (Trumbull 2001; Consumers International 1995). The corporatist structure in Japan, too, has also largely weakened the impact of consumer protection, thanks to the greater entrenchment of producer interests within the central state bureaucracy. Japanese consumer groups have not been able to challenge the political power of producer groups, and indeed many have argued for measures that support the manufacturers: thus, "a disproportionate amount of their criticisms of business are criticisms of the practices of foreign businesses" (Vogel 1992). By arguing for greater food standards and self-sufficiency in agriculture, for instance, Japanese consumers have actually fought against their own immediate economic interests, which could be served by cheaper imports. However, when there have been divisions and disputes in national politics, Japan's highly mobilized consumer movement has often been able to achieve notable successes (such as the Product Liability Law in 1994), and its relationship with government has been marked less by co-option and more by conflict (Maclachlan 2002).

Care must be taken in seeking to classify consumer politics in any one country, especially if a focus on government initiatives, regulations, and institutions masks the history of conflict often bubbling under the surface, conflicts that often go to the heart of the definition of a consumer. In Germany, the producer bias of the corporatist framework has resulted in a system that privileges better information for the individual. Consumer protection remains largely market oriented as a consequence. In Britain, the model of the consumer that has largely won out is that of an economic being, to whom more information ought to be presented so that he or she can make better individual choices. Arguably, this model was enshrined in the legislation following the Report of the Molony Committee on Consumer Protection in 1962, in the Office of Fair Trading in 1973, and in the privatization schemes and their regulatory shadows from the 1980s. Yet activists also presented the consumer as a social being, to whom states and businesses should respond, ensuring that not only individuals but also consumers as a collective be provided with basic goods and services as well as with access to all the sorts of information and resources crucial to the exercise of good citizenship.

Likewise, in the United States, care must be taken in identifying consumer protection solely as a market-oriented, individualistic regime. Certainly, the primacy of the market cannot be denied, nor the faith held in it as a solver of consumer problems. But American consumer politics also embraces other forms of protection. Because the individual consumer is also a rights-based citizen, these rights politicize his or her actions in a manner distinct from the associational tendencies of Scandinavian social democracy. Thus, in the late 1960s, a regulatory framework emerged in the United States often far more rigorous than that achieved in European economies. Consequently, regulatory agencies such as the Federal Trade Commission and the Federal Energy Administration were strengthened, and new agencies such as the Environmental Protection Agency, the Occupational Safety and Health Administrations, the Consumer Safety Commission, and the National Highway Traffic Safety Administration were launched (Nadel 1971).

It is important not to classify too rigorously the consumer protection regime of any one country. States have learned and copied from one another, resulting in ad hoc measures that, collectively, betray the ideal types of many different consumer protection systems. Furthermore, over time states have changed their policies and adapted consumerism both to the demands of the consumer movement itself and the more general ideologies of the political party in power. In France, for example, a strong central state has enabled many experiments in consumer protection. Initially, the limited resources of the National Consumption Committee, created in 1960, matched the powerlessness of the British Consumer Council rather than anything seen to exist in Scandinavia. Following the lead taken by the German Stiftung Warentest and the relative weakness of French comparative testing organizations, the government created the National Consumption Institute in 1967, which soon began publishing results of its own tests as well as advising on a much broader range of issues. In the 1970s, a model of consumer protection based on representation and corporatist negotiation began to appear following pressure from a highly motivated and better resourced grassroots consumer movement. A secretariat of state for consumption was established in 1976, and a flood of consumer protection acts began to appear. The Socialist government quadrupled funding to consumer protection and attempted to place consumers on an equal footing with producers, ultimately culminating with the establishment of a full Ministry of Consumption in 1981. Although these initiatives were eventually scaled back, the centralized state of France created a framework for the establishment of the consumer as a highly politicized aspect of citizenship (Chatriot 2005).

It is important not to classify too rigorously the consumer protection regime of any one country.

So much of consumer protection owes as much to the efforts of consumers as it does to government. It is difficult to reduce the characteristics of protection regimes solely to the political economic context of each individual state. In Britain, for instance, the existence of an extremely impressive private comparative testing magazine has partially excused the state from taking on an advocacy role for consumers. Likewise, Consumentenbond in the Netherlands has also enjoyed an extremely impressive popularity among Dutch consumers, perhaps ensuring the dominance of an information-based model of consumer protection. Had Consumentendbond's magazine, *Consumentengids*, not penetrated so many Dutch households, then the state may have been forced to step in on behalf of consumers to a far greater extent than it did. And if consumer protection is broken down into its constituent parts—into advertising regulation, trade descriptions, price controls, and so on—then ever-greater disparities from national norms emerge. The point is, therefore, less that rigid differences can be determined from cross-national comparisons but that consumer protection had become an international phenomenon from which states learned from one another and adopted measures that took best practices from different contexts. The most important point about consumer protection is not that it was implemented in different ways throughout the world but that consumer protection existed at all.

Consumer protection was clearly an international trend, appearing in liberal capitalist, mixed, and social market economies. As many of these systems were fundamental to the pursuit of the cold war, consumption also became an aspect of a broader geopolitical framework. In many ways, the Soviet bloc had to be seen to be responding to the U.S. pursuit of the standard of living, but members of communist bureaucracies were also influenced by international developments in consumer protection. In this regard, the consumer movement and consumer protection were global trends that cut across cold war politics pointing to alternative narratives of globalization within contemporary world history. Posited as a neutral political movement, consumerism avoided a polarization across the ideological divide and instead served to harmonize and globalize consumer protection regimes behind the scenes of any such controversy of the kind found in Nixon and Khrushchev's kitchen debate of 1959.

Undoubtedly, consumption did play a role in the cold war. While both sides pursued the goal of greater standards of living and the provision of necessities for all, ultimately capitalism proved more effective at providing comfort and luxury than the command economies of the Soviet bloc. The communism of the party-state failed to either predict or satisfy consumer wants even after several decades of industrialization and economic planning (Bryson 1984; Steiner 1998). Yet advocates of consumer protection emerged within economic planning departments. In East Germany, leaders had to contend with the Soviet emphasis on production goods while acknowledging that many of their citizens looked favorably upon the new prosperity being enjoyed in the West. A distinct consumer lobby emerged in the 1950s in the Ministry for Trade and Provisioning, which found expression in specialized journals dealing with domestic trade and which developed "a language and a set of goals aiming toward building a more articulated consumption regime, toward a wider and richer array of consumption offerings" (Landsman 2005).

Within the confines of the German Democratic Republic, though, the consumer lobby was never able to enjoy a persistent power base or a sustained role in the planning of consumption. But in more open societies, a fuller recognition of the consumer could take place. Yugoslavia had, perhaps, the strongest tradition of consumer protection stretching back to 1957 and the state-run Federal Board of Family and Households. In 1969, this was reorganized to become the Association of Consumers, a state-funded but reasonably autonomous body with the remit to encourage better quality and lower-priced products (Macgeorge 1997). Later, other communist countries were known to take advantage of the worldwide consumer movement. In China and Cuba, consumer organizations were created from above as deliberate means to contain the political ill will of consumers in an economy of shortages. Yet in more liberal or reformist regimes, the commitment to the consumer was genuine. In countries such as Hungary, experiments were conducted in decentralization and "marketized" socialism, while more foolhardy borrowing from Western governments took place to increase imports to satisfy consumer demand. As a wider commitment to liberalization, a more grassroots consumer organization even emerged in Hungary in 1982 as an offshoot of the Patriotic People's Front, an umbrella for various civil movements (Koźminski 1992).

In Poland, as in East Germany, the party-state followed the Soviet productivist model, which occasionally paid lip service to the consumer but which ultimately focused on the dictates of production. However, consumption could nevertheless be an important focus for broader political grievances, and many of these concerns were taken up by a consumer lobby within the Institute for Domestic Trade and Services from the late 1950s that also looked to learn from the consumer protection regimes of the West. During the later stages of Polish communism, this consumer lobby was able to transform itself into a more genuine consumer movement. Amid the events of the early 1980s—those associated with Solidarity—a more independent form of consumer activism emerged. The Federation of Consumers (Federacja Konsumentów, or FK), established in 1981, was neither an official arm of the state nor the product of ordinary forms of consumer interaction with the world of goods. It was an association of experts drawn from the civil service and the professions and that bore much in common with the increasingly professionalized nongovernmental organizations and new social movements of the West. The concerns and interests of the consumers attached to FK were no longer focused solely on improving consumer supply under a command economy, but were adapted also from an emerging global discourse of consumer rights and protection to which they, as educated professionals, had access. It reflects the extent to which the experts of FK behaved not as cold war warriors, championing one ideological system over another, but as an intermediary cohort of citizens concerned with the condition of their society and economy from a perspective influenced by the international exchange of consumerist thought. Their work points to the growing internationalization of consumer protection and organized consumerism that traversed established divisions of twentieth-century history (Hilton and Mazurek 2007).

Indeed, the twentieth century witnessed a harmonization of the language of consumer protection. For instance, the standardization movement facilitated trade and commerce while also offering basic protections for consumers. National bodies formed at the beginning of the twentieth century came together in 1947 to create the International Organization for Standardization. Such bodies have been tied into broader process of westernization and even Americanization. The Organization for Economic Cooperation and Development (OECD), for example, began as a facilitator of the Marshall Plan in 1948 and has subsequently become an important focal point for the communication of consumer protection measures. The OECD's Committee on Consumer Policy has reviewed measures undertaken in member states on an annual basis, also providing ten-year summaries that act as reference guides for those wishing to learn about what has been enacted in other contexts. It has helped bring a convergence in consumer policies by focusing member states' attention on common goals particularly, for the OECD, in developing global markets to increase consumer choice (OECD 1995).

But harmonization of consumer policy has also come through the intervention of supranational bodies concerned with the regulation of trade and markets. Resolution 543 of May 17, 1973, by the Council of Europe established a Consumer Protection Charter, based around the five established consumer movement concerns of protection, redress, information, education, and representation first articulated by President Kennedy in the United States. This paved the way for the first Programme for Consumer Protection in 1975, which directed European consumer policy in subsequent decades. The modifications and additions made in the second program in 1981 did not detract from the underlying rights-based spirit, and no substantial changes were made under the

Single European Act of 1987 that led to the consolidation of the internal market. Indeed, the third consumer program of 1986, A New Impetus for Consumer Portection Policy, was couched within the broader objective of the internal market, and if anything, the rhetoric of rights was toned down as greater competition and choice were held to offer the main protections to the consumer (Weatherill 1997; Commission of the European Communities 1986; Consumers in the Europe Group 1999).

The supranational framework provided by Europe both harmonized consumer protection and narrowed it as a concept. European codification of consumer law amid a process of economic integration has ensured that individual member states have adopted protection mechanisms pioneered in other countries. It has meant that Europe has had a tremendous impact on national consumer protection regimes, ensuring that the differences between countries such as France and Germany have been blurred. It has also meant that in those states where consumer protection was weak or underdeveloped, such as Greece, Spain, Italy, and Portugal, a ready-made model for consumer protection has been provided. But increasingly, that model of consumer protection has been dictated by the wider goal of market reform, ensuring that consumerism as a regulatory regime has been diluted if not replaced with a notion of consumerism emphasizing choice, competition, and ever-expanding markets.

European consumer policy therefore followed a largely information-based approach, whereby consumers were protected through the provision of better information, making them more efficient and rational and, in turn, improving the operation of the market (Hadfield, Howse, and Trebilock 1998). Ultimately, their interests were seen to lie in more choice and expanding markets, rather than the greater supply of public goods, a more equitable distribution of commodities, or the ability of all consumers to participate on a more equal footing. Admittedly, as in the United States and throughout the OECD, extremely strong regulatory protections were made available on matters of consumer safety and food sovereignty, especially as witnessed in the reactions to bovine spongiform encephalopathy (BSE, or mad cow disease) (Vos 2000; Ringstedt 1986). But generally, harmonization of consumer protection policy was attendant with a reduction to the lowest common denominator. While different traditions of consumer activism and the political-economic structure of an individual state might therefore have created very different consumer policy regimes across America, Europe, and the Pacific region, the work of supranational bodies such as Europe served to override these differences. And they did so by positing the most global of consumer interests—choice—as the main target of consumer protection. The Europe of the 1990s therefore reflected only one aspect of the vision of consumer society held by those who sought to reconstruct Europe after 1945. As consumer protection regimes first came into existence, there had been a concern to ensure all were protected, with protection meaning access as well as choice. By the 1990s, Europe had much less to say for those who could not actually afford choice.

The consumer society being built by states at the end of the twentieth century was very different from that which had driven reconstruction in postwar Europe.

In the 1950s, politicizing consumption came to be as much about access to afflu-ence as it was about choice for those already enjoying comfort and luxury. Particularly after the Second World War, consumption offered the basis for a new social contract for populations eager to move forward from the austere environ-ment of deprivation and devastation. No matter that the critiques of commodity capitalism persisted and the liberal left remained uneasy with an amoral accep-tance of luxury, the consumer societies created in the 1950s steered their public toward an area between necessity and luxury, hunger and excess: a mass con-sumption, comfortable, affluent middle ground that all could enjoy.

But as states responded to citizens as consumers, consumers themselves were acknowledged to be an incredibly diverse entity. Standing in as substitutes for the public, consumers were as varied as society itself. Very different overall systems therefore came into being in Europe, America, and the wider world. These did not all follow the consumer democracy of the United States; nor did they agree on the definition of the citizen supposedly at the heart of consumer society: he or she could be a social democratic participant in civil society; a co-opted interest within a corporatist structure; a utility-maximizing individual eager to improve his or her own well-being at one and the same time as the efficiency of industry; or a highly politicized rights-seeking individual capable of making demands of, and gaining intervention by, successive governments in the marketplace.

Standing in as substitutes for the public,
consumers were as varied as society itself.

For all that the organized consumer movement might like to see in twentieth-century consumer protection a progressive narrative of success built upon suc-cess, these great differences in the models of the consumer-citizen warn against such a history. Consumer activists have often liked to argue that their heyday was in the 1960s and 1970s; if they have declined as a political and social force there-after, it is due to their having achieved many of their own goals. To some extent, they have a right to be so contented. Compared to the fledgling technocratic age of the 1950s, commodities no longer break down as soon as they are taken home, guarantees and standard contracts ensure that forms of redress are available to dissatisfied customers, advertisements might well continue to exaggerate but there are restrictions on overtly false claims, sources of information are available to shoppers other than those provided by the manufacturer or retailer, and most dramatically, the danger of death and injury from negligently assembled products has declined.

Yet in all the measures that have been successfully implemented, there has also been a narrowing of the vision of consumer protection. As states have borrowed best practices from one another, or avoided the mistaken experiments conducted by each other, consumer protection has become harmonized. However, as the European experience demonstrates, this harmonization has taken place around narrowly defined rights to choice and ever-expanding markets. These were crucial elements of the demands of so many consumer groups, but they were not all. Consumers and states had imagined a consumer society open to everybody, in which all could participate and in which all could operate fairly. These were the driving factors behind many of the consumer protection measures introduced just as the affluent society was coming to fruition. They were designed to ensure that protection existed so that every citizen could enjoy the good life.

But in the later focus on choice, protection became unevenly distributed. Those who can afford to choose alternatives, can bear the costs of deceptive practices, and can simply live to spend another day have their own protection mechanisms. But for the poor and disadvantaged, access to such protection is less readily available, and their participation in consumer society comes at a struggle and a cost. This runs against the internationalist vision of consumption promoted in the postwar years when, at the height of the cold war, the advocates and practitioners of communism and capitalism argued the relative merits of each system in bringing more goods to more people. Particularly since consumer society has continued to have a global remit, stretching beyond the industrialized nations of the world and toward Southeast Asia, Latin America, and ultimately Africa, these aspects of consumption have remained crucial. But if the definition of the consumer was restricted to choice, then the implications for less developed countries could be profound. The difficulties faced by consumers in the developing world could be very different from those faced by the affluent, but the solutions that have come to be proposed have not emphasized the same rights to access, participation, and improved standards of living as those that defined the consumer societies of Europe and North America in the 1950s and 1960s.

References

Boulat, R. 2005. Jean Fourastié at la naissance de la societé de consummation en France. In *Au nom du consommateur: Consommation et politique en Europe et aux États-Unis au xxe siècle*, ed. A. Chatriot, M.-E. Chessel, and M. Hilton. Paris: La Découverte.

Bryson, P. J. 1984. *The consumer under socialist planning: The East German case*. New York: Praeger.

Chatriot, A. 2005. Qui defend le consommateur? Associations, institutions et politiques publiques en France, 1972-2003. In *Au nom du consommateur: Consommation et politique en Europe et aux États-Unis au xxe siècle*, ed. A. Chatriot, M.-E. Chessel, and M. Hilton. Paris: La Découverte.

Cohen, L. 2003. *A consumers' republic: The politics of mass consumption in postwar America*. New York: Knopf.

Commission of the European Communities. 1986. *Ten years of community consumer policy: A contribution to a people's Europe*. Luxembourg: Office for Official Publications of the European Communities.

Consumers in the Europe Group. 1999. *EU consumer protection policy: A review of European Union consumer programmes, EU consumer protection legislation and European Commission consumer initiatives*. London: Consumers in the Europe Group.

Consumers International. 1995. *Balancing the scales, part 2: Consumer protection in the Netherlands and Germany*. London: Consumers International.

de Grazia, V. 2005. *Irresistible empire: America's advance through twentieth-century Europe*. Cambridge, MA: Balknap.

Donohue, K. G. 2003. *Freedom from want: American liberalism and the idea of the consumer*. Baltimore: John Hopkins University Press.

Furlough E., and C. Strikwerda, eds. 1999. *Consumers against capitalism? Consumer co-operation in Europe, North America and Japan, 1840-1990*. Oxford, UK: Rowman & Littlefield.

Goodwin, L. S. 1999. *The pure food, drink, and drug crusaders, 1879-1914*. Jefferson, NC: McFarland.

Hadfield, G. K., R. Howse, and M. J. Trebilock. 1998. Information-based principles for rethinking consumer protection policy. *Journal of Consumer Policy* 21:131-69.

Hilton, M. 2003. *Consumerism in twentieth-century Britain: The search for a historical movement*. Cambridge: Cambridge University Press.

Hilton, M., and M. Mazurek. 2007. Consumerism, Solidarity and communism: Consumer protection and the consumer movement in Poland. *Journal of Contemporary History*, 42 (2): 313-41.

Horowitz, D. 2004. *The anxieties of affluence: Critiques of American consumer culture, 1939-1979*. Boston: University of Massachusetts Press.

Koźminski, A. K. 1992. Consumers in transition from the centrally planned economy to the market economy. *Journal of Consumer Policy* 14:351-69.

Landsman, M. 2005. *Dictatorship and demand: The politics of consumerism in East Germany*. Cambridge, MA: Harvard University Press.

Macgeorge, A. 1997. Yugoslavian consumer movement. In *Encyclopaedia of the consumer movement*, ed. S. Brobeck, R. N. Mayer, and R. O. Herrmann. Santa Barbara, CA: ABC-CLIO.

Maclachlan, P. L. 2002. *Consumer politics in postwar Japan: The institutional boundaries of citizen activism*. New York: Columbia University Press.

Mayer, R. N. 1989. *The consumer movement: Guardians of the marketplace*. Boston: Twayne.

Nadel, M. V. 1971. *The politics of consumer protection*. New York: Bobs-Merrill.

Organization for Economic Cooperation and Development. 1995. *A global marketplace for consumers*. Paris: OECD.

Ringstedt, N. 1986. OECD, safety and the consumer. *Journal of Consumer Policy* 6:57-64.

Steiner, A. 1998. Dissolution of the "dictatorship over needs"? Consumer behaviour and economic reform in East Germany in the 1960s. In *Getting and spending: European and American consumer societies in the twentieth century*, ed. S. Strasser, C. McGovern, and M. Judt. Cambridge: Cambridge University Press.

Theien, I. 2006. Shopping for the "People's Home": Consumer planning in Norway and Sweden after the Second World War. In *The expert consumer: Associations and professionals in consumer society*, ed. A. Chatriot, M.-E. Chessel, and M. Hilton. Aldershot, UK: Ashgate.

Thorelli, H. B., and S. V. Thorelli, eds. 1974. *Consumer information handbook: Europe and North America*. New York: Praeger.

———. 1977. *Consumer information systems and consumer policy*. Cambridge, MA: Ballinger.

Trumbull, G. 2001. Strategies of consumer group mobilisation: France and Germany in the 1970s. In *The politics of consumption: Material culture and citizenship in Europe and America*, ed. M. Daunton and M. Hilton. Oxford, UK: Berg.

———. 2006a. *Consumer capitalism: Politics, product markets and firm Strategy in France and Germany*. Ithaca, NY: Cornell University Press.

———. 20006b. National varieties of consumerism. *Jahrbuch für Wirtschaftsgeschichte* 1:77-93.

Vogel, D. 1992. Consumer protection and protectionism in Japan. *Journal of Japanese Studies* 18 (1): 119-54.

Vos, E. 2000. EU food safety regulation in the aftermath of the BSE crisis. *Journal of Consumer Policy* 23:227-55.

Weatherill, S. 1997. *EC consumer law and policy*. London: Longman.

Zweiniger-Bargielowska, Ina. 2000. *Austerity in Britain: Rationing, controls and consumption, 1939-1955*. Oxford: Oxford University Press.

Buying into Downtown Revival: The Centrality of Retail to Postwar Urban Renewal in American Cities

By
LIZABETH COHEN

This article argues that the link between consumption and civic engagement has an important local, not just national, history and that retailers' involvement in the downtown urban renewal of American cities in the post-WWII era offers a particularly fruitful avenue of investigation. The article focuses on New Haven, Connecticut, and Boston, Massachusetts, where Edward J. Logue served as development chief from 1954 to 1967. His record over these fourteen years, when he was a national leader in federally funded urban renewal, offers a revealing case of how consumption and civic culture intersected at the local level. Although the power given to retailers varied starkly in the redevelopment of these two cities, in both cases department stores were deemed essential to the viability of the central business district. That priority ultimately limited the success of downtown revitalization, given the department store sector's growing suburban orientation and steady economic concentration from the 1960s on.

Keywords: downtown; urban renewal; department stores; retail; Edward J. Logue; New Haven; Boston

In September and October of 1947, 385,000 Philadelphians took the elevator to the fifth floor of Gimbel's flagship downtown department store with no purchase in mind. Instead, they came to view a massive "Better Philadelphia Exhibition" that had been a year and a half in the planning. Taking up two full floors and costing $340,000 (equivalent to about $840,000 in

Lizabeth Cohen is the Howard Mumford Jones Professor of American Studies in the History Department of Harvard University. This article builds on her current book project, a study of Edward J. Logue and the rebuilding of American cities after World War II. She is the author of Making A New Deal: Industrial Workers in Chicago 1919-1939 *(Cambridge University Press, 1990);* A Consumers' Republic: The Politics of Mass Consumption in Postwar America *(Knopf, 2003); and, with David Kennedy,* The American Pageant *(Houghton Mifflin 1998, 2002, 2006). She has received fellowships from the Guggenheim Foundation, ACLS, NEH, and the Radcliffe Institute.*

DOI: 10.1177/0002716206298744

today's dollars), the exhibition, according to an admiring review in *The Architectural Forum*, used "every device known to the display artist" to show "what is wrong with Philadelphia and what, specifically, can be done about it." In an experience "strikingly reminiscent of the Futurama at the [New York] World's Fair," visitors encountered a huge 30 × 14 foot aerial photo map, where synchronized with a narration, sections of present-day Philadelphia flipped over to show proposed improvements; a diorama of an imagined "Better Philadelphia" in 1982; and three-dimensional models, murals, wall panels, and full-size replicas of an actual dingy street corner and a typical row house with a remodeled backyard garden. In one particularly compelling exhibit, "the shadow of blight" spread gradually over the heart of the city as a pendulum swung across a map of Philadelphia. Not only did Gimbel's Philadelphia store host the exhibition, it lent its vice president, Arthur Kaufman, to serve as an officer of the "Better Philadelphia" project, along with the president of the Citizens' Council on Planning, the president of the Philadelphia Chamber of Commerce, and the vice president of a major insurance company (who was also a descendent of the prominent eighteenth-century Philadelphian Dr. Benjamin Rush) ("Philadelphia Plans Again" 1947).

The deep investment of Gimbel's Department Store in the future viability of Philadelphia during the late 1940s may come as a surprise today. We live in an era when the total number of department stores is sharply decreasing, and the survivors are likely to be national chains unidentified with any local community, located in suburban and exurban malls rather than center cities. As recently as November 17, 2006, a *New York Times* front-page story predicting a comeback for department stores after four decades of decline made it clear that consumers were patronizing stores in suburban shopping centers, not downtown. Although we may associate Gimbel's with New York's Macy's, its once fierce competitor in Herald Square, in fact the store had deep Philadelphia roots. Adam Gimbel established his Philadelphia store in 1894, fourteen years before opening his New York City branch. And until it went out of business in 1984, Gimbel's remained a stalwart fixture among Philadelphia's major department stores, long sponsoring that city's Thanksgiving Day Parade the way Macy's did in New York ("Gimbel's," http://en.wikipedia.org/wiki/Gimbel's; see also Fischer n.d.).

Much of the literature on consumption and civic culture after World War II focuses on the national level, whether tracking the emergence of a mass-consumer-oriented postwar economy, the application of marketing techniques to political campaigns, or the embrace of socially conscious consumption. The case of department stores' involvement in the enormous effort by American cities to revitalize themselves after World War II—after fifteen years of urban stagnation accompanying the Great Depression and the war and in the face of the explosion of suburbanization that immediately followed—demonstrates that the link between consumption and civic engagement has an important local history as well.

One visitor who enthusiastically viewed the Better Philadelphia Exhibition on a trip back to his hometown went on to make a career of rebuilding cities. From 1954 until almost 1968, Philadelphia-born and Yale-educated Edward J. Logue was a pivotal figure in the urban renewal of two economically troubled northeastern cities, New Haven, Connecticut, and Boston. As the powerful development administrator in New Haven from 1954 to 1961, he pioneered many of the strategies of attracting federal funding for massive urban rebuilding that other cities would later imitate. Under the watch of Logue and his partner Mayor Richard Lee, New Haven received more federal money per capita than any other city in the United States, by 1965 more than two and a half times greater than the next highest, Newark, New Jersey (Rae 2003, 324). Applauded nationally for his talent at making big plans and finding others to pay for them, Logue caught the eye of new Boston Mayor John Collins, elected in 1959 with a promise to reverse the half-century stagnation of one of the nation's oldest cities. In 1961, Ed Logue became Development Administrator in Boston, armed with unprecedented centralized authority over the city's planning and redevelopment and compensated—at his demand—at a salary higher than any other public official in the state. When Logue moved on to a powerful new statewide position created for him by Governor Nelson Rockefeller of New York in 1968, he left behind a fourteen-year record of overseeing urban renewal in two cities during the key years of federally funded and locally implemented urban renewal. In both of these cities, retail was a key component of the downtown renewal plan. Logue's legacy thus offers a unique opportunity to follow over a decade and a half the role that retailers like Gimbel's played in the successes and failures of urban renewal and thereby to probe the interconnection of private capital and public investment in the reconstruction of American cities in the postwar era.

Edward J. Logue was a pivotal figure in the urban renewal of two economically troubled northeastern cities, New Haven, Connecticut, and Boston.

In New Haven and Boston, as in most American cities, downtown department store owners and executives played central roles in urban renewal efforts, while their stores became important sites for redevelopment projects. From their founding in the late nineteenth century, department stores had been the lifeblood of downtown development—a destination for mass transit, an anchor for other commerce, a provider of jobs, an icon for the city. Beginning in the Great Depression and accelerating after World War II, however, the number of downtown stores steadily declined, their share of metropolitan shoppers and their dollars likewise shrinking (Friedan and Sagalyn 1997). When it became clear that the severe housing shortage facing the United States at the end of the war would be addressed through massive building of suburban dwellings, panic set in. How would the central business district fare as more city residents moved out? How should managers prioritize improvements in downtown "trunk" stores versus expansion through suburban "branches?" Still strongly identified with their home cities, department stores clamored for help sustaining downtown retail. They called for thousands more off-street parking spaces, the streamlining of traffic flow in congested retail centers, new roadways that sped shoppers directly from their suburban homes into downtown, improvements in mass transportation, slum clearance of "gray belt" neighborhoods bordering retail cores, and updated shopping environments that resembled the new modern malls beginning to appear in suburban rings. They also complained of high real estate taxes that overburdened them with costs that suburban stores did not share, aggravating the tax advantage already given to suburban stores beginning in 1954 for greater write-offs of accelerated depreciation on new construction than renovations of existing structures (Isenberg 2004, 166-202; Hanchett 1996). Richard C. Bond, president of John Wanamaker of Philadelphia, called his department store colleagues to arms in 1960: if America's great cities are not to become ghost towns, merchants "should be heading the list of dedicated, aroused and enlightened business leaders, for we have more at stake than perhaps any other group to see that our cities thrive rather than shrink and die." Only a multi-billion-dollar program of federal spending, Bond argued, can "check this urban erosion before it reaches catastrophic proportions" ("Pressure by Business Urged" 1960).

From their founding in the late nineteenth century, department stores had been the lifeblood of downtown development—a destination for mass transit, an anchor for other commerce, a provider of jobs, an icon for the city.

Understandably convinced of the wisdom of calls like Bond's to rebuild downtowns around dynamic retail with large, well-established department stores at its core, Ed Logue and Mayor Richard Lee made plans for the "model city" of New Haven accordingly. First, the New Haven Redevelopment Authority leveled the dilapidated Oak Street neighborhood adjoining downtown, inhabited by poor immigrants and blacks, to make room for a complex of luxury apartment towers and the "Oak Street Connector," an expansive highway extension designed to bring cars from the Connecticut Turnpike (Route 1/95) and later the state's new north-south Route 91 right into the city center. The thinking went that middle-class New Havenites would now have the option of modern living downtown or a quick trip back in if they insisted on moving to the suburbs.

New Haven's redevelopers then turned to their next big project: rebuilding downtown around a three-block commercial complex with two major department stores, an attached two-block-long fifteen-hundred-car garage designed by prominent architect and Yale Architecture School Dean Paul Rudolph, a modern three-hundred-room hotel, new up-to-date office space, and the Chapel Square Mall bordering the historic New Haven Green. What became known as the "Church Street Project" was the first federal urban renewal project to focus on a commercial district, and it was trendsetting in using federal dollars to restructure land use, parking, and traffic circulation in order to recentralize a region's retail activities in its major city's downtown core. A ninety-three-acre site of small stores and service establishments, many owned by Jewish and Italian immigrants or their descendants, was to be leveled to make way for the rebirth of downtown New Haven (Lowe 1967, 427-63; Talbot 1967, 116-35; Longstreth 2006, 11-13; Hardwick 1996; Garvin 2002, 160-61, 261-62; Sternlieb 1963, 111).

What became known as [New Haven's] "Church Street Project" was the first federal urban renewal project to focus on a commercial district.

But Lee and Logue's fantasies of creating a mini–Herald Square or Fifth Avenue or even nearby Hamden Plaza Shopping Center in downtown New Haven seriously misjudged what it would take to revitalize the city. So committed were the planners, politicians, and developers to attracting high-prestige retail to put New Haven back on the map that they overlooked the true base of New Haven retail, the small stores, personal services, restaurants, and professional offices downtown that created bustling sidewalk traffic and urban ambiance. With eyes focused on a total remaking of downtown New Haven as a regional retail center capable of competing with newly sprouting suburban malls, Logue and his colleagues made inadequate plans, indeed almost forgot to consider the relocation of small businesses until the new mall was ready. Only when a group of 120 small downtown merchants—hastily allied as the Central Civic Association to meet this sudden threat to their livelihoods—sued the city in 1958 were temporary quarters in prefabricated metal structures provided. Some stores moved in, while others—estimated at 20 percent—went out of business, unable to afford the transition costs and the long wait for permanent new quarters. Still others ironically moved out to the suburban shopping centers ("New Haven Offers Stand-By Sites" 1958).

The project's planners had vaguely assumed many small stores would come into the Chapel Square Mall when it was finished, but they made no allowance for how they would survive until then or find the capital to relocate in such expensive real estate, even with the 10 percent rental discount promised after the merchants protested. Most were renters who would not even get eminent domain compensation for the taking of their stores by the city. A letter sent to Mayor Lee by Leo S. Gilden, president of "Gilden's, Inc., Jewelers for Four Generations" and the president of the Central Civic Association, bitterly outlined the group's complaints: they had never been informed of the project before the public announcement; they were not even invited to the luncheon disclosing the plans to the public and "first learned of all this via radio and newspaper"; and they—as taxpayers and servers of the New Haven public for many years—took great offense at the mayor's statement "that you realize that perhaps some of the smaller businessmen could not survive this change but that in the long run the city would benefit by it." Reminding the mayor "that this is a democracy we live in," Gilden insisted that "certainly the livelihoods and welfare of the thousands of people involved in this must be considered before the interests of outside capital," referring to the project's New York developer Roger Stevens and the New York department store Lee hoped to attract (Logue 1957). One Church Street merchant, jeweler Robert R. Savitt, whose two-story property was slated for demolition at a compensation lower than he felt he deserved, embroiled the city in a major suit that delayed the entire project for a couple of years. By the fall of 1961, all that stood in the huge mud and rubble wasteland that had once been the heart of downtown New Haven was Rudolph's massive municipal garage—ultimately completed at a price tag of $6 million, twice what had been budgeted.

It also proved frustratingly more difficult than anyone had expected to line up the two anchor department stores. Although Edward Malley Company, the largest still-viable department store in downtown New Haven, had intended to remain in its original location facing the Green, adjacent to but not part of the Chapel Square Mall, its management was convinced to build a new store on a site closer to the Oak Street Connector and the parking garage, thus freeing its prime spot for a hotel. Malley's was already opening its new store in the fall of 1962 before Mayor Lee was finally able to announce triumphantly that he had at last found it a partner in Macy's, notably in time for the 1963 mayoral election. (Having watched his plurality over his Republican challenger dangerously decline to 4,000 votes in 1961 from almost 14,000 in 1959 with the delays in the Church Street Project, Lee was greatly relieved that delivering Macy's helped him win by 11,345 votes in the 1963 election [Powledge 1970, 42, 44, 46].) It had been a long, difficult search for a New York department store willing to move into downtown New Haven, even with the massive garage in place. Macy's, a store that was aggressively expanding into suburban shopping centers, ultimately agreed to the New Haven proposition in a calculation that this three-story, 320,000-square-foot store would give it a foothold in the Connecticut market, a part of the metropolitan New York area it had yet to enter. That Macy's managers felt a downtown store would enhance its suburban strategy attests to the power that the trunk-and-branches paradigm still held (Macy's 1964).

So convinced were New Haven's redevelopers of the superiority of suburban-type store design that in planning the new downtown they forgot what made the urban experience unique. Yes, shoppers could travel from highway to parking garage to a chosen department store floor without even entering the real city. But horizontal, sleek, modernist department stores and a mall designed around an interior central courtyard put up large, solid-wall exteriors, isolating customers inside and pedestrians and drivers outside on sidewalks and streets made much less interesting and safe. Very possibly, New Haven commerce would have declined anyway, given Connecticut's huge suburban growth and a tax structure that gave little relief to cities. But the New Haven urban renewers' unwavering vision for saving downtown by putting suburban-style, department-store-dominated retail at the center ignored—and ultimately destroyed—the true base of New Haven commerce, the small shops that an observer at the time noted were often loyally "supported by particular ethnic and racial groups." With the long project delays caused by the Savitt suit, the developer's difficulties securing financing, and the problem attracting a second department store, the Chapel Square Mall did not open until March 1967, a full decade after the project's announcement, giving New Haven–area consumers plenty of time to develop new suburban patterns of shopping. Soon it also became clear that the Oak Street Connector, designed to deliver shoppers to the doorstep of the downtown stores, could just as easily facilitate the exodus of middle-class New Haven residents. It became all the easier to live in the suburbs, work downtown, and shop near home where store hours were longer, parking was free and easy, and malls featured a convenient mix of small and large stores. Moreover, poorer, ethnically and racially diverse customers, who were increasingly dominating New Haven's population, found fewer and fewer attractions downtown as upscale shopping designed for wealthier suburbanites gradually replaced demolished stores.

So by the time Malley's closed in 1982, Macy's in 1993, and the Chapel Square Mall went into a fatal dive not long thereafter, there was little of the old New Haven urban fabric left to close over the huge hole ripped out of the city's heart. Talk once again turned to seeking department stores to fill the gap, prompting a longtime observer of the New Haven scene to deride the city for what he called its "Shartenberg Syndrome," referring to another local department store that had closed in 1962. Charging that "the department store was an unfortunate symbol for that longing [to feel] their city was special" and "distinctive," the syndrome "made city policymakers spend more than thirty years seeking downtown department stores as anchors for urban renewal." Driven by nostalgia rather than hard-headed realism, they used the department store "to re-create the past," he argued, rather than thinking creatively about a new kind of future for downtown New Haven (Bass n.d.).

Edward Logue took on the job of redeveloping Boston in 1961, having learned some important lessons in New Haven. When he left, six years after planning had begun on the Church Street Project and four years from its public announcement, downtown New Haven looked more, not less, abandoned. He thus made sustaining, even increasing, the number of white-collar jobs downtown his priority in Boston, recognizing that keeping workers in the city's core would bolster the retail and personal service economy along with the city's tax base, even if people moved their residences to the suburbs. Accordingly, the Government Center Project—a sixty-acre complex of federal, state, and municipal headquarters and private commercial space built on the site of Scollay Square, Boston's former red-light district—became the jewel in Boston's urban renewal crown. Aware that the federal and state governments were willing to build new office towers somewhere in downtown Boston, the Boston Redevelopment Authority (BRA) conceived, with the planning expertise of architect I. M. Pei, of a campus of government buildings in which a new city hall would be the centerpiece. A massive concentration of public employees in the center of Boston—in Government Center alone, twenty-five thousand where there previously had been six thousand—promised to provide a ready market for downtown retail ranging from department stores to restaurants. By design, the project's centerpiece—the enormous and architecturally acclaimed Kallman, McKinnell & Knowles Boston City Hall—had no cafeteria or dining hall within it, to force employees to leave the premises and patronize local restaurants and other businesses. The physical renovation of the city's retail district may not have explicitly been the BRA's top priority, but ensuring the survival of downtown commerce certainly was high on its list (O'Connor 1993; Garvin 2002, 88-90).

Logue delegated the task of planning the structural modernization of Boston's downtown shopping district to a group of local businessmen recruited for the purpose, organized in 1962 as the Committee for the Central Business District, Inc., or CCBD. The committee was headed by veteran civic leader Charles A. Coolidge, a Boston Brahmin senior partner in the prominent law firm of Ropes and Gray and former head of the Greater Boston Chamber of Commerce. On its Executive Board sat the chairmen of the two major department stores, Jordan Marsh and Filene's, and the president of Boston's third largest, Gilchrist's. Gun-shy from the traumas of his New Haven experience, Logue let the retailers recommend to the BRA how dramatic the redevelopment should be, the most desirable mix of large and small stores, and solutions to the sticky problem of temporary relocations. Blessed with a financially healthier group of retailers in Boston's larger market, Logue began by asking the CCBD's members to pay for a major study of the central business district's problems and feasible solutions, which would later make applying for federal redevelopment funds easier. CCBD members came up with a quarter million dollars to hire famed commercial architect and urban planner Victor Gruen as well as a Washington economist, Robert

Gladstone, to estimate potential growth in the downtown Boston market (Logue 1962-1967).

In his treatise of 1964, *The Heart of Our Cities; The Urban Crisis: Diagnosis and Cure*, Gruen enthused about the "pattern of cooperation" between Boston's CCBD and the BRA. No stranger himself to the kind of internecine conflicts that had wracked cities like New Haven and Fort Worth, Texas, where he had struggled unsuccessfully to win adoption of his own ambitious, futuristic city plan, Gruen took great comfort in the city and citizen committee's agreement "that whatever is planned and implemented must be acceptable to both parties" (pp. 321-26; see also Hardwick 2004, 166-92). Likewise, the *Boston Herald* remarked on Logue's uncharacteristic handling of planning for the retail core, commenting that his statements and actions revealed "a caution untypical of his usual drive to get things done, now if not sooner," as if there was "a 'proceed cautiously' sign on the central business district so as to disrupt its operations as little as possible" (Saint 1965). Logue admitted as much to his BRA board chairman, Monsignor Francis Lally, in a progress report shortly before the CCBD was announced. Promising that all the pieces would soon be in place to begin "planning for the retail core," Logue acknowledged that it had taken longer than he would have liked "but I think the result has been to get support and depth from the retailers" (Logue 1962).

[T]he Boston Herald *remarked on Logue's uncharacteristic handling of planning for the retail core, commenting that his statements and actions revealed "a caution untypical of his usual drive to get things done, now if not sooner."*

In *The Heart of Our Cities*, Gruen (1964, 321) also touted the CCBD's broad base, "embrac[ing] in its membership retail establishments of all types and sizes, including Jordan Marsh Company and Wm. Filene's Sons Co., real estate owners, utility companies, banks, newspaper publishers, hotel operators, restaurateurs, movie house operators, and others." While representatives from a wide range of businesses sat on the full seventy-five-member CCBD, in reality the department stores, particularly the chiefs of Filene's and Jordan Marsh, controlled the powerful CCBD Executive Committee. According to an influential 1964 article in *Fortune* assessing the prospects for urban redevelopment in

Boston, "Boston: What Can a Sick City Do?" Walter McQuade described the CCBD as dominated by the chief executives of Jordan Marsh and Filene's. "These two mighty merchants put their renowned rivalry aside temporarily and together made the round of the stores, the banks, the newspapers, and other businesses in the area 'hat in hand' . . . and came back with a good hatful of funds—$250,000—for replanning the whole district" (p. 166). Indeed, these two major department stores remained very identified with the city, even as both had begun expanding into suburban branch stores, though with different strategies: Jordan's spread its branches at some distance from the CBD to preserve its flagship store's business, while Filene's built within the inner ring and sacrificed downtown sales (Sternlieb 1962, 162-70).

Boston's retailers may have had deep pockets and that "depth" of commitment to downtown renewal that Logue remarked on to Monsignor Lally, but they also were extremely cautious about change, aware of the damage that dislocations like New Haven's urban redevelopment could have on city-based retail business, already losing its stronghold on metropolitan sales. When Gruen's preliminary planning called for constructing a multilevel mall from Government Center all the way along the main shopping fare of Washington Street and another traverse mall from Tremont Street to South Station—in essence incorporating blocks of the city's core into a central shopping structure—Coolidge, speaking for his Executive Committee, protested the proposal as "too big, too much." Instead, the CCBD sent Gruen back to the drawing board to come up with a more modest plan providing for an underground truck delivery system, some exclusively pedestrian areas, the improvement of traffic circulation through straightening several key streets and making them one-way, the addition of more parking garages, the establishment of a few new store sites in place of ones considered substandard, and the possible commercial development of the South Station property. When making a westbound thoroughfare required the taking of the budget-priced Raymond's Department Store at the corner of Franklin and Washington, great concern was expressed about how best to house Raymond's and other smaller enterprises temporarily. Over and over at the unveiling of the plans for downtown revitalization in May 1967, Mayor Collins, BRA Board Chairman Monsignor Lally, and CCBD President Charles Coolidge reiterated the strength of this plan for "propos[ing] changes which are dramatic, but which . . . are not too disruptive to business within the district. The retailer's business must continue or else the retailer may be forced out of business by his customers going elsewhere" ("Four Hundred Million Plan for Downtown Revitalization" 1967, 412). Boston's plan was a far cry from Logue's oversight of the total demolition of New Haven's downtown retail core. The most drastic proposals called for a pedestrian mall in the heart of the retail district, which later proved problematic, and a raised walkway above Summer Street from South Station all the way to the Boston Common, which was never constructed ("Four Hundred Million Plan for Downtown Revitalization" 1967, 409-12; BRA 1967a; BRA 1967b, 34-45).

Despite all the care that Logue took to involve the major retail players in the planning process and not to disrupt downtown commerce, the viability of

Boston's central business district continued to diminish. To some extent, conventional midprice downtown department stores were eclipsed everywhere, first by branches in suburban malls and then, starting in the 1960s, by a segmentation of the consumer market with the growth of discount department stores for price-conscious buyers (usually located in the suburbs), on one hand, and high-end specialty and department stores for the affluent (sometimes downtown), on the other (Bluestone et al. 1981, 18-27). The latter phenomenon might have bolstered Boston's central shopping district had not another component of Boston's urban renewal program—initiated before Logue arrived, but pushed by him to completion—undercut it. The first step in the commercial urban redevelopment of Boston had taken place under Mayor Collins's predecessor, John Hynes, in the late 1950s. On the heels of the West End fiasco, where a forty-eight-acre working-class residential neighborhood labeled as "blighted" and "slum" was bulldozed for luxury high-rise apartments aimed at keeping the middle class in the city (and then left leveled for years awaiting their construction), Hynes sought a site free of controversy. He fixed on abandoned rail yards located between the city's Back Bay and South End neighborhoods and near Copley Square as the ideal location for a major retail and office complex, what eventually became the Prudential Center. Although "the Pru" did not threaten downtown on its own, it became the core of a thriving, upscale shopping district around Newbury Street in the Back Bay, dominated by expensive specialty stores and restaurants located on a traditional urban street grid (Sternlieb 1962, 111).

As the satellite Prudential–Back Bay area flourished, affluent consumers found less and less reason to shop in the old retail core, particularly since the downtown department stores were disappearing, not only into the suburbs but also into each other. Beginning in the 1960s and accelerating in the 1980s and 1990s, existing national retail holding companies like Federated Department Stores, Allied Stores Corporation, the May Department Stores Company, and Dayton-Hudson Corporation began aggressively acquiring more stores and then merging among themselves, leaving behind abandoned brick and mortar corpses in cities throughout the country (Friedan and Sagalyn 1997, 78-86). Even as Boston prospered in the 1980s and 1990s as a corporate center, retail in the old downtown declined. The Back Bay shopping district thrived, though over time specialty chains increasingly replaced independently owned stores, making it less distinguishable from an upscale mall. Today, Boston's old central business district, now known as "Downtown Crossing," remains home to only one traditional department store, the national chain of Macy's, as the result of repeated retail consolidations. Jordan Marsh became Macy's in 1996; and just this past year, Macy's parent company, Federated, bought Filene's and converted all surviving stores to Macy's as part of a $17 billion takeover of regional chains to create a vast national retail empire of more than eight hundred stores. Although Boston's central retail core is certainly prospering more than New Haven's—where the closest thing today to a department store is the Yale Coop, run by Barnes & Noble—it is once again causing anxious hand-wringing by the present mayor and his BRA. "Makeover for 'Tired' District" read a *Boston Globe* headline on

September 8, 2006, announcing the city's hiring of yet another consulting firm to devise strategies for revitalizing Downtown Crossing. Poor and moderate-income consumers without easy access to suburban discount stores and unable to afford the Back Bay shops have been the mainstay of Downtown Crossing, but here, as previously in New Haven, they are not seen as a desirable solution to the latest downtown crisis. Rather, the thousands of white-collar workers downtown and the future upper-class residents of new luxury condos being planned nearby are Mayor Thomas Menino's preferred target audience. Sound familiar?

What can we learn from this tale of downtown urban renewal in New Haven and Boston? Several conclusions are worth noting. Although redevelopment administrator Edward Logue brought experience from one city to his work in another and changed his strategies along the way, giving retailers a greater role in Boston than they had had in New Haven, in both cases department stores were viewed as the solution to downtown's ills. As major commercial developer James Rouse put it, in discussing his frustrating eight-year struggle to redevelop the center of Norfolk, Virginia, in the mid- to late 1960s, "There was no alternative [to the department store as anchor], at least in anybody's mind" (Friedan and Sagalyn 1997, 81). But whether it was professional planners, Washington bureaucrats, or local businessmen doing the betting during the 1950s and 1960s, it seems that they put their money on a vulnerable horse. Department stores' insistence on suburban-style store designs often undermined the uniqueness of the urban experience and encouraged the construction of enormous, self-contained, superblock projects that were rarely adaptable to other purposes should the need arise. That inflexibility proved increasingly problematic as the department store sector underwent extraordinary restructuring over the decades that followed. Tragically, while urban planners and policy makers focused their efforts and public money on making downtown districts more appealing to consumers, economic decisions in board rooms far outside their control were ultimately shaping events, whether it was disinvesting in downtown stores in the 1960s or consolidating local and regional stores into a smaller number of identical national chain outlets in the 1990s. Meanwhile, smaller merchants who had managed to survive the lack of interest and support of urban renewers in the 1950s and 1960s found themselves struggling against the rapid expansion of specialty chains in the latter decades of the twentieth century.

In 2006, as in 1947 when Philadelphians flocked to the "Better Philadelphia Exhibition," commerce provides a major base to any city's economy and vitality, just as consumption figures significantly in the nation's GDP. Like it or not, prosperity in our postindustrial American society depends on consumption of goods and services. I would hope that this history of retail and urban renewal suggests that cities make critically important decisions when they favor some merchants and retail environments over others. The cases of downtown New Haven and Boston testify to the importance of preserving a mix of commerce and a diversity of consumers to protect cities from falling victim to the internal restructuring of any one commercial sector or the shifting loyalties of any particular group of consumers.

But we may draw a deeper lesson about the way governments and corporations have been entwined in shaping the urban built environment. As federal urban renewal took shape from the 1950s through the early 1970s, that public-private partnership between city planners and downtown merchants became a major component of the redevelopment formula all over the country. Enormous amounts of federal, state, and local dollars all went toward buttressing old, and creating new, infrastructure to support downtown commerce. This huge public investment, however, did not keep the tax code from favoring new suburban mall construction or major retailers from ultimately reneging on that partnership by abandoning downtown stores and engaging in mergers and acquisitions that fundamentally changed the physical landscape of postwar retail. Much as it was with the building of the railroads across the continent in nineteenth-century America, the age of urban renewal gave deep public roots to the flowering of private capital in the realm of commerce. The advocates of urban renewal may have miscalculated what was possible in reviving downtowns, but we might rightfully ask what obligation these retail corporations had—and still have—to the urban citizens whose tax dollars have underwritten their postwar development.

I have written elsewhere about how, over the course of the post–World War II era, Americans came to live in a Consumers' Republic (Cohen 2003). While that may be the inescapable reality, we nonetheless retain some choice about where it is located, how it looks and feels physically, and which consumer citizens are invited to participate.

References

Bass, Paul. N.d. Shartenberg Syndrome, R.I.P. http://old.newhavenadvocate.com/articles/hit11.o6.html (accessed August 28, 2006).

Bluestone, Barry, Patricia Hanna, Sarah Kuhn, and Laura Moore. 1981. *The retail revolution: Market transformation, investment, and labor in the modern department store*. Boston: Auburn House Publishing Company.

Boston Redevelopment Authority (BRA). 1967a. *Boston/The plan for the central business district*. Boston: BRA.

———. 1967b. *Seven years of progress: A final report by Edward J. Logue, Development Administrator*. August. Boston: BRA.

Cohen, Lizabeth. 2003. *A consumers' republic: The politics of mass consumption in postwar America*. New York: Knopf.

Fischer, John. N.d. *Gone but not forgotten. About greater Philadephia/New Jersey*. http://philadelphia .about.com/od/history/a/strawbridges.htm (accessed August 24, 2006).

Four hundred million plan for downtown revitalization called creative, bold, realistic. 1967. *City Record* 59 (May 27): 409, 411-12.

Friedan, Bernard J., and Lynne B. Sagalyn. 1997. *Downtown, Inc.: How America rebuilds cities*. Cambridge, MA: MIT Press.

Garvin, Alexander. 2002. *The American city: What works, what doesn't*. 2nd ed. New York: McGraw-Hill.

Gruen, Victor. 1964. *The heart of our cities; the urban crisis: Diagnosis and cure*. New York: Simon & Schuster.

Hanchett, Thomas W. 1996. U.S. tax policy and the shopping-center boom of the 1950s and 1960s. *American Historical Review* 101 (October): 1082-1110.

Hardwick, M. Jeffrey. 1996. A downtown utopia? Suburbanization, urban renewal and consumption in New Haven. *Planning History Studies* 10 (Winter): 41-54.

————. 2004. *Mall maker: Victor Gruen, architect of the American dream*. Philadelphia: University of Pennsylvania Press.

Isenberg, Alison. 2004. *Downtown America: A history of the place and the people who made it*. Chicago: University of Chicago Press.

Logue, Edward J. 1957. Papers. July-August. Series 5, Box 7, Folder 596. Yale University Manuscripts and Archives, New Haven, CT.

————. 1962. Letter to Monsignor Lally. March 23. Papers. Series 6, Box 152, Folder 481. Yale University Manuscripts and Archives, New Haven, CT.

————. 1962-1967. Papers. Series 6, Boxes 152-153, Folders 481-513. Yale University Manuscripts and Archives, New Haven, CT.

Longstreth, Richard. 2006. The difficult legacy of urban renewal. *CRM: The Journal of Heritage Stewardship* 3 (Winter): 11-13.

Lowe, Jeanne R. 1967. *Cities in a race with time: Progress and poverty in America's renewing cities*. New York: Random House.

Macy's, R. H., & Company. 1964. *Annual report for the fiscal year ended August 1 1964*. New York: R. H. Macy.

McQuade, Walter. 1964. Boston: What can a sick city do? *Fortune*, June, p. 70.

New Haven offers stand-by sites for displaced stores. 1958. *Women's Wear Daily*, May 27.

O'Connor, Thomas H. 1993. *Building a new Boston: Politics and urban renewal 1950 to 1970*. Boston: Northeastern University Press.

Philadelphia plans again. 1947. *Architectural Forum*, December, pp. 66-88.

Powledge, Fred. 1970. *Model city: A test of American liberalism: One town's efforts to rebuild itself*. New York: Simon & Schuster.

Pressure by business urged for U.S. aid to urban areas. 1960. *Women's Wear Daily*, February 8.

Rae, Douglas. 2003. *City: Urbanism and its end*. New Haven, CT: Yale University Press.

Saint, Irene. 1965. Downtown business area changes made cautiously. *Boston Herald*, November 30.

Sternlieb, George. 1962. *The future of the downtown department store*. Mimeograph, Joint Center for Urban Studies of the Massachusetts Institute of Technology and Harvard University, Cambridge, MA.

————. 1963. The future of retailing in the downtown core. *Journal of the American Institute of Planners* 29 (May): 102-12.

Talbot, Allan R. 1967. *The mayor's game: Richard Lee of New Haven and the politics of change*. New York: Harper & Row.

Should
Consumer
Citizens Escape
the Market?

This article uses a sociological perspective to question the validity of critiques of consumer culture. First, the author examines the debate over whether consumers possess true freedom of action, reviewing problems critics find in the notion of "agency." Second, the author proposes that anticonsumption ideology is class-based, anachronistic, and sometimes confuses consumption with materiality. Third, the author examines what it may mean to "escape" from consumerism, using an example from a marginalized African community deprived of the means of consumption. The notions of "the market" and "marketing" are reviewed as institutions and practices with ancient roots that assume varying forms in different cultural contexts rather than as sources of pathology. Finally, the author suggests that marketing and consumerism may be enlisted for the practice of citizenship and engagement in progressive political action.

Keywords: consumption; critical sociology; materiality; political action; Romantic utopia

By
ERIC J. ARNOULD

Just as medieval society was balanced on God and the Devil, so ours is balanced on consumption and its denunciation.
—Baudrillard (1970/1998, 196)

Critiques from the right and left, from sociological to religious perspectives, inveigh against market capitalism and contemporary consumerism. As Baudrillard's epigraph suggests, the denunciation of consumption is characteristic of our age, and the choir of voices has increased in amplitude as the scope of consumerism has expanded geographically and culturally without altering its ritually evoked positions. This article analyzes the meanings of the concepts of "consumers," "citizens," and "markets" in an effort to move beyond the highly ritualized arguments surrounding consumerism and capitalism. First, I review some positions on action in consumer research and suggest the term "agency" is conceptually problematic. Second, I discuss the term "consumers" and propose that the anticonsumption ideology is anachronistic,

DOI: 10.1177/0002716206298698

class-based, and confused with the question of materiality. Third, I examine the idea of "escape," where we confront a Romantic idea, the apotheosis of which is the utopian dream. The dangers of escape are illustrated with an example from a marginalized African community deprived of the means of consumption. Next, I discuss the notions of "the market" and "marketing" and try to disassociate them from capitalism. Finally, I suggest some implications of the discussion for citizen consumers.

Should?

Many social theorists argue that progressive social action would be more likely if consumers would seek escape from the strictures of the current consumption paradigm (Ewen 1976/2001; Halton 2000; Klein 2000; D. Miller 1988; Ritzer 1993; Schor 1998, 2004). Implied in their arguments is the notion of agency—the physical or mental ability, skill or capability that enables actors to do something. The actor is assumed to proceed under his or her own volition, or at least without the permission of another.

Such views can be traced to Marx, who argued that producers, those who sold their labor to capitalists to make their living, should escape the market as a condition of reclaiming the full value of their labor. Producers were thus urged to return to a consumption regime that featured authentic use values over fetishized exchange values. A socialist revolution that returned the means of production to the control of the working class, according to Marx, was the precondition for this happy event (Marx 1887/1977).

However, there is a doubtful tone in some contemporary writing about the prospects for autonomous consumer action. Bourdieu's (1977, 1984) theory and subsequent consumer research (Allen 2002; Holt 1998) argue that consumers invest in, exchange, and deploy various kinds of capital resources. Furthermore, one kind or resource, cultural capital, is said to be basically class-distributed knowledge of various sign systems and consumption practices, inevitably subordinate to the logic of market capitalism. How people consume through historically determined, class-distributed, and embodied presuppositions defines and differentiates them as social categories and actors.

Baudrillard (1970/1998) argued that autonomous consumer action has become impossible. He wrote, "Differentiation may then take the form of the rejection of

Eric J. Arnould is PETSMART Distinguished Professor in the Norton School of Family and Consumer Sciences at the University of Arizona. He received a Ph.D. in social anthropology from the University of Arizona. He investigates service relationships, channels structure and market organization, households, consumer culture theory, and multimethod research.

NOTE: The author thanks Risto Moisio for significant intellectual contributions. Christina Goulding and Michael Saren's invitation to present to the Critical Marketing Seminar at the University of Wolverhampton led to this article's development.

objects, the rejection of 'consumption,' and yet this still remains the very ultimate in consumption" (p. 90). Baudrillard rejected the possibility of successful social change in ideas like eco-consumerism, green consumption, religious asceticism, voluntary simplicity, downsizing, going off the grid, and other such differentiating practices that may well be rationalized by actors in terms of a folk understanding that such actions constitute choices to escape from the market. The reason for his pessimism, articulated at length in *The Consumer Society*, is that the consumer economy forecloses the possibility of escape, because all action is subordinate to the logic of the consumption of signs. In consumer culture, "the solution to social contradiction is not equalization but differentiation. No revolution is possible at the level of a code" (Baudrillard 1970/1998, 94). In other words, sign value has replaced use value. But Baudrillard's vision is conservative, and it rejects consumers' capability for progressive political action implied in the word "should."

There is a doubtful tone in some contemporary writing about the prospects for autonomous consumer action.

Firat and Venkatesh (1995) offered a more optimistic appraisal of the situation confronting the postmodern consumer who, living in a fragmented society, enjoys more potential choice of maneuver than under the realm of modernism. They claimed that "much consumption does take place outside the market system" (p. 258), citing as examples flea markets and swap meets that are typically organized, although not exclusively, in terms of market logic (Belk, Wallendorf, and Sherry 1989; Herrmann 1997).

De Certeau (1984) offered a possibility of *détournement* or reappropriation of market resources to ends not envisioned by marketers, and often through mundane or playful everyday practices (Aubert-Gamet 1997). In this view, consumers gradually but inevitably erode marketers' control through microemancipatory practices that decenter market-determined subjectivity and accelerate fragmentation of the acting subject (Firat and Venkatesh 1995, 255).

Maffesoli (1996, 18) focused not on the individual, but on sociability, or when "the collective sensibility which arises from the aesthetic form results in an ethical connection between acting subjects." This ethical connection, linked to the logic of the gift in the tradition of the French Anti-Utilitarian Social Movement (M.A.U.S.S.), creates heterotopia. In other words, "communal sensibility . . . offers an alternative to both the production and distribution of goods (economic or symbolic)" (Maffesoli 1996, 17). Social movements that reappropriate marketer-produced resources and limit marketers' access to them (Cova and Cova 2002), or that assume marketing functions and graft them onto a communitarian ethos, might be read as evidence of escapes (Muniz and Schau 2005).

In this vein, agapic (selfless or altruistic) love and storgic (affectionate, friend-ship-based) love are often experienced and practiced (Belk and Coon 1993) in terms of the logic of the gift, offering escape from market logic even if, as Illouz (1997) has shown, romantic (agapic/storgic) love is in essence a consumption form. Similarly, D. Miller (1998) found elements of agapic love and also religious sacri-fice that eludes market logic in mundane shopping and housekeeping. Similar, the anti-utilitarian logic of the gift persistently influences contemporary social relation-ships, informal market exchanges, and inheritance practices (Caillé 1994/2005; Cheal 1988; Curasi, Prince, and Arnould 2004; Herrmann 1997; Mauss 1925).

According to Ozanne and Murray (1995), real consumer emancipation requires the reflexively defiant consumer. Emancipation is possible if one develops a reflexive distance from the marketing code (i.e., becomes code conscious), acknowledging its structuring effects rather than living within the code unwary (Ozanne and Murray 1995, 522-23; D. Miller 2005, 9). Contra Baudrillard, consumers can fend off the marketer-imposed code if they are able to disentangle marketer's artifice from the value in use of marketer-supplied resources.

Postmodern consumers' ability to act for themselves comes through recogni-tion that one is "a participant in an ongoing, never ending process of construction that includes a multiplicity of moments where things (most importantly as sym-bols) are consumed, produced, signified, represented, allocated, distributed and circulated" (Firat and Venkatesh 1995, 250; see also D. Miller 2005, 9). Notice that these authors stressed consumers' proactive, productive, or prosumptive behaviors in contrast with the passive consumers of modernist social theory (Ewen 1976/2001; Halton 2000; Packard 1957). Cyberspace may offer yet more freedom of action if one believes that in cyberspace the consumer is freed from constraints which hamper freedom of action in the sociophysical world (Venkatesh 1998; "Living a Second Life" 2006).

Problems with Consumer Agency

The ideas referred to above may suggest that "consumers have free reign in the play of signs to piece together a collage of meanings that express the [indi-vidual's] desired symbolic statements" (Murray 2002, 428). This agency questions the institutional ordering mechanisms discussed in some consumption sociology (Packard 1957; Ewen 1976/2001; Ritzer 1993), but it evades the problem of structuring habitus in Bourdieu's theories and sign systems in Baudrillard's. Instead, researchers employ agency or some synonym to express an optimistic view of consumer freedom, for example, autonomy (Thompson and Haytko 1997, 16); free will (Belk, Ger, and Askegaard 2003, 331); and ability to produce culture

(Peñaloza 2001, 393), to produce producer's products (Kozinets et al. 2004, 671), and to transform brands into symbolic markers of cultural categories (Fournier 1998, 367).

Unfortunately, the agency construct encounters some fundamental conceptual problems despite attempts to rescue it (Emirbayer and Mische 1998). First, the notion of agency attributes (mostly post hoc) some form of innate capacity, ability, or intention to actors and their action (Fuchs 2001; Loyal and Barnes 2001). In this way, the construct relies on an historical and particularly Western view of the autonomous self (Meyer and Jesperson 2000) that is an artifact of the Western market-driven economy, rooted in earlier developments in Western theology (Campbell 1987; Meyer and Jesperson 2000). Agency is really about the institutional authority to act, and thus agentic action is ultimately derived from actors' class-based institutional roles within consumer society rather than freedom from them. Agentic behaviors can hardly exist apart from cultural templates that authorize and guide action. As Bourdieu (1977, 1984) and others (e.g., Swidler 1986) have shown in some detail, culture always shapes peoples' habitus or strategies for action and understanding, and if they live in a consumer culture, those strategies cannot be prior to or elsewhere than this shaping process.

A second problem with the agency construct is the impossibility of separating empirically autonomous, or "free," from "determined" behaviors (Loyal and Barnes 2001). Unfortunately, social action can be explicated with reference to elements of choice or causation depending upon the scale of analysis. In other words, there is no difference in the characteristics of action that "could have been otherwise" and those that "could not have been otherwise" thus deciding in favor of freedom or determination.

In the end, the critique finds consumer agency is little more than a folk model. In other words, if people act agentically, they are agentic (Fuchs 2001). And it celebrates a Western version of actorhood and evokes value-laden notions of freedom, constraint, and transcendence of constraint via choice, constructed using cultural resources. We may doubt consumers' ability to emancipate themselves, to develop reflexive distance from the marketing code by acknowledging its structuring effects, or to fend off the marketer-imposed code because action is always institutionally authorized by market-mediated institutions.

Consumers

The next issue to consider is whether "consumers" should escape the market in the pursuit of citizenship. On this point, many sociological theorists seem doubtful of their prospects. Consumers are thought to exist in a permanent state of longing deluded by empty commercial promises that cannot satisfy these desires (Elliott 1997, 292). From Packard (1957) to Ewen (1976/2001), and on to Ritzer (1993) and Schor (1998, 2004), there is a sociological cottage industry devoted to the proposition that consumers as consumers cannot escape their degraded condition as pawns in a marketing power game. In extreme forms, this position is determinist and its implications dystopian (Halton 2000), recalling nightmarish fictional depictions of modern society (Huxley 1932/1946).

While progressive in intent, this work makes some fundamental mistakes that miscast consumers. This work unintentionally distorts the lived experience of consumer culture because of the use of analytic methods that generally rely on aggregate data. First, this leads to a confusion of causes with effects; for example, massive expenditures on advertising and marketing must be constricting consumer imaginations, diverting consumers from what "really matters"—typically family, community, and/or nature—and creating a dominated consumer subject (Ewen 1976/2001; M. C. Miller 1988; Packard 1957; Schor 1998, 2004). And yet abundant case studies show some consumers building relationships and community and sometimes turning both media and marketer provided resources to their own, sometimes political, ends (Kozinets 2001, 2002; Kozinets and Handelman 2004). Yet purists decry the emergence of community whenever consumerist forms are detected, as is evident in the debate over megachurches (Colson 1992; Johnson 2005; "Learn on Sundays" 2006).

Second, this work sometimes infers causal paths between consumption and social and environmental pathologies from correlational data (e.g., Schor 1998, 2005). In a context of market fragmentation and consumer *détournement* and *bricolage* (Marion 2003; Peñaloza 2001; Thompson and Haytko 1997), absent detailed knowledge of consumer projects, it is incautious at best to infer general social tendencies from aggregate data, for example, hours spent watching television, annual expenditures in a government-defined product category, hours per day spent online, or even a divergence between growth in GDP and subjective quality of life.

A third problem with the portrayal of consumers in much of the critical sociology of consumption is implicit class bias. Baudrillard (1970/1998, 91) argued, "There is also a full-blown syndrome of anti-consumption, a very modern phenomenon . . . which is, at bottom, a metaconsumption and acts as a cultural indicator of class. . . . *It is on the basis of luxury that the lost simplicity is consumed* [italics added]." Baudrillard's critique of the critique of consumption is basically that the critics speak from a middle-class subject position, and their arguments for voluntary simplicity (Elgin 1993) or even involuntary simplicity (Schor 2005) are steeped in the modernist critique of materialism by middle- and upper-class North Americans (Vanderbilt 1996), one often directed at the supposed consumer excesses of the masses (Scott 2005). And as Baudrillard presciently discerned, voluntary simplicity and other such alternatives indeed take the form of luxury consumption, whether of money or time.

From a different standpoint, one may wish to critique the anachronism and essentialism implicated in the social science construct "consumer." Producer and consumer are essentialized binaries that derive from a model of industrial capitalism in which these two actors are divided by capital. But even if this model was once descriptive, there is reason to question its usefulness today. Persons who employ free-floating firm-provided resources to construct avatar-like online persona (Schau and Gilly 2003); who remake and remanufacture firm-provided resources (Muniz and Schau 2005); who open workshops in the Second Life virtual community to sell claws, paws, and wings and then convert the Linden dollars earned there into U.S. dollars ("Living a Second Life" 2006; Venkatesh 1998); or who willingly transform themselves through technological, biological, or biotechnological prostheses (Schroeder 1994; Wood 1998) surely require us to rethink what consumer "does" and who consumer "is." In short, if consumers conform to the "dupe" model, meaningful political engagement seems problematic; if not, perhaps the opportunities are greater.

Some authors may have confused the problems of consumption with another problem, that of objectification. Critics often argue that marketing promotes too much social division and too much consumption, but from the perspective of materiality, the problem is elsewhere. First,

> Proper materialism is one that recognizes the irreducible relation of culture, which through production . . . creates persons in and through their materiality. [True, c]apitalism splits culture and person apart into commodities separated from their intrinsic person-making capacities, and the illusion of pure humanism outside of materiality. (D. Miller 2005, 17)

In other words, both society at a macro-level and persons at an individual level are created in and through the material forms that are projected into the world; in our culture, through market-mediated consumption (D. Miller 1987). Then the logic of capitalism deludes us into thinking there is a human essence separate from material forms because so many such forms do confront us in an alienated commodity form (Marx 1887/1977). Nevertheless, everything from Klingon clothing to financial derivatives are created by humans but created according to emergent strategies of action embedded in marketing-mediated culture. In turn, their existence produces us as "Klingons" or merchant bankers (Kozinets 2001; Miyazaki 2005).

All societies proceed through the creation of external forms, and all societies are threatened by such forms developing autonomous momentum that threatens people with estrangement and in capitalism with alienation (D. Miller 1987, 180). This is as true of premarket peoples drawing images on a cave wall as it is of those of us who live in late capitalism threatened by the apparatus of marketing, advertising, franchising, market research, and the like that we ourselves animate.

Because capitalism splits persons from commodities through the apparatus of markets, when successful, consumers' postacquisition appropriative behaviors constitute a negation of the alienated commodity and its transformation into culturally meaningful objects (Kopytoff 1986; D. Miller 1987, 191-93). Thus, well-being is determined by the capacity for self creation by a society or individual through objects' appropriation (Miller 2005, 20). So we can view the proliferation of identity practices and lifestyle consumption communities not as marketer-provoked social manipulation but as consumption-fuelled reappropriation of differentiated selves (Thompson and Haytko 1997; Willis 1990).

Therefore, the proliferation of consumer goods is sometimes implicated in the creation of social worlds and identities that are generative of the sociality

Maffesoli (1996) imagined in a global capitalist context. Middle-class Indonesian men described by Keane (2005) do not have too many consumer goods, even though they have many outfits; they are not victims of consumer culture gone mad. Instead, a diverse repertoire of costume enables them to define themselves effectively relative to the differentiated, globalized social order they inhabit. Were they deprived of some of this array, their capacity to participate in contemporary Indonesian life would be constrained, as would their capacity for self-definition (Douglas 1992). These things are constitutive of sociality, not superficial symbols, Keane argues.

Escape

Next I turn to the question of escape in the interest of social and political engagement. No doubt the rich symbolic resources generated by market capitalism provide for all sorts of sign experimentation; "even as the market makes its profits, it supplies some of the materials for alternative or oppositional symbolic work" (Willis 1990). However, we have seen Baudrillard (1970/1998) argue that there is no escape at the level of the code. So perhaps it is worth reflecting on the idea of escape itself. And soon we realize that this idea of escape is largely a product of modernity and, as argued extensively elsewhere, a specifically Romantic response to it (Campbell 1987; Brown, Doherty, and Clarke 1998). Moves to reclaim personal "authenticity" (Arnould and Price 2000), the Dionysian ecstasies of anticonsumerist festivals (Kozinets 2002), the nostalgia of retroscapes (Brown and Sherry 2003), the socially engaged projection of utopia (Kozinets 2001; Macalaran and Brown 2005), or politically motivated ecotourism (Shultis and Way 2006) are forms of Romantic consumerism. Thus, the utopian spirit, however progressively motivated, is colonized by market logic.

Are there examples of escape from the market? A case can be made, but my example is dystopian. In 1999, I had occasion to revisit the sites of research conducted in the 1970s in Zinder, Niger Republic, on contending consumer globalizations (Arnould 1989). Zinder's agriculturally based economy has long been integrated into global circuits of production and consumption, but by the turn of the millennium this was no longer true. Structural adjustment programs have done their work (Gervais 1995); Zinder's economy is now marginalized from these circuits. Exports of value are reduced to things like sheep exported seasonally to Nigeria to celebrate the Muslim festival of Eid. Millet, sorghum, and cowpeas, for which there is no significant world market, are all that can be cultivated in this increasingly arid environment. Hence, Zinderois have virtually no economic resources; illiteracy and innumeracy ensure that they have virtually no skills to sell; they have no control of the political-economic agenda. One old friend frantically pled for the few cents needed to repair a bicycle tire, his only means of livelihood. This level of desperation and evident deprivation of the means of consumption is consummate. A former field assistant remarked, "One bad harvest and they are all dead men." This kind of escape is clearly not the kind envisioned by the critics of market capitalism, and yet it is hard to imagine a realistic alternative.

The Market

Market capitalism is attacked as the primary contemporary source of all kinds of social pathology. As mentioned, these attacks fix advertising (Ewen 1976/2001), brands (Klein 2000), commercial electronic media (Halton 2000), marketing research (Dávila 2001), and marketing formula (Rimke 2000; Ritzer 1993) squarely in their sights. Consumer conformity, loss of autonomy, falsity, materialism, kitsch, ecological collapse, routinization, global poverty, addiction, and obesity (Schor 2004) flow from the expanding reach of the market.

For an anthropologist, the demonization of markets and marketing is strange. The form of these attacks has changed little since Marx's economic, Thoreau's spiritual, and first-wave feminist social reformers' moral warnings in the nineteenth century. These echo today in the anti-McDonald's and voluntary simplicity movements (Keane 2006; Ritzer 1983; Scott 2005). The demonization of the market thus repeated is nicely summarized in Baudrillard's (1970/1998) epigraph and makes one wonder whether, despite its merits, the academic criticism of markets and consumption stems from critics' reactance to finding themselves objects of marketing or from a desired return to the comfortable master narratives of modernity (Bauman 1994).

[M]arkets and marketing are institutions and practices with ancient roots that assume varying forms in different cultural contexts.

But markets and marketing are institutions and practices with ancient roots that assume varying forms in different cultural contexts from the time of the Mesopotamian empires, in the trans-Saharan African caravan trade, or in pre-Conquest America (Brumfiel 1980; Meillassoux 1971; Polanyi, Arensberg, and Pearson 1957). Markets and marketing are not synonymous with capitalism; that is why we terminologically separate the industrial capitalism of Marx's day from the consumer-driven market capitalism of today. With Ilouz (1997, 1-2), we may recognize that late market capitalism democratizes the space of consumption, but at the cost of social fragmentation, a growing gap between rich and poor, and exacerbation of the effects of economic externalities such as pollution and resource depletion. However, because markets are an institutional apparatus that can be put to many social ends, they also provide space for progressive political action. This separation is also why theorists (e.g., Baudrillard 1970/1998; Firat and Venkatesh 1995) can argue for the predominance of consumption over production in the current economic order.

For all of this, many groups are consumers to a far lesser extent than others, as in the Niger example (see also Chin 2001). Their interests are therefore unduly underrepresented in global consumptionscapes (Appadurai 1990), and this indeed results in a material culture constructed in the image of groups alien to the underrepresented. One may say that such groups are denied the means of consumption and hence the means to realize themselves through material cultural forms. When people are unable to perceive the means of self-creation, or because objective conditions prevent self-creation through consumption, it is here that alienation and social pathology emerge, not from the engagement with the market or consumption or objects themselves (Miller 1987, 189).

Some Implications for the Practice of Citizenship

I have suggested via my deconstructive conceit that, until scholars and activists recognize that we live in a historical moment in which market-mediated consumer culture is the dominant social fact, mode of action and interpretation, moral denunciations of consumption, and marketing are bound to repeat ritualized forms. Also, the proposed solutions may appear to "the masses" as displays of elite cultural capital. The point I want to make here is that successful, progressive practices of citizenship "should" take place through market-mediated forms in our culture because these are the templates for action and understanding available to most people. Let me first give an example from the more apolitical end of the spectrum of social movements, the microbrewery industry:

> Microbreweries and brewpubs have attempted to define cognitively the specialty beer segment in ways that exclude major brewers and contract brewers. In our view, these oppositional identity strategies work in this context because the microbrewery movement actually resembles a true social movement in many respects. (Carroll and Swaminathan 2000, 731-32)

The loosely integrated producer-consumer microbrewery movement has significantly impacted the profitability and even mortality of contract brewers, premium brands produced by the major brewers, and the profitability and legitimacy of the major brewers (Carroll and Swaminathan 2000). The independent coffee house movement illustrates similar tendencies (Thompson and Arsel 2004). The point is that a form of social activism (infused with a marketplace logic of status marking and the play of specialized cultural capital [Holt 1998]) nonetheless functions as a practice of self-conscious resistance with material repercussions for oligopolistic industries.

[S]uccessful, progressive practices of citizenship "should" take place through market-mediated forms in our culture because these are the templates for action and understanding available to most people.

Further toward the overtly political end of the political action spectrum, I might evoke the Fair Trade (FT) movement. FT is a sourcing strategy primarily for agricultural commodities produced in tropical or subtropical developing countries, such as coffee, chocolate, tea, bananas, and sugar among others. Sourcing is undertaken by an international confederation of nonprofit organizations, one of which is TransFair USA. FT organizations seek to reduce the layers of middlemen between producers in the developing world and consumers in the developed world by handling a number of marketing, logistics, and product certification functions. The goal is to move value shares up the market channel so that producers in developing countries receive a greater share of consumers' purchase price. FT is a also a self-taxing scheme for concerned consumers who pay higher prices in return for the promise that producers will benefit directly from increased prices. Extensive survey research conducted in Guatemala, Peru, and Nicaragua indicates that across numerous standard social indicators, participants in TransFair USA marketing schemes reap positive benefits from this growing social movement. May we applaud that at a rate of 67 percent a year as compared to 12 percent growth for organic coffee, FT coffee is the fastest-growing segment of the U.S. coffee market, and that it has a 60 percent retail-location growth from 2003 to 2004 to thirty-five thousand locations in the United States (Arnould, Plastina, and Ball forthcoming)?

Finally, consider social movements at the most political end of the spectrum. In a book that received a lot of media attention, Hamburger and Wallsten (2006) argued for the permanence of Republican government based on nothing more than garden variety, data-based, mass-customized, target marketing of the type that reaches very small niche markets with precisely tailored messages and that make commercial—in this case Republican—messages seem attractive. And it works because marketized modes of action and address are part of American culture. In other words, marketing engenders shared forms of habitus and effective strategies for action and interpretation available to anyone.

But of course, all marketing campaigns are vulnerable to competition. Thus, one reads laudatory accounts on the left of marketing campaigns competitive with those of the Republican right, such as the "retail politics" of Sherrod Brown, who successfully ran for U.S. Senate in 2006. Brown engaged in mass-customizing the Democratic message and target marketing to disaffected white ex-manufacturing workers and Ohio-based CEOs alike. As John Nichols (2006, 11) wrote, "He recognizes that he will not crack the political codes of blue-collar counties that voted for Bush by repeating the talking points produced by a Democratic strategist in Washington."

More broadly, active participation in contemporary commercial media plays a complex social and potentially liberatory political role and is thus at odds with the sociology of marketing and consumption supportive of the dupe theory (Jong and Stammers 2005; Pickard 2006; Strangelove 2005). Sherrod Brown won; the Democrats also won the 2006 election, challenging the Republican oligopoly much as the microbrewery industry challenged the brewing oligopoly. Retail politics in a consumer-friendly form can challenge political hegemonies.

[T]o engage in progressive political action,
consumer citizens need to escape neither
consumption nor the market.

While the above argument may seem fanciful, it is not far from Slater and Tonkiss's (2001) recognition of the complex cycling and recycling of cultural forms through the market, a characteristic of advanced market-mediated consumer culture. Furthermore, these critical sociologists also recognize the importance of discriminating markets as an ideological idealization of neoliberals (p. 201) and as social and political forms whose effects and purposes are susceptible to influence through discourses and practices in which state, corporation, national, and global regulatory bodies as well as citizen activists all play a governance role, if often unequal ones (p. 145). In other words, marketing is an apparatus that may be enlisted in a variety of political projects.

Conclusion

This article sought to question some of the more ritualized approaches to the relationship between consumer culture and progressive social action. First, I reviewed some positions on the consumers' freedom of action, and I suggested that imputations of agency are conceptually problematic. Second, I discussed the term "consumers" and proposed that the anticonsumption ideology that seems to underlie the title's overarching question is an anachronistic and essentializing class-based ideology. I then considered more fundamental questions of materiality and objectification that tend to get unhelpfully bundled with markets and marketing in some critical sociology. Third, I examined the idea of escape. Here I reminded readers that escape is a Romantic idea, a response to the modern machine age, the apotheosis of which is the utopian dream. The dangers of real escape were illustrated with an example from a part of the globe set adrift by globalization (Appadurai 1990). Next, I invited readers to unbundle the concept of marketing from the critique of capitalism. Finally, I circled back to the question of political action and suggested that progressive politicized action is entirely possible within the framework of a mass-market mediated consumer culture. In other words, to engage in progressive political action, consumer citizens need to escape neither consumption nor the market.

References

Allen, Douglas E. 2002. Toward a theory of consumer choice as sociohistorically shaped practical experience: The fits-like-a-glove (FLAG) framework. *Journal of Consumer Research* 28 (March): 515-33.

Appadurai, A. 1990. Disjuncture and difference in the global cultural economy. *Public Culture* 2 (2): 1-24.

Arnould, E. J. 1989. Toward a broadened theory of preference formation and the diffusion of innovations: Cases from Zinder Province, Niger Republic. *Journal of Consumer Research* 16 (September): 239-67.

Arnould, E. J., A. Plastina, and D. Ball. Forthcoming. Market disintermediation and producer value capture: The case of fair trade coffee in Nicaragua, Peru and Guatemala. In *Product and market development for subsistence marketplaces: Consumption and entrepreneurship beyond literacy and resource barriers*, ed. J. A. Rosa and M. Viswanathan. New York: JAI/Elsevier.

Arnould, E. J., and L. L. Price. 2000. Authenticating acts and authoritative performances: Questing for self and community. In *The why of consumption: Contemporary perspectives on consumers motives, goals, and desires*, ed. S. Ratneshwar, D. G. Mick, and C. A. Huffman. New York: Routledge.

Aubert-Gamet, V. 1997. Twisting servicescapes: Diversion of the physical environment in a re-appropriation process. *International Journal of Service Industry Management* 8 (1): 26-41.

Baudrillard, J. 1970/1998. *The consumer society: Myths and structures*. London: Sage.

Bauman, Z. 1994. Is there a postmodern sociology? In *The postmodern turn: New perspectives on social theory*, ed. S. Seidman. Cambridge: Cambridge University Press.

Belk, R. W., and G. S. Coon. 1993. Gift giving as agapic love: An alternative to the exchange paradigm. *Journal of Consumer Research* 20 (3): 393-418.

Belk, R. W., Guliz Ger, and Soren Askegaard. 2003. The fire of desire: A multisited inquiry into consumer passion. *Journal of Consumer Research* 30 (December): 326-51.

Belk, R. W., M. Wallendorf, and J. F. Sherry Jr. 1989. The sacred and the profane in consumer behavior: Theodicy on the odyssey. *Journal of Consumer Research* 16 (1): 1-38.

Bourdieu, P. 1977. *Outline of a theory of practice*. Cambridge: Cambridge University Press.

———. 1984. *Distinction: A social critique of the judgment of taste*. Cambridge, MA: Harvard University Press.

Brown, S., and J. F. Sherry Jr. 2003. *Time, space, and the market: Retroscapes rising*. Armonk, NY: M.E. Sharpe.

Brown, S., A.-M. Doherty, and B. Clarke. 1998. *Romancing the market*. London: Routledge.

Brumfiel, E. M. 1980. Specialization, market exchange, and the Aztec state: A view from Huexotla. *Current Anthropology* 21 (4): 459-78.

Caillé, A. 1994/2005. *Don, intérêt et désintéressement: Bourdieu, Mauss, Platon et quelques autres.* Paris: Editions La Découverte/M.A.U.S.S.

Campbell, C. 1987. *The romantic ethic and the spirit of modern consumerism.* New York: Blackwell.

Carroll, G. R., and A. Swaminathan 2000. Why the microbrewery movement? Organizational dynamics of resource partition. *American Journal of Sociology* 106 (3): 715-62.

Cheal, D. 1988. *The gift economy.* London: Routledge.

Chin, E. 2001. *Purchasing power: Black kids and American consumer culture.* Minneapolis: University of Minnesota Press.

Colson C. 1992. Welcome to McChurch. With E. S. Vaughn. *Christianity Today* 36 (14): 28-33.

Cova, B., and V. Cova. 2002. Tribal marketing: The tribalization of society and its impact on the conduct of marketing. *European Journal of Marketing* 36 (5/6): 595-620.

Curasi, C., L. Price, and E. Arnould. 2004. How individuals' cherished possessions become families' inalienable wealth. *Journal of Consumer Research* 31 (3): 609-22.

Dávila A. 2001. *Latinos, inc.: The marketing and making of a people.* Berkeley: University of California Press.

De Certeau, M. 1984. *The practice of everyday life.* Berkeley: University of California Press.

Douglas, M. 1992. Why do people want goods? In *Understanding the enterprise culture*, ed. S. Hargreaves and A. Ross. Edinburgh, UK: Edinburgh University Press.

Elgin, D. 1993. *Voluntary simplicity: Toward a way of life that is outwardly simple–inwardly rich.* New York: William Morrow.

Elliott, R. 1997. Existential consumption and irrational desire. *European Journal of Marketing* 31 (3/4): 285-96.

Emirbayer, M., and A. Mische. 1998. What is agency? *American Journal of Sociology* 103 (4): 962-1023.

Ewen, S. 1976/2001. *Captains of consciousness: Advertising and the social roots of the consumer culture.* 25th anniversary ed. New York: Basic Books.

Firat, A. F., and A. Venkatesh 1995. Liberatory postmodernism and the reenchantment of consumption. *Journal of Consumer Research* 22 (3): 239-67.

Fournier, S. 1998. Consumers and their brands: Developing relationship theory in consumer research. *Journal of Consumer Research* 24 (4): 343-73.

Fuchs, S. 2001. Beyond agency. *Sociological Theory* 19:24-40.

Gervais, M. 1995. Structural adjustment in Niger: Implementations, effects & determining political factors. *Review of African Political Economy* 22 (63): 25-40.

Halton, E. 2000. Brain suck. In *New forms of consumption*, ed. M. Gottdiener. Lanham, MD: Rowman & Littlefield.

Hamburger T., and P. Wallsten. 2006. *One party country: The republican plan for dominance in the 21st century.* New York: Wiley.

Herrmann, G. M. 1997. Gift or commodity: What changes hands in the U.S. garage sale? *American Ethnologist* 24 (4): 910-31.

Holt, D. B. 1998. Does cultural capital structure American consumption? *Journal of Consumer Research* 25 (1): 1-26.

Huxley, A. 1932/1946. *Brave new world.* New York: Harper & Row.

Illouz, E. 1997. *Consuming the romantic utopia.* Berkeley: University of California Press.

Johnson, L. L., II. 2005. Niche marketing lures the "unchurched." *Marketing News* 39 (12): 14.

Jong, W., M. Shaw, and N. Stammers, eds. 2005. *Global activism, global media.* London: Pluto Press.

Keane, W. 2005. Signs are not the garb of meaning: On the social analysis of material things. In *Materiality*, ed. D. Miller. Durham, NC: Duke University Press.

Klein, N. 2000. *No logo: Taking aim at the brand bullies.* Toronto, Canada: Knopf.

Kopytoff, I. 1986. The cultural biography of things: commoditization as process. In *The social life of things*, ed. A. Appaduradi, 64-94. Cambridge: Cambridge University Press.

Kozinets, R. V. 2001. Utopian enterprise: Articulating the meaning of Star Trek's culture of consumption. *Journal of Consumer Research* 28 (1): 67-89.

———. V. 2002. Can consumers escape the market? Emancipatory illuminations from Burning Man. *Journal of Consumer Research* 29 (1): 20-38.

Kozinets, R. V., and J. M. Handelman. 2004. Adversaries of consumption: Consumer movements, activism, and ideology. *Journal of Consumer Research* 31 (3): 691-704.

Kozinets, R. V., J. F. Sherry Jr., D. Storm, A. Duhachek, K. Nuttavuthisit, and B. Deberry-Spence. 2004. Ludic agency and retail spectacle. *Journal of Consumer Research* 31 (December): 658-72.

Learn on Sundays, deepen faith at midweek services. 2006. *Marketing News* 40 (9): 15-17.

Living a second life. 2006. *The Economist*, September 30, pp. 77-79.

Loyal, S., and B. Barnes. 2001. "Agency" as a red herring in social theory. *Philosophy of the Social Sciences* 31 (4): 507-24.

Maclaran, P., and S. Brown. 2005. The center cannot hold: Consuming the utopian marketplace. *Journal of Consumer Research* 32 (2): 311-24.

Maffesoli, M. 1996. *The time of the tribes: The decline of individualism in mass society.* London: Sage.

Marion, G. 2003. Apparence et identité: Une approche sémiotique du discours des adolescents à propos de leurs expérience de la mode. *Recherche et Applications en Marketing* 18 (2): 1-29.

Marx, K. 1887/1977. *Capital: A critique of political economy.* Translated by D. Fernbach. New York: Vintage Books.

Mauss, M. 1925. *The gift: Form and functions of exchange in archaic societies.* New York: Norton.

Meillassoux C., ed. 1971. *The development of indigenous trade and markets in West Africa.* London: Oxford University Press.

Meyer, J. W., and R. L. Jesperson. 2000. The "actors" of modern society: The cultural construction of social agency. *Sociological Theory* 18 (1): 100-120.

Miller, D. 1987. *Material culture and mass consumption.* Oxford, UK: Basil Blackwell.

———. 1998. *A theory of shopping.* Ithaca, NY: Cornell University Press.

———. 2005. Materiality: An introduction. In *Materiality*, ed. D. Miller. Durham, NC: Duke University Press.

Miller, M. C. 1988. *Boxed in: The culture of TV.* Evanston, IL: Northwestern University Press.

Miyazaki, H. 2005. The materiality of finance theory. In *Materiality*, ed. D. Miller. Durham, NC: Duke University Press.

Muniz, A., and H. Schau. 2005. Religiosity in the abandoned Apple Newton brand community. *Journal of Consumer Research* 31 (4): 737-48.

Murray, J. B. 2002. The politics of consumption: A re-inquiry on Thompson and Haytko's (1997) "speaking of fashion." *Journal of Consumer Research* 29 (3): 427-40.

Nichols, J. 2006. What can Sherrod Brown do for the Democrats? *The Nation*, October 2, pp. 11-14.

Ozanne, Julie L., and Jeff B. Murray. 1995. Uniting critical theory and public policy to create the reflexively defiant consumer. *American Behavioral Scientist* 38 (February): 516-26.

Packard, V. O. 1957. *The hidden persuaders.* New York: D. McKay Co.

Peñaloza, L. 2001. Consuming the American West: Animating cultural meaning and memory at a stock show and rodeo. *Journal of Consumer Research* 28 (3): 369-98.

Pickard, V. W. 2006. United yet autonomous: Indymedia and the struggle to sustain a radical democratic network. *Media, Culture & Society* 28 (3): 315-36.

Polanyi, K., C. M. Arensberg, and H. W. Pearson, eds. 1957. *Trade and market in the early empires: Economies in history and theory.* Glencoe, IL: Free Press.

Rimke, H. M. 2000. Governing citizens through self-help literature. *Cultural Studies* 14 (1): 61-78.

Ritzer, G. 1993. *The McDonaldization of society.* Thousand Oaks, CA: Pine Forge Press.

Schau, H. J., and M. C. Gilly. 2003. We are what we post? Self-presentation in personal web space. *Journal of Consumer Research* 30 (3): 385-404.

Schor, J. B. 1998. *The overspent American: Upscaling, downshifting, and the new consumer.* New York: Basic Books.

———. 2004. *Born to buy: The commercialized child and the new consumer culture.* New York: Scribner.

———. 2005. Prices and quantities: Unsustainable consumption and the global economy. *Ecological Economics* 55:309-20.

Schroeder, R. 1994. Cyberculture, cyborg post-modernism and the sociology of virtual reality technologies. *Futures* 26 (5): 519-28.

Scott, L. M. 2005. *Fresh lipstick: Redressing fashion and feminism.* New York: Palgrave Macmillan.

Shultis, J. D., and P. A. Way 2006. Changing conceptions of protected areas and conservation: Linking conservation, ecological integrity and tourism management. *Journal of Sustainable Tourism* 14 (3): 226-37.

Slater, D., and F. Tonkiss. 2001. *Market society.* Malden, MA: Polity.

Strangelove, M. 2005. *The empire of mind: Digital piracy and the anticapitalist movement*. Toronto, Canada: University of Toronto Press.

Swidler, A. 1986. Culture in action: Symbols and strategies. *American Sociological Review* 51 (2): 273-86.

Thompson, C. J., and Z. Arsel. 2004. The Starbucks brandscape and consumers' (anticorporate) experiences of globalization. *Journal of Consumer Research* 31 (December): 631-43.

Thompson, C. J., and D. L. Haytko. 1997. Speaking of fashion: Consumers' uses of fashion discourses and the appropriation of countervailing cultural meanings. *Journal of Consumer Research* 24 (1): 15-42.

Vanderbilt, T. 1996. It's a wonderful (simplified) life. *The Nation* 262 (3): 20-22.

Venkatesh, A. 1998. Cybermarketscapes and consumer freedoms and identities. *European Journal of Marketing* 32 (7/8): 664-87.

Willis, P. 1990. *Common culture: Symbolic work at play in the everyday cultures of the young*. Milton Keynes, UK: Open University Press.

Wood, M. 1998. Agency and organization: Toward a cyborg-consciousness. *Human Relations* 51 (10): 1209-27.

A Carnivalesque Approach to the Politics of Consumption (or) Grotesque Realism and the Analytics of the Excretory Economy

BY
CRAIG J. THOMPSON

Politics of consumption analyses often evince a moralistic subtext that traces to the nineteenth-century fusion of Calvinism and patriarchal sexual politics. This spermatic legacy has channeled these critical discourses in a therapeutic direction that attenuates their realpolitik relevance. Drawing from Bakhtin's account of the carnivalesque, the author argues for an analytics of the excretory economy that eschews therapeutic goals in favor of muckraking scholarship that critically analyzes specific market systems and their constitutive networks of power relationships and material consequences. The author concludes by discussing some ways in which muckraking scholarship can mobilize citizen-consumers to the activist cause of transforming structural conditions that render specific facets of commercial culture problematic.

Keywords: muckraking scholarship; grotesque realism; moral critiques of consumption; therapeutic consumption

This article addresses the moral critique of consumption—culturally canonized by Veblen's (1899) stinging indictments of conspicuous consumption—as a profligate pursuit, driven by status emulation, leading to indolence, insipidness, and invidious comparison. As this grim postindustrial tale goes, personal well-being, family life, aesthetic virtues, natural resources, and the inhabitability of the planet are all being sacrificed on the altar of status-chasing consumerism, as consumers vainly waste their time and money trying to emulate the voluptuous lifestyles of media celebrities (e.g., De Graaf, Wann, and Naylor 2001; Frank 1999; Kasser 2002; Lasn 1999; Putnam 2000; Schor 1998, 2000; Taylor 2003).

Craig J. Thompson is Churchill Professor of Marketing at the University of Wisconsin–Madison. His research focuses on the cultural shaping of consumer-marketing relationships, the construction of identity though consumption, postmodern trends in consumer culture, and the marketing implications of consumer culture theory. He is on the editorial boards of the Journal of Consumer Research; Journal of Public Policy & Marketing; *and* Consumption, Markets, & Culture.

DOI: 10.1177/0002716207299303

Contemporary social critics seldom consider the historical roots of this Veblenesque legacy, in large part because they are applying this critical viewpoint to macro-level problems that appear self-evident in terms of their significance and consumptive etiology: escalating consumer debt levels, the rampant commercialization of childhood, ecological degradation, a looming peak oil crisis, and global warming (Schor 2000). Under these crisis conditions, why worry about antiquarian origins if this critical viewpoint can precipitate solutions to these consumption-driven dilemmas and avert impending disasters? However, a genealogical reflection raises the unsettling prospect that Veblenesque moralizations—which after a hundred-plus years have done little to slow the accelerating pace and mushrooming scale of consumerism—are further affirmation of Foucault's (1978) paradoxical interpretation of the repressive hypothesis: that is, a seminal discourse that produces a self-perpetuating dialectic of discipline and desire.

The moral critique of consumption is intimately connected to the normative discourses and ascetic practices of the spermatic economy (the belief that sperm ought to be conserved and not squandered) and its ideological fusion of patriarchal sexual politics and the Calvinist emphasis on diligent work and self-abnegation (Haraway 1994). As discussed by Barker-Benfield (1972), Freud's influential ideas regarding the sublimation of libidinal energy crystallized beliefs that had been in cultural circulation throughout much of the eighteenth century. In this proto-Freudian folk theory, seminal fluid represented an *élan vital* that flowed through the body (and body politic), which men needed to judiciously conserve if they were to have the energy and strength to succeed in an increasingly competitive economic marketplace (Kimmel 1996). This spermatic conception drove the moral panics over masturbation and promiscuous sexuality that raged throughout the latter half of the nineteenth century and into the early years of the twentieth century.

During this period, sexual continence functioned as a potent metaphor for the Protestant (and capitalist) ideals of wealth accumulation and productive investments in one's entrepreneurial calling—both deemed to signal that one had been predestined for salvation (see Weber 1905/2002)—and the concomitant Calvinist censures of extravagant spending and social displays of wealth (Freedman 1982). Rosenberg (1973) contended that this bourgeois sublimation of sexual desire enhanced the social standing of middle-class men by forging a symbolic distinction to the servant class and working-class laborers, who were portrayed as lacking self-control and being prone to wasteful intemperance.

As the twentieth century dawned, the middle- and upper-class segments of American culture came to fear that the psychic stresses, bureaucratic constraints, and proliferating material comforts of the bourgeois household were draining men of their vitality, leaving them enervated and ill prepared to assume their patriarchal responsibilities in the family and society at large. The idolatry of Teddy Roosevelt and his embodiment of the vigorous outdoor life stands as the therapeutic counterpart to this spermatic economy construction of masculinity and its anxious quest to regain phallic potency (see Kimmel 1996; Haraway 1994). This crisis-of-masculinity narrative shifted the spermatic economy to a psychological register, no longer tied to the literal conservation of semen. Accordingly, professional-class American men immersed themselves in commercial recreations of atavistic masculinity via mythic stories about the American West (though the frontier had long been closed); retreated to homosocial enclaves that reproduced the fraternal order of the guild tradition; sought revitalization through hunting and other primal experiences of nature; and ardently participated in virile sports, such as boxing and body building (Kimmel 1994).

This therapeutic orientation also forged a broader cultural association between consumption and humanistic ideals of self-expressiveness, self-development, and self-fulfillment that reverberates to the present day (Lears 1994).[1] Over the course of the twentieth century, therapeutic consumption became an increasingly prominent marketplace narrative, widely propagated by advertising, mass media, business leaders, journalists, and politicians who campaigned on promises of endless prosperity and implemented government policies that facilitated this fertile coupling of mass consumerism, cultivated individuality, and corporate capitalism (Cohen 2004; Cross 2000). As copiously documented by Roland Marchand (1985), this therapeutic framing of consumption would also become integral to American cultural conceptions of democracy. Rhetorical appeals to the democracy of goods and the democratizing forces of capitalist markets are now central themes of neoliberal punditry and its relentless praise singing for deregulated global corporate capitalism (see Frank 2000).

In this article, my aim is to retheorize the politics of consumption in carnivalesque terms (Bakhtin 1965/1984) that circumvent the moralistic and ideological tropes of the spermatic economy. Following Bakhtin (1965/1984), the carnivalesque is a linguistic and embodied social practice that "degrades" culturally rarefied discourses by transferring these texts, which speak in the language of the "high, spiritual, and abstract," to their material grounding in the "bodily lower stratum" (pp. 19-20). As a bit of foreshadowing, my carnivalesque theorization poaches a degrading phrase from Paul Willis (1978, p. 170), who characterized commercial culture as "the shit of production," a genuinely unseminal conception I shall unabashedly bend to suit my carnivalesque agenda.

The Carnivalesque and the Excretory Economy

According to Bakhtin (1965/1984), medieval carnivals exuberantly conjoined eating, drinking, copulating, and shitting in a pagan cosmology that celebrated the fertility of the Earth and the maternal body, the procreative power of sex, the fecund nature of excrement, and the corporeal fate of returning to the Earth as organic matter. The carnivalesque body is equally copulative and excretory, salacious and scatological, vibrant and on the way to becoming decomposing humus that feeds the earth. Thus, the carnivalesque decenters subjectivity and directs attention toward the web of transpersonal and ecological interconnections that sustain an indissoluble cycle of degeneration and regeneration.

FIGURE 1
DISCURSIVE DIMENSIONS OF THE CARNIVALESQUE

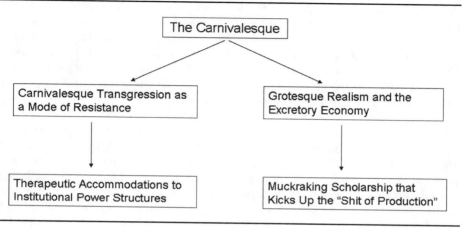

As illustrated in Figure 1, Bahktin's (1965/1984) portrayal of the carnivalesque is structured by two dimensions: transgressive resistance and grotesque realism. In these postmodern times, the transgressive dimension has been enthusiastically embraced as an emancipatory practice through which consumers can elude and defy the ideological imperatives, conformist mandates, and materialistic temptations of the capitalist marketplace (Debord 1967; Firat and Dholakia 1998; Lasn 1999). In contrast, academic writings on the politics of consumption have studiously ignored the implications of grotesque realism and the degrading project of critically situating socioeconomic relationships of power, and their ennobling rationalizations, in the excretory economy. My overriding agenda is to assert the generative power of this latter dimension for developing realpolitik critiques of commercial culture and mobilizing consumer-citizens to take transformative actions. As a preliminary step, however, I need to clear the theoretical ground by clarifying the utopian sensibilities that have equated the carnivalesque almost exclusively with transgressive practices while omitting the dimension of grotesque realism.

Carnivalesque transgression as resistance and all that utopian shit

In this utopian formulation, transgressive consumers are a geographically and temporally dispersed counterdominant force that provocatively subverts the conventions and norms of bourgeois consumerism and instigates a critical consciousness toward market capitalism (Debord 1967; Lasn 1999). Some proposed exemplars of carnivalesque resistance include defiant consumers who, a la the Situationist movement (Debord 1967), proactively reject prepackaged experiences and identities (Firat and Dholakia 1998); the stridently antimaterialistic, "no spectators allowed" community that annually congregates at the Burning Man festival (Kozinets 2002); Lesbian and Gay Pride parades whose exaggerated displays of camp and vamp mock the heterodominance of mainstream consumer culture (Kates and Belk 2001); the unruly cybercommunities of digital file sharers who jam their iPods with pirated music (Giesler and Pohlmann 2003); fantasy reenactors who retreat into anachronistic worlds that predate corporate capitalism, such as the Mountain Man Rendezvous (Belk and Costa 1998); and neopagan festivals that contest technocracy and commercialism through archaic polytheistic rituals and incantations (Pike 2001).

Some of these studies do address ways in which carnivalesque transgressions (and festive gatherings) remain paradoxically intertwined with commercial culture (e.g., Giesler and Pohlmann 2003; Kates and Belk 2001; Kozinets 2002). However, their prevailing argument is that these transgressive (and marginally perceptible) communities, identities, and social practices are effecting at least a partial resistance to corporate capitalism's ideological hailings and, thereby, afford consumer experiences that are more intense, authentic, and libratory. This qualified utopianism is further buttressed by Romantic jargon about the indomitable spirit of human freedom. Owing to these predilections, theoretical accounts of transgressive consumer resistance often meld therapeutic accommodations to institutional power with collective struggles to transform the means of production, the circuits of distribution, and the modalities of consumption (Thompson 2003). This dilemma can be brought into clearer relief by considering Bakhtin's (1965/1984) sociohistoric motivations for (mis)attributing revolutionary potential to these defiantly unregenerate folk rituals.

According to Bakhtin (1965/1984), the medieval carnival was a configuration of space and time in which oppressive rule was forced to confront the irrepressible will of the people. Carnivalesque practices ritualistically mocked the sanctimonious authority of the church and court, transgressed the sacred boundaries and aesthetic norms imposed by these disciplinary regimes, and asserted a collective refusal toward regal and papal subjugation. These ribald parodies exposed that not only do the king and the pope have no clothes, they shit just like everyone else, and no amount of pomp and circumstance will save them from the universal fate of death and decay. This inalienable knowledge gave the folk a collective power that could not be contained by oppressive authority.

Yet Bakhtin's (1965/1984) lionization of carnivalesque resistance was a utopian allegory that poetically envisioned a collective revolt against Stalinism, rather than a historical reality (see Clark and Holquist 1986). As Stallybrass and White (1986), among others, have noted, the Church and the court came to embrace the medieval carnival as a means to incorporate pagan traditions into the liturgy of Catholicism and to gradually distance these Saturnalian rituals from their historical roots. In the eighteenth and nineteenth centuries, the emerging bourgeoisie ideologically justified their sociopolitical dominance by representing the proletariat as a grotesque body of odors, boisterous laughter, drunkenness, and licentiousness, uniquely suited to life in the shop floor, the alehouse, and coarse conditions of poverty (Stallybrass and White 1986). In symbolic contrast, bourgeois consumers claimed the intellectualizing mantles of transcendent rationality, Kantian aesthetics, and civilizing mannerisms (Elias 1939/2000). In this same historical time frame, the commercial realm became more carnivalesque, as the rationalizing demands of industrialization instilled a recurrent need for (temporally and spatially bounded) moments of bacchanalian release. During the latter half of the nineteenth century, religious observances, most notably Christmas and Easter holidays, were also reconfigured as carnivalesque festivals, and the medieval celebration of St. Valentine's Day was reborn as an impassioned frenzy of consumer romanticism (Schmidt 1997). In sum, the commercial and the carnivalesque make for not-so-strange bedfellows.

These paradoxical dynamics raise perplexing questions about who is actually shitting on whom during these transgressive power struggles. In academic discourses, however, this dialectical complexity is typically buried under a pile of polemics. Theorists enamored with the glassy-eyed visage of the "disenchanted" or "alienated" consumer excrete thick narratives recounting how the forces of global capitalism are weakening the moral fiber of society by making consumers more materialistic, more harried, less civil, and less civically engaged (Putnam 2000). Theorists who are captivated by the carnivalesque image of the "defiantly elusive" consumer are similarly stricken with logorrhea: effusively spewing forth about how these carnivalesque transgressions and myriad acts of *détournement* are rendering corporate capitalism impotent and ineffectual (Debord 1967; Lasn 1999).

Bridging this chasm between the politics of consumption (as commonly formulated in academic discourse) and the reeking reality of corporate capitalism's shit requires that critical theorists abandon moralistic preoccupations with consumers' well-being, their existential states, their creative defiance, or slack-jawed submissions to the interpellations of the marketplace. Reflections on the travails or triumphs of the consumer provide a convenient intellectual path for tiptoeing around the shit of production; we may catch an unpleasant fetid waft here and there, but we can hold our noses and neatly avoid tracking any unpleasant substances into our pristine ivory towers. By forgoing this detour, we have to traipse through the fields of capitalist production and confront the question of just what to do about all this shit.

Grotesque realism and the shit of production

> The essential principle of grotesque realism is degradation, that is, the lowering of all that is high, spiritual, and abstract; it is a transfer to the material level, to the sphere of Earth and body in their indissoluble unity. . . . To degrade also means to concern oneself with the lower stratum of the body, the life of the belly and the reproductive organs; it therefore relates to acts of defecation and copulation, conception, pregnancy, and birth. Degradation digs a bodily grave for a new birth; it has not only a destructive, negative aspect, but also a regenerating one. (Bakhtin 1965/1984, 19-21)

To illustrate these peculiar notions of grotesque realism and degrading critical analysis, let us consider a bane of politics of consumption discourses: the automobile. From Galbraith's (1958) indictment of Cadillac tailfins as an icon of wasteful stylistic obsolescence to contemporary condemnations of gas-guzzling, greenhouse-gas-spewing, status-symbolizing SUVs, the automobile has been a potent symbol for the presumed ills of consumer society. This spermatic critique overlooks the degrading historical fact that the automotive transformation of urban metropolises had little to do with status competition or the Machiavellian machinations of the marketing apparatus. Rather, the automobile was initially hailed as a public health innovation and a major boon to urban living. At the turn of the century, American metropolises were being suffocated by the sickening miasma of horse manure and rotting dead horses. As McShane and Tarre (1997) explained,

> While the nineteenth century American city faced many forms of environmental pollution, none was as all encompassing as that produced by the horse. The most severe problem was that caused by horses defecating and urinating in the streets, but dead animals and noise pollution also produced serious annoyances and even health problems. The normal city horse produced between fifteen and thirty-five pounds of manure a day and about a quart of urine, usually distributed along the course of its route or deposited in the stable. While cities made sporadic attempts to keep the streets clean, the manure was everywhere, along the roadway, heaped in piles or next to stables, or ground up by the traffic and blown about by the wind. Citizens frequently complained about the "pulverized horse dung" which blew into their faces and houses and which covered the outside displays of merchants. The paving of streets accelerated the problem, as wheels and hoofs ground the manure against the hard surfaces and amplified the dust. Writing in *Appleton's Magazine* in 1908, Harold Bolce argued that most of the modern city's sanitary and economic problems were caused by the horse. Bolce charged that each year 20,000 New Yorkers died from "maladies that fly in the dust, created mainly by horse manure." (pp. 105-6)

[T]he automobile was initially hailed as a public health innovation and a major boon to urban living.

Under these material conditions, automobiles were a genuine breath of fresh air that made for a much better technological complement to the urban environment. By 1915, the major metropolises of New York, Paris, and London had largely replaced horses and carriages with automobiles and electric trolleys as the dominant modes of urban transportation (McShane and Tarre 1997). In our contemporary era, the gas-powered automobile is functionally equivalent to the horse and carriage of old, and it has precipitated new constellations of societal problems ranging from greenhouse gases to the health-threatening stresses of urban congestion. However, the current market system is structured and entrenched in ways that are not nearly as conducive to the rapid transformations enacted by our horse-and-carriage forebears. Structural barriers to enacting necessary changes in the material organization of commercial culture constitute a significant problem worthy of academic attention. More to the point, the resulting critical insights need to be publicized in ways that bring consumer-citizens to their "I am not taking this shit any more!" tipping point and productively inform activist strategies.

An important implication of grotesque realism is that nothing mobilizes consumer-citizens to social activism more than shit in the face. Rather than trying to cure consumers from affluenza or save their souls from materialistic seductions, an analytics of the excretory economy gets down and dirty into the degrading flows of shit (both productive and toxic) that circulate within specific market systems—linking consumers, producers, suppliers, laborers, advertisers, media, and regulators in particular networks of power relations—and then throws this institutional shit back in the collective face of the consumer-citizenry.

The Excretory Economy and Muckraking Scholarship

The theoretical and realpolitik differences that distinguish the politics of consumption, in its moral/therapeutic form, and an analytics of the excretory economy can be demonstrated through a comparison of two parallel critiques of commercial culture, one that is unabashedly spermatic in moral tenor and the other that digs into the excretory muck: George Ritzer's (1993) *The McDonaldization of Society* and Eric Schlosser's (2002) *Fast Food Nation*.

As a quick review of the McDonaldization thesis, Ritzer (1993, 1998) argued that the rationalizing principles that made McDonald's a global goliath—efficiency, calculability, predictability, and control through standardization—have come to dominate many other sectors of society ranging from tourism, education, politics, and medicine. Ritzer conceded that these dominant principles have yielded tangible benefits to society, but, echoing Weber (1905/2002), he warned that these gains have come at the high cost of spiritual disenchantment and the rationalized circumscription of creativity and freedom. From Ritzer's standpoint, McDonaldization has displaced authentic human relationships with scripted interactions, leaving workers and consumers with little or no opportunity to exercise genuine creativity in this world of standardized actions and prefabricated choices. To escape this postindustrial iron cage, Ritzer (1993) provided a trickster action plan: eat lunch at a local greasy spoon rather than a McDonaldized establishment, pay with cash rather than credit, make more meals from scratch, assiduously avoid corporate chains for any kind of service provision, boycott television with the exception of PBS programming, refuse to patronize domed sports stadiums, and read the *New York Times* rather than *USA Today*.[2]

Ritzer delivers a clever cultural reading of the homogenizing trajectories at work in global commercial culture that can spark a disconcerting sense of intuitive recognition. However, his emancipatory strategies are oriented toward therapeutic goals. Absent from this individuated politics of consumption is the realpolitik agenda of mobilizing consumer-citizens to hold corporations accountable for their actions and to reform their problem-inducing structures of operation (Kelly 2001; Klein 2002a). In fairness, Ritzer (1993, 1998) did enjoin consumer-citizens to collectively organize for certain political purposes such as keeping corporate fast food out of school cafeterias and creating work conditions that allow for more creativity and personal autonomy.

Much like proposals for downshifting and voluntary simplicity, however, Ritzer's (1993, 1998) action strategies seek to place some (therapeutic) boundaries on the corporate colonization of everyday life, but they do not challenge the underlying structural conditions that make these encroachments possible and problematic. For example, the persistent underfunding of public school systems has greatly facilitated the corporatization of education (Klein 2002b). Furthermore, America's overprocessed and cost-driven public food culture has resulted in unappealing and nutritionally suspect meals being standard fare in (noncorporatized) school cafeterias (Pollan 2006). In other words, keeping McDonald's out of school cafeterias may not improve the nutritional profile of the meals being served, and it most likely would lessen the culinary enjoyment of the students.

A more efficacious strategy would be to pressure fast-food providers to shift away from their standard cost-saving ingredients (such as corn syrup and hydrogenated vegetable oils) that unnecessarily increase the health risk of fast-food consumption and to invest more resources in effectively marketing healthier menu options. As Gladwell (2001) astutely noted, the first rule of successful fast-food marketing is to never promote something as "healthier" (even when it is), owing to the negative taste connotations that this phrase invokes. Another viable option would be to confront plans (and standard rationales) for McDonaldizing school lunch programs with countercases such as the Appleton Central Charter High School initiative (in Appleton, Wisconsin), which successfully implemented a whole foods lunch program. This holistic approach entailed nutritional education; an extended lunch period with a calmer and more relaxed atmosphere; the removal of vending machines from school grounds; and most important of all, well-prepared lunches consisting of a fresh entrée, free of additives or chemicals, fresh fruit, a salad bar, whole grain breads, low-fat cookies for dessert, and an energy drink and/or milk (see Keeley and Fields 2004).

To create positive alternatives to the McDonaldization of the diet (rather than just rely on prohibition strategies), consumer-citizens need to understand the institutional intricacies through which McDonaldization has been implemented and perpetuated and to what effects. In other words, they need concrete answers to the questions of how and why this shit is produced in this form and with this mix of consequences. In the spirit of excretory analysis, Schlosser (2002) did not make moral presumptions about what kind of food consumers should be eating or lament their moral failings for frequenting McDonaldized restaurants. He even acknowledged that this shit tastes pretty good, even when these enticing flavors and aromas have been chemically engineered. Instead, Schlosser explicated how the fast-food industry became such an ubiquitous economic and cultural force in the United States and the world at large.

Schlosser (2002) teased out, in remarkable detail, how this globally pervasive market system arose from an ensemble of tax policies, labor laws, suburban development initiatives, technological infrastructure, corporate alliances (e.g., McDonald's and Disney), media and advertising saturation, and strategies of vertical integration—all of which have been underwritten by incessant and quite successful corporate lobbying, revolving-door employment schemes, and other tactics of political influence. Schlosser illuminated how this institutional configuration has diminished the role of unions throughout the fast-food industry, thereby creating perpetually depressed industry wage scales and high-risk working conditions (particularly for meat packers) (also see Brueggemann and Brown 2003) and systematically compromising the economic positions of farmers, beef producers, meat packers, and restaurant workers. Schlosser also documented the fast-food industry's harmful material effects on the environment, animal welfare, and yes, consumers. In this latter case, however, his concern is not whether consumers are being disenchanted by standardized cuisine; rather, it is why fast-food consumers are routinely sickened by exposure to *e. coli* and other food-borne pathogens.

[I]nstitutional erasure of investigative journalism . . . is a major structural impediment to consumer citizenship and democratic dialogue.

I cannot think of a more fitting coda for this article than the most memorable line from *Fast Food Nation:* "eating a hamburger can now make you seriously ill [because] there is shit in the meat" (Schlosser 2002, 197). Though not quite horse manure in the face, this circumstance has sparked considerable public interest in the backstage production processes of the fast-food industry. If you tell consumers that they are being disenchanted and dehumanized by McDonaldized cuisine, they probably will not look up from their ketchup-stained Big Mac wrappers. If you tell them that they may literally be eating shit, they will see a different kind of red. Such grotesque realizations tend to pierce the veil of habit, complacency, and corporate ideology.

By exposing all this corporate shit, Schlosser (2002) has fostered greater critical awareness among consumers about the grotesque realities of fast-food production and laid the groundwork for political actions that can transform these industry practices. Indeed, consumer and worker rights groups are aggressively pushing key institutional players in the fast-food industry and government to redress these workers' rights, ecological, animal rights, and nutritional infractions. In responding to these diverse grassroots movements and multiple boycotts—further energized by Morgan Spurlock's (2004) supersized shit bomb—McDonald's has taken steps to make substantive improvements in its menu, labor policies, environmental footprint, and supply chain sources, though U.S. franchises still lag behind those in the European Union in terms of the pace and scale of these reforms (BBC News 2005).

An action-oriented insight that academics can glean from Schlosser (2002) is the importance and realpolitik value of investigating a defined market system within commercial culture, rather than making sweeping generalizations that presuppose the operation of a singularly dominant ideology (e.g., McDonaldization) or a pathological zeitgeist (e.g., affluenza). Teasing out these complexities calls for muckraking scholarship that unpacks critical institutional details about how a market system functions and the specific effects that emanate from its organizational structures and processes.

Owing to a confluence of ideological, economic, and institutional forces, investigative exposés of exploitive corporate practices have become one kind of informative shit that media conglomerates almost never produce. In the increasingly consolidated world of corporate-controlled media, shareholder imperatives to increase profits (which often entails cutting costs), "if it bleeds it leads" sensationalism, and, more subtly, an obsequious stance toward the official stories espoused by corporate advertisers and their lobbied advocates in government have made muckraking investigative journalism (of the Upton Sinclair, I. F. Stone, or Erwin Knoll variety) too expensive, too risky, and too controversial for mainstream media (see McChesney 2004).

This institutional erasure of investigative journalism—which can shine a critical light on all the shit that corporate power brokers would just as soon remain out of public view—is a major structural impediment to consumer citizenship and democratic dialogue. If the "fourth estate" is suffering from investigative constipation, being unable to move muckraking exposés past the colonic blockages of ideology, economics, and institutional disincentives, then some roles for academics are to leverage their skills and cultural authority to bring institutional power structures to light, to critically interrogate the network of relationships and alliances through which they operate, and to identify their institutional contradictions and susceptibilities to various kinds of change strategies. For this reason, an analytics of the excretory economy does not tolerate the intellectual conceit that the mere act of writing academic papers and books can instigate social change. Rather, this critical shit has to be distributed in the fields of political action through linkages with activist social networks and the strategic use of popular media forms, such as information pamphlets, Web sites, blogs, popular press books, documentaries, and radio talk shows, to name a few.

Media studies scholar Robert McChesney (1993, 2000, 2004) exemplifies this muckraking orientation. McChesney is Marx meets McCluhan meets Mother Jones: the medium is the power structure, and this dominant condition calls for a rabble-rousing message. His historical analyses map out the institutional alliances among corporations, politicians, and government regulators and the arrays of policies, strategies, and tactics that have enabled the public airwaves to be thoroughly colonized and consolidated by corporate power. McChesney adroitly interjects this academic research into the public sphere through his radio talk show, *Media Matters*, which is distributed through a network of NPR and community radio stations (and podcast through http://will.uiuc.edu/am/mediamatters/default.htm) and his Free Press organization (http://www.freepress.net), which functions as an information clearinghouse for media activism.

[A]n analytics of the excretory economy does not tolerate the intellectual conceit that the mere act of writing academic papers and books can instigate social change.

By transgressing conventional boundaries between academics and activism, critically minded researchers can facilitate grassroots political action and empower consumer-citizens with realpolitik knowledge for collectively redressing specific failings, excesses, abuses, and exploitations of a given market system. The incentive for consumers-citizens to actively participate in these (institutionally anchored) activist projects is also provided by the excretory economy: it is about the only way they can make sure that the shit stays out of the meat.

Notes

1. This therapeutic motif also enables redemptive "anticonsumerist" practices, such as downshifting and voluntary simplicity (Schor 1998; Taylor 2003), to be commodified as a minimalist aesthetic, indicative of refined consumption tastes, and marketed to affluent consumers as a status-conveying lifestyle (see Holt 2000).

2. This moralistic privileging of certain consumption practices—consumers should eat food prepared in this manner, read this kind of literature, watch this kind of media programming, and go to these kinds of retail establishments—steps right into the elitist tirades that critics of commercial culture are always having to scrape off their Blackspot sneakers (see, for example, Heath and Potter's [2004, 133-34] ad hominem lambasting of Naomi Klein and her *de rigueur* loft apartment and lifestyle preferences for artsy bohemian neighborhoods).

References

Bakhtin, M. 1965/1984. *Rabelais and his world.* Trans. H. Iswolsky. Bloomington: Indiana University Press.

Barker-Benfield, B. 1972. The spermatic economy: A nineteenth century view of sexuality. *Feminist Studies* 1:45-74.

BBC News. 2005. McDonald's praised for happy cows. http://news.bbc.co.uk/2/hi/business/4338308.stm.

Belk, R. W., and J. A. Costa. 1998. The mountain myth: A contemporary consuming fantasy. *Journal of Consumer Research* 25 (3): 218-40.

Brueggemann, J., and C. Brown. 2003. The decline of industrial unionism in the meatpacking industry: Event-structure analyses of labor unrest, 1946-1987. *Work and Occupations* 30 (3): 327-60.

Clark K., and M. Holquist. 1986. *Mikhail Bakhtin.* Cambridge, MA: Harvard University Press.

Cohen, L. 2004. *A consumers' republic: The politics of mass consumption in postwar America.* New York: Vintage.

Cross, G. 2000. *An all-consuming century: Why commercialism won out in America.* New York: Columbia University Press.

Debord, G. 1967. *The society of the spectacle.* Detroit, MI: Red and White.

De Graaf, J., D. Wann, and T. Naylor. 2001. *Affluenza: The all-consuming epidemic.* San Francisco: Berrett-Koehler.

Elias, N. 1939/2000. *The civilizing process: Sociogenetic and psychogenetic investigations.* Rev. ed. Trans. E. Jephcott. New York: Blackwell.

Firat, A. F., and N. Dholakia. 1998. *Consuming people: From political economy to theaters of consumption.* London: Routledge.

Foucault, M. 1978. *The history of sexuality.* Vol. 1. New York: Random House.

Frank, R. H. 1999. *Luxury fever: Money and happiness in an era of excess.* Princeton, NJ: Princeton University Press.

Frank, T. 2000. *One market under god: Extreme capitalism, market populism, and the end of economic democracy.* New York: Anchor Books.

Freedman, E. B. 1982. Sexuality in nineteenth-century America: Behavior, ideology, and politics. *Reviews in American History* 10 (4): 196-215.

Galbraith, J. K. 1958. *The affluent society.* New York: Houghton Mifflin.

Giesler, M., and M. Pohlmann. 2003. The social form of Napster: Cultivating the paradox of consumer emancipation. In *Advances in consumer research,* vol. 30, ed. P. A. Keller and D. W. Rook. Provo, UT: Association for Consumer Research.

Gladwell, M. 2001. The trouble with fries. *The New Yorker,* March 5. http://www.gladwell.com/2001/2001_03_05_a_fries.htm.

Haraway, D. 1994. Teddy bear patriarchy: Taxidermy in the Garden of Eden, New York City, 1908-1936. In *Culture/power/history,* ed. N. B. Dirks, G. Eley, and S. B. Ortner. Princeton, NJ: Princeton University Press.

Heath, J., and A. Potter 2004. *Nation of rebels: Why counterculture became consumer culture.* New York: HarperBusiness.

Holt, D. B. 2000. Postmodern markets. In *Do Americans shop too much?* ed. J. Cohen and J. Rogers. Cambridge, MA: Beacon.

Kasser, T. 2002. *The high price of materialism.* Cambridge, MA: MIT Press.

Kates, S. M., and R. W. Belk. 2001. The meanings of Lesbian and Gay Pride Day: Resistance through consumption and resistance to consumption. *Journal of Contemporary Ethnography* 30 (4): 392-429.

Keeley, J., and M. Fields. 2004. *Case study: Appleton Central Alternative Charter High School's nutrition and wellness program.* Michael Fields Agricultural Institute. www.michaelfieldsaginst.org/programs/food/case_study.pdf.

Kelly, M. 2001. *The divine right of capital: Dethroning the corporate aristocracy.* San Francisco: Berrett-Koehler.

Kimmel, M. S. 1994. Consuming manhood: The feminization of American culture and the recreation of the male body, 1832-1920. *Michigan Quarterly Review* 33 (Winter): 7-36.

———. 1996. *Manhood in America.* New York: Free Press.

Klein, N. 2002a. *Fences and windows: Dispatches from the front lines of the globalization debate.* New York: Picador Press.

———. 2002b. *No logo: No space, no choice, no jobs.* New York: Picador Press.

Kozinets, R. V. 2002. Can consumers escape the market? Emancipatory illuminations from Burning Man. *Journal of Consumer Research* 29 (1): 20-38.

Lasn, K. 1999. *Culture jam: The uncooling of America.* New York: William Morrow.

Lears, T. J. J. 1994. *Fables of abundance: A cultural history of advertising in America.* New York: Basic Books.

Marchand, R. 1985. *Advertising the American dream: Making way for modernity, 1920-1940.* Berkeley: University of California Press.

McChesney, R. W. 1993. *Telecommunications, mass media, and democracy: The battle for the control of U.S. broadcasting, 1928-1935.* New York: Oxford University Press.

———. 2000. *Rich media, poor democracy: Communication politics in dubious times.* New York: New Press.

———. 2004. *The problem of the media: U.S. communication politics in the twenty-first century.* New York: Monthly Review Press Books.

McShane, C., and J. A. Tarre. 1997. The centrality of the horse to the nineteenth-century American city. In *The making of urban America*, ed. R. Mohl. Wilmington, DE: Scholarly Resource Books.

Pike, S. 2001. *Earthly bodies, magical selves: Contemporary pagans and the search for community.* Berkeley: University of California Press.

Pollan, Michael. 2006. *The omnivore's dilemma.* New York: Penguin.

Putnam, R. D. 2000. *Bowling alone: The collapse and revival of American community.* New York: Simon & Schuster.

Ritzer, G. 1993. *The McDonaldization of society.* Thousand Oaks, CA: Sage.

———. 1998. *The McDonaldization thesis: Explorations and extensions.* Thousand Oaks, CA: Sage.

Rosenberg, C. E. 1973. Sexuality, class, and role in nineteenth-century America. *American Quarterly* 35 (May): 131-53.

Schlosser, E. 2002. *Fast food nation: The dark side of the all-American meal.* New York: Perennial.

Schmidt, L. E. 1997. *Consumer rites: The buying and selling of American holidays.* Princeton, NJ: Princeton University Press.

Schor, J. B. 1998. *The overspent American: Upscaling, downshifting, and the new consumer.* New York: Basic Books.

———. 2000. The new politics of consumption. In *Do Americans shop too much?* ed. J. Cohen and J. Rogers. Boston: Beacon.

Spurlock, M. 2004. *Super size me.* Los Angeles: Samuel Goldwyn Films.

Stallybrass, P., and A. White. 1986. *The politics and poetics of transgression.* Ithaca, NY: Cornell University Press.

Taylor, B. 2003. *What kids really want that money can't buy: Tips for parenting in a commercial world.* New York: Warner Books.

Thompson, C. J. 2003. Natural health's narratives of healing and the ideological production of consumer resistance. *Sociological Quarterly* 44 (Winter): 81-108.

Weber, M. 1905/2002. *The protestant ethic and the spirit of capitalism (and other writings).* Ed. and trans. P. Baehr and G.C. Wells. New York: Penguin.

Willis, P. 1978. *Profane culture.* London: Routledge & Kegan Paul.

Veblen, T. B. 1899. *The theory of the leisure class.* Project Gutenberg On-line Reader. http://www.gutenberg.org/catalog/world/readfile?fk_files=37643&pageno=1.

Why Not Share Rather Than Own?

By
RUSSELL BELK

Sharing is an alternative form of distribution to commodity exchange and gift giving. Compared to these alternative modes, sharing can foster community, save resources, and create certain synergies. Yet outside of our immediate families, we do little sharing. Even within the family, there is increased privatization. This article addresses impediments to sharing as well as incentives that may encourage more sharing of both tangible and intangible goods. Two recent developments, the Internet and intellectual property rights doctrines, are locked in a battle that will do much to determine the future of sharing. Businesses may lead the way with virtual corporations outsourcing the bulk of their operations. Whether virtual consumers sharing some of their major possessions are a viable counterpart remains an open question.

Keywords: sharing; property; possessions; ownership; intellectual property; Internet

Lone commuters in private vehicles travel billions of miles each day. Not only do these private vehicles contribute to airborne pollution and global warming, but the increased stress of time spent in traffic results in a tripling of heart attack risk a short time later (Peters et al. 2004). By individually sharing via carpooling (or better still, bike-pooling) or by jointly sharing via supporting and using public transportation, these negative consequences could be substantially ameliorated. So why do more of us not share our cars and other individual possessions? Is this an inevitable tragedy of the commons (Hardin

*Russell Belk is the Kraft Foods Canada Chair of Marketing in the Schulich School of Business at York University. He is past president and a fellow of the Association for Consumer Research and past president of the International Society of Marketing and Development. He has received the Paul D. Converse Award, the Sheth Foundation/*Journal of Consumer Research *Award for Long Term Contribution to Consumer Research, two Fulbright Fellowships, and four honorary professorships. He is the cofounder of the Association for Consumer Research Film Festival and has more than 350 publications. His research involves the meanings of possessions, collecting, gift giving, and materialism.*

DOI: 10.1177/0002716206298483

1968) that only state mandates, rewards, and punishments can affect? Or is there hope for sharing outside of our immediate families? A pessimistic view would suggest that we are headed toward *less* rather than *more* sharing. What were once the family radio, the family car, and the family television are increasingly privatized property of individuals within households. And the family meal is becoming a quaint memory. In this article, I explore the nature of sharing and ask whether a more optimistic view is possible.

Sharing is an alternative to the private ownership that is emphasized in both marketplace exchange and gift giving. In sharing, two or more people may enjoy the benefits (or costs) that flow from possessing a thing. Rather than distinguishing what is *mine and yours*, sharing defines something as *ours*. Thus, we may share a vacation home, a park bench, or a bag of jelly beans. We may also share more abstract things like knowledge, responsibility, or power. In each case, all of those involved in the sharing have something (a share) of the costs or benefits of a thing. Sharing, as used here, includes voluntary lending, pooling and allocation of resources, and authorized use of public property, but not contractual renting, leasing, or unauthorized use of property by theft or trespass. We can share not only places and things, but also people and animals (to the extent they are ours to share), as well as our ideas, values, and time. I do not include the simple coincidences that we may "share" a common language, place of birth, or set of experiences. These are all involuntary coincidences that do not depend on volitional sharing. Instead, I mean the act and process of distributing what is ours to others for their use as well as the act and process of receiving something from others for our use. The receipt of shared goods may be for an indefinite or prescribed period of time. And our share may be for our exclusive use or for use by us as well as others. Individuals, groups, and even nations can share. Just as consumption units may share in consuming something, production units may share in producing something, through profit sharing, employee-owned corporations, stock share ownership, and other joint ownership of the means of production. But the focus here is on shared consumption.

Although giving and receiving are involved in sharing, they differ from the giving and receiving involved in commodity exchange and gift giving. In economics' ideal form of commodity exchange, strangers barter or use money as a medium of exchange. Even though notions of customer relationship management might have it otherwise, in economic theory commodity transactions are balanced with no lingering indebtedness and no residual feelings of friendship. In Marshall Sahlins's (1972) terms, these transactions constitute either the tit-for-tat equivalence of balanced reciprocity, or negative reciprocity in which exchange partners seek to get more than they give. In both cases, the underlying model is that of the egoist who is the ideal "economic man." To be self-canceling, these transactions are simultaneous rather than sequential or staggered over time. This dissolves the relationship such that each partner can walk away without needing to ever see the other again. Therefore, Simmel (1990, 227) suggested that money transactions should be between strangers, not between friends or enemies.

If we conceive of a continuum involving these constructs, commodity exchange lies at one end and sharing at the other, with gift giving somewhere in the middle.

End points may be variously conceived as egoism-altruism, stinginess-generosity, and impersonality-personality. Gift exchange in Mauss's (1967) view is, like commodity exchange, based on reciprocity, and the gift cycle is driven by societal obligations to give, receive, and reciprocate. In Gregory's (1982, 1997) formulation, gift giving is the opposite of commodity exchange in that gift exchanges establish qualitative relationships between people and entail encumbrances or debts, whereas commodity exchanges establish quantitative relationships between objects and annul indebtedness (see also Frow 1997; Miller 2001; Osteen 2002). Gift exchange is ideally staggered so that balance is never achieved and therefore a debt always exists. It may even involve Sahlins's (1972) generalized reciprocity in which givers and receivers do not attempt to keep accounts, but rather give without thought to the balance or imbalance of any would-be accounts. Gifts have a highly ritualized character and are normally given with special wrappings and sometimes with special songs, food, clothing, and presentation traditions (Belk 1979, 1996; Sherry 1983). The gift exchange takes on a character that is more social than economic and may even come to involve agapic love (Belk and Coon 1993; Belk 1996). However, as Derrida (1992) and others (e.g., Sherry, McGrath, and Levy 1992, 1993) have reminded us, gifts are often more egoistic than altruistic. On the other hand, Granovetter (1985) and others (e.g., Carrier 1995; Silver 1990) have found reason to believe that many forms of business exchange involve embedded relationships and are better characterized as gift exchanges than commodity exchanges. Furthermore, although money has been found to be taboo in a number of gift exchange relationships (Webley, Lea, and Portalska 1983; McGraw, Tetlock, and Kristel 2003; Belk 2005), there are exceptions, as when giving downward in age or social class. However, despite such exceptions, clear conceptual boundaries between gifts and commodities remain.

Although it has not been well distinguished in the literature, sharing is a third form of distribution that is distinct from both marketplace commodity exchange and gift giving. Although some things can be distributed by any of these three means, there are some things that we can only share, including both positive things like a sunset, correspondence, and quietness as well as negative things like guilt, shame, and the proceeds of a crime in which we participate.

One prototype for positive sharing is income pooling and resource sharing within the family. While anthropologists like Sahlins (1972) and Godbout and Caille (1998) treated giving to close kin as gift giving, in most instances such giving is better construed as sharing. Especially within affluent cultures, this type of sharing is taken for granted. Young children need not work for their food, clothing, and shelter; nor are these things presented as gifts with all the ritual presentation that gifts involve. Children need not ask permission to enter their parents' home; they are not accused of theft if they take food from the refrigerator; nor will they be sued for trespass if they sit on the "family" sofa. They will not be presented with a bill for the expenses their parents have incurred on their behalf. Rather, the Marxian ideal of "from each according to his abilities; to each according to his needs" is very closely approximated within the family, even if there is sometimes disagreement about what each family member "needs" and which of these desires should have the highest priority. Despite the previously suggested exceptions involving privatization within the family, this does not imply that family members are self-sufficient and indifferent to one another's needs and desires. Sharing remains the norm.

Another prototype of sharing that is even more basic than the family is the mother. She literally shares her body with the fetus and her mother's milk with the infant. It is generally unthinkable that she would either charge for these services as commodities or regard them as the special gifts that some suggest (e.g., Godbout and Caille 1998; Vaughan 1997). However, surrogate motherhood and wet nurses show that even these very personal forms of sharing can be outsourced. Furthermore, with access to birth control and abortion, the mother is able to choose whether to share her body in these ways. Unless she was artificially inseminated or has adopted her child, she has also chosen to share her sexualized body with a male partner to become pregnant. That commoditized sex (prostitution) also has an ancient heritage does not eliminate the highly intimate mutual sharing of having sex, giving birth, and child rearing.

Issues in Sharing

A recent hotbed of sharing activity and discussions involves the Internet (e.g., Coyne 2005; Ghosh 2005). Sharing with others online includes open-source code writing; sharing information on Internet bulletin boards (BBs) and chat rooms; publishing blogs (Weblogs), vlogs (video logs), and Web sites; contributing to collaborative online games; helping create or improve entries in online encyclopedias like Wikipedia; participating in P2P (peer-to-peer) file sharing (e.g., Giesler 2006); maintaining listservs; and responding to e-mail requests. Those who make use of these online resources are a part of Internet sharing regardless of whether they make similar contributions themselves. Some see such sharing as the burgeoning of a new age of altruism brought about by the magic of cyberspace, while others suggest that such acts are largely egoistic. The altruistic explanation is closer to the original democratizing ethos of the personal computer (Belk and Tumbat 2005) and the view of computer hackers as heroic champions bringing power to the people. Thus, a key issue in such sharing is the extent to which it is altruistic and the extent to which we may be entering a new age of altruism.

Sharing has been the norm since the Scientific Revolution in the "open science" model of rapid disclosure and dissemination of new inventions and discoveries (David 2005). Prior to this time, the scientific model, especially in alchemy, involved secrecy in the quest to discover "nature's secrets." But starting in the seventeenth century, scientists began to realize that science would advance much more rapidly with the free and open sharing of information. This model now holds for academics generally. But the same Internet revolution that some see as fostering a new age of altruism is also fostering a new age of expanding intellectual property rights (IPR) that threatens to replace the altruism of sharing with the egoism of commoditization. At the present time, this battle is especially fierce regarding digital information (e.g., books, papers, music, films, software) and medical products (e.g., pharmaceuticals, genetic products, and bioprospecting—Hayden 2005; Kelty 2005). Similar issues arise in sharing human organs, eggs, semen, and blood and personal information (e.g., government surveillance, data mining, and identity theft). At issue here is what can or cannot be shared and under what conditions.

Sharing is a culturally learned behavior. The same is true of possession and ownership (Furby 1976). In the West, children learn about possession and ownership first and only learn to share as they get older (Furby 1978). But because of their nomadic heritage, Australian Aborigines learn sharing at an earlier age and more thoroughly than they learn possessiveness (Gould 1982; Testart 1987). Possessions are a burden in a nomadic society. Sharing such things as food, weapons, and tools is imperative for survival. The vestigial and strongly ingrained sharing ethos among Aborigines led to a number of problems following the introduction of automobiles (Gerrard 1989) and European private property laws in Australia (Maddock 1972).

Sharing is also more the prescribed norm in China with the concept of *zhanguang* (share the light). It is illustrated by the expectation that a villager who smokes in a public place should bring enough cigarettes or tobacco for everyone (Yan 1996). There are many prescribed instances of sharing in Japan as well, as with someone who gets a hole in one in golf being expected to share his or her good luck by buying gifts for the entire golf club (Rupp 2003). It is even possible to get insurance to indemnify such a "lucky" golfer. And there is a strong tradition in Africa that those who do well should share their wealth with extended family, to the extent of housing and feeding relatives who might come to town for months at a time (Belk 2000).

It is easiest to envision more sharing of intangible goods like information, opinions, images, and ideas, especially when these things are in digital form and we do not lose them by sharing them.

Thus, sharing is an interpersonal process and is sanctioned and prescribed by culture. Sharing by a giver can be judged as generous or stingy, altruistic or selfish, and fair or unfair, all according to cultural norms. We can feel that we have gotten our fair share, more than our fair share, or less than our fair share. Sharing can reduce envy and create feelings of community, or it can create dependency and foster feelings of resentment and inferiority. When someone shares with us, we can perceive his or her action as a sincere effort to please us or as an insincere sop designed to pacify and placate us (Foster 1972). Sharing can take place under conditions of excess, but it can also occur under conditions of insufficiency. And we may share broadly with anyone and everyone or narrowly within a couple, a family, or a business corporation.

Impediments to Sharing

For there to be sharing, there must first be feelings of possession, if not ownership. Otherwise, we have nothing to share. In communes, kibbutzim, cooperatives, and communism, possession and ownership may be to hold things in common for those who wish to use them. These contexts bear reexamination, but they will not be considered here.

We can come to feel possessive about and have a sense of ownership toward things that are not our property—a panoramic view, our children, a seat in a classroom, and even our beliefs (Abelson 1986). If ownership allows sharing, feelings of possessiveness and attachment toward the things we own or possess discourage sharing (Belk 1992; Kleine and Baker 2004; Wallendorf and Arnould 1988). To the extent that we feel a possession is a part of our extended self, we are more likely to wish to retain it (Belk 1988; Kleine, Kleine, and Allen 1995). For example, the more we cathect or feel that a particular bodily organ is a part of our identity, the less willing we are to become an organ donor or pledge to donate the organ in the future (Belk 1987, 1990).

Another factor that inhibits sharing is materialism, defined as the importance a person attaches to possessions. Materialists believe that possessions are the key source of happiness or unhappiness in life (Belk 1985). One of three operational components in this conception of materialism is nongenerosity, suggesting a partial explanation for why those who are more materialistic are also less willing to share.

Another impediment to sharing is the perception that resources are scarce and if we share we may miss something we might have enjoyed. Consider the case of fine art. It might be argued that there is only so much truly fine art and that even apart from its unaffordability, there is simply not enough to go around. But public art museums, reproductions, and copies provide democratized access to fine art, as André Malraux (1967) proposed. In its early history, the Boston Museum of Fine arts displayed copies of sculptures (DiMaggio 1982). Eventually, however, the reproductions were relegated to the basement of the museum and only originals were publicly displayed. One reason may be found in Walter Benjamin's (1968) lament that we lose the "aura" of the original when we substitute a mechanical reproduction. Another explanation, however, is that we lose the status-conferring power of the scarce original when we attempt to substitute a reproduction. We may disparage such copies with the labels forgery, fake, or counterfeit.

Incentives to Share

Incentives to share intangibles

Despite such impediments to sharing, sharing occurs beyond the immediate family in virtually all cultures. Consider the culture of academic scholarship. We claim ownership of our academic ideas by presenting them and publishing them. If we instead borrow "others' ideas," we may be accused of plagiarism. To seek to profit from our academic ideas rather than to freely share them with others is generally viewed with disdain. The scholar is supposed to be motivated by the joy of creating and sharing ideas. So, we freely participate in a giant potlatch of ideas with our colleagues and students, often from a sincere and joyous desire to share our discoveries, creative theories, and critical interpretations. We are satisfied with the fame or reputation that may result and the people we may inspire, even if we enjoy indirect economic benefits through the promotions, fame, and salary increases that may accrue.

Although sharing our data (Sieber 1991) could make research much easier, eliminate redundant data collection, allow specialists to collect data, and subject our insights to triangulation by multiple others, we are reluctant to do this, unless forced. We may be part of a community of scholars, but we would rather that our scholarly neighbors come over and admire our flower garden rather than borrow our seeds, tools, and potting soil. Nevertheless, this sharing of primary data is exactly what has been done with DNA sequences in the Human Genome Project, and this has led to great breakthroughs in biology and medicine that could never have occurred without such data sharing (Love and Hubbard 2005).

There are, however, some things that we can share or give away without losing them—a song, a joke, a story, our bodies, things we put up on our Web sites, or music files shared on the Web. Even with earlier information goods like books, journals, and videos, it is possible to make copies that can be shared freely (Varian 2000). Unlike some other works of art, these copies are virtually indistinguishable from the originals. With the advent of the Internet and e-mail, some have suggested that consumerism is being replaced by the gift economy (Pinchot 1995), the hi-tech gift economy (Barbrook 2005), or the society of the gift (Coyne 2005). But here, too, these forms of give and take are better characterized as sharing than gift giving in that they lack the ritual presentation of the gift and because donors and recipients are often anonymous and unknown. With open source software like Linux, numerous people contribute source code anonymously and freely (Bergquist 2003; Bergquist and Ljungberg 2001). Benkler (2005) called this "commons-based peer production." Other examples include music and video file sharing (Giesler 2006), software or "freeware" sharing (Raymond 2001), and a variety of virtual communities sharing information via online bulletin boards, chat rooms, and Web sites (Barbrook and Cameron 2001; Rheingold 2000).

Coyne (2005) considered possible motives for giving away our possessions and productions on the Internet. One is "cheap altruism": although we give away the digital equivalent of a song, computer program, photograph, or text file, we still have it. In Annette Weiner's (1992) terms, it is a way of keeping while giving. But this does not explain why someone would contribute at all rather than act as a free rider. A second explanation that Coyne offered is that this is true altruism and a return to tribal society in a digital age. In this view, the Internet is leading to a global community of sharing, communicating, and giving, with a free flow of information providing equality of access. A related view that Coyne most fully embraced is that the Internet precipitates something that has always remained beneath the surface in humans—the primordial and playful gift economy. But once again, the concept of the gift is less apt than the concept of sharing. Just as the parent who shares with intimately known others in the family seldom packages the things they give as a gift, contributors to open source code or Internet bulletin boards help anonymous others because they can. The apt model here is that of a cornucopia. Motivations may include the notions of somehow "paying back" the benefits previously received from the Internet. Although keeping while giving is not irrelevant, the sense of paying back and at the same time keeping the cornucopia flowing is the factor that is needed to explain why many people choose the giving involved in sharing over being a free rider. Although he was speaking in terms of gifts, Hyde (1983) suggested an imperative for constant movement. We are impelled to continue to share when someone has shared with us, although not necessarily with the same person. Thus, if someone allows us to merge into heavy traffic (effectively sharing the road with us), we may be more inclined to do the same for others. We might also apply this to our own academic giving in reviewing papers, for example.

There is also the motivating effect of feeling a part of a community of kindred spirits. Possessions not only symbolize the self, they can act as marker goods (Douglas and Isherwood 1979) that symbolize membership in a group or class. The joint possession of certain goods can also convey status and power by demonstrating the group's command of what are taken to be scarce resources. And consumer goods may be expressive of lifestyle affiliations, some of which may take on cultlike characteristics centered around a brand such as the cult of Macintosh computer aficionados (Muñiz and O'Guinn 2001; Belk and Tumbat 2005). Expressing a similar affection for this particular brand rather than another marks us as belonging to a group of like-minded people. Within brand cults, there is also a sense of sharing a secret: that of the wonder of the brand. And as with sharing secrets and self-disclosure generally, mutual sharing of secrets deepens and reinforces relationships. Perhaps the ultimate bonding form of sharing secrets is to share one's body sexually with another. Yet at the same time, this too is a case of keeping while giving as long as we do not damage our sense of self-worth in the process.

Incentives to share tangibles

Few of us would be churlish enough to decline a request to give directions to a stranger who is lost or to deny someone who asks for the time of day. Sharing such intangible knowledge is often a case where we can keep while giving. But what of sharing tangible goods? In ancient times like those of Homer's Greece, a stranger seeking hospitality would commonly be granted food and shelter (Reece 1993). In the Middle Ages, hospitals extended an unconditional welcome and hospitality to those in need (Roberts 1996). In sixteenth-century France, the tables and beds of high-ranking households were open to visits without notice, although this was restricted to friends, neighbors, and kin (Davis 2000). While such hospitality may still exist with regard to extended family (e.g., Jones 1996), strangers are now less welcome. Fiske (1991) and Komter (2005) saw communal sharing as a model of resource allocation that applies primarily within the immediate family. Why should we share our material possessions outside of our immediate family? Consider the analogy of school girls or boys sharing clothing. Each student gains an apparently larger wardrobe at no cost other than that of risking damage to or nonreturn of their clothing that is lent out. Each has effectively leveraged her or his lifestyle without increasing her or his wardrobe expenditure. An institutionalized version may be found in a service called Bag Borrow or Steal that rents designer handbags for a $50 per month fee, with users being able to trade in for another model anytime they wish (Windfield 2005). Some local car sharing co-ops operate on this principle to make cars available to others when they need them without the costs of unnecessary parking and maintenance. We may also belong to larger groups that share possessions in the case of time-share vacation homes, collectively owned sailboats, shared institutions like museums, and shared resources like national parks. Here, too, we leverage our lifestyles beyond individual possibilities. We get most of the benefits of ownership in each case.

A different explanation is needed for cases like picking up a hitchhiker or giving to a beggar since we are unlikely to have the favor returned by those we befriend. Here, the sense of paying back for one's prior good fortune is one possibility. But so is genuine altruism and helping others to nourish a self-image that we are generous and helpful. Such sharing can be spoiled by money. A dinner guest who pulls out his checkbook at the end of the meal rather than offering flowers or wine to be shared during the meal will be unwelcome in the future (Benkler 2005).

Materialism, possessive individualism, and the conviction that self-identity must be developed by extension into possessions are all factors that inhibit sharing.

A further incentive for sharing tangible things is an extension of the keeping-while-giving motivation identified with nontangible things. Here, the keeping may either be literal as in lending someone a tool that we expect to be returned, or symbolic as in believing that more will come our way. Suppose we are walking on a beach and find some interesting-looking shells that we pick up. A child comes along and admires the shells, so we give her one. We do this in the belief that we are likely to encounter more such shells on our walk. The principle has been called "unlimited good" (Foster 1969). As with the cornucopia image used earlier, as long as we believe that the supply of good things is unlimited, we are happy to share with others. It is only when we believe that the supply is fixed that we become selfish and try to retain our possessions. That is, when we construe life as a zero-sum game, we are less likely to share. And even when we view the supply of a good as limited, there may be an inclination to share when it would otherwise go to waste. This would apply to an unrefundable ticket to a performance that we cannot attend as well as to the leftovers from a harvest that gleaners may be invited to make use of. A countercase involves concert recordings of the Grateful Dead. For years, the band allowed "tapers" to record and trade tapes of their performances, as long as they did not sell them for a profit. But in late 2005, the band made an effort to stop the free downloading of this music from both their own Web site (www.gdstore.com) and a site called Live Music Archive (www.archive.org). As one account of the proposed end of sharing the Dead put it, the attempt to commoditize the concert recordings invoked a vision of the Internet not as cornucopia, but as a pay-per-play cash cow (Pareles 2005). Boyle (2005) has compared this and other attempts to enclose the "commons" of cyberspace to the fifteenth-century closure of the agricultural commons.

As with intangibles, yet another incentive to share tangibles is when our extended sense of self embraces other people outside of our immediate family (Belk 1988). As Etzioni (1988) suggested, when we feel a shared identity with others—whether in our neighborhood, group, city, state, or nation—we feel a common sense of moral obligation toward them. And in the broadest sense, we all share a common humanity that may provoke sharing with others with whom we can empathize in their time of need. This sense of commonality is especially relevant to those things that can only be owned in common, as is the case with our stewardship of planetary resources.

Conclusions

This is a preliminary framing of the issues about sharing. Much remains to be done. In the case of the Internet, we shall see whether the increase in sharing or the simultaneous increase in intellectual property rights it has inspired will ultimately predominate in cyberspace. Still, some tentative conclusions may be offered.

As we have replaced social security with financial security, trust in money and things have supplanted trust in people, and economic capital has become more important than social capital. We continue to share resources within our nuclear families, but even families share less these days, as possessions within the family are privatized. Individual bank accounts and credit cards are growing as joint accounts and cards decline. And that part of traditional Christian wedding vows that professes "I do thee endow with all my worldly goods" is negated by the addendum, "Except as stipulated by prenuptial agreements." Perhaps it is because of the decline in sharing within our intimate attachments that we seem to increasingly seek virtual communities online. Ironically, we are becoming more likely to share our deepest secrets, insights, information, and loyalties with someone whom we know only by an online pseudonym than we are with our partners or with other members of our families.

It is easiest to envision more sharing of intangible goods like information, opinions, images, and ideas, especially when these things are in digital form, and we do not lose them by sharing them. But there are limits here as well. As I have argued, academics can only gain credit for their work by freely sharing it. But we are largely unwilling to share their raw data with others. Many of the things we might wish to share are legally protected by intellectual property laws, as illustrated by the prosecution of the music file-sharing site, Napster. The film industry is also battling to stop the online distribution of "pirated" films. And patents, copyrights, and other legal protections are further impediments to freely sharing many ideas.

There are burdens to possession, as any home owner can attest. And with the increasingly rapid pace of technological change, we may see a shift toward shared ownership.

With tangible goods, there are also many laws to protect private property from sharing, while there are other laws granting free shared access through private lands to beaches, fields, and forests. But the larger barrier to sharing material goods is attitudinal. Materialism, possessive individualism, and the conviction that self-identity must be developed by extension into possessions are all factors that inhibit sharing. Although Inglehart (1981) contended that affluent societies are moving into an age of postmaterialism and Pine and Gilmore (1999) suggested that we are becoming an experience economy that values doing over having, there is very little indication that we are ready to sever our attachments to things and become more defined by our attachments to people. We cling to an identity forged in the crucible of materialism. Those who call for downshifting (e.g., Schor 1998), dematerializing (e.g., Hammerslough 2001), or voluntary simplicity (e.g., Elgin 1998) need to confront the tenacity with which we seem to cling to possessions (see also Boyle 1998).

Interestingly, it is business that shows a trend toward less possessiveness and materialism. Virtual corporations retain the right to their intangible brand names but freely outsource everything else from production to management, marketing, and customer service. It is more economical and necessary to remain competitive. By, for instance, belonging to an automobile cooperative rather than owning an individual car, consumers can leverage their lifestyles in a similar manner. Still, it seems that the virtual consumer has less allure than the virtual corporation. But there may be reasons for hope. There are burdens to possession, as any home owner can attest. And with the increasingly rapid pace of technological change, we may see a shift toward shared ownership. For a growing number of car sharing cooperatives like AutoShare of Toronto, the question being raised is, Why own when you can share?

References

Abelson, R. P. 1986. Beliefs are like possessions. *Journal for the Theory of Social Behavior* 15:223-50.

Barbrook, R. 2005. The hi-tech gift economy. *First Monday*. http://www.firstmonday.org/issues/issue3_12/barbrook/index.html (accessed November 1, 2006).

Barbrook, R., and A. Cameron 2001. Californian ideology. In *crypto anarchy, cyberstates, and pirate utopias*, ed. P. Ludlow. Cambridge, MA: MIT Press.

Belk, R. 1979. Gift-giving behavior. In *Research in marketing*, vol. 2, ed. J. N. Sheth. Greenwich, CT: JAI.

———. 1985. Materialism: Trait aspects of living in the material world. *Journal of Consumer Research* 12 (3): 265-80.

———. 1987. Identity and the relevance of market, personal and community objects. In *Marketing and semiotics: New directions for the study of signs for sale*, ed. Jean Umiker-Sebeok. Berlin: Mouton de Gruyter.

———. 1988. Possessions and the extended self. *Journal of Consumer Research* 15:139-68.

———. 1990. How perceptions of the body influence organ donation and transplantation: Me and thee versus mine and thine. In *Psychological research on organ donation*, ed. J. Shanteau and R. J. Harris. Washington, DC: American Psychological Association.

———. 1992. Attachment to possessions. In *Human behavior and environment: Advances in theory and research*, vol. 12, *Place attachment*, ed. I. Altman and S. Low. New York: Plenum.

———. 1996. The perfect gift. In *Gift giving: A research anthology*, ed. C. Otnes and R. F. Beltramini. Bowling Green, OH: Bowling Green University Popular Press.

———. 2000. Consumption patterns of the new elite in Zimbabwe. *Journal of Macromarketing* 20:204-5.

———. 2005. Exchange taboos from an interpretive perspective. *Journal of Consumer Psychology* 15 (1): 16-21.

Belk, R., and G. Coon. 1993. Gift giving as agapic love: An alternative to the exchange paradigm based on dating experiences. *Journal of Consumer Research* 20:393-417.

Belk, R. and G. Tumbat. 2005. The cult of Mac. *Consumption, Markets and Culture* 8:205-18.

Benjamin, W. 1968. The work of art in the age of mechanical reproduction. In *Illuminations*, ed. H. Arendt, trans. Harry Zohn. New York: Harcourt, Brace & World.

Benkler, Y. 2005. Coase's penguin, or, Linux and the nature of the firm. In *Code: Collaborative ownership and the digital economy*, ed. R. Ghosh. Cambridge, MA: MIT Press.

Bergquist, M. 2003. Open source software development as gift culture: Work and identity formation in an Internet community. In *New technologies at work: People, screens, and social virtuality*, ed. C. Garsten and H. Wulff. Oxford, UK: Berg.

Bergquist, M., and J. Ljungberg. 2001. The power of gifts: Organizing social relationships in open source communities. *Information Systems Journal* 11:305-20.

Boyle, J. 2005. Fencing off ideas: Enclosure and the disappearance of the public domain. In *Code: Collaborative ownership and the digital economy*, ed. R. Ghosh, 235-58. Cambridge, MA: MIT Press.

Boyle, T. C. 1998. Filthy with things. In *T. C. Boyle stories*. London: Penguin.

Carrier, J. 1995. *Gifts and commodities: Exchange and Western capitalism since 1700*. London: Routledge.

Coyne, R. 2005. *Cornucopia limited: Design and dissent on the Internet*. Cambridge, MA: MIT Press.

David, P. A. 2005. From keeping "nature's secrets" to the institutionalization of "open science." In *Code: Collaborative ownership and the digital economy*, ed. R. Ghosh. Cambridge, MA: MIT Press.

Davis, N. 2000. *The gift in sixteenth-century France*. Madison: University of Wisconsin Press.

Derrida, J. 1992. *Given time. I, Counterfeit money*. Trans. P. Kamuf. Chicago: University of Chicago Press.

DiMaggio, P. 1982. Cultural entrepreneurship in nineteenth-century Boston: The classification and framing of American art. *Media, Culture and Society* 4:303-22.

Douglas, M., and B. Isherwood. 1979. *The world of goods: Towards an anthropology of consumption*. New York: Norton.

Elgin, D. 1998. *Voluntary simplicity, revised edition: Toward a way of life that is outwardly simple, inwardly rich*. New York: Harper.

Etzioni, A. 1988. *The moral dimension: Toward a new economics*. New York: Free Press.

Fiske, A. P. 1991. *Structures of social life: The four elementary forms of human relations, communal sharing, authority ranking, equality matching, and market pricing*. New York: Free Press.

Foster, G. M. 1969. Peasant society and the image of limited good. In *Applied anthropology*, ed. G. M. Foster. Boston: Little, Brown.

———. 1972. The anatomy of envy: A study of symbolic behavior. *Current Anthropology* 13:165-82.

Frow, J. 1997. *Time and commodity culture: Essays in cultural theory and postmodernity*. Oxford, UK: Clarendon.

Furby, L. 1976. The socialization of possession and ownership among children in three cultural groups: Israeli kibbutz, Israeli city, and American. In *Piagetian research: Compilation and commentary*, vol. 1, ed. S. Modgil and C. Modgil. Windsor, UK: NFER Publishing.

———. 1978. Sharing: Decisions and moral judgments about letting others use one's personal possessions. *Psychological Reports* 93:595-609.

Gerrard, G. 1989. Everyone will be jealous for that mutika. *Mankind* 19 (2): 95-111.

Ghosh, R., ed. 2005. *Code: Collaborative ownership and the digital economy*. Cambridge, MA: MIT Press.

Giesler, M. 2006. Consumer gift system: Netnographic insights from Napster. *Journal of Consumer Research* 33:283-90.

Godbout, J. T., and A. Caille 1998. *The world of the gift*. Trans. D. Winkler. Montreal, Canada: McGill-Queen's University Press.

Gould, R. A. 1982. To have and have not: The ecology of sharing among hunter-gatherers. In *Resource managers: North American and Australian hunter-gatherers*, ed. N. M. Williams and E. S. Hunn. Boulder, CO: Westview.

Granovetter, Mark. 1985. Economic action and social structure: The problem of embeddedness. *American Journal of Sociology* 91 (November): 481-510.

Gregory, C. A. 1982. *Gifts and commodities*. London: Academic Press.

———. 1997. *Savage money: The anthropology and politics of commodity exchange*. Amsterdam: Harwood Academic.

Hammerslough, J. 2001. *Dematerializing: Taming the power of possessions*. Cambridge, MA: Perseus Publishing.

Hardin, G. 1968. The tragedy of the commons. *Science* 162:1243-48.

Hayden, C. 2005. Benefit-sharing: Experiments in governance. In *Code: Collaborative ownership and the digital economy*, ed. R. Ghosh. Cambridge, MA: MIT Press.

Hyde, L. 1983. *The gift: Imagination and the erotic life of property*. New York: Random House.

Inglehart, R. 1981. Post-materialism in an environment of insecurity. *American Political Science Review* 75:880-900.

Jones, A. 1996. Philanthropy in the African American experience. In *Giving: Western ideas of philanthropy*, ed. J. B. Schweewind. Bloomington: Indiana University Press.

Kelty, C. 2005. Trust among the algorithms: Ownership, identity, and the collaborative stewardship of information. In *Code: Collaborative ownership and the digital economy*, ed. R. Ghosh. Cambridge, MA: MIT Press.

Kleine, S. S., and S. M. Baker. 2004. An integrative review of material possession attachment. *Academy of Marketing Science Review* 1:1-39.

Kleine, S. S., R. E. Kleine III, and C. T. Allen. 1995. How is a possession "me" or "not me"? Characterizing types and an antecedent of material possession attachment. *Journal of Consumer Research* 22:327-43.

Komter, A. E. 2005. *Social solidarity and the gift.* Cambridge: Cambridge University Press.

Love, J., and T. Hubbard. 2005. Paying for public goods. In *Code: Collaborative ownership and the digital economy*, ed. R. Ghosh. Cambridge, MA: MIT Press.

Maddock, K. 1972. *The Australian Aborigines: A portrait of their society.* London: Penguin.

Malraux, A. 1967. *Museums without walls.* Ed. S. Gilbert and F. Price. Garden City, NY: Doubleday.

Mauss, M. 1967. *The gift: Forms and functions of exchange in archaic societies. I.* Trans. Ian Cunnison. New York: Norton.

McGraw, A. P., P. E. Tetlock, and O. V. Kristel. 2003. The limits of fungibility: Relational schemata and the value of things. *Journal of Consumer Research* 30:219-29.

Miller, D. 2001. Alienable gifts and inalienable commodities. In *The empire of things: Regimes of value and material culture*, ed. Fred R. Myers, 91-115. Oxford, UK: School of American Research Press.

Muñiz, A. M., Jr., and T. O'Guinn. 2001. Brand community. *Journal of Consumer Research* 27:412-33.

Osteen, M. 2002. Gift or commodity? In *The question of the gift: Essays across disciplines*, ed. Mark Osteen. London: Routledge.

Pareles, J. 2005. The Dead's gamble: Free music for sale. *New York Times* (online edition), December 3.

Peters, Annette, Stephanie von Klot, Margit Heier, Ines Trentinaglia, Allmut Hörmann, H. Erich Wichmann, and Hannelore Löwel. 2004. Exposure to traffic and the onset of myocardial infarction. *New England Journal of Medicine* 351 (17): 1721-30.

Pinchot, G. 1995. The gift economy. *Context: A Quarterly of Humane Sustainable Culture.* http://www.context.org/ICLIB/IC41/PinchotG.htm (accessed November 1, 2006).

Pine, J. B., II, and J. H. Gilmore. 1999. *The experience economy: Work as theatre and every business a stage.* Boston: Harvard Business School Press.

Raymond, E. S. 2001. The hacker milieu as gift culture. *Future Positive.* http://futurepositive.synearth.net/stories/storyReader$223 (accessed November 1, 2006).

Reece, S. 1993. *The stranger's welcome: Oral theory and the aesthetics of the Homeric hospitality scene.* Ann Arbor: University of Michigan Press.

Rheingold, H. 2000. *The virtual community: Homesteading on the electronic frontier.* Cambridge, MA: MIT Press.

Roberts, S. 1996. Contexts of charity in the Middle Ages: Religious, social, and civic. In *Giving: Western ideas of philanthropy*, ed. J. B. Schweewind. Bloomington: Indiana University Press.

Rupp, K. 2003. *Gift-giving in Japan: Cash, connections, cosmologies.* Stanford, CA: Stanford University Press.

Sahlins, M. 1972. *Stone age economics.* Chicago: Aldine-Atherton.

Schor, J. B. 1998. *The overspent American: Upscaling, downshifting, and the new consumer.* New York: Basic Books.

Sherry, J. F., Jr. 1983. Gift giving in anthropological perspective. *Journal of Consumer Research* 10:157-68.

Sherry, J. F., Jr., M. A. McGrath, and S. J. Levy. 1992. The disposition of the gift and many unhappy returns. *Journal of Retailing* 38 (1): 40-65.

———. 1993. The dark side of the gift. *Journal of Business Research* 28:225-44.

Sieber, J. E. 1991. *Sharing social science data: Advantages and challenges.* Thousand Oaks, CA: Sage.

Silver, A. 1990. Friendship in commercial society: Eighteenth-century social theory and modern Sociology. *American Journal of Sociology* 95:1474-1504.

Simmel, G. 1990. *The philosophy of money.* Trans. Bottomore and D. Frisby. London: Routledge.

Testart, A. 1987. Game sharing systems and kinship systems among hunter-gatherers. *Man* 22 (2): 287-304.

Varian, H. R. 2000. *Buying, sharing and renting information goods.* http://www.sims.berkeley.edu/~hal/Papers/sharing.pdf (accessed November 1, 2006).

Vaughan, G. 1997. *For-giving: A feminist critique of exchange.* Austin, TX: Plain View Press.

Wallendorf, M., and E. J. Arnould. 1988. "My favorite things": A cross-cultural inquiry into object attachment, possessiveness, and social linkage. *Journal of Consumer Research* 14:531-47.

Webley, P., S. L. Lea, and R. Portalska. 1983. The unacceptability of money as a gift. *Journal of Economic Psychology* 4:223-38.

Weiner, A. 1992. *Inalienable possessions: The paradox of keeping-while-giving.* Berkeley: University of California Press.

Windfield, Nick. 2005. In a dizzying world, one way to keep up: Renting possessions. *Wall Street Journal,* October 17, p. A1.

Yan, Y. 1996. *The flow of gifts: Reciprocity and social networks in a Chinese village.* Stanford, CA: Stanford University Press.

Downshifting Consumer = Upshifting Citizen? An Examination of a Local Freecycle Community

By
MICHELLE R. NELSON,
MARK A. RADEMACHER,
and
HYE-JIN PAEK

Critics suggest that contemporary consumer culture creates overworked and overshopped consumers who no longer engage in civic life. The authors challenge this conventional criticism against consumption within an individualistic lifestyle and argue instead that consumers who are "downshifting" do engage in civic life. In particular, this research examines downshifting attitudes among members of freecycle.org, a grassroots "gift economy" community. Results of an online survey show that downshifting consumers are indeed less materialistic and brand-conscious. They also tend to practice political consumption (e.g., boycotts, buycotts). Most important, they tend to engage in a digital form, but not a traditional form, of civic and political participation. The authors contend that alternative forms of consumption might be a new form of civic engagement.

Keywords: downshifting; Web community; civic engagement; political consumption; materialism

Critics claim that overworked individuals and unchecked consumption erode civic life. According to a conventional critique, "distracted by material things and out of touch with social health, [consumers] watch community life from the sidelines" (De Graaf, Wann, and Naylor 2001, 62). Most critiques emphasize the privileging of acquisition over community, along with a time displacement of priorities (Putnam 1995). Indeed, according to New American Dream: A Public Opinion Poll, 93 percent of Americans surveyed agreed with the statement, "Too many Americans are focused on working and making money and not enough on family and community" (2004; see http://www.newdream.org/about/PollResults.pdf).

Nevertheless, in response to hyperconsumption and the stress, overtime, and psychological expense that may accompany it, a growing number of people (estimated at 19 percent of the U.S. population; Schor 1998) are simplifying their lifestyle. These are "downshifters"—people

DOI: 10.1177/0002716206298727

who voluntarily choose to work less and/or consume less. Downshifting behaviors are often considered a form of the voluntary simplicity movement. Both emphasize regaining balance in life (more leisure time, less work) by reducing clutter and emphasizing personal fulfillment and connections to others over economic success (Etzioni 1998; Mazza 1997). As a result of reduced incomes or a desire for a less materialistic life, downshifters try to repair, reuse, share, and make goods rather than buy them. Instead of "getting and spending" to give lives order and meaning, downshifters may focus on civic reengagement (Schor 1998).

Alternative forms of consumption might be a new form of civic engagement.

Although increased civic engagement is often implied as a motivator or a consequence of downshifting (Etzioni 1998), research has not empirically examined these relationships. Accordingly, the purpose of this study is to investigate whether people who simplify their lives or downshift their work and/or consumption behaviors then "upshift" or increase their civic life.

Previous research has identified downshifters, in part, as those who choose good-quality secondhand goods (Shaw and Newholm 2002). In this article, we examine a previously unstudied community of people who actively seek out

Michelle R. Nelson is an associate professor in the Department of Advertising at the University of Illinois at Urbana-Champaign. Her research focuses on advertising and consumer culture. She studies the sociocultural and psychological factors that regulate commercial media effects on individuals' values, attitudes, and behaviors. She has authored articles in journals such as Journal of Consumer Psychology, Journal of Consumer Behaviour, *and* Journal of Advertising.

Mark A. Rademacher is a doctoral student in the School of Journalism and Mass Communication at the University of Wisconsin–Madison. Broadly construed, his research focuses on media and consumer culture. Specifically, he studies the influence of media, consumption, and peer culture in college students' identity development and maintenance. He has presented numerous papers on these topics at major communication and consumer research conferences. In 2006, he was selected to attend the National Communication Association's National Doctoral Honors Seminar.

Hye-Jin Paek is an assistant professor in the Grady College of Journalism and Mass Communication at the University of Georgia. Her topical research interests include health campaigns, socially responsible consumer behavior and advertising, and communication research methods. Her theoretical orientation focuses on how promotional media messages influence individuals' beliefs, attitudes, and behaviors and how such influences are augmented by social perceptions, social interactions, and social contexts. She has published her research in major communication journals such as Communication Research, Journalism & Mass Communication Quarterly, *and* Mass Communication & Society.

secondhand goods as a way to investigate the relationships among downshifting attitudes, consumer and political consumption values, and acts of civic and political engagement. The community is freecycle.org—an international, grassroots group committed to participating in a "gift economy" based on the free exchange of goods. Members of local freecycle groups actively post messages to give away (e.g., "Offer: children's clothes, all sizes") or request consumer goods from others in the community (e.g., "Wanted: good working lawn mower"). Thus, they are reusing and recycling secondhand goods.

Analyzing survey data collected from this type of downshifter, we examine the following research questions: (1) What are the motivations of joining freecycle.org and what are these downshifters' consumption values? and (2) To what extent do they engage in traditional and nontraditional forms of civic participation? As we argue, the critique that consumption erodes civic life is too simple. Rather, emerging and alternative modes of consumption are positively related to new forms of civic participation.

Critiques of consumer culture

Despite consumer culture's contribution to America's economic stability and success, it is also viewed with underlying anxiety. Critics have argued that the increased availability of consumer goods partnered with increased disposable income has resulted in hedonistic, individualistic consumers (e.g., Bell 1976; Bellah 1975; Galbraith 1958; Lasch 1979; see Horowitz [2004] for a review). Instead of using consumption to achieve social equality and other collective social goals, these types of consumers are viewed as seeking personal satisfaction through goods at the expense of democracy.

The dichotomy between consuming for personal satisfaction and for the communal good became most apparent during World War II. Many public intellectuals viewed the government-imposed restrictions on consumption as an expression of a new moralism, in which citizens rationed and sacrificed a standard of living for the soldiers and for "the health of postwar democracy" (Horowitz 2004, 20). The new moralism linked consumption with democracy and community. Through self-restraint, consumption could transcend individualism to serve the public good. Despite this optimistic view, in the postwar era individualistic consumption returned as Americans experienced both incremental gains in income and the availability of mass-produced goods (Cohen 2003). The behavior of consumers during this period "undermined . . . [the efforts] to make a convincing link between democracy, the reform of capitalism, and lessened consumption" (Horowitz 2004, 21). Furthermore, it laid the foundation for beliefs that the rising aspiration and associated consumption helped drive the postwar economy; indeed, the links between patriotism, consumption, and democracy remain intact today. An op-ed piece in *USA Today* commented on retail sales on Veteran's Day and suggested, "We are a nation that conflates patriotism and shopping, our role as citizens and our role as consumers. We know our economy depends on consumer confidence and spending. Shopping is good for America; therefore, it's patriotic" (Roth-Douquet 2006).

Whether for political or personal reasons, many American middle-class consumers have, quite literally, "shopped till they dropped." In a recent critique of consumer culture, Schor (1998) cited statistics that show increased work hours, credit card balances, and stress levels and decreased household savings and quality-of-life indicators such as time spent with family and happiness. Thus, to escape this "work-and-spend" cycle, some individuals are seeking other ways of living by reducing their work hours and consumption—these are the downshifters. Downshifters do not escape the marketplace (Arnould 2007 [this volume]) but are voluntarily engaging in alternative forms of work, consumption, and play because of the individual gratifications they receive. Thus, in contrast to some anticonsumption simplifiers (e.g., "radical greens" who isolate themselves in communes; Moisander and Pesonen 2002), the mainstream downshifters tend to operate inside consumer and civic culture.

Downshifting and the simple life

The "simple living" movement, with its roots in material restraint, dates back to at least the colonial era (Shi 1985). The movement rests on the de-emphasis on acquiring money and goods to focus on "the purity of the soul, the life of the mind, the cohesion of the family, or the good of the commonwealth" (Shi 1985, 3-4).

Contemporary simplifiers seek to minimize their consumption, although they are not required to live in poverty or isolation from others nor to deny technological progress or the existence of material beauty. Specifically relevant to the freecycle community, voluntary simplifiers remove clutter and complexity in their personal lives by giving away or selling those possessions that are seldom used and that could be used productively by others (Elgin 2000). Downshifters seek out those secondhand goods (Shaw and Newholm 2002).

The reasons for downshifting relate to wanting more time and experiencing less stress and more balance in life. Thus, the primary motivations for these people are, first, to gain time by working less and, second, to escape from the work-and-spend cycle. Two forms of downshifting emerge: *work downshifting*, voluntarily decreasing the number of hours of employment; and *consumption downshifting*, consciously reducing spending.

Downshifters are primarily white consumers with middle- to upper-middle-class incomes from Western, affluent countries (Schor 1998; Zavestoski 2002). As a group, these consumers are concerned with environmental, social, and animal welfare issues (Shaw and Newholm 2002). They are also more likely to value the functional utility of goods over the ability to convey status (Craig-Lees and Hill 2002; Schor 1998). Thus, we can expect these types of consumers to be less brand-conscious and materialistic than hedonistic consumers (Etzioni 1998).

Downshifting consumption and upshifting participation?

Scholars have argued that contemporary American culture is witnessing the decline of civic mindedness. The critique primarily stems from the belief that contemporary culture represents individualistic and self-serving consumption behavior, as well as the fact that media increasingly pervade daily life. As the argument goes, both of these conditions ultimately distract citizens from more community-focused activities. The most ardent proponent of this decline thesis is political scientist Robert Putnam (2000), who argued that the privatization of social life has resulted in a decline in social capital and, therefore, a decline in the social cohesiveness of communities (see also Bellah et al. 1985). In essence, Putnam and others (e.g., Bennett 1998, 2000) have argued that the evolution from a civic culture to an "uncivic" culture represents "a fundamental threat to the survival of healthy communities and democratic political systems" (Stolle and Hooghe 2004, 153).

But the decline thesis has faced strident opposition from a number of scholars in various disciplines. Most critiques characterize the decline thesis as pessimistic, based on nostalgia for a time when civic engagement was the norm, and nearsighted in its conceptualization of civic engagement (Stolle and Hooghe 2004). Some scholars advocate for the inclusion of new forms of civic participation such as socially conscious consumption and consumer activism (e.g., boycotts and buycotts) (e.g., Klein 2000; Scammell 2003; Stolle, Hooghe, and Micheletti 2005). The primary difference is that these forms of engagement focus on the politicization of lifestyle concerns instead of organizational politics (Bennett 1998; Stolle and Hooghe 2004). Other scholars focus on the Internet's potential to build social networks and communities organized around branded goods (Muniz and O'Guinn 2001) or to help people organize, discuss, or provide opinions related to political or civic matters (Shah et al. 2005).

The ultimate response to the decline thesis, then, is that civic engagement has evolved to include a wider range of activities, including debating and seeking political information online and political consumption. The politicizing of consumption has consequently transformed some consumers into people who consciously consider the consequences of consumption—and routinely ask how, where, and by whom a product is made. Such consumers attempt to use purchasing power to bring about social change and to be socially responsible (Webster 1975).

One group of consumers who must confront their values and new lifestyles and identities when faced with consumer choices are downshifters (Schor 1998). By living more consciously and being aware of where and how goods are made, downshifters are likely to engage in forms of political consumption by boycotting goods and services of companies whose actions or policies they consider unethical (Elgin 2000) or by buycotting goods and services of companies that practice social responsibility. Indeed, through their reduction in consumption and reuse of secondhand goods, downshifters are helping the environment. Those who partake in such practices are also more likely to engage in other green consumption activities, such as buying solar heating equipment (Stern 1984). Yet as noted by Etzioni (1998), the consequences of downshifting for social justice and society are not known and warrant further examination.

Taking up this issue, we explore downshifting attitudes and measures of civic participation. The downshifters here are part of a Web community (freecycle.org), people who use the Internet to build and leverage social networks to share their goods. In fact, such virtual communications are viewed by the broader simplicity movement as a way to reach out to similar others, who become submerged between networked communities and commercialized communities (Cherrier and Murray 2002). These virtual spaces help create feelings of belonging and solidarity and support for alternate ways of living. Schor (1998) suggested that such peer reference groups are necessary for downshifter survival in a consumer society. But does membership in a consumption community (albeit secondhand consumption) suffer from time displacement critiques noted above? Will freecyclers use their online propensity to engage in online political or civic activities, or will they fall prey to the critiques of Internet use as described by de Vreese (2007 [this volume])? We examine a local downshifting group that builds community on the Web to help us explore and revisit the conceptualization of what it means to be civically and politically engaged in contemporary (consumer) culture.

Method

Survey

A survey was conducted among members of the Madison, Wisconsin, chapter of freecycle.org in July 2005. Freecycle.org is predicated on the idea of a gift economy with the express goal of environmental activism and community (i.e., "to build a worldwide gifting movement that reduces waste, saves precious resources & eases the burden on our landfills while enabling our members to benefit from the strength of a larger community"; www.freecycle.org). As of November 8, 2006, freecycle.org expanded from a small group in Tucson, Arizona, in 2003 to a current global membership of 2,792,052 people comprising 3,811 communities in 77 countries.

In partnership with the local chapter's moderators, an online survey was distributed to the 7,507 members of the Madison and Dane County freecycle community. A link to the survey was embedded in a post on the community's Web site that mirrored the format of a typical "Wanted" post. In total, 183 freecycle members completed the survey. This response rate (2.4 percent) is low. But it should be noted that our main purpose is not to generalize our findings to the entire freecycle.org community but rather to take this group of people as a unique case of downshifters and to examine their motivations and practices related to consumption and civic participation.

The participants consisted of 75 percent females and 89 percent Caucasians with a mean age of 39.4 years. A little less than 60 percent of the respondents were married, and just more than 63 percent of respondents owned their home. Their median income falls into the $40,000 to $49,999 bracket, and their average education level is between some college and college degree (see Table 1 for demographic profiles).

TABLE 1
DESCRIPTIVE CHARACTERISTICS OF VARIABLES USED (N = 183)

Variable	Mean	Standard Deviation
Predictor variables		
Demographics		
Sex (female)[a]	74.9 (137)	—
Race (white)[a]	89.1 (163)	—
Married[a]	59.6 (109)	—
Home ownership[a]	63.4 (116)	—
Age	39.38	10.83
Education[b]	3.81	1.61
Income[c]	8.00	3.74
Values		
Brand consciousness	2.39	1.02
Materialism	2.47	1.27
Civic/consumption activities		
Political consumption	4.93	1.28
Offline civic participation	1.99	1.78
Online civic participation	1.72	1.49
Criterion variables		
Work downshifting	4.88	1.26
Consumption downshifting	5.19	1.23

a. The variables are measured with a dichotomous scale that indicates 1 as the label's value (i.e., female, white, married, own a home) and 0 as other (i.e., male, other races, combination of other marital status, and rent); numeric values indicate proportion with sample size in parentheses.
b. The education variable was measured with a 6-point ordinal scale ranging from *high school degree* to *graduate or terminal degree*. The mean represents an education level between some college and undergraduate degree.
c. Income was measured with an 11-point ordinal scale with a $9,999 increase per bracket (starting under $10,000). The numeric value indicates median (instead of mean), which represents the $40,000 to $49,999 bracket.

Measures

The variables used in the present analysis can be categorized into four groups: (1) the criterion variables—work and consumption downshifting; and the predictor variables: (2) consumption values—brand consciousness and materialism; (3) online (non-traditional) and offline (traditional) civic participation and political consumption; and (4) the demographic variables—gender, race, marital status, homeownership, age, education, and income. The variables measured with multiple items were examined with exploratory factor analysis (EFA) for a factor structure and with Cronbach's alpha reliability for internal consistency. Table 1 reports descriptive statistics of all the variables. The appendix also reports all the items that construct the respective variables, EFA results and alpha coefficients, and question wording.

To identify motivations of joining the community, the survey asked members this question: "What prompted you to become a member of freecycle?" Two coders initially classified respondents' open-ended responses into one of ten distinct categories. When some respondents stated multiple reasons for joining the community, only their first response was considered in the coding procedure. The interreliability coefficient using Perreault and Leigh's (1989) Index (P/L Index)—known to be most appropriate when there are only two coders and items with nominal scales—was .85, which represents fairly good reliability (Rust and Cooil 1994). One of the researchers settled disagreements between the two coders. The original ten categories were then collapsed into four distinct categories that more accurately reflected the emergent themes in the respondents' answers: simple life (e.g., decluttering), environmental concerns, self-orientation (e.g., "want free stuff"), and other-orientation (e.g., help others by giving away goods).

Then we analyzed two sets of hierarchical regression models to examine the associations between the two forms of downshifting (work and consumption) and each of the consumption values, political consumption, and civic participation measures. With work downshifting and consumption downshifting as dependent variables in each regression model, predictors were entered in hierarchical regression models in the following order: first, the seven demographic variables for control purposes; second, the two consumption value variables; and finally, the two forms of civic participation and political consumption. Since some of the variables that are entered in the same block have a strong correlation (e.g., between the two consumption values and between the two forms of civic participation) and therefore may cancel out one another's effects, we also looked at the size and direction of beta-in coefficients as well as those of beta-final coefficients. As shown in Table 2, the first column reports "beta-final coefficients" from the final equation in which all the predictors are controlled; the second column reports each "beta-in coefficient" in which demographic variables only are controlled.

Results

Motivations for joining freecycle

Our first research question asked why people joined the freecycle community. The most frequent answer given (33 percent of respondents) related to elements of a "simple life," which echoes the mission of the community and adheres to characteristics of voluntary simplicity. Answers that fall into this category include de-cluttering or getting rid of stuff. For example, one member said, "I had a lot of stuff in my house that was very useable, but I didn't want it anymore"; another indicated, "We were moving and had a ton of stuff to get rid of. Plus, I'm a reformed packrat, so now need to clean the basement." Others saw freecycle as a viable alternative to donating the items to local thrift shops or paying for them to be removed.

TABLE 2
HIERARCHICAL REGRESSION ANALYSES THAT PREDICT
TWO FORMS OF DOWNSHIFTING (N = 183)

Variable	Work Downshifting		Consumption Downshifting	
	Beta Final[a]	Beta In[b]	Beta Final[a]	Beta In[b]
Demographics				
Sex (female)	−.044	—	−.110	—
Race (white)	−.061	—	.052	—
Married	.080	—	−.032	—
Home ownership	.265°°°	—	.096	—
Age	−.174°°	—	−.061	—
Education	.153°°		.185°°	
Income	−.166°		−.153°	
Incremental R^2		.176°°°°		.127°°°
Consumption values				
Brand consciousness	−.109	−.225°°°	−.294°°°°	−.374°°°°
Materialism	−.270°°°°	−.339°°°°	−.194°°	−.358°°°°
Incremental R^2		.119°°°°		.179°°°°
Civic/consumption activities				
Political consumption	.150°°	.212°°°	.229°°°	.271°°°°
Offline civic participation	−.080	.085	.003	.114
Online civic participation	.172°°	.183°°	.047	.113
Incremental R^2		.045°°		.053°°
Total R^2		.339°°°°		.359°°°°

NOTE: All betas are standardized regression coefficients.
a. Betas are taken from the final equation with all the predictors entered.
b. Betas are taken from "beta in" after the control variables (demographic variables).
°$p \le .10$. °°$p \le .05$. °°°$p \le .01$. °°°°$p \le .001$.

The next two most frequent answers were related to self-oriented needs and wants (27 percent) and environmental concerns (27 percent). For those whose answers fall into the "self-orientation" category, responses were related to their own functional or economic purposes (e.g., save money) or their own wants/desires (e.g., love a bargain, free stuff, or mere curiosity). For environmental concerns, responses typically explicitly included the "recycling purpose" or "keep stuff out of landfill" rationale. Many also noted that their goods still had "life left in them." Compared to the self-oriented reasons, other-oriented reasons were less frequent (8 percent). The respondents whose answers belong to this category appeared interested in helping others (e.g., "hoping their stuff goes to someone who needs it") or feeling a sense of bonding/community.

Consumption values and political consumption and civic participation

We also examined the association between downshifting practices and each of the consumption values, political consumption, and civic participation measures. As shown in Table 2, materialism and brand-consciousness values were quite strongly and negatively related to both of the downshifting practices. Those who engage in work downshifting—by valuing personal growth over financial growth—and those who engage in consumption downshifting are significantly less materialistic. They also tend to place less emphasis on the importance of designer names and heavily advertised brands. Although the beta-final coefficient of the brand consciousness variable becomes nonsignificant at the p-value = .05 level (beta final = $-.109$, $p = .17$), its beta-in coefficient shows that the association remains significant when demographic variables only are controlled and materialism is not controlled (beta in = $-.225$, $p < .01$). Given the significant correlation between brand consciousness and materialism ($r = .425$, $p < .001$), it seems that the beta final coefficient of brand consciousness is cancelled out in the regression model for work downshifting. This finding may indicate two points: one, materialism may be a stronger negative predictor of work downshifting than brand consciousness; two, nevertheless, brand consciousness is also statistically and negatively related to work downshifting. Compared to the regression model for work downshifting, the regression model for consumption downshifting indicates that the two consumption values are quite robust predictors. Overall, these two consumption values explain about 12 percent of total variance in the work-downshifting model and about 18 percent in the consumption-downshifting model.

The two forms of downshifting practices are also quite significantly related to political consumption and civic participation. First, political consumption, represented by boycotting (e.g., I will not buy a product from a company whose values I do not share) and buycotting (e.g., I make a special effort to buy from companies that support charitable causes), are strongly and positively related to both downshifting practices. It is interesting to note that the relationships are somewhat stronger for consumption downshifters than for work downshifters. Those who are consciously limiting consumption may also think more about political ramifications of purchases than those limiting work hours.

Meanwhile, two types of civic participation—online and offline—have different levels of associations with the two downshifting practices. Online civic participation—for example, organizing community activities, discussing politics, expressing own views to politicians by e-mail or on Web sites—is significantly and positively related to work downshifting but not to consumption downshifting. In this case, perhaps the time gained by limiting employment is used for civic purposes. By contrast, there is no significant association between offline civic participation—for example, attending a club meeting, volunteering, or working on a community project—and either of the two downshifting practices. Noteworthy is that, at the bivariate level (i.e., simple correlations between variables), the two forms of civic participation are significantly and positively related to both of the downshifting practices at the $p = .05$ level, although online participation appeared more strongly related ($r = .231$, $p = .002$, for work downshifting; $r = .189$, $p = .011$, for consumption downshifting) than offline participation ($r = .141$, $p = .058$, for work downshifting; $r = .163$, $p = .029$, for consumption downshifting) to the two criterion variables. But in the hierarchical regression models where other major predictors are controlled, the strength of the associations became weaker.

Overall, this civic engagement block in the hierarchical regression models explained about 4.5 percent of total variance in work downshifting and 5.3 percent in consumption downshifting. In addition, including the total variance explained by the first block of the demographic variables (18 percent in the work downshifting and about 13 percent in the consumption downshifting), the overall hierarchical regression models explained about 34 percent of total variance in work downshifting and about 36 percent in consumption downshifting.

Discussion

We examined freecycle.org members as an interesting case because their practice in reusing consumer goods is characteristic of voluntary simplicity and downshifting. Findings indeed showed that the freecycle survey respondents engaged in downshifting practices by limiting consumption (i.e., "consumption downshifting") and choosing personal growth over economic growth and time over money (i.e., "work downshifting"). As might be expected, the two forms of downshifting were highly correlated ($r = .52$).

The profile of the Madison, Wisconsin, freecycle community was similar to that of other downshifters (Schor 1998) in their high education profiles, but not in their lower incomes (see Table 2). This inconsistency may be due to the low response rate of our online survey, which may not represent all community members. It is also possible that the freecyclers in our sample have less income because they have already downshifted their work hours and incomes. Indeed, for nearly one-third of the members, participation in freecycle stemmed from a desire for obtaining goods. For example, one member commented, "We are retired and on a limited budget. Free things are a real help"; and another person joined to "save money on things that I want to buy and cannot." It appears for these consumers, freecycle allowed them to engage in consumer culture despite their limited economic capital. Such motivations remind us that not all downshifters have "deep closets" of possessions to unload (Schor 1998). Indeed, in a study of consumers who engage in alternative consumption practices in the United Kingdom, Williams and Windebank (2005) noted that some are shopping at secondhand stores or carboot sales for fun, while others are doing so out of economic and material necessity.

Though economic and material necessity may explain why some respondents joined freecycle, the motivations for membership among our local group varied. While the explicit motto of freecycle.org relates to a social movement dedicated to "changing the world one gift at a time," the primary motivations for membership

were fairly balanced between self-oriented motivations and environmental reasons. That is, by de-cluttering and simplifying their lives, members' personal lives
improve. Yet it was also true that the manner of de-cluttering—by giving goods
"to a good home" rather than filling the landfill—was also important to freecyclers.

Despite both self-oriented and environmental motivations for joining, it
is obvious that freecyclers hold consumption values different from the ones critics assign to hedonistic consumers. Unlike consumers who view consumption objects
as a reflection of self (Belk 1988) or as a means of maintaining social hierarchies
(Veblen 1899/1965), consumers seeking to truly engage in de-cluttering or downshifting material possessions must be able to dispose of goods and decouple
notions of "identity" from goods (Belk 2007 [this volume]). This means dematerializing and valuing goods for function and not for branded or lifestyle values. In
keeping with Etzioni's (1998) claims about the larger voluntary simplicity movement, the downshifters in our freecycle community also appeared to devalue
materialism and brand conscious values, at least according to the self-report measures in our survey. This may suggest that downshifters maintain a distinctly different relationship with consumer culture than the general population.

*[C]onsumers seeking to truly engage in
de-cluttering or downshifting of material
possessions must be able to dispose of goods
and decouple notions of "identity" from goods.*

Our findings also support the assertion made by Elgin (2000) that those who
engage in work and consumption downshifting are also likely to express their personal values and political orientation through consumer activism such as boycotts
and buycotts. The politicizing of consumption has transformed some consumers
into individuals who consciously consider the consequences of consumption—
and who routinely ask how, where, and by whom a product is made.

Although the data cannot answer whether freecyclers consume in this fashion
to achieve communal and social goals or to express personal lifestyle concerns,
future research should explore the question of whether political consumption is
motivated by communal or hedonistic goals (or both).

Some insight into this question, however, can be gleaned from the fact that our
analysis indicates that downshifters in general are likely to be civically engaged.
Both offline and online measures of civic participation are positively related to downshifting attitudes. Thus, it is noteworthy that despite belonging to a community
devoted to consumption, albeit an alternative form of consumption, freecyclers

are active members of civic life. A more nuanced examination of the findings, however, reveals that online civic participation seems to be more strongly related to work downshifting than offline, traditional civic participation. The finding makes sense because the freecycle community itself is maintained in a digital world. Consequently, freecyclers may view themselves as part of a larger, global digital community and use the Web to engage in community issues across geographic boundaries. This explanation is fairly speculative, but it presents an empirically testable question for future research—that is, which communities do individuals consider most worthy of their civic efforts: the geographic area of residence or the digital community in which they live? Regardless, the Internet as a new public sphere may provide opportunity for people to engage in socially responsible consumption such as downshifting and to engage civically in Web and geographic communities. Thus, spending time online should not be viewed as automatically detrimental to civic life. Rather, instead of asking how much time people spend online (i.e., time displacement), it is more beneficial to ask *what* they are doing online (de Vreese 2007).

[D]espite belonging to a community devoted to consumption, albeit an alternative form of consumption, freecyclers are active members of civic life.

We acknowledge that our findings on the association between downshifting practices, political consumption, and civic participation should not be considered conclusive due to our limited sample drawn from a particular subsegment of the downshifting community. More population-level research should follow this case study to see whether the associations it observed can apply to other consumers and to the larger downshifting community as a whole. In addition, as in efforts to measure the effectiveness of other acts of political consumerism (e.g., boycotts, buycotts, talk; Micheletti and Stolle 2007 [this volume]), future research should also look at various forms of downshifting and their consequences in terms of individual and collective well-being and civic culture.

Overall, the findings of this study imply that the critique of consumption eroding civic life is too simplistic to truly capture the nuanced roles of consumption and civic life in contemporary society. As the case of freecycle illustrates, individuals brought together around consumption acts can have a positive relationship with both consumption and civic life. The ultimate effect of alternative consumption communities like freecycle on consumer or civic culture, however, is yet to be realized. As Arnould (2007) has illustrated, it is virtually impossible to exist outside of the marketplace. And as addressed above, this is not the down-shifters' goal. But by engaging in alternative forms of consumption while holding antimaterialist and anti-brand-conscious values, by engaging in political consumption, and by participating in civic life, downshifters may ultimately serve as "moral agents" (Shi 1985) who, through their behavior, challenge the hegemonic position of consumer culture from within.

[O]nline civic participation seems to be more strongly related to work downshifting than offline, traditional civic participation.

Appendix
Variable Construction and Question Wording

Variable and Items	Question Wording
Work downshifting (EFA = 67.2 percent, alpha = .73)[a]	I would like to (or I choose to) work fewer hours, even if it means a drop in earnings Time is more important than money I am interested in personal growth more than economic growth
Consumption downshifting (EFA = 71.6 percent, alpha = .78)[a]	I try to limit my consumption I believe in material simplicity (i.e., buying and consuming only what I need) I believe in "small is beautiful" (e.g., I prefer smaller cars over larger cars)
Brand consciousness (EFA = 65.2 percent, alpha = .72)[a]	A recognizable brand name on a product is a good indication of quality The fact that a product is heavily advertised is a good indication of quality I prefer products with designer names
Materialism (EFA = 78.1 percent, interitem correlation = .56)[a]	Material affluence is very important to happiness I believe that money can buy you happiness

(continued)

Political consumption (EFA = 76.2 percent, interitem correlation = .53)[b]	I will not buy a product from a company whose values I do not share I make a special effort to buy from companies that support charitable causes
Offline civic participation (EFA = 69.2 percent, alpha = .84)[b]	Went to a club meeting Did volunteer work Worked on a community project Worked on behalf of a social group or cause
Online civic participation (EFA = 52.7 percent, alpha = .87)[b]	Used e-mail to organize community activities Discussed politics or news events using e-mail E-mailed a politician or editor to express my views Visited a Web site of a social group or cause Forwarded a news article to someone over e-mail Visited the Web site of a politician or political party Sought opinions and analysis about politics online (e.g., blogs) Expressed my political opinion in chat rooms or online polls

NOTE: In parentheses beside each variable constructed by the respective items, EFA indicates exploratory factor analysis that shows clearly one factor for all the variables (percentage total variance explained), alpha indicates Cronbach's alpha coefficient (for multiple items) and interitem correlation for two items.

a. On a 7-point scale (*strongly disagree* to *strongly agree*).

b. The question was asked, "How often during the past 3 months?" with 6-point scales ranging from *0 times* (1) to *10 or more times* (6).

References

Arnould, Eric J. 2007. Should consumer citizens escape the market? *Annals of the American Academy of Political and Social Science* 611:96-111.

Belk, Russell W. 1988. Possessions and the extended self. *Journal of Consumer Research* 15 (September): 139-68.

———. 2007. Why not share rather than own? *Annals of the American Academy of Political and Social Science* 611:126-40.

Bell, Daniel. 1976. *The cultural contradictions of capitalism*. New York: Basic Books.

Bellah, Robert N. 1975. *The broken covenant: American civil religion in time of trial*. New York: Seabury Press.

Bellah, Robert N., Richard Madsen, William M. Sullivan, and Ann Swidler. 1985. *Habits of the heart: Individualism and commitment in American life*. Los Angeles: University of California Press.

Bennett, W. Lance. 1998. The uncivic culture: Communication, identity, and the rise of lifestyle politics. *PS: Political Science and Politics* 31:741-61.

———. 2000. Introduction: Communication and civic engagement in comparative perspective. *Political Communication* 17:307-12.

Cherrier, Helen, and Jeff Murray. 2002. Drifting away from excessive consumption: A new social movement based on identity construction. *Advances in Consumer Research* 29:245-47.

Cohen, Lizabeth. 2003. *A consumers' republic: The politics of consumption in postwar America*. New York: Knopf.

Craig-Lees, Margaret, and Constance Hill. 2002. Understanding voluntary simplifiers. *Psychology & Marketing* 19 (2): 187-210.

De Graaf, John, David Wann, and Thomas H. Naylor. 2001. *Affluenza*. San Francisco: Berrett-Koehler.

de Vreese, Claes H. 2007. Digital renaissance: Young consumer and citizen? *Annals of the American Academy of Political and Social Science* 611:207-16.

Elgin, Duane. 2000. Voluntary simplicity and the new global challenge. In *The consumer society reader*, ed. Juliet B. Schor and Douglas B. Holt. New York: New Press.

Etzioni, Amitai. 1998. Voluntary simplicity: Characterization, select psychological implications, and societal consequences. *Journal of Economic Psychology* 19:619-43.

Galbraith, John Kenneth. 1958. *The affluent society*. New York: Houghton Mifflin.

Horowitz, Daniel. 2004. *The anxieties of affluence: Critiques of American consumer culture, 1939-1979*. Amherst: University of Massachusetts Press.

Klein, Naomi. 2000. *No logo: Taking aim at the brand bullies*. New York: Picador.

Lasch, Christopher. 1979. *The culture of narcissism: American life in an age of diminishing expectations*. New York: Warner Books.

Mazza, P. 1997. Keeping it simple. *Reflections* 36 (March): 10-12.

Micheletti, Michele, and Dietlind Stolle. 2007. Mobilizing consumers to take responsibility for global social justice. *Annals of the American Academy of Political and Social Science* 611:157-75.

Moisander, Johanna, and Sinikka Pesonen. 2002. Narratives of sustainable ways of living: Constructing the self and other as a green consumer. *Management Decision* 40 (4): 329-42.

Muniz, Albert, and Thomas C. O'Guinn. 2001. Brand community. *Journal of Consumer Research* 27 (March): 412-32.

Perreault, William D., and Laurence E. Leigh. 1989. Reliability of nominal data based on qualitative judgments. *Journal of Marketing Research* 26 (May): 135-48.

Putnam, Robert D. 1995. Tuning in, tuning out: The strange disappearance of social capital in America. *PS: Political Science and Politics* 28:664-83.

———. 2000. *Bowling alone: The collapse and revival of civic America*. New York: Simon & Schuster.

Roth-Douquet, Kathy. 2006. Shopping can be patriotic, but citizenship requires more. *USA Today*, November 8. http://www.usatoday.com/news/opinion/editorials/2006-11-08-veterans-day-edit_x.htm (accessed November 15, 2006).

Rust, Roland T., and Bruce Cooil. 1994. Reliability measures for qualitative data: Theory and implications. *Journal of Marketing Research* 31 (February): 1-14.

Scammell, Margaret. 2003. Citizen consumers: Towards a new marketing of politics? In *Media and the restyling of politics: Consumerism, celebrity and cynicism*, ed. J. Corner and D. Pels. London: Sage.

Schor, Juliet B. 1998. *The overspent American: Why we want what we don't need*. New York: Harper Perennial.

Shah, Dhavan V., Jaeho Cho, William P. Eveland Jr., and Nojin Kwak. 2005. Information and expression in a digital age: Modeling Internet effects on civic participation. *Communication Research* 32 (5): 531-65.

Shaw, Deirdre, and Terry Newholm. 2002. Voluntary simplicity and the ethics of consumption. *Psychology & Marketing* 19 (2): 167-85.

Shi, David E. 1985. *The simple life: Plain living and high thinking in American culture*. New York: Oxford University Press.

Stern, Paul C. 1984. *Energy use: The human dimension*. New York: Freeman.

Stolle, Dietlind, and Marc Hooghe. 2004. Inaccurate, exceptional, one-sided or irrelevant? The debate about the alleged decline of social capital and civic engagement in western societies. *British Journal of Political Science* 35:149-67.

Stolle, Dietlind, Marc Hooghe, and Michelle Micheletti. 2005. Politics in the supermarket: Political consumerism as a form of political participation. *International Political Science Review* 26 (3): 245-69.

Veblen, Thorstein. 1899/1965. *The theory of the leisure class*. New York: A. M. Kelley.

Webster, Frederick E., Jr. 1975. Determining the characteristics of the socially conscious consumer. *Journal of Consumer Research* 2:188-96.

Williams, Colin C., and Jan Windebank. 2005. Why do households use alternative consumption practices? *Community, Work and Family* 8 (3): 301-20.

Zavestoski, Stephen. 2002. The social-psychological bases of anticonsumption attitudes. *Psychology & Marketing* 19 (2): 149-65.

Mobilizing Consumers to Take Responsibility for Global Social Justice

This article studies the antisweatshop movement's involvement in global social justice responsibility-taking. The movement's growth (more than one hundred diverse groups) makes it a powerful force of social change in the new millennium. The rise of global corporate capitalism has taken a toll on political responsibility. As a response, four important movement actors—unions, antisweatshop associations, international humanitarian organizations, and Internet spin doctors—have focused on garment-production issues and mobilized consumers into vigilant action. The authors examine these actors, their social justice responsibility claims, and their views on the role of consumers in social justice responsibility-taking. The authors determine four paths of consumer action: (1) support group for other causes, (2) critical mass of shoppers, (3) agent of corporate change, and (4) ontological force for societal change. The authors find that the movement mobilizes consumers through actor-oriented and event-specific (episodic) framing and offer a few results on its ability to change consumer patterns and effect corporate change.

Keywords: responsibility-taking; political consumerism; antisweatshop movement; effectiveness

By
MICHELE MICHELETTI
and
DIETLIND STOLLE

Over the past decade, the political consumerist antisweatshop movement has become a major political claim maker and transnational advocacy network. Not only have the number and kind of actors, networks, and organizations included in it diversified, matured organizationally, and grown in number and strength, but with the help of the Internet, it has professionalized its activities and strengthened its potential to frame its claims, mobilize support, and push change on corporations. It can even boast a series of victories. Through its framing of the sweatshop problem and its information campaigns, the movement is increasingly convincing consumers that sweatshops are social injustices and that certain actors have responsibility to solve sweatshop problems. In so doing, it challenges conventional views of political responsibility by going beyond government and calling

DOI: 10.1177/0002716206298712

on citizens and on corporations to play their part. The movement is thus expanding the arenas and spheres where global political responsibility is practiced to include the market. Although experts debate its effectiveness in solving sweatshop problems, it should be considered a significant movement in the new millennium and part of a more general political process of creating new forms of responsible governance locally, nationally, and globally (Micheletti 2007; Smith and Johnston 2002).

Through its framing of the sweatshop problem and its information campaigns, the movement is increasingly convincing consumers that sweatshops are social injustices and that certain actors have responsibility to solve sweatshop problems.

Global Social Justice Responsibility-Taking

Severe violations of human and workers' rights have been found in the global garment industry. Watchdog fact-finding offers long lists of labor violations in facto-

Michele Micheletti is a professor of political science at Karlstad University, Sweden. She has written books on corporatism, interest groups, civil society, democratic auditing, and political consumerism. Her general research focus is citizen engagement in politics. Her writings have been published in English, Swedish, French, and German and have appeared in Scandinavian Political Studies, International Review of Political Science, Journal of Behavioral and Social Sciences, Governance, Sociologia Ruralis, Electoral Studies, West European Politics, *and* Sciences del al Société *as well as in several edited volumes.*

Dietlind Stolle (PhD, Princeton University, 2000) is an associate professor in political science at McGill University, Montréal, Canada. She conducts research and has published on voluntary associations, trust, institutional foundations of social capital, and new forms of political participation, particularly political consumerism. She is also the principal investigator of a unique longitudinal comparative youth survey (with Marc Hooghe). Her work has appeared, for example, in the journals British Journal of Political Science, International Review of Political Science, Political Behavior, *and* Political Psychology *as well as in various edited volumes. She has also edited a book on social capital and one on political consumerism.*

NOTE: This research is funded by the Swedish Council of Research. We thank Valérie-Anne Mahéo for research assistance.

ries used by well-known global garment logo giants. A 2004 report on outsourcing in China documents, for instance, that young women work a double shift seven days a week to sew clothing for an average wage of 22 cents (USD) an hour, sixteen-year-old girls apply toxic glue with a toothbrush and their bare hands to build shoes for the Western market, garment factory temperatures are often over 100 degrees Fahrenheit, and garment workers are threatened and coached to lie to factory auditors asking about their working conditions (see National Labor Committee, www.nlcnet.org/campaigns/archive/report00/introduction.shtml). These and other violations of workers' social justice are the reasons for the existence of an encompassing claim-making activist antisweatshop movement whose strategy, tactics, and support are explained by the fact that governments across the board are unable or unwilling to act effectively.

Government inaction on global social justice responsibility is of central interest in political science. It shows that existing political institutions charged with caring for the world are not proving that they can successfully take responsibility for global problems. "Earth has no CEO. No Board of Directors. No management team . . ." is how the United Nations Development Programme, United Nations Environment Programme, World Bank, and World Resources Institute (2003) summed up the general situation. This discouraging conclusion suggests that traditional government political responsibility, which is premised on the existence of state authority (jurisdiction) for problem solving and identifiable actors that can be made legally accountable for their specific actions, are ill suited to take charge of solving pressing complex global problems. The traditional political responsibility process seems only to work well when government is mandated to enact strong laws that allow it to establish who is to blame for intentional wrongdoings concentrated in time and room (Jordan, Wurzel, and Zito 2003). However, in global garment making as well as other areas alluded to in the quote above, these aspects of good government are seldom in place. It is difficult to prove intentionality of injustice and wrongdoings by the numerous and often hidden commodity chain actors involved in the global production, sale, and consumption of affordable fashion. Even if good laws are in place, governments in developing countries for different reasons may not have the capability or willingness to prosecute transnational garment corporations for wrongdoings. And without good laws, it is not even possible to hold wrongdoers legally accountable for their actions (International Council on Human Rights [ICHRP] 2002).

Corporations use opportunities opened up by economic globalization and free trade to lower their costs and improve their consumer markets. In itself, this is not a problem. However, in weakly regulated settings as in global garment manufacturing, corporate conduct frequently creates social justice and environmental problems. Time and time again, corporate conduct has been shown to be harmful and morally dubious but not necessarily illegal and, therefore, not really solvable through national and international law (ICHRP 2002). Numerous are the examples of transnational garment corporations shaking off reports about unsatisfactory working and environmental conditions in the countries where they are operative. When first asked about their role in causing and treating the problems that have developed because of their presence in other countries, corporations have answered that they are unaware of the problems and that they lie outside their scope of responsibility. Although this kind of corporate blame avoidance has lessened because of concerted civil society and consumer action, responsibility-taking is still debated and in need of institutional formulation and implementation. These developments show the difficulty in applying conventional models of responsibility-taking because their logic of accountability assumes (1) a governmental regulatory framework and (2) an intimate link between problem cause and problem solving that allows government and citizens to bring wrongdoers to court and be sanctioned and forced to right their wrongs (Young 2006).

Weaknesses in the conventional model of political responsibility and increasing disappointment with the World Trade Organization (WTO) policy on free trade have led scholars, policy analysts, activists, and consumers to develop new ways to fill the responsibility vacuum created by government inaction and corporate negligence. They may use public law and pressure governments to enact better laws. However, their mission focuses more on improving corporate policy and practice as well as changing the consumers' worldview about the role of consumption in society as a whole. This strategic and conscious choice is explained by the more structural nature of complex global social justice problems, which is "a consequence of many individuals and institutions acting in pursuit of their particular goals and interests, within given institutional rules and accepted norms" (Young 2006, 114). This ambitious responsibility-taking mission demands creative cooperation among a vast array of actors and a highly innovative repertoire of skills, communication, and arenas for action. For the antisweatshop movement, it means turning to global capitalism and logo corporations.

This ambitious responsibility-taking mission demands creative cooperation among a vast array of actors and a highly innovative repertoire of skills, communication, and arenas for action.

Today, large garment corporations are vulnerable targets for antisweatshop activism. Their buyer-driven character forces them to survive in highly competitive markets. To make a profit, they must compete with other sellers over increasingly fickle (non–brand loyal) consumers looking for good-quality clothing at very affordable prices. To maintain and even improve their market shares and profit margins, they outsource their manufacturing to countries where labor is inexpensive and devote considerable resources into competitive logo and image marketing. In the weakly regulated setting of outsourced garment manufacturing, worker welfare is jeopardized by fast and flexible production needed to keep up with fashion-craving consumers (Smith 1997; Gereffi 2001). This creates serious social justice problems. At the same time, the antisweatshop movement can use the vulnerable and competitive image situation of the buyer-driven corporate world to push to improve garment workers' rights and social justice. Wanting profits and a good image among consumers, logo garment corporations are now forced to address sweatshop problems.

To maintain profits and a good image among consumers, logo garment corporations are now forced to address sweatshop problems.

Development of Antisweatshop Political Consumerism

The metaphor "sweatshop" was coined in the late 1800s to call attention to problems at workshops or factories using "sweated labor" (people who worked long hours with poor pay and conditions) to produce goods. Even then, the piece-work tailoring trade was singled out as a mode of manufacturing open for "sweaters" to employ vulnerable workers and treat them badly. Particularly "sweatable" groups were children and especially women immigrants working in the garment trade in large cities. Reformers, as antisweatshop activists were then called, made political claims about sweatshop wrongdoings. They criticized workplace safety and low workers' wages, demanded that institutions and individuals involved in these industries take responsible action, and offered a few highly innovative solutions that used the market as an arena for politics. Early on, they emphasized the role of consumers. New York working women lobbied Josephine Shaw Lowell, charity reformer and founder of the New York Consumers' League in 1891, who testified publicly that consumers were behind "some of the worst evils from which producers suffer" and that they had the duty "to find out under what conditions the articles they purchase are produced and distributed, and to insist that these conditions shall be wholesome and consistent with a respectable existence on the part of the workers" (quoted in Boris 2003, 205). In similar fashion, Florence Kelley used her platform as general secretary of the National Consumer's League to formulate a new model of political responsibility that gave consumers a central role: "No one except the direct employer is so responsible for the fate of these children as the purchasers who buy the product of their toil" (quoted in Sklar 1998, 27).

Antisweatshop reformers used a variety of tactics to promote their cause. They investigated sweatshops, informed and educated the public, publicized sweatshop problems, offered "buycott" or best-practice shopping guides, pressured government to purchase "no-sweat" wear for its employees, mobilized public support for political responsibility-taking, supported unionization, entered partnerships with business, and even established a very early innovative no-sweat labeling scheme (the U.S. White Label Campaign 1898-1919) (Boris 2003; Sklar 1998). The rich scholarship on the history of sweatshops shows that their main goal was to pressure government to take political responsibility and enact government-enforced labor standards to stamp out sweatshops (Stott 1999; Rosen 2002).

This happened. Scholars of American history agree that the "New Deal Order" with its focus on federal regulatory authority took political responsibility to end sweatshops. It promoted unionization, legislative labor standards, and consumer preference for union-made goods. Something else happened. Corporations sought ways to avoid regulation. Many of them dodged unionization by moving their manufacturing to southern states where unions were weak. Later, they moved their manufacturing abroad—first to Latin America and then Asia. Corporate handling of sweatshop responsibility provoked unions whose initial response was protectionistic and involved blocking imports and supporting economic nationalistic calls on consumers to "buy American." They even tried to hide the fact that sweatshops existed in the United States (Boris 2003, 212). Once garment manufacturing was outsourced, the third world movement became involved. Its cause was not protectionism but third world solidarity through fair trade shopping. The alternative trade movement began in the 1950s with third world stores (now world shops) selling goods from developing countries. Perhaps surprising given their different reasons for engaging in antisweatshop activism and even showing current tensions in the movement on how to solve sweatshop problems, unions (that first promoted protectionism and later with outsourced manufacturing broadened their cause to global solidarity) and third world groups wanting to advance global solidarity through shopping form the root of today's antisweatshop movement.

Contemporary antisweatshop activism came to a boil in the 1990s. Two events in 1995 were crucial formative events in North America: the establishment of the amalgamated Union of Needle, Industrial, and Technical Employees (UNITE! and now UNITE HERE!) and the police raid of domestic sweatshops in El Monte, California. UNITE triggered a new union activism that used consumer power to pry open space for organizing. The El Monte raid was a wake-up call for U.S. civil society and created a media sensation with ripple effects far into the future (data not shown). In Europe, clothing became high civil society politics a bit earlier and in a different way. The formative event was a lockout of women workers demanding a legal minimum wage in a clothing factory in the Philippines, which startled European international solidarity activists who had not previously considered the politics of clothes, the plight of women workers in developing countries, and the potential to hold Western consumers and producers responsible for bad working conditions in foreign garment factories. People in Europe expressed their outrage publicly; the media became interested. This led to the establishment of the leading European antisweatshop organization, the Clean Clothes Campaign (CCC) in 1990. CCC states retrospectively that the lockout "struck a nerve" and that "campaigning for 'Clean Clothes' provided a concrete way of taking up the political demands of women's and labour organizations in the south and, at the time, of changing the behaviour and the policies of TNC's [transnational corporations] and governments in the North, since they are responsible for the way people in the south live and work" (Ascoly and Zendenrust 1999).

Shortly afterwards, the antisweatshop movement gained momentum. Old, established civil society organizations learned to spice up their traditional social justice message with the help of spin-doctor, PR-oriented Internet-based advocacy groups like Global Exchange (from 1988). Global Exchange used its media talents to focus public and media attention on celebrity corporate leaders—in particular, Nike CEO Phil Knight and Kathie Lee Gifford, U.S. talk show host with her own brand name clothes—whose corporations were key targets of antisweatshop activism (Bullert 2000). This concentration on logos and CEO celebrities used buyer-driven corporate vulnerabilities well and gave the sweatshop problem cultural resonance by showing the relationship between important consumer symbols in the cultural environment and social justice responsibility-taking (cf. Kubal 1998). Validation of the movement's hook into popular culture came and comes in a variety of forms, two of which are the Doonesbury comic strips in 1997 on outsourced Nike manufacturing in Vietnam that triggered a wave of university student activism and a joke by Jay Leno about Nike sweatshops on the Tonight Show in 1998. Within a few years, culture jamming with the encouragement of Adbusters Media Foundation, a global network of artists, activists, writers, pranksters, students, educators, and entrepreneurs wanting to advance what it calls the "uncooling of consumption," would exploit corporate vulnerabilities more fully by expressing antisweatshop sentiments in more humorous and radical ways.

Old and new civil society teamed up in the antisweatshop cause. Figure 1 shows that the movement globally includes more than one hundred organizations representing church groups; student groups; think tanks; policy institutes; foundations; consumer organizations; international organizations; local to global labor unions; labor-oriented groups; specific antisweatshop groups; no-sweat businesses; business investors; and international humanitarian and human rights organizations, networks, and groups. Several antisweatshop actors (particularly the ones from old civil society) have a broader agenda than antisweatshop political consumerism. For them, political consumerism is one strategy to reach their general

FIGURE 1
CONTEMPORARY ANTISWEATSHOP MOVEMENT'S MAIN GROUPS,
ORGANIZATIONS, AND NETWORKS

Academic Consortium on International Trade	Fair Trade Center	MaisonInternationaal Huis (MINTH)	SA 8000 (Social AccountabilityInt'l.)
Adbusters	Fair Wear	Maquiladora Health and Safety	Scholars Against SweatshopLabor
Alberta Nike Campaign	FLO-International (Fairtrade	Support Network	Smithsonian Sweatshop Exhibition
American Center for International Labor Solidarity	Labelling Organizations Int'l.)	Maquila Solidarity Network	Stichting Onderzoek Multinationale Ondernemingen
American Apparel	Gapsucks.org	Multinational Resource Center	(SOMO,Centre for Research on
Asia Monitor Resource Center	Garment Worker Center		Multinational Corporations)
Asian Network for the Rights of	Get Ethical	National Interfaith Committee	Students Against Sweatshops,
Occupational Accident Victims	Global Alliance for Workers	for Worker Justice	Canada
Attac	and Communities	National Labor Committee for	Sweatshop Journal
	Global Exchange	Worker and Human Rights	Sweatshop Watch
Behind The Label (UNITE)	Globalise Resistance	National Mobilization Against	SweatX (union cut and sew shop)
Boycott Nike	Global Solidarity, Irish	Sweatshops	
	Congress of Trade Unions	Nike Wages Campaign	TCFU Australia
Campaign for the Abolition of	Global Solidarity Dialogue	Nike Watch (Oxfam, AUS)	Thai Labor Campaign
Sweatshops and Child Labor	Global Unions	NorthSouth Institute	Transnational Information
Campaign for Labor Rights		No Sweat: The UK Campaign	Exchange-Asia (TIE-Asia)
Carnegie Council on Ethics and	HomeNet	Against Sweatshops	Transnationale Organization
International Affairs	Hong Kong Christian	No Sweat Shop Labeling Campaign	
Catholic Institute for	Industrial Committee		Union Label and Service Trades
International Relations	Human Rights for Workers:	Olympic Living Wage Project:	(part of AFLIO)
Child Labor Coalition	The Crusade Against Global	Starving for the Swoosh (2001)	Union Mall
Child Labor Bulletin	Sweatshops	Oxfam's campaign "Make	Union Wear
Christian Aid	Human Rights First	Trade Fair" -involved in	Unite! Union of Needle trades,
Clean Clothes Campaign		Fair Play at the Olympics	Industrial and Textile Employees
Community Aid Abroad	International Committee for		United Students Against Sweatshops
"Just Stop It"	Trade Union Rights	Peace Through Interamerican	US/Labor Education in the
Coop America	International Confederation of	Community Action	Americas Project (US Leap)
CorpWatch	FreeTrade Unions	People-Centered Development	
	International Federation for	Forum	Verite (non-profitsocial auditing)
Development and Peace	Alternative Trade	People's Global Action	Vietnam Labor Watch
Diamond Cut Jeans	International Labor Organization	Play Fair at the Olympics	
	International Labor Rights Fund	Press for Change	Witness for Peace
Educating for Justice			Women in Informal Employment
Ethical Consumer	Just Act: Youth ACTion for	Responsible Shopper, Co-Op	Globalizing and Organizing
Ethicalshopper.net	Global JUSTice	America	Women Working Worldwide
Ethical Threads	Just Do It! Boycott Nike!	Resource Center of the Americas	Workers Rights Consortium
Ethical Trading Initiative	Just Shoppers'Guide to		World Development Movement
European Association of National	Sport Shoes		Worldwide Responsible Apparel
Organisation of TextileRetailers	Labour Behind the Label		Production
European Fair Trade Association	LINK Etc.		
Fair Labor Association	LINK-label		
Fairtrade Foundation			

SOURCES: Individual websites; http://depts.washington.edu/ccce/polcommcampaigns/nikecampaignsites.htm
NOTE: The snowball method was used to collect information from Internet searches, information from individual Websites and their linking functions, and previous research. Many of the movement actors were accessed over a period of four years. The figure does not include actors with corporate social responsibility as their main theme, e.g., Amnesty Business, the United Nation's Global Compact, and European Commission's Social Agenda. Neither does it include personal blogs, individuals' Websites nor European country-specific groups affiliated with pan-European ones as the Clean Clothes Campaign. It includes all movement actors focusing on social justice responsibility-taking in the global garment sector, though many of the groups have goals as well.

goals. Many of the newer groups focus on the market as an arena for politics and have "clean clothes" as a main focus while others concentrate exclusively on unsatisfactory conditions in the garment industry. The groups dedicating themselves entirely to garment sweatshops have robust, creative, and expressive names. Some are Behind the Label, Ethical Threads, Sweat Gear, and the "Just Stop It" campaign, which is a culture jam of a famous Nike marketing slogan.

Noteworthy is the less common cooperation between unions and consumers, as illustrated by the UNITE and the National Consumers League's Stop Sweatshop campaign that reached out to more than 50 million consumers globally (Golodner 1997) and the coalition between the AFL-CIO, UNITE, and students that led to the establishment of the United Students Against Sweatshops (USAS from 1998), now a central actor in the antisweatshop movement. USAS's time-consuming and at times violent struggle to get college and university procurement officers to use their shopping choices to ensure that academic sports equipment and college products are sweat-free is glorified in *The Nation*, media reports, journal articles, books, and on the USAS Web site. USAS (2006) formulated its role in social responsibility-taking this way: "Many universities directly profit from the exploitation of the women and men around the globe who make the clothes that bear their logo. To stop this cycle of indignity, we, as students, started to demand that our universities take responsibility for the conditions under which their licensed apparel is made by adopting Codes of Conduct to regulate the behavior of their manufacturers."

Sweatshop concerns and the need to develop innovative tactics and solutions for global social responsibility-taking is giving new life to social-justice-oriented old civil society, whose methods and missions were out of touch with younger generations (Levi 2003; Ascoly and Zendenrust 1999). Creative forms of individualized collective action, attention to the role of production and consumption in global politics, and use of the Internet facilitate the building of bridges and coalitions between traditional membership groups and those groups whose legitimacy and support are crafted online. This lets the movement reach out to heterogeneous groups of consumers—from inner-city youth to blue-collar workers, soccer moms, university students, film and pop music stars, and government procurement officers. With the help of innovative campaign framing and methods, it reveals the policies and practices of global garment corporations and asks consumers to consider how their seemingly private consumer choice is connected to and, therefore, responsible for garment workers' labor rights and safety. Once this consciousness-raising about the politics of clothes is in motion, the movement then offers supporters ideas about how they can take social justice responsibility for their choices of clothes and shoes, resources to pressure corporations to take social justice responsibility, and information to reconsider how they value consumption as part of their social lives.

Role of Consumers in the Antisweatshop Movement

Consumers are important actors for all parts of the antisweatshop movement. However, a study of documents and interviews with key movement actors (UNITE HERE!, Global Unions, CCC, USAS, Oxfam, Global Exchange, and Adbusters Media Foundation) representing important parts of the movement (unions, specific antisweatshop associations, international humanitarian organizations, and Internet spin doctors) shows that these organizations mobilize consumers to play different roles in the antisweatshop struggle.[1] We identify and discuss four distinct consumer roles below. They are (1) support group for a broader cause, (2) critical mass of fair trade shoppers, (3) "spearhead force" of corporate change, and (4) ontological agent of societal change.

What unites the heterogeneous organizations into a movement is their agreement that the common goal is improved workers' rights in the global garment industry. This does not mean that there is no disagreement or tension within the movement. Currently the movement is debating whether unionization, codes of conduct and independent monitoring, or "no-sweat" clothing is the best way to go to end sweatshops (Ballinger and Connor 2005; Johns and Vural 2000). The consumer role is part of this tension.

For unions, consumers are supporters that help them to solve sweatshop problems through increased unionization, which they argue will empower workers and give them a formal platform to negotiate with employers and sign collective agreements that guarantee decent wages and working conditions, thus making sweatshops history. Consumers are a "broad, ideologically benign community" that can be used in a political strategy "to make the struggle for justice for workers more palatable to the public in an antilabor climate" (Golodner 1997). Unions ask consumers to join union-called boycotts of corporations, support their urgent appeals, and follow union-formulated good purchasing practices. With this amassed consumer support, they believe that unions will be able to harness globalization and develop themselves into a countervailing power forceful enough to challenge sweatshop work and corporate globalization (Global Unions 2000). To get consumers on board, North American unions have even established a special unit. UNITE's Behind the Label (see http://www.behindthelabel.org/about.asp) multimedia news magazine and online community (sponsored by an alliance of clothing workers, religious leaders, human rights advocates, consumers, and students) has as its mission to raise consciousness about sweatshop abuses and get consumers to buy union-made apparel. Thus, contemporary unions (as their historical cousins) want consumers to let corporations know they are being watched through a union lens.

Even though most other antisweatshop activists support the union cause, they also want consumers to play a more dynamic and independent role. For them, consumers—not unions—can become the countervailing power to corporations. The consumer role of critical shopping mass is cultivated by international humanitarian and human rights organizations as well as USAS to accomplish this. For them, when consumers better their consumer practice, they promote the development of a market for sweat-free goods and indirectly influence corporate policy and practice. These organizations believe that critical mass shopping is an important step toward a more equitable world. Oxfam International (2006) stated that aware and mobilized consumers can "use their purchasing power to tilt the balance, however slightly, in favour of the poor." It asks consumers to help alleviate poverty by using fair trade labeling schemes, participating in fair trade holiday shopping campaigns, and becoming involved in different online and offline campaigns to show garment corporations the seriousness of their mission (Oxfam Australia 2006a, 2006c). The international human rights group Global Exchange (2006), which harshly criticized the WTO for "systematically [undermining] democracy around the world" in its free trade policy and creating a situation where consumers are confronted with "products at the store [that] may seem like a bargain, but they come with a very high human price for the workers that made them," now uses its spin-doctoring talents to sell fair-traded consumer goods and to mobilize sweat-free communities because "organizing communities of consumers can make sweatfree purchases dynamic and effective" (Global Exchange 2005; Moller 2006). For USAS, educational institutions can become critical mass "no-sweat" consumers. Its efforts in mobilizing students to pressure procurement officers first made global garment corporations mad. Over the years, they learned to respect USAS's knowledge and ability to change higher education's procurement practices. USAS's efforts are now imitated by other antisweatshop actors.

An even more independent and dynamic role is consumers as a spearhead force of corporate change. This role is an important fundament of the CCC, identifying itself as a European consumer pressure group and consumer campaign whose strength comes from consumer power and people becoming a "community of consumers" rather than just "autonomous shoppers" (Golodner 1997). Buyer-driven corporate vulnerabilities are very consciously and explicitly used as good opportunities for spearhead consumer action to hit corporations where it hurts most, because "brand name companies compete intensely for consumer loyalty, and therefore consumers can influence how these companies operate" (CCC 2006). Interestingly, the CCC did not plan this consumer role. Rather "using the consumer angle to raise awareness . . . worked far beyond our original expectations" and "holds true for all the countries that the campaign has spread to" (Ascoly and Zendenrust 1999; Merk 2006). It also acknowledges that consumers can support trade unions, but spearheading political consumerism is the most dominant role. Now it even stresses the importance of government as a consumer of work wear in its clean clothes communities campaigning. Here its focus differs from the critical shopping mass perspective because government consumers are seen as a role model (a spearhead) for individual consumers to learn how they can directly take responsibility for the impact of their consumption on the complex global garment commodity chain (Clean Clothes Communities 2005).

The most independent, forceful, and radical consumer role is found in the part of the antisweatshop movement wanting most to "shake up consumer culture" (Lasn 2006). For Adbusters Media Foundation, consumers as an ontological force for paradigmatic societal change means that a transformation in their predispositions and worldview about consumer culture and corporations will facilitate grand social and political reform. Its founder Kalle Lasn is convinced that new consumer thinking about consumption can shift present power alliances, shake up governments, and force corporations to change. Without contacts with other parts of the antisweatshop movement, Adbusters dedicates itself to reaching this goal by helping consumers liberate themselves from their "media-consumer trance" and "megacorporations," which are identified as "the largest single psy-chological project ever undertaken by the human race" (Lasn 2000, 19). Only enlightened and reformed consumers can play this powerful role because unions are stuck in "an old leftist paradigm" that promotes workers' self-interests and unsustainable economic growth and are therefore unable to solve pressing global problems, and mobilizing consumers into a critical mass of fair trade shoppers only "scrapes at the surface" of the problems created by corporate globalization and overconsumption (Lasn 2006).

Rounding Up Consumers: Global Antisweatshop Movement Campaigning

No matter what the consumer role, the movement uses two types of frames, episodic and thematic, to get consumers to see and act on the connections between their apparel choices and the realities of outsourced manufacturing for garment workers (cf. Iyengar 1999). Episodic campaigns focus on particular issues and put responsibility claims on specific wrongdoers. They aim at trigger-ing consumers to take immediate action. Thematic campaigns penetrate the underlying mechanisms leading to social justice responsibility vacuums, and they depict the sweatshop problem more broadly and abstractly by embedding it in the larger context of the pervasive role of consumption in our lives. They aim at changing consumer thinking about consumer society and culture.

Not surprisingly given the consumer roles characteristic of much of the move-ment, most antisweatshop mobilizing activism stresses episodic campaigning and focuses on high-profile specific events because, as CCC (2005, 36) explained, "It is by taking action in our everyday lives, by provoking consumers to question what they are buying and as they buy, that we will move forward." Antisweatshop movement actors believe that episodic consumer campaigning can convince cor-porations to accept unions and collective bargaining, improve their codes of con-duct, allow for third-party monitoring of their implementation, and in the end help alleviate social injustices in the global garment industry.

Here, personalization of sweatshop problems is important to drive the mes-sage home to consumers. Workers' testimonials and video clips on key movement actors' Web pages ask consumers to take a good look at the individuals who sew their clothes and shoes and the corporations that hire them. A Global Unions (2006) spotlight feature started thematically by asking consumers rhetorically, "What's the link between the top brand of jeans you may be wearing and Haiti, the poorest country in the Americas?" It answered immediately that it is the "day-to-day exploitation of workers in the export processing zones of the Dominican Republic and Haiti, where they produce clothing for leading international brands." Then the frame becomes episodic. Consumers in three short minutes get to know union activist Haitian Georges Macès, who sews the hems of Levi's and other brand-name jeans. They see Georges riding his bike to work and then at his workplace, where he explains his situation, his union's efforts, and his need for a decent living wage. Toward the end of the clip, Georges "appeals to all those far away from Haiti who wear the jeans I make" and states that "it is important that customers know that our sweat and blood goes into these jeans." The aim of this and other episodic framing is to prompt individual consumers to participate in time-limited campaigns with urgent appeals drafted as e-mail letters ready to send to corporate executives, politicians, decision makers, or even other consumers to engage in organized demonstrations outside flagship retail stores and to use fair trade shopping hints for purchases at the holiday season. When all this happens, the movement has coordinated individualized and more organized antisweatshop collective action in a forceful way. The Nike Corporation and its retailers' Niketowns have provided particularly important opportunities for the movement to use episodic framing to promote both individualized and organized consumer collective action.

[P]ersonalization of sweatshop problems is important to drive the message home to consumers.

Targeting big sports is increasingly important for the movement. Millions of people follow these high-media-profile events, which antisweatshop actors use to play on the virtues of fair play and fair competition associated with sports (Oxfam Australia 2006b, 3) and which make sportswear companies easy targets "because the consumer link is even stronger—for example, they sponsor events" (CCC 2006). The Olympics and European soccer have been important antisweatshop arenas. Examples are Foulball (1997), following the publicity wave after *Life* magazine's article on child labor in a Nike soccer factory; Play Fair at the Olympics (Oxfam 2004); Play Fair in Europe (World Football Cup 2000); Sportwear Industry Still Not Playing Fair (World Cup 2002); Red Card to Child Labor (World Cup 2004); mobilizing efforts before, during, and after the 2006 World Cup resulting in the report "Offside"; and even now major league baseball (Zirin and Tyner 2006). Each campaign targets logo corporations showcased at the sporting events, presents documentation of their corporate wrongdoings, personalizes worker treatment with the help of pictures and testimonials, and offers consumers a toolbox of tips to take action individually and collectively as well as internationally and locally. About thirty-five countries participated in about five hundred innovative and conventional actions during the 2004 Olympics including press conferences, street theater performances, parades, bike rides to the

Olympic city (Athens), worker testimonial tours, demonstrations outside the Olympic committee, petitions, reinterpretation of the Olympic torch-carrying event, intervention in sportswear corporate events, a "sew-in" near the Acropolis, student athletes displaying "playfair" symbolism, lobbying, politician contacts, Web site sweatshop sports computer games to attract younger people, and awards of gold medals to garment workers. In countries where outsourcing manufacturing takes place, activists held demonstrations outside Nike corporate offices, marched to parliament buildings, and even took garment workers to upmarket shopping malls to see the retail prices of their labor. The campaign is a trophy proudly displayed on antisweatshop Web sites.

For Adbusters Media Foundation, episodic campaigns, though moving corporations toward more responsibility-taking, are what its founder Kalle Lasn (2006) called antisweatshop "complaint-making." Today, Adbusters believes that episodic framing does not mobilize the true force of consumers and does not use capitalism effectively to change the corporate "genetic code" and consumers' predisposition and worldview. Although held in awe, supported by more than one hundred thousand registered culture jammers, and with about fifteen to twenty thousand Web visitors daily, Adbusters was criticized by Lasn in the same way. Its specific product and corporate culture-jamming memes (episodic framing) that recontextualize corporate messages in humorous ways to send "a chill down the spine of corporations" and its Buy Nothing Day asking consumers to stop shopping on one day each year are mere "tweakings of the king's nose" (Lasn 2006). After 9/11, President George W. Bush's reelection, increased disappointment with the WTO and other important globe-shaping events, Adbusters made the strategic decision to focus more on attempting to challenge corporations by "playing the capitalist game." It established Blackspot Anticorporation, a sweat-free shoe manufacturing operation that has sold twenty thousand pairs of sneakers as of September 2006, as its thematic campaign frame and hopes it will evolve into a local worldwide consumer cooperative "to reassert consumer sovereignty over capitalism" and combine "our passion for social activism with grassroots antipreneurial [sic] zeal and rearrange the ugly face of megacorporate capitalism" (Adbusters 2006). This thematic strategy is seen as a better way to change consumers' predispositions, downshift consumption, and promote sustainable development. It even includes mobilization of students to demand a new economic paradigm (true cost economics) in university economic courses as well as engagement in struggles for access arenas reserved for free (noncommercial) speech. With these efforts, Adbusters wants to reach its goal of creating space for consumers to reconsider the role of consumption in their lives to build up capitalism anew from the grassroots level.

Assessing Antisweatshop Activism

Is the antisweatshop movement mobilizing consumers effectively to take responsibility for global social justice and to pressure corporations to do likewise? Are corporations responding to this pressure? "No real impact" is the critics' answer. Garment sweatshops still exist. Consumer power cannot be harnessed effectively, and even if it can, this says nothing about how changes in consumer thinking and purchasing practices affect corporations (Vogel 2005). Other observers are less pessimistic. Prominent business scholars remind us of corporate vulnerabilities: "Skeptics may doubt that survey responses translate into choices at the shopping mall, but high-profile multinational corporations take the polling data seriously" (Fung, O'Rourke, and Sabel 2001). Antisweatshop activism can be powerful because buyer-driven brands have reputations at risk (deWinter 2001).

Measuring the effectiveness of political activism is always tricky. It is even more difficult when activism, as in the present case, is (1) controversial and understudied; (2) not solely collectively organized; (3) not delimited to one target, issue, and time frame; and (4) focused on corporations that, unlike many governments, are not required to reveal important information for scholarly assessments. To study market-based political activism, we need to develop measures of effectiveness that take these problems into account. This means assessing the entire activism cycle—from activists' problem formulation and problem recognition and mobilization among consumers, the media, and civil society to the ability of the antisweatshop movement to get their issues on the corporate policy agenda and incorporated in their policy making and implementation. Finally, it is important to assess the ability of the movement to create positive concrete outcomes for garment workers domestically and globally.

A few preliminary results on antisweatshop effectiveness are offered here. The antisweatshop movement has succeeded in formulating the sweatshop problem in a way that resonates well in Western democratic cultures. With the metaphor "sweatshop" as its common master frame, the movement has been able to communicate complex information in an easily understandable way. It has even developed innovative resources to convince consumers, journalists, civil society, and governments that sweatshop problems demand new models of responsibility-taking. Since the mid-1990s, numerous journalists have covered logo garment corporations' sweatshop problems closely; a peak of reporting on sweatshop issues accumulated around the year 2000 in the *New York Times* (data not shown; Greenberg and Knight 2004). The word *sweatshop* has also entered consumer thinking, as witnessed by the global resonance of the Nike Email Exchange, a culture jam that used the word *sweatshop* to toy with Nike's marketing image and, in doing so, made national and international news. These and other examples demonstrate the ability of the antisweatshop movement to create a "community of consumers"—individual, institutional, and governmental ones—and to convince them that they can become "a link in a chain of change which will lead to action" (Stolle and Micheletti n.d.). Survey data validates that citizens who use the market as an arena for politics find it to be an effective way to take personal responsibility and, therefore, facilitate societal change (Boström et al. 2004).

But the critics are right when they say that high visibility and recognition of sweatshop problems and even a mobilized consumer spirit up-and-ready for personal responsibility-taking do not automatically lead to corporate change. Other measures of effectiveness are necessary to make this assessment. Has the movement convinced garment corporations that sweatshops are *their* problem to solve? Has it led to changes in corporate policy making? Has corporate policy making been implemented in garment factories? Ongoing research finds that corporations are developing more antisweatshop friendly policies and practices. The movement has been able to force reluctant and formerly blame-avoiding corporations to take social justice responsibility and adopt codes of conduct. A good case in point is Nike, which after years of sustained antisweatshop criticism improved its code of conduct, issued its first Corporate Responsibility Report, opened up to independent monitoring, disclosed its outsourced factory locations, increased minimum wage requirements, and improved health and safety conditions (Arnold and Hartman 2005). Other logo garment corporations are slowly following suit or at least are moving to preempt antisweatshop movement targeting.

Still, these policy changes may just be "sweatwash," meaning that logo corporations change their policy to manage activism and dodge activist and media criticism. How serious are corporations about solving sweatshop problems? And, most important, has antisweatshop targeting and activism improved the working life of global garment workers? Here, findings are mixed and often refer to specific situations. Limited space allows, therefore, for only a few examples. Probably the most successful antisweatshop episodic consumer campaign was against child labor, which has basically disappeared in foreign companies in parts of the developing world that trade with OECD countries (Edmonds and Pavcnik 2006). In districts in Indonesia where activists concentrated their efforts on mobilizing consumer awareness on certain logo brands' treatment of workers, a 15 to 20 percent higher rate of compliance with the minimum wage is reported (Harrison and Scorse 2006). Other efforts are less successful. Codes of conduct are generally not implemented fully: workers are often ill-informed about their existence, monitoring of them is sporadic and often internal rather than independent, all corporations do not disclose their overseas factories, and there are few real attempts to improve wage levels (Fair Trade Center 2006; Applebaum et al. 2000; Gereffi, Garcia-Johnson, and Sasser 2001; Dirnback 2006). But it would be wrong to conclude that code implementation problems mean that working conditions have not improved. They have. Workers in outsourced factories manufacturing for logo garment corporations are better off because of antisweatshop activism and other developments like the legal frameworks associated with trade agreements (Edmonds and Pavcnik 2006).

The conclusion to date is that antisweatshop activism has bite—even if change comes slowly, unevenly, very incrementally, and if doubt still exists about both logo and particularly nonlogo corporations' dedication to social justice responsibility-taking. The question is how sharp antisweatshop's teeth are and how big of a bite it really can make into corporations. To succeed, the movement must continue to mobilize consumers as supporters, as critical shopping mass, as a spearhead force of corporate change, and as ontological agents of deeper structural societal change. Both episodic and thematic campaigns seem to be necessary to keep the sweatshop issue in the public mind and to create general public awareness on the social connections between consumer choice and global social injustices. The big difference from earlier decades is that these problems do not go unnoticed by consumers, civil society, the media, government, and most important, garment corporations themselves.

Note

1. Organizers were chosen with the help of a reputational influence method, that is, reference to them in academic and popular scientific publications as well as cross-references to them on other antisweatshop actors' Web sites. All represent main movement parts: unions (Union of Needle, Industrial, and Technical Employees [UNITE HERE!], Global Unions), international humanitarian organizations (Oxfam, Global Exchange), Internet spin doctors (Global Exchange, Adbusters Media Foundation), and specific anti-sweatshop groups (United Students against Sweatshops [USAS], Clean Clothes Campaign [CCC]). Information on them was collected from their own original documents, interviews with their representatives (telephone or e-mail in fall 2006), and secondary literature.

References

Adbusters Media Foundation. 2006. *Philosophy behind the shoes.* http://adbusters.org/metas/corpo/blackspotshoes/aboutblackspot.php.

Applebaum, R. P., E. Bonacich, J. Esbenshade, and K. Quan. 2000. *Fighting sweatshops: Problems of enforcing global labor standards.* http://repositories.cdlib.org/cgi/viewcontent.cgi?article=1000&context=isber.

Arnold, D. G., and L. P. Hartman. 2005. Beyond sweatshops: Positive deviancy and global labour practices. *Business Ethics: A European Review* 14 (3): 206-22.

Ascoly, N., and I. Zendenrust. 1999. *The code debate in context: A decade of campaigning for clean clothes.* http://cleanclothes.org/codes/99-3-11.htm.

Ballinger, J., and T. Connor. 2005. Internet publicized e-mail exchange between Ballinger, founder of Press for Change, and Connor, NikeWatch, Oxfam Australia. Unpublished material.

Boris, E. 2003. Consumers of the world unite! In *Sweatshop USA. The American sweatshop in historical and global perspective,* ed. D. D. Bender and R. A. Greenwald. London: Routledge.

Boström, M., M. Follesdal, M. Klintman, M. Micheletti and M. P. Sörensen. 2004. *Political consumerism: Its motivations, power, and conditions in the Nordic countries and elsewhere.* www.norden.org/pub/velfaerd/konsument/sk/ TN2005517.asp?lang=6.

Bullert, B. J. 2000. Strategic public relations, sweatshops, and the making of a global movement. Working Paper no. 14, John Shorenstein Center on the Press, Politics and Public Policy, Seattle, WA.

Clean Clothes Campaign (CCC). 2005. *Made by women.* www.cleanclothes.org.

———. 2006. *An introduction to the clean clothes campaign: What does the clean clothes campaign do? What are its main objectives and activities?* www.cleanclothes.org.

Clean Clothes Communities. 2005. *Working towards ethical procurement of work wear.* http://www.cleanclothes.org/ftp/05-10-ethicalpublicprocsemreport.pdf.

deWinter, R. 2001. The anti-sweatshop movement: Constructing corporate moral agency in the global apparel industry. *Ethics & International Affairs* 15 (2): 99-115.

Dirnback, Erik. 2006. Strategic Affairs Department, UNITE HERE! Telephone interview, October 10.

Edmonds, E. V., and N. Pavcnik. 2006. International trade and child labor: Cross-country evidence. *Journal of International Economics* 68. www.nber.org/papers/W10317.

Fair Trade Center. 2006. *Klädbranschen 2006. Bakgrundsmaterial från Fair Trade Center. De fullständiga svaren från företagen.* www.fairtradecenter.se.

Fung, A., D. O'Rourke, and C. Sabel. 2001. Realizing labor standards: How transparency, competition, and sanctions could improve working conditions worldwide. *Boston Review,* February/March. http://bostonreview.net/BR26.1/fung.html.

Gereffi, G. 2001. Beyond the producer-driven/buyer-driven dichotomy: The evolution of global value chains in the Internet era. *IDS Bulletin* 32 (3): 30-40.

Gereffi, G., R. Garcia-Johnson, and E. Sasser. 2002. The NGO-industrial complex, *Foreign Policy,* 125:56-65.

Global Exchange. 2005. *Sweatfree toolkit. How your community can help end sweatshops*. www.globalexchange
.org/campaigns/sweatshops/sweatfreetoolkitintro.pdf#search=%22consumer%20sweatshop%22.

———. 2006. *Socially responsible shopping and action guide* and *World Trade Organization*. www
.globalexchange.org/campaigns/sweatshops/ftguide.html and www.globalexchange.org/campaigns/wto/.

Global Unions. 2000. *Employed children, unemployed adults*. www.global-unions.org/displaydocument
.asp?DocType=PressRelease&Index=991209053&Language=EN.

———. 2006. *Spotlight with Georges Macès*. www.icftu.org/displaydocument.asp?Index=991223109&
Language=EN.

Golodner, L. F. 1997. *Apparel industry code of conduct: A consumer perspective on social responsibility*.
www.nclnet.org/research/workersrights/apparel_industry_code_of_conduct.htm.

Greenberg, J., and G. Knight. 2004. Framing sweatshops: Nike, global production, and the American news
media. *Communication and Critical/Cultural Studies* 1 (2): 151-75.

Harrison, A., and J. Scorse. 2006. Improving the conditions of workers? Minimum wage legislation and
anti-sweatshop activism. *California Management Review* 48 (2): 140-60.

International Council on Human Rights (ICHRP). 2002. *Beyond voluntarism. Human rights and the
developing international legal obligations of companies*. Versoix, Switzerland: ICHRP.

Iyengar, S. 1999. Framing responsibility for political issues. *Annals of the American Academy of Political
and Social Science* 546:59-70.

Johns, R., and L. Vural. 2000. Class, geography, and the consumerist turn: UNITE! and the Stop Sweatshops
Campaign. *Environment and Planning Annual* 32:1198-1200.

Jordan, A., R. K. W. Wurzel, and A. R. Zito. 2003. New instruments of environmental governance: Patterns
and pathways of change. *Environmental Politics* 12 (1): 1-26.

Kubal, T. J. 1998. The presentation of political self: Cultural resonance and the construction of collective
action frames. *Sociological Quarterly* 39 (4): 539-54.

Lasn, K. 2000. *Culture jam: How to reverse America's suicidal consumer binge—And why we must*.
New York: Quill.

———. 2006. Founder, Adbusters Media Foundation. 2006. Telephone interview, September 22.

Levi, M. 2003. Organizing power: The prospects for an American labor union. *Perspectives on Politics*
1 (1): 45-68.

Merk, Jeroen. 2006. Expert, Clean Clothes Campaign Headquarters. E-mail interview, October 4.

Micheletti, M. 2007. The moral force of consumption and capitalism: Anti-slavery and anti-slavery. In
Citizenship and consumption, ed. K. Soper and F. Trentmann. London: Palgrave Macmillan.

Moller, K. 2006. Executive director, Global Exchange. E-mail interview, October 17.

Oxfam. 2004. *Play fair at the Olympics*. www.oxfam.org.uk/what_we_do/issues/trade/playfair_olympics_
eng.htm.

Oxfam Australia. 2006a. *Big noise*. www.maketradefair.com/en/index.php?file=bignoise.htm.

———. 2006b. *Offside*. www.oxfam.org.au/campaigns/labour/06report/statements_from_footballers_
associations.html.

———. 2006c. *Prove consumers care*. www.oxfam.org.au/campaigns/labour/06report/action.html.

Oxfam International. 2006. *Fair trade and you*. www.maketradefair.com/en/index.php?file=25032002111113
.htm&cat=4&subcat=1&select=1.

Rosen, E. 2002. *Making sweatshops: The globalization of the U.S. apparel industry*. Berkeley: University
of California Press.

Sklar, K. K. 1998. The consumers' White Label campaign of the national consumers' league 1898-1919. In
Getting and spending: European and American consumer societies in the 20th century, ed. S. Strasser,
C. McGovern, and M. Judt. Cambridge: Cambridge University Press.

Smith, J., and H. Johnston, eds. 2002. *Globalization and resistance: Transnational dimensions of social
movements*. Lanham, MD: Rowman & Littlefield.

Smith, P. 1997. Tommy Hilfiger in the age of mass customization. In *No sweat: Fashion, free trade, and
the rights of garment workers*, ed. A. Ross. New York: Verso.

Stolle, D., and M. Micheletti. N.d. *The expansion of political action repertoires: What an Internet campaign can tell us about political participation*. Manuscript under review.

Stott, R. 1999. Between a rock and a hard place: A history of American sweatshops, 1820-present. *Journal
of American History* 86 (1): 186-91.

United Nations Development Programme, United Nations Environmental Programme, World Bank, and World Resources Institute. 2003. *World resources 2002-2004.* www.wri.org/governance/pubs_description .cfm?pid=3764.

United Students Against Sweatshops (USAS). 2006. *History and formation.* www.studentsagainstsweatshops .org//index.php?option=co_content&task=view&id=21&Itemid=50 USAS.

Vogel, D. 2005. *The market for virtue: The potential and limits of corporate social responsibility.* Washington, DC: Brookings Institution.

Young, I. M. 2006. Responsibility and global justice: A social connection model. *Social Philosophy and Policy* 23:102-30.

Zirin, D., and D. Tyner. 2006. Baseball begins to listen to sweatshop foes. *The Nation,* July 31. www.thenation .com/doc/20060731/zirintyner.

Political Brands and Consumer Citizens: The Rebranding of Tony Blair

By
MARGARET SCAMMELL

It has become commonplace to speak of political parties and brands. This article looks at the rise of the brand and explains how branding has become the cutting edge of commercial marketing. It examines how the brand concept and research techniques are used in politics and focuses in particular on the rebranding of Tony Blair in the run up to the 2005 U.K. general election. More broadly, it argues that branding is the new form of political marketing. If market research, spin, and advertising were the key signifiers of marketed parties and candidates in the 1980s and 1990s, "branding" is the hallmark now. It will argue that the brand concept has analytical value. It is not simply a convenient and fashionable term for image. Furthermore, it is a demonstration that we are moving from a mass media model to a consumer model of political communication.

Keywords: political communication; political brands; marketing and elections; Tony Blair

Political parties are the ultimate brands.
—Burkitt (2002)

This article describes how and why branding is used in politics. It focuses in particular on the rebranding of Tony Blair in 2005. However, more broadly, it argues that branding is the new form of political marketing. If market research, spin, and advertising were the key signifiers of marketed parties and candidates in the 1980s and 1990s, "branding" is the hallmark now. The article will argue that the brand concept has analytical value. It is not simply a convenient and fashionable term for image. Furthermore, it is a demonstration that we are moving from a

Margaret Scammell is a lecturer in media and communications at the London School of Economics and Political Science. She has also been a lecturer at the School of Politics and Communications at the University of Liverpool and a research fellow at Joan Shorenstein Center for Press/Politics at the John F. Kennedy School of Government, Harvard University. Before joining the academy, she worked as a journalist for newspapers, magazines, and television.

DOI: 10.1177/0002716206299149

mass media model to a consumer model of political communication. Before moving to the politics, however, it is important to get a firmer grip on the concept of the brand.

Brands: What Are They?

Our common if loose understanding that brand refers to image and reputation is more or less right. As consultants Anholt and Hildreth (2004) put it, "A brand is nothing more . . . than the good name of something." In marketing, a brand is defined as "the psychological representation" of a product or organization: its symbolic rather than tangible use-value. At a basic level, the brand acts as a shortcut to consumer choice, enabling differentiation between broadly similar products. Most intriguing for marketers, however, is the way brand image works, appearing to add a layer of emotional connection that operates over and above the functional use-value of a product. Thus, in the classic example of brand power, "two thirds of cola drinkers prefer Pepsi in blind tests, yet two thirds *buy* Coke" (Burkitt 2002). Although brands, most famously Coca-Cola, have existed as household names for more than a century, the brand idea acquired its contemporary ubiquitous importance over the past twenty years. The term *brand* is everywhere now, applied not just to products, companies, organizations, and celebrities but also to cities, nations, and even private individuals, such that job seekers, for example, are encouraged to "consider yourself a brand" to impress interviewers (Whitcomb 2005). There are four main reasons for the contemporary rise of the brand: first, economic, and the recognition that a respected brand name translates into financial value; second, promotional, and growing skepticism about the efficacy of mass advertising in a world of media abundance and audience fragmentation; third, the perception of increasing consumer power as the new consumerism of the turn of the century brings together heightened demands for value-for-money and new concerns for corporate social responsibility; and fourth, consumer research, which insists on the importance of emotional engagement in shopping behavior, especially in explanations of repeat purchases.

The economic imperative stemmed from the phenomenal increase in the value of intangibles over the last quarter of the twentieth century. Intangibles are equivalent roughly to the gap between companies' "book values" (such as material assets, equity, and return on investment) and their stock market valuations. "The brand is a special intangible that in many businesses is the most important asset," according to Jan Lindemann (2004) of Interbrand, a consultancy that together with the magazine *BusinessWeek* publishes league tables of top global brands. The precise financial value of brands is notoriously difficult to measure by orthodox accounting practices. However, international stock markets recognize the value of intangibles in takeover claims (sometimes called "acquired goodwill") on the balance sheets. It is now beyond dispute that brands contribute massively to corporate worth. An Interbrand study, conducted in association with

JP Morgan, concluded that brands account for more than one-third of share-holder value, on average, while for some leading brands (for example, Coca-Cola and McDonald's) the brand is worth well over 50 percent of stock market value. In cash terms, the figures are truly staggering. Google, the hottest mover in Interbrand/*Businessweek*'s 2006 league table, has an estimated brand value of $12.38 billion. Coca-Cola, still the world's top brand, was put at $67 billion, while the number two brand, Microsoft, was valued at $56.9 billion.

The term brand *is everywhere now, applied not just to products, companies, organizations, and celebrities but also to cities, nations, and even private individuals.*

Recognition of this market power has led to the development of "brand man-agement" as a specialist function within companies, supplemented by a boom in brand consultancy as a new branch of marketing expertise. Brand consultancies are frequently staffed by people previously employed in advertising (Burkitt 2002), who often employ similar qualitative research techniques but who now see their work as more fundamental, and always prior to any advertising campaigns. It is increasingly common for former advertisers to talk of the "postadvertising age." Al and Laura Ries's influential book *The Fall of Advertising and the Rise of PR* (2002) argued that the hard sell of advertising was insufficient for the business of brand building. Advertising cannot substitute for the longer-term, more wide-ranging creation of reputation through sustained public relations. Maurice Saatchi (2006) went further, enlisting neuroscience to explain the "strange death of mod-ern advertising." Constant exposure to a vast array of digital media has effectively "rewired" the brains of the under-twenty-five-year-olds; they respond faster but recall less, Saatchi said. This is why teenagers can digitally multitask at rapid speeds, receive and send a text message, play a game, and download music all in the space of the typical thirty-second commercial. Neuroscience calls it "continu-ous partial attention," and the result is that "day-after recall scores for television advertising have collapsed, from 35 percent in the 1960s to 10 percent today."

A common thread in the marketing literature is that brand image is not, nor can it be, the simple creation of advertising. The peculiar property of the brand, as distinct from the product, is that it is not under the sole authorship of the owner companies. The brand emerges also from customer experience and per-ception. Promise, the agency that Labour commissioned to conduct research prior to the 2005 General Election, claims that "brands belong to everyone . . . shaped by millions of conversations which take place every day between a company and its customers . . . customers and non-customers" (Trevail, 2004). Ultimately, the brand is "only as good as the grapevine says it is." The customer contribution is known as brand equity. Brand equity is effectively a gift that customers may bestow or withhold; thus, it is a complex source of strength and weakness for companies. It may add billions to corporate worth; equally, it is acutely sensitive to competition and highly vulnerable even to small shifts in consumer perception and behavior.

Brand equity is effectively a gift that customers may bestow or withhold; thus, it is a complex source of strength and weakness for companies.

Thus, the surge of consumer activism of the past decade created new anxieties and opportunities in the boardrooms. Companies faced a diverse and intensified range of pressures from both the traditional consumer watchdog wing of activism, buttressed by mounting attention from the news media (scrutiny of value-for-money, product quality, and honesty of claims) and from activists, championed famously by Naomi Klein and Anita Roddick, with demands for social responsibility and ethical corporate behavior in human and animal rights and the environment. The climate of heightened consumer activism simultaneously increased the vulnerability of brands and their potential value. A good brand name is a tremendous asset as consumers become more demanding, but equally a reputation built over years may be dismantled virtually overnight by scandal, evidence of misdeed, or even simply competition from a smarter rival. Consequently, all aspects of brands, their definition, research, communication, and methods of economic evaluation, have become increasingly sophisticated as management invests in brand development and research while consultancies compete to sell brand-building formulas. On the economic side, statistical models contend to demonstrate the importance of brand equity, linking financial values to equity indicators, such as consumer awareness, preference, satisfaction and scores on specific image attributes and, increasingly, perceived social responsibility. On the definition and research side, marketers draw on cognitive and neuropsychology to make sense of consumers' emotional responses and attachments to brands. It has led to a burgeoning marketing interest in emotional intelligence

TABLE 1
WHAT MAKES A BRAND DISTINCTIVE?

Cultural	"symbol of our society"	Brand differentiators
Social	"grew up with it"	
Psychological	"says something about me"	
Economic	"value for money"	Boundary conditions
Functional	"works better"	

and the ways that reason and emotion work in consumers' purchase decisions (Heath 2001; Franzen and Bouwman 2001; Goleman 1996; Woods 2004).

James Donius's influential model (cited in Woods 2004; see Table 1) distinguished between "boundary conditions" (the basic economic and functional performance of a brand) and "brand differentiators" (cultural, social, and psychological associations) in consumer choice. In mature markets, where many products meet the basic boundary conditions of reliable functionality and acceptable pricing, consumer choice is decided overwhelmingly by the less tangible attributes of brand differentiation.

[T]he skill of brand research is to make explicit that which is normally unexpressed and to convert it into a prioritized order that can assist brand development and promotion.

The task of brand research lies in discovering how differentiators operate in consumers' perceptions and in finding patterns of differentiation. A common theme is that, while brand differentiators emerge from multiple and diverse experiences and psychological associations, they often work at a low level of consumer attention. Consumer psychology, drawing from cognitive psychology, calls this low-involvement processing (Heath 2001). Moreover, "many of the encounters that each of us has with a brand are experienced beneath the radar of conscious attention. The tiny details that do contribute to brand image such as the quality of plastic carrier bags, the information on a till receipt . . . sneak into our brains invisibly" (Gordon, quoted in Burkitt 2002). Hence, the skill of brand research is to make explicit that which is normally unexpressed and to convert it into a prioritized order that can assist brand development and promotion.

Brand research is primarily qualitative, seeking of necessity to delve beneath the surface evidence of quantitative polling. Burkitt (2002) described two traditions of consumer qualitative research: first, the behaviorist school, which seeks explanations through direct observation of consumer behavior rather than through questioning respondents; and second, the human psychology school, which is premised on the assumption that people can and do understand their own motivations, although they may need help ("moderation") to access and make explicit "views and values that people have not thought about in a very conscious way or do not normally admit to." The latter school is commonly equated with the focus group, although according to Burkitt, British market researchers prefer "qualitative research" since the purpose is to encourage respondents to speak as freely as possible, rather than restrict them to a narrow product focus. It enlists enabling and projective techniques from counseling and self-development to uncover respondents' normally unspoken intuitive associations and hard-to-admit private feelings. Typical techniques include "mood boards" (collections of pictures/images that evoke emotional territories, lifestyle, and feeling); "concept statements," in which respondents are asked to write down their views before discussing them; and party-game-type associations, which are probably the best known among the brand researcher's bag of tricks. The result is questions such as "If product X was a car/fruit/football team what kind of car/fruit/football team would it be?" Beyond this, and as we shall see in the case of Tony Blair, researchers call upon techniques of psychoanalysis to access respondents' most privately held or even repressed opinions.

"Reconnecting the Prime Minister": Political Branding in Action

The strategy to "reconnect" Tony Blair with disaffected voters prior to the 2005 U.K. General Election offers a sharp illustration of the centrality of brand thinking in politics. Labour, although consistently ahead in the polls, approached the campaign nervously, worried at their ability to mobilize their own supporters and concerned at the depth of anger toward Blair, especially among women voters. Moreover, Labour, as the party of government for eight years, was particularly susceptible to rising public cynicism. Politicians, Philip Gould (2003) said, were talking to an "empty stadium"; voters felt powerless and ignored and were looking for a more interactive engagement with politicians. The 2001 contest had produced the lowest postwar turnout at 59 percent, and Labour strategists feared that another record low rendered them vulnerable to a hung Parliament or worse should the Conservatives motivate their base through anti-Blair appeals and promises of tough immigration policy and lower taxes.

This was the context in which Labour, in January 2005, enlisted the services of Promise plc, a commercial consultancy specializing in brand building. Promise detailed its work in an unusually frank paper for a Market Research Society conference (Langmaid, Trevail, and Hayman 2006). The following account and quotations come from their paper, unless otherwise stated. Promise came to Labour's attention in December 2004 through a *Financial Times* article written by Charles Trevail, one of the company's founders. Trevail had argued that Labour was a "premium brand"—a high-cost, high-service product that, precisely because it raised consumer expectations to high levels, was especially vulnerable to credibility problems. Promise runs an annual index tracking the fit between consumer expectations and experience of leading brands. It had concluded its 2004 survey with the finding that two-thirds of brands failed to live up to their promises and that "premium brands were especially likely to let customers down." This, said Promise, was "the pain of premium": premium products offered high quality to customers and their very success brought with it the risk that consumers may "idealize these brands—they imbue them with lots of positive qualities they'd like them to have, and which they cannot always live up to." Trevail's argument was spotted by Shaun Woodward, former Conservative communications director, who had defected and been elected as a Labour MP in 1997. Woodward arranged a meeting between Promise executives and Labour campaign strategists Philip Gould and Sally Morgan at Number 10 Downing Street in December 2004. At the meeting, Gould said "they needed a new perspective on the New Labour brand."

Promise conducted preliminary research for Labour, involving standard focus groups of Labour loyalists and former Labour voters who were now undecided. Although it mainly confirmed what Labour already knew, the party's campaign team was impressed, especially with the analysis of respondents' "relationships with Blair personally" and how these fed into overall attitudes. Promise was commissioned to devise a strategy to counteract the Conservatives and crucially to recommend ways to "reconnect" Tony Blair to the electorate. Thereafter, Promise focused only on undecideds, particularly groups of women who had previously voted Labour. The focus was in line with Gould's surveys, which found that the hostility to Blair and Labour was especially keen among women and "might severely damage their showing at the polls." Promise attempted to isolate the Blair factor through the numerical scaling it uses in its brand index, asking respondents to award marks out of ten to parties and leaders on the basis of two attributes: reputation and delivery. It then asked respondents to score Labour and Conservatives against their own set of ideal attributes (competence, leadership, teamwork, integrity, in touch, understand, interactive). "Worryingly for New Labour, the Tories outperformed them"; and worse for the prime minister, he scored lower than his own party. Overall, Promise concluded that the New Labour brand was undermined by constant media attacks, the Iraq war, and the perception that Blair had lied about weapons of mass destruction. A key finding was that Blair personally was crucial to brand perceptions and that there was a marked deterioration over time, from enthusiastic welcome of the young Blair to resentment and anger at the later tough Blair.

To probe the link between perceptions of Blair and the party brand, Promise used expressive techniques, including asking respondents to write a letter to

TABLE 2
LETTERS TO BLAIR (FROM UNDECIDED WOMEN VOTERS)

Key Phrases	Underlying Emotional Experience	Desires/Wishes/Direction
Theme 1: You've left me!		
"you should have come home" (Tsunami); "your country needed you"; "where were you when the disaster happened"; "all the promises you made that never came to fruition"	Abandoned and unimportant	Put us first Get back in touch Get more involved with us
Theme 2: Too big for your boots/celebrity		
"a president with Cherie"; "globe-trotting holiday makers"; "celebrity hero worship (Bush)"; "thought you were a people's person, not a movie star."	His self-importance and global lifestyle leaves me feeling inferior/ undervalued	Reorder priorities Get back to basics Get real
Theme 3: Reflect and change		
"take time to think"; "how foolish you've been"; "you've lost sight of reality."	Not held in mind Uncontained Out of control	Think, reflect—are you still the bloke we elected; have you moved on to bigger things?

SOURCE: Langmaid, Trevail, and Hayman (2006).

Mr. Blair, "to let him know what they thought and more importantly how they felt," assuring them that "we would place the content of their letters before him, as we did." Promise summarized the emotional experiences of Blair under three broad headings (see Table 2): "you've left me," "you've become too big for your boots," and "you need to reflect on what you've done and change." From these broad emotional themes, they then drew on Gestalt psychology and the "two-chair" exercise, asking a volunteer to act out both parts of a two-way conversation between herself and Blair. The conversation was reported as follows:

Woman voter to Blair: "I thought you were one of us. A people person. Yet you were more interested in sucking up to people more famous than yourself. To do that you even put our boys' lives at risk in Iraq even though more than a million people had marched against that war. Why didn't you listen? Why are you spending so much time away from us? Why didn't you come home straight away after the tsunami? How could you stay on holiday when our people were dying?"

Blair to woman voter: "I'm afraid you've only got part of the picture. From where I sit the war in Iraq was crucial to the cause of world peace. But I understand that it's difficult to see the whole thing for you. [Boos from the group!] You put me in charge and I must do what I think to be the right thing. I am sure that history will prove us right in the end."

After group discussion of the imaginary conversation, the woman returned to the chair tasked to be Blair saying what she would *like* to hear from him. This is what she said:

> *Blair to woman voter:* "I understand your feelings and I realize that there are many who do not agree with me over Iraq. . . . I still believe on balance that we did the right thing, though I have been shocked to appreciate the depth of frustration among those who disagree with me. I solemnly promise to spend more time at home in contact with our own people and to debate these issues more seriously before we launch on such an endeavor again."

It was a relatively small difference in Blair's response, but it produced an extraordinary reaction, one woman even shouting out, "We love you." This was the crucial moment in the strategy to rebrand Blair. The women's anger toward Blair stemmed not so much from opposition to the Iraq war, although that was deeply unpopular, but from perceptions of Blair's patronizing tone and self-justificatory response to criticism. Promise researchers had been taken aback by the "degree of aggression—even hatred" directed at Blair. Moreover, the strength of hostility was related to the warmth of their welcome to the younger Blair, who had seemed so "fresh," "approachable," "modern, progressive and easy to look at and listen to."

The task, as Promise saw it, was to integrate the two Tonys, the young, hopeful Tony and the older tough Tony, into a new "mature Tony."

Promise concluded, "There appeared to be almost two completely separate Mr. Blairs out there in the public's consciousness. The one, ideal, almost perfect as a leader and source of hope; the other almost equally mendacious, even wicked as a source of disillusionment and despair." Ideal Tony had become Terrible Tony. Respondents reacted to Blair "with the feelings of jilted lovers: He had become enthralled by someone else, a figure more powerful than ourselves, the resident of the White House. . . . Therefore feeling rejected ourselves we must start to reject him." The task, as Promise saw it, was to integrate the two Tonys, the young, hopeful Tony and the older tough Tony, into a new "mature Tony"; and the two chair exercise suggested that it was possible to do this through communication style and tone.

Simultaneously with the Blair focus groups, the Promise team worked on a new brand model for Labour, approaching the issue "as they would any other large brand," exploring the environment in which the brand existed, how it was promoted, and most important, what it meant to consumers. New Labour had emerged out of a sophisticated brand strategy, driven by intimate contact with voters, the party's customers. But by 2005 it was badly tarnished: "The brand lens through which people viewed the party had become clouded by the Iraq war and constant media attacks on the government. . . . The research categorically stated [that] New Labour had a problem with their leader, but so influential was he as an icon of the brand, the party also had a problem that reached the very core of the brand." The New Labour brand, personified by Blair, had stopped listening, it was too reliant on him, but without him seemed lightweight, all spin rather than substance. The Conservatives' brand, despite being perceived as outdated, felt "more real"; the Tories had more substantial "brand equity."

The depth of dissatisfaction on three core attributes, competence, integrity, and teamwork, "could not be reversed over the twelve-week period before the election. However, we realized that the brand did have an opportunity to address issues of integrity and teamwork head-on. . . . We recommended a strategy that portrayed members of the Cabinet working as a team; something that was very much lacking for the Tories." Promise suggested the rebranding of New Labour as "progressive realists": passionate, friendly, and inclusive for the benefit of all. It needed to show strength in depth by promoting a greater range of spokespeople and competence through highlighting management of the economy. It also needed to emphasize public services ("this brand is about *we*, not *me*") and communications that looked "in touch." For Blair, this meant showing that he understood why people were angry and that he should drop the much-resented "I know best" stance in favor of "we can only do this together."

From "Tough Tony" to "Mature Tony": The Masochism Election Strategy

The plan to "reconnect the prime minister" got its first airing two weeks later (February 2006) with Tony Blair's speech to the Labour Party Spring Conference at Gateshead, in northeast England. To the delight of Promise and Labour campaigners, sound bites chosen by the media highlighted the new, "mature Tony" approach: "I understand why some people are angry, not just over Iraq but many of the difficult decisions we have made, and, as ever, a lot of it is about me," said Blair. "So this journey has gone from 'all things to all people,' to 'I know best' to 'we can only do this together.' And I know which I prefer. A partnership. Forward together. It's your choice."

Promise's main recommendations appeared in Labour's campaign war book: "TB must connect with the electorate . . . and make it clear that he has not abandoned them"; he should show greater candor, humility, and willingness to listen (as cited in Kavanagh and Butler 2005, 57). This emerged publicly as the "masochism strategy," in which the prime minister increased his appearances on television in the run-up to the election, deliberately seeking out aggressive interviewers and asking TV shows to find hostile audiences to question him. The strategy, with its underlying analogy of a rocky marriage, provoked considerable press interest and no little contempt as the prime minister was subjected to some humbling encounters. He was repeatedly lambasted over Iraq; while in the most excruciating confrontations a hospital worker asked the prime minister if he would be prepared to "wipe someone's backside for £5 an hour," and on the popular Saturday night show *Ant and Dec's Takeaway* a child asked him, "My dad says you're mad. Are you mad?" As the pro–New Labour commentator Andrew Rawnsley (2005) noted, much of the press did indeed think that the strategy was madness: "The traditional campaign playbooks say that leaders should always be displayed among crowds of cheering supporters affirming their goodness and greatness. And predictably conventional reporting has depicted these TV trials as evidence that the wheels are already coming off a 'humiliated' Prime Minister's campaign."

Nonetheless, the masochism strategy was central to Labour's campaign, as was the attempt to showcase a united leadership team. The latter was easier said than done, requiring a concerted effort from Labour campaigners to heal the much-reported rift between Labour's most powerful figures, Blair and Gordon Brown, the chancellor of the exchequer. Labour's longest-serving campaigners, Philip Gould and Alastair Campbell, were convinced that Brown's inclusion was indispensable to electoral success. Brown would ensure focus on the party's key assets, management of the economy and public services, and without Brown, Blair would look isolated and vulnerable. As one Labour insider said, "I think Philip and Alastair were both kept awake at night by the thought that if Gordon did not come back, Tony would be humiliated" (as cited in Kavanagh and Butler 2005, 58). After weeks of negotiation, the pair was persuaded to bury their differences, at least for the duration. The reuniting of the Lennon and McCartney of British politics was signaled in the party's first election broadcast (PEB) of the campaign. Directed by filmmaker Anthony Minghella *(The English Patient)*, the PEB featured Blair and Brown chatting together about their common values and achievements; it was a "soft-sell about a 'partnership that's worked' " (Harrison 2005, 111). Remarkably, this was the only PEB under Blair's leadership that had highlighted any Labour politician other than him. In general, Labour's advertising and promotional material was far less Blair-focused than in the previous two elections. Instead, the team theme continued with Brown repeatedly at Blair's side on the campaign trail.

Branding: Its Value for Political Campaigners

Branding as a concept and research method has both particular and general value for campaigners. The particular value is demonstrated in the "reconnection strategy"; its general usefulness becomes clear in the evolution of political marketing thinking.

The reconnection strategy was a strikingly different way to deal with the problem of leader unpopularity. Margaret Thatcher, although widely respected as a strong leader, was also deeply disliked by a large minority of the population. The Conservative solution for her in the 1987 election was a presidential campaign that highlighted her advantages as an experienced and strong leader but made little attempt to alter entrenched public perception that she was "out of touch" and "talked down" to ordinary people. Labour in 1992 had the opposite problem with then-leader Neil Kinnock, and its remedy was to protect Kinnock as far as possible from exposure to hostile questioning from the press and public (Scammell 1995). Neither course completely fitted the campaigners' bill for Blair in 2005. It would have been impossible to shield him from the scrutiny of the press, much of which treated the campaign as a referendum on the prime minister (Scammell and Harrop 2005, 131). The option of protecting him from the public, with a Thatcher-like presidential campaign, was considered seriously (Langmaid, Trevail, and Hayman 2006, 6), but it was riskier for Blair than it had been for Thatcher. First, being seen as in touch was the essence of the New Labour brand and, until the Iraq war, had been personified by Blair. He personally and the party generally had more to lose than Thatcher had. Moreover, his closest advisers, including Gould and Campbell, were concerned to bolster his authority in the party. The "Tough Tony" was largely responsible for the party's current image problems; he should be seen to be spearheading the solutions. Promise's contribution was not that it introduced Labour campaigners to brand ideas; rather, it provided solutions, including language and tone, that resonated with existing thinking. New Labour itself, as Promise stated, had been widely accepted as a triumph of branding, indeed marveled at by the business world (Scammell 1999, 737), but campaigners recognized it was vulnerable and in need of constant adaptation. The general thrust of Promise's recommendations, to demonstrate that the party was still in touch and listening, had informed Labour's 2003 mass consultation exercise, The Big Conversation, while Blair in the same year argued for a "rebranding" of the "progressive political project" (Blair 2003).

The general value of branding to campaigners is both conceptual and practical. It provides a conceptual framework to distinguish and fathom links between the functional perceptions of parties and leaders (the "boundary conditions"), such as economic management, policy commitments and the competence to deliver, and the emotional attractions ("boundary differentiators"), such as "one of us," authenticity, approachability, and attractiveness to the ear and eye. It brings together the emotional and intellectual, rational and irrational ("sometimes *disturbingly* irrational" [Burkitt 2002, 9]), the big and tiny details that feed into overall brand images. Branding is underpinned by the insight that these images are highly vulnerable, constantly changing, and rarely under complete control. The near-permanence of change has become a Gould mantra and the foundation of one of his key criticisms of political science analysis: that it is so "static"; it can explain admirably a moment in time but cannot capture the "messy unpredictable and often random nature of politics as it happens" (Gould 2002). Thus, "reassurance" was a key task of the brand in 1997, as Labour's research demonstrated that target voters were unconvinced that New Labour really was *new* (and would not go back to the old ways of special interests, tax raising and a too close relationship with trade unions). However, by 2001, reassurance had turned into perceptions of caution and excessive concern with opinion polls, and so Labour had to refresh the brand, be prepared to show bold leadership, be "less nervous of unpopularity," be far less concerned with the press "and, dare I say it, opinion polls" (Gould 2002). By 2005, *new* New Labour needed to change tack again and reestablish "Tough Tony" as the listening, caring, in-touch leader that target voters thought he was when they first elected him.

---

*The general value of branding to campaigners
is both conceptual and practical.*

Arguably, branding is now the permanent campaign. The original model of the permanent campaign, as first used by President Carter's strategist Pat Caddell (Blumenthal, 1982), was characterized inter alia by continuous polling, intense news management, and constant attention to media images. This model, says Gould (2002), "has had its day." It may once have been an understandable reaction to a "relentlessly intrusive media" and, he admitted, it had characterized the early years of the first New Labour government. However, spin and news management were not only insufficient to maintain political leadership; they ultimately "contaminated" the Labour brand and undermined public trust. In a similar vein, Needham (2005) argued that the brand concept, rather than the permanent campaign, is the more useful to understand communication in the governments of Blair and Bill Clinton. The permanent campaign focuses on the instruments of media politics; the brand concept uncovers the underlying strategic concerns of efforts to maintain voter loyalty through communication designed to provide reassurance, uniqueness (clear differentiation from rivals), consistency of values, and emotional connection with voters' values and visions of the good life.

The practical attraction of branding for campaigners is its familiarity. Branding emerged from marketing concepts and methods that have been employed in politics on both sides of the Atlantic since the 1970s. Its emphasis on image is a more developed version of service marketing's key concern for reputation, based on record and credible promises, which for politicians is pretty much the only thing of substance that they can offer to voters before election. Its qualitative research techniques, designed to tap into emotional connection, are essentially an extension of the type of methods long used in political advertising research. However, the crucial added value of branding is that it provides a conceptual structure to link advertising insight into all aspects of the brand, positioning, development, and promotion; and unlike advertising, it is not wedded to a particular form of communication. Paradoxically given the shared methods, the marketing turn to branding has coincided with shaken faith in advertising itself as capable of encompassing all the details, big and small, that create brand image. And Philip Gould is one of those former advertisers who now claim we are living in a postadvertising world.

Political Branding: A Consumer Model of Political Communication

It is not possible here to explore all the consequences of consumer politics, still less all the normative questions that naturally arise. However, here are a few preliminary conclusions:

Consumer model of political communication. The mass-media dominated, agenda-setting, advertising-driven model of political campaigning, while far from dead, is in decline. Media-centered explanations are decreasingly able to encompass the strategic logic and promotional changes of either election campaigns or government communication. Branding is both a cause and effect of the shift toward a thoroughly consumerized paradigm of political communication. This is evident not just in campaigns and the rebranding of Blair, but also in U.K. government communications over the past fifteen years. Brand research and promotion is now commonplace for government departments (Needham 2003, 17), while the Government Information and Communication Service has for some time been considering ways to develop a corporate brand image for government itself.[1] It is a progression of the process of the remodeling of the government-citizen relationship along consumer lines that has been a marked feature of "modernization" on both sides of the Atlantic since the early 1990s (Cohen 2003; Hilton 2001; Needham 2003; Scammell 2003).

Branding is both a cause and effect of the shift toward a thoroughly consumerized paradigm of political communication.

There is a perfect circle in the brand approach: campaigners research citizens as though they were consumers, and their research tells them that citizens' attitudes toward politics are profoundly shaped by their experience as consumers.

This is made clear in Gould's 2003 brand environment analysis titled "The Empty Stadium: The World Turned Upside Down," in which he argued for a new campaign paradigm. The analysis posited a fundamental mismatch between people's experience as confident consumers and insecure citizens. Affluence and choice had empowered people as consumers, but globalization, threats of terrorism, and environmental erosion had led to insecure citizens. Individuals' greater control as consumers exacerbated their sense of loss of control as citizens. Conventional politics was blamed for the rising climate of insecurity and social fracture, while being considered irrelevant to a "new consumer world of empowerment, self-actualization," and personal values. Consumer power had led to a paradigm shift within marketing, from "interruption marketing" (unasked for, unwelcome) to "permission marketing" (anticipated, relevant, personal). All interruption marketing was resisted, said Gould, but political communication was the most resisted of all. Political campaigns must follow marketing and develop more personal, interactive messages: "if we play the game as we have always done," the stadium will continue to empty.

Brand connection. A driving concern of branded politics is connection. Gould says of his work that it is all about connection; he represents the "voice of the electorate" in Labour strategy meetings. Recent moves toward a more personal and interactive communication (including, e.g., Howard Dean's fabled open-source campaign) suggest a positive role for consumer politics. However, it is also true that the voice Gould represents is not the electorate but a small part of it, primarily the soft supporters and undecideds that constitute target voters. Party members, hard-core supporters, and those who say they are unlikely to vote are rarely the subject of focus groups (Burkitt 2002). Political brand equity, in other words, is largely defined by the undecideds. It means almost inevitably that political brand equity has shallow roots and is easily buffeted. This is a striking difference from commercial branding where much of the effort is directed at retaining the loyalty of existing customers.

Hard and soft politics. Branding theoretically should include both the hard politics (policies, issues, record of performance) and the soft (emotional connection, values, likeability). It does not necessarily lead to a wholesale flight from hard, "proper" politics, the perennial complaint against political marketing. However, the example of the reconnection strategy shows how branding may muddy these waters. It dealt with the hardest of hard issues, the decision to go to war, and resulted in a strategy that compelled Blair to account for his actions before fierce public scrutiny. Yet at the core of the strategy was the softest of politics: that merely by appearance, communication style, and tone, he could draw much of the sting of public anger. A generous reading of the reconnection strategy might be that it displayed a refreshing attention to the emotional intelligence of voters. A more damning verdict is that branding is yet another step on the road to *Politics Lost.* Journalist Joe Klein's decades-spanning acquaintance with U.S. elections and political consultants led him unequivocally to that conclusion. For

Klein, no one was more cynically nonpolitical than George W. Bush's strategist Karl Rove, for whom there were only three basic questions that matter to voters: Is the candidate a strong leader? Can I trust him? Does he care about people like me? The hard politics of specific issues were only useful as sticks to beat opponents or as illustrations of candidate brand values (Klein 2006, 144-45).

However, branding is not easily categorized as a force for either good or ill. It does not, any more than any other marketing technique in politics, supply single-route solutions. Its research results, like any other, must be interpreted and negotiated by the relevant political actors. Its application, as for any commercial brand, will be shaped by consideration of the environment, the structural, social, and cultural factors that affect people's choices. Much like the citizen-consumer debate itself, it is double edged, offering new potential and creating new anxieties.

[B]randing is not easily categorized as a force for either good or ill.

Note

1. James Humphreys, formerly head of the Strategic Communication Unit, initiated the "government brand" communication effort.

References

Anholt, S., and J. Hildreth. 2004. *Brand America: The mother of all brands*. London: Cyan Books.

Blair, A. 2003. Where the Third Way goes from here. *Progressive Governance*. www.progressive-governance .net/php/print_preview.php?aid=35.

Blumenthal, S. 1982. *The permanent campaign*. New York: Simon & Schuster.

Burkitt, Catherine. 2002. Are you less emotionally intelligent than Blair? And if so why should you care? Paper presented to the annual conference of the Political Studies Association, Aberdeen, UK.

Cohen, Lizabeth. 2003. *A consumers' republic*. New York: Knopf.

Franzen, Giep, and Margot Bouwman 2001. *The mental world of brands: Mind, memory and brand success*. Henley-on-Thames, UK: World Advertising Research Centre.

Goleman, Daniel. 1996. *Emotional intelligence*. London: Bloomsbury.

Gould, Philip. 2002. What "permanent campaign"? BBC Online. http://news.bbc.co.uk/1/hi/uk_politics/ 2499061.stm.

———. 2003. The empty stadium: The world turned upside down. Presentation to a political communication class, London School of Economics, March.

Harrison, M. 2005. On air. In *The British General Election of 2005*, ed. Dennis Kavanagh and D. Butler. Basingstoke, UK: Palgrave.

Heath, R. 2001. *The hidden power of advertising*. London: Admap Publications.

Hilton, M. 2001. Consumer politics in post-war Britain. In *The politics of consumption: Material culture and citizenship in Europe and Asia*, ed. M. Daunton and M. Hilton. Oxford, UK: Berg.

Kavanagh, D., and D. Butler. 2005. *The British General Election of 2005*. Basingstoke, UK: Macmillan.

Klein, Joe. 2006. *Politics lost*. New York: Doubleday.

Langmaid, R., C. Trevail, and B. Hayman. 2006. Reconnecting the Prime Minister. Paper presented at the annual conference of the Market Research Society, London.

Lindemann, Jan. 2004. *The social value of brands*. http://www.brandchannel.com/papers_review.asp?sp_id=342.

Needham, C. 2003. *Citizen-consumers: New Labour's marketplace democracy*. London: The Catalyst Forum.

———. 2005. Brand leaders: Clinton, Blair and the limitations of the permanent campaign. *Political Studies* 53 (2): 343-61.

Rawnsley, A. 2005. Tony Blair wants a good kicking. *The Observer*, February 20. http://observer.guardian.co.uk/comment/story/0,6903,1418478,00.html.

Ries, Al, and L. Ries. 2002. *The fall of advertising and the rise of PR*. New York: HarperCollins.

Saatchi, M. 2006. The strange death of modern advertising. *Financial Times*, June 21. http://www.ft.com/cms/s/117b10ee-014b-11db-af16-0000779e2340.html.

Scammell, M. 1995. *Designer politics*. Basingstoke, UK: Macmillan.

———. 1999. Political marketing: Lessons for political science. *Political Studies* 47 (4): 718-39.

———. 2003. Citizen consumers: Towards a new marketing of politics? In *Media and the restyling of politics*, ed. J. Corner and D. Pels. London: Sage.

Scammell, M., and M. Harrop. 2005. The press: Still for Labour despite Blair. In *The British General Election of 2005*, ed. D. Kavanagh and D. Butler. Basingstoke, UK: Macmillan.

Trevail, C. 2004. *There's more to brands than Coca-Cola*. Promise Corporation. http://www.promisecorp.com/thinking/thinking.htm.

Whitcomb, S. 2005. *Interview magic*. Indianapolis, IN: JIST Works.

Woods, Richard. 2004. Creating emotional maps for brands. Paper presented to the annual conference of the Market Research Society, London.

Logo Logic: The Ups and Downs of Branded Political Communication

By
W. LANCE BENNETT
and
TASO LAGOS

Activists often have difficulties getting messages to larger publics. This is particularly challenging in the U.S. press/politics system, where the mainstream media tend to open the news gates only after government institutions engage with issues. Yet there are signs in recent years that activists are finding creative ways of publicizing their causes by attaching political messages to familiar corporate brands. For example, complex messages about labor conditions in foreign factories making shoes and apparel may travel more easily when attached to a major brand, for example, Nike sweatshop. The first part of this analysis examines how branded political communication works and how it may be effective. The second part looks at possible downsides of getting consumer audiences to actually grasp the larger import of the politics behind the brands and getting targeted companies and industrial sectors (fashion, food, forest products, etc.) to change their offending behaviors.

Keywords: political communication; logo campaigns; consumer politics; product certification; culture jamming; corporate social responsibility

Activists have long lamented the difficulties of getting their messages to larger publics. The broad distribution of activist messages can be particularly challenging in the United States. Mainstream news organizations tend to open the news gates to activists only after government has begun to engage publicly with their issues in legislative, executive, or legal institutions (Bennett 1991). True, protest activities may make news, but the coverage is typically in terms that portray activists as civilly disobedient and disruptive forces—a pattern applied to many voices critical of economic globalization (Bennett et al. 2004). Further complicating matters, issues such as sustainable development, workers' rights, and environmental degradation often fall beyond the will of governments to act. As a result, some global justice activists are attempting to create nonstate governance and regulatory systems (Beck 2000; Cashore, Auld, & Newson 2004).

DOI: 10.1177/0002716206298484

The general idea of activists trying to develop nongovernmental regulatory systems—complete with standards and certification processes for socially responsible production and consumption—is breathtaking in its ambition. The emergence and proliferation of so-called logo campaigns that attach political messages to corporate brands (e.g., Nike sweatshop) have become central tactics in mobilizing consumer power to get companies to accept such regulation (Klein 1999). This article explores the broad logic of logo campaigns as a means of developing political relationships among activists, consumers, producers, and corporations with the aim of regulating the global product chains that increasingly drive national economies and personal lifestyles. The first part of this analysis examines how branded political communication works. The second part looks at conditions that can make this form of messaging effective in reaching consumer audiences. The third part looks at the downside of trying to harness consumer power to get targeted companies and industrial sectors to change their offending behaviors.

Logo Logic: How Branded Communication Works

Attacking corporate brands is not in itself a new thing. Labor unions have long promoted boycotts and "buycotts" to use consumers to discipline the labor policies of companies. NGOs and activist groups have also used campaigns to get corporations such as Nestlé to stop offending practices such as distributing powdered infant milk formula to places where water contamination threatened the babies who consumed it (Keck and Sikkink 1998). Traditional *corporate campaigns* still occur under conditions of collective identification (such as union membership) and/or support from powerful institutions (such as the United Nations, which provided help to the Nestlé campaign). By contrast, contemporary globalization activists typically face low ideological commitment among consumers and little support from authoritative institutions in promoting regulatory standards. Indeed, consumer publics are often escaping formal politics and unpleasant issues within their lifestyle cocoons (Bennett 1998).

As a result, activists are learning to tap into personal identification with brands and recognizing the importance of lifestyles as the organizers of personal meaning in everyday life. Building on these social identity principles, the central elements of "logo logic" are (1) attaching political messages to so-called lifestyle brands that have already captured the collective attention of individual consumers; (2) communicating these branded messages through both digital and mass media, finding different gate-keeping points than the ones that filter conventional political

W. Lance Bennett is a professor of political science and Ruddick C. Lawrence Professor of Communication at the University of Washington, where he directs the Center for Communication and Civic Engagement (www.engagedcitizen.org).

Taso Lagos received his PhD in communication from the University of Washington in 2004 and is now a lecturer in the Department of Communication.

news; and (3) using the (often negative) publicity about the brand to develop political relationships with corporations.

Attaching political messages to lifestyle brands

As citizens in postindustrial societies—particularly younger generations—are detaching from parties and group-based memberships, many of them are finding new ways to connect more directly with issues (environmentalism, social justice, health care, privacy, morality) that impact how they live their personal lives (Inglehart 1997; Bennett 1998). For example, the deforestation of coffee plantations in far-off lands by desperate farmers who are not paid a living price for their beans is seen by many conservationists as having a direct negative effect on the habitats of songbirds that migrate to North America. Hence, campaigns for "shade coffee" have direct personal links to issues such as bird watching, hiking, and other forms of nature appreciation that are associated with lifestyle values. If a so-called lifestyle brand such as Starbucks coffee can be associated with the destruction of bird habitat, consumers can be brought to the issue in ways that avoid conventional political action yet express personal values (Eliasoph 1998). Even if consumer pressure does not increase directly, a sustained public challenge to an otherwise strong lifestyle brand may produce a response from the company.

[A]ctivists are learning to tap into personal identification with brands and recognizing the importance of lifestyles as the organizers of personal meaning in everyday life.

Logo politics rely on the corporate target's having already done the difficult and costly work of reaching its consumer audience with branding. The brand is the key because, increasingly, what is being sold by corporations is less the product than the brand image (Klein 1999). In an era of global production systems, the manufacture of many products has become outsourced. Shoes and fashion for major brands such as Nike and Reebok or Gap may be produced in the same Vietnamese, Indonesian, or Chinese contract factories that are not owned by the companies.

In noisy media environments that bombard independent consumers with attractive choices, branding has become the byword for keeping products competitive. A brand's familiarity keeps loyal customers coming back despite growing competition, but it may also make them pay attention when disturbing messages are attached to it. Thus, organic consumer activists who have trouble drawing broad public attention to the bovine growth hormones in milk, or to the genetic modification of soybeans and other foods, may have more success alerting Starbucks customers to the trouble lurking within their cappuccinos or soy lattes. Turning the familiar mermaid logo into a parody of Edvard Munch's *Scream* and playing on the brand name as "Frankenbucks" becomes a "culture jam" raising problematic aspects of lifestyle choices (Lasn 1999).

Logo politics rely on the corporate target's having already done the difficult and costly work of reaching its consumer audience with branding.

As a result of its attention-getting potential, branded communication can ease the audience problem that often plagues activists. Branded political messages often travel easily across media layers, from e-mail, to webzines and blogs, and even into the mass media through gates different than the ones that screen ordinary political news. These diffusion paths often begin with digital media content controlled by activists themselves.

New media rules

The advance of digital communication technologies enables activists to "Be the Media," as the slogan for Indymedia puts it. This capacity to participate in the production and distribution of media content is enabled at low cost by the proliferation of digital media technologies. Yet not all content travels equally. Branded messages cross diverse social networks more easily than conventional political content. For example, so-called culture jams often travel virally on the Internet, inviting recipients to click on links or go to Web sites where they can learn more about issues. Recipients may forward these jams on to friends, either out of concern or just because they are fun.

The viral transmission, network jumping, and media boundary crossing of Jonah Peretti's famous Nike sweatshop culture jam has become legendary. At the core of Peretti's "Nike sweatshop e-mail adventure" was a merger of content and media. The short, catchy, easily imitated and shared messages (called "memes") are the stuff of digital diffusion (Peretti n.d.). His online order for a pair of sneaks customized with the word "sweatshop" produced a hilarious exchange with a representative from Nike, which Peretti forwarded to some friends. The friends and their chain of contacts forwarded it in turn, until, by one estimate, 11.4 million people received it. In the process, the exchange was posted on numerous blogs and Web sites in what Peretti calls the "middle media" where larger audiences gather, including commentators, producers, and journalists from the mass media who seek trends and new material. Soon, Peretti and his Nike/sweatshop message were featured in mainstream media around the world, including an invitation to appear on *The NBC Today Show* (Peretti 2004).

In many cases, branded messages that would not pass through media gates as hard news may be picked up as humor, consumer news (in the increasingly important category of "news you can use"), or as business stories about troubled companies. In these paths to publicity, branded communication finds the equivalent of "wormholes" in the news universe—a universe that is otherwise resistant to reporting radical political messages straight up. In short, globalization activists may still be disparaged or ignored in mainstream political news, but they may have greater success in getting their messages across by other means. As a result, hard-to-communicate messages about global coffee markets, sustainable agriculture, or community development in far-off lands may gain greater visibility when delivered through logo campaigns to pressure Starbucks to sell fair trade coffee, or to buy from shaded coffee farms that provide habitats for migratory birds. Similarly, hard-to-sell messages about labor conditions in foreign factories become easier to deliver when simplified and paired with a brand that already travels far and wide: Nike sweatshop. The next question is whether getting such messages into the consumer environment makes a difference in achieving activists' political goals.

[G]lobalization activists may still be disparaged or ignored in mainstream political news, but they may have greater success in getting their messages across by other means.

Developing political relationships

The ultimate goal of much of this communication is to use consumer power to pressure companies and industries to change their behaviors. This is a tall order. Getting companies to mouth the words of social responsibility is one thing, but evaluating and certifying their actual practices is something else. Indeed, corporate codes of conduct have swept many industries on the wings of public relations counsel that they are low cost and publicity-friendly first responses. However, it is far more difficult to get companies to disclose actual production or resource acquisition practices, or even to divulge the locations of factories. Even when companies cooperate, activists must find resources to conduct effective monitoring and certification of compliance. In short, there is a long chain of political relationships between getting the attention of consumers and using that attention to develop effective industry standards and certification systems that work. The next sections of the article explore the ups and downs of these complicated relationships that begin with the deceptively simple process of branded communication.

The Upside: Have Logo, Will Travel

There are several levels of thinking about what works in logo campaigns: (1) increasing the awareness of consumers; (2) holding a brand hostage in the media; (3) running low-cost, long-term "permanent" campaigns to sustain the threat to the brand; (4) using this sustained pressure to build political relationships with companies; and (5) creating regulatory mechanisms to actually induce change in corporate practices.

Consumer awareness

The question of how much consumers may understand about the politics behind a brand as a result of a logo campaign is often difficult to answer. Some more conventional consumer campaigns clearly achieve high levels of attention and awareness, as happened in the European case of the Brent Spar oil platform that Shell UK planned to dispose of by sinking off the coast of Scotland. Greenpeace organized a campaign and promoted a boycott of Shell gas stations. The issue made big news throughout Northern Europe when Greenpeace activists occupied the platform. It is likely that substantial awareness about the issue developed, in part because the perceived threat was immediate, and because publics had prior experience with devastating oil spills. This large-scale awareness led to what Micheletti (2003) called individualized collective action in the form of a boycott of Shell.

However, it is less clear if such levels of awareness and mobilization typically develop around the complex issues behind many logo campaigns. The relationship between Nike and its suppliers or Starbucks and its growers is much more ambiguous than connecting Shell to a possible oil spill. It is not clear how deep the consumer understanding goes in such logo campaigns. Indeed, this is an important area for future research. Even at the height of the campaign against Nike in the period from 1995 to 1998, it is impossible to untangle sales and profit drops from a series of larger structural problems that hit the entire industry ("Hitting the Wall" 2000). What does seem clear is that seeing their precious brand receive such negative publicity led corporate officers to address activist demands. Holding the brand hostage may be a more important political lever in many campaigns than raising consumer consciousness.

Holding the brand hostage

In logo logic, it may not be necessary—or even possible—to get masses of consumers to fully grasp the politics behind the brand. What may matter more is the prospect of consumers developing a vague sense that the brand is no longer cool. The prospects of a brand "losing its cool" may travel quickly through the image tribes who swarm to trendy lifestyle images, and run away just as quickly (Turow 1997). Thus, companies may not wait to see if consumers are forming deeper understandings about politics at the sites of production—that might be too late. Suggestions of trouble in brand-land often produce preemptive reactions from targeted companies. The challenge for activists is to keep campaigns going long enough to extract meaningful responses.

Sustaining pressure through permanent campaigns

Labor activist Jeff Ballinger had been working to publicize the downside of Nike's business model since the late 1980s. His one-person campaign buzzed around Nike for several years until the activist networking organization Global Exchange joined forces in the mid-1990s and stepped up the pressure. The centerpiece of their campaign was a low-budget national tour for Indonesian factory workers who had been fired for demanding that factory owners pay the minimum wage. Simple public relations measures alerted journalists along the tour route that a press event would occur, often outside a Niketown. Activists were mobilized through e-mail networks to organize the protests. In addition, columnist Bob Herbert was sold on the story and became a loud national voice.

The result was the wave of publicity shown in Figure 1, which reflects a search of the *New York Times* and *Washington Post* in the Nexis database for "Nike and Indonesia" between 1991 and 1998. This time span corresponds to the period from the first wire reports of abuses of workers in Nike contract factories in Indonesia (accompanied by Nike CEO Phil Knight's denials), to Knight's eventual public admission of responsibility for the problems and a vow to correct them.[1] As indicated, the dominant news framing at the peak of the campaign adopted the activists' preferred term of *sweatshop*, followed by business and consumer frames that typically linked the sweatshop problem to core areas of company vulnerability.[2] The volume of stories peaked between 1995 and 1997, when Global Exchange became central to the campaign. Suddenly, Nike went from being a business success story to having a sweatshop problem that threatened its business image.

It is typical of logo campaigns that the entry of even one activist networking organization with modest resources can make a huge difference. As Ballinger put it, "Global Exchange turned my rundown, VW bus of a campaign into an 18 wheeler" (Bullert 2000, 8). Yet Global Exchange stepped back from the campaign

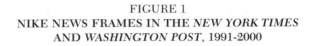

FIGURE 1
NIKE NEWS FRAMES IN THE *NEW YORK TIMES*
AND *WASHINGTON POST*, 1991-2000

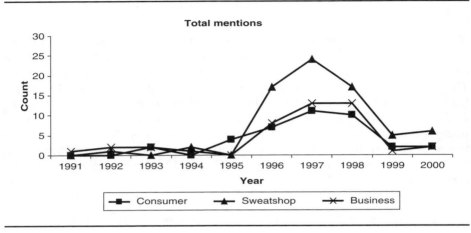

following Knight's public promise to address the problems. In more centralized issue campaigns, this might mean the end of the attack on Nike. However, many logo campaigns develop a loosely organized, open structure that enables new organizations to enter and continue the campaign on new fronts. For example, in the late 1990s Students against Sweatshops led a campaign to get apparel companies such as Nike to join the Worker Rights Consortium (WRC), a certification system for fair labor practices. The campaign received another wave of publicity as activists pressed colleges to sell campus gear from sweatshop-free companies. As of this writing, 158 colleges (including the entire University of California system) had joined the WRC ("Codes Don't Work" 2006).

Despite the success of the campaign at getting buy-in from many schools that control apparel licensing for large student markets, Nike resisted joining the WRC. The company affiliated, instead, with a competing certification organization, the Fair Labor Association (FLA). Many movement activists regard the FLA as a corporate shield rather than a prod to higher social responsibility. Our concern here is not to settle these different perceptions among activists but to point out the potential for slippage between campaign success at one level (in this case, publicity) and failure to establish desired political relationships with targets. Indeed, the competition between different standards systems is a common issue facing activists who are trying to do it by themselves.

Political relationships

As the Nike campaign suggests, the goal for activists is to get leading corporations to change their behavior (Manheim 2001). However, activists may disagree on just how responsive a target has been. As a result, changes of corporate behavior may be regarded as victories by some activists and as public relations ploys by others. As mentioned above, Global Exchange turned down its pressure in the Nike campaign after the wave of publicity it helped to generate moved company founder and CEO Phil Knight to deliver a 1998 speech at the National Press Club in which he made the extraordinary admission that "the Nike product has become synonymous with slave wages, forced overtime, and arbitrary abuse." He also promised a number of sweeping reforms, which, if implemented, would make Nike a leader in setting responsible global labor standards ("Hitting the Wall" 2000, 11). Knight's dramatic public confession notwithstanding, the subsequent decision by Nike to affiliate with the FLA and not the WRC left many activists convinced that Nike would not become fully committed to the highest standards of labor justice. As a result, activists, including Jeff Ballinger and Students against Sweatshops, continued the campaign to press for Nike to join the WRC.

No matter how one regards Nike's affiliation with one certification regime over another, the fact is that these campaigns have helped create fledgling systems for regulating corporate behavior in distant reaches of the world. A similar story could be told about the Clean Clothes Campaign in Europe (http://www.cleanclothes .org/). The establishment of such regulatory systems in the absence, or with only peripheral involvement, of government is an interesting and important development in its own right.

Regulation without government

Many product sectors now have functioning standards certification systems. A common model is to support these certification processes through fees paid by companies to certification organizations. As part of their certification, companies or other profitable middle organizations in a chain of consumption may also be required to pay premiums or commit resources directly to producers or suppliers to help achieve various goals, such as offering coffee growers a fair price for their crops, or giving factory workers training and support in making labor rights claims. In the fair trade (FT) coffee sector, for example, there is an international Fairtrade Labeling Organization (FLO) that works with affiliated NGOs in various nations to seek compliance from businesses and to develop markets for fair trade products. When a company such as Starbucks is certified by an FLO affiliate such as TransFair, the company can display an official certification trademark on bags or products containing the certified coffee. FLO affiliate Max Havelaar operates similarly in various European countries. (For an overview of this process in the United States, see http://www.transfairusa.org/content/certification/ producer_certification_guide.php.) Coffee is the oldest fair trade product in the United States (1989), and the most successful, with sales in the United States (the leading fair trade nation) rising from roughly $89 million in 2001, to $369 million in 2004, and $500 million in 2005 (Fair Trade Federation 2004; Wilkinson 2006, 17). To put this in perspective, Proctor and Gamble alone made roughly $1 billion in profits from its Folgers brand in 2001 and continues to resist the campaign against it, as explained below (Organic Consumers Association 2001).

In short, despite encouraging developments in industries from food, to fashion, to forest products, there are also problems inherent in using logo campaigns to leverage nongovernmental regulatory schemes. Despite the appeal of branded communication, logo campaigns may also send mixed messages due to lack of coordination among different organizations. The lack of (governance) mechanisms to reconcile differences may result in the proliferation of different and sometimes competing standards systems. Where this makes for confusing signals to consumers, the chain of communication power driving these systems may be broken.

The Downside of Branded Political Communication

As noted above, one of the greatest challenges to branded consumer politics is the frequent lack of coordination among activists targeting the same companies, often resulting in the proliferation of different messages and a confusing array of regulatory systems in many areas. This can lead to a cascade of other disconnections down the chain linking consumer power to improving conditions at the sites of production.

Multiple messages and competing regulatory systems

Many certification systems compete for the regulation of coffee alone. The primary systems include Bird Friendly (shade and habitat protection), Organic (regulating pesticides, chemicals, soil, and growing practices), Rainforest Alliance (forest preservation, sustainable agriculture), Fair Trade (paying a fair price and developing sustainable local grower communities), and Utz Kapeh (good agriculture and worker welfare). A similar profusion of what Cashore, Auld, and Newson (2004) called nonstate market-driven governance systems (NSMD) has occurred in the forest products sector. The fashion sector has also followed a familiar path with the proliferation of multiple systems, ranging from the FLA and WRC in the United States to a number of others internationally. Even when particular systems are successful, as in the case of FT coffee, problems with them can be traced to inherent limitations of logo logic.

Disconnects in the chain of consumer power

One undesirable result of the proliferation of certification regimes is that some large companies may decide to join standards systems, yet not post the trademarks on products for fear of confusing branded consumers (Consumers International 2005). This breaks the chain of communication-driven political pressure: if consumers do not receive continuing signals about the products they buy, awareness and demand break down. Another related problem is that some campaigns may target companies effectively, yet not reach consumers to increase awareness of the underlying issues. For example, activists targeted Home Depot with demands to carry lumber products certified by the Forest Stewardship Council. Holding the Home Depot logo hostage led to an agreement to sell certified products, yet the campaign probably did not educate many Home Depot consumers about the deeper politics or issues of forest certification (de Graf 2006). By contrast, public service ads on public television in the Netherlands resulted in high levels of consumer awareness about sustainable forest management. In the latter case, consumer awareness feeds back into the chain of demand for certified products and, in addition, may grow the ranks of activists spreading the cause (de Graaf 2006).

Limits to lifestyle brands

Another challenge to logo campaigns is the inherent limitation of lifestyle brands in some sectors. Nike is clearly a lifestyle brand that is also an industry leader with the capacity to set a new tone in the apparel sector. By contrast, even if Starbucks became a leader in fair trade coffee, it is not clear that other, far larger, brands would follow; their consumers simply may not be having the same kind of lifestyle experiences with mass consumption coffee. For example, Kraft (Maxwell House) has been targeted with fair trade campaigns, yet its code of conduct remained a conservative affirmation of belief in the free market as the best regulatory mechanism (Oxfam International 2002, 28). Following this logic, Proctor and Gamble agreed to make its lifestyle brand Millstone fair trade, but it has resisted converting its dominant brand, Folgers. Millstone represents just 5 percent of Proctor and Gamble's $1 billion profit on coffee. The campaign against Folgers goes on as of this writing, but there seems little way to reach its consumers with messages that worked for Starbucks (Organic Consumers Association 2003). The limits of using logo communication to expand the scope of consumer pressure are fairly clear in the cases of these nonlifestyle brands.

Conclusion

Branded political communication uses the work already done by advertising to send messages to audiences. The merger of political content and familiar brand identifications may help activist messages clear the first threshold of public communication: getting the attention of a desired audience or at least making the media in ways that get the attention of corporate managers. By contrast, more conventional communication can make activists sound shrill and preachy to people who actively seek to avoid the unpleasantness of political intrusions in their private lives.

While branding communication may help messages travel, do those messages actually raise consumer awareness about the politics beyond the brands? Here the answer seems a bit mixed. On the plus side, the growth of certification systems seems clear. For example, world Fair Trade sales have grown steadily since the inception of organized FT some two decades ago. In addition to adding a social justice dimension to the act of consumption in the north, people in the global south seem to be benefiting as well. FT currently benefits some 5 million people, including five hundred producer groups and 1 million farmers in forty-nine countries according to FLO data (Wilkinson 2006, 27). However, the story becomes a bit less clear when we consider the diversity of certification systems and issue frames that may end up confusing the very consumers whose continuing demand is so important to the effectiveness and growth of the process itself. Even the informed consumer may not find it easy to make political choices among the dizzying array of trademarks on coffee in stores.

While branding communication may help messages travel, do those messages actually raise consumer awareness about the politics beyond the brands?

Some of these coordination problems can be traced to the absence of binding (e.g., governmental) means of reconciling different standards systems. In the absence of institutional support, the viability of many systems depends on finding the resources to pay for the monitoring and certification of corporate compliance, and to expand markets for certified goods so that companies may eventually self-regulate on grounds that it is simply good for business. Yet the uphill struggle in these systems is that companies often initially prefer those systems that demand the least, which weakens the strength of subsequent signaling to consumers. For example, in the apparel sector, the FLA, like many certification organizations, is supported largely by company contributions, which, in the view of some activists, gives companies too much leverage over standards. Not surprisingly, most U.S. apparel companies that have joined a certification system have joined the FLA, which also included 194 colleges and universities as of this writing (FLA 2004, 2005). Even when colleges seek to comply with stronger apparel certification criteria of the WRC, the absence of many corporate members or other stable source of revenue means that few resources are available to monitor factories or train workers in claiming and defending their rights ("Codes Don't Work" 2006). The grand dilemma is that logo campaigns and culture jamming may win public attention and success at some levels, but there are many other links in the process that must be joined in order to create a successful system for producing "clean" clothes or "just" coffee.

Notes

1. For a timeline of events in the Nike campaign, see the chronology at the Center for Communication and Civic Engagement, http://depts.washington.edu/ccce/polcommcampaigns/NikeChronology.htm.

2. Based on thirty-two *Washington Post* and seventy-two *New York Times* stories and editorials gathered in a Nexis search of "Nike and Indonesia" between 1991 and 2000. Coder reliability calculated by Cohen's kappa based on two independent coders was .91 for the sweatshop code, 1.0 for the business code, and .7 for the consumer code, indicating good to excellent reliability across the three reported codes.

References

Beck, Ulrich. 2000. *What is globalization?* Cambridge, UK: Polity.

Bennett, W. Lance. 1991. Toward a theory of press-state relations. *Journal of Communication* 40 (2): 103-25.

———. 1998. The uncivic culture: Communication, identity, and the rise of lifestyle politics. Ithiel de Sola Pool Lecture, American Political Science Association. *PS: Political Science and Politics* 31 (December): 41-61.

Bennett, W. Lance, Victor Pickard, David Iozzi, Carl Schroeder, Taso Lagos, and Courtney Caswell. 2004. Managing the public sphere: Journalistic construction of the great globalization debate. *Journal of Communication* 54 (3): 437-55.

Bullert, B. J. 2000. Strategic public relations, sweatshops and the making of a movement. Joan Shorenstein Center on the Press, Politics, and Public Policy, Working Paper 2000-14. Kennedy School of Government, Harvard University, Cambridge, MA. http://www.ksg.harvard.edu/presspol/Research_Publications/Papers/Working_Papers/2000_14.PDF#search=%22bullert%20nike%22 (accessed November 21, 2006).

Cashore, Benjamin, Graeme Auld, and Deanna Newson. 2004. Legitimizing political consumerism: The case of forest certification in North America and Europe. In *Politics, products, and markets: Exploring political consumerism past and present*, ed. Michele Micheletti, Andreas Follesdal, and Dietlind Stolle. New Brunswick, NJ: Transaction Publishers.

Codes don't work. 2006. Inside Higher Education, September 28. http://www.workersrights.org/press/InsideHigherEd_Sept-28-06_CodesDontWork.pdf (accessed October 18, 2006).

Consumers International. 2005. *From bean to cup: How consumer choice impacts upon coffee producers and the environment*. London: Consumers International. www.consumersinternational.org.

de Graaf, John. 2006. *Buyer be fair: The promise of product certification* (Film). Fox-Wilmar Productions. http://www.buyerbefair.org/index.html (accessed October 20, 2006).

Eliasoph, Nina. 1998. *Avoiding politics: How Americans produce apathy in everyday life*. New York: Cambridge University Press.

Fair Labor Association. 2004. *Nike, Inc. labor compliance program in year two*. http://www.fairlabor.org/2004report/companies/participating/complianceProgram_nike.html (accessed October 18, 2006).

———. 2005. *About us*. http://www.fairlabor.org/all/about/ (accessed October 18, 2006).

Fair Trade Federation. 2004. *Fair trade trends in North America and the Pacific Rim. Executive summary*. Washington, DC: Fair Trade Federation.

Hitting the wall: Nike and international labor practices. 2000. Harvard Business School, Case Study Number N1-007-047. http://ww.hbsp.harvard.edu (accessed October 18, 2006).

Inglehart, Ronald. 1997. *Modernization and post-modernization: Cultural, economic, and political change in 43 societies*. Princeton, NJ: Princeton University Press.

Keck, Margaret, and Katharyn Sikkink. 1998. *Activists beyond borders: Advocacy networks in international politics*. Ithaca, NY: Cornell University Press.

Klein, Naomi. 1999. *No logo: Taking aim at the brand bullies*. New York: St. Martins/Picador.

Lasn, Kalle. 1999. *Culture jam: How to reverse America's suicidal consumer binge—And why we must*. New York: HarperCollins.

Manheim, Jarol B. 2001. *The death of a thousand cuts: Corporate campaigns and the attack on the corporation.* Mahwah, NJ: Lawrence Erlbaum.

Micheletti, Michele. 2003. *Political virtue and shopping: Individuals, consumerism and collective action.* New York: Palgrave.

Organic Consumers Association. 2001. *National day of action against Folgers.* http://www.organicconsumers.org/Starbucks/folgers.cfm (accessed October 24, 2006).

———. 2003. *National day of action for fair trade coffee.* http://www.organicconsumers.org/starbucks/022103_fair_trade.cfm (accessed October 20, 2006).

Oxfam International. 2002. *Mugged: Poverty in your coffee cup.* London: Oxfam International.

Peretti, Jonah. 2004. The Nike sweatshop email: Political consumerism, Internet, and culture-jamming. With Michele Micheletti. In *Politics, products, and markets: Exploring political consumerism past and present,* ed. Michele Micheletti, Andreas Follesdal, and Dietlind Stolle, 127-42. New Brunswick, NJ: Transaction Publishers.

———. n.d. *Culture jamming, memes, social networks, and the emerging media ecology: The "Nike sweatshop email" as object-to-think with.* http://depts.washington.edu/ccce/polcommcampaigns/peretti.html (accessed October 20, 2006).

Turow, Joseph. 1997. *Breaking up America: Advertisers and the new media world.* Chicago: University of Chicago Press.

Wilkinson, John. 2006. Fair trade moves centre stage. The Marian and Arthur Edelstein Virtual Library, Working Paper 3 (September). http://www.centroedelstein.org.br/wp3_english.pdf (accessed October 24, 2006).

This article explores the relationship between Internet use among young people, their political consumption, and their political participation. The study widens the notion of online civic and political engagement and includes measures of active and passive forms of participation. To test a number of hypotheses developed on the basis of extant research, a survey was conducted in 2006 among 2,404 young Dutch respondents (aged sixteen to twenty-four). The results demonstrate the importance of the Internet for political activities for young people. They also show that most online activities (ranging from news use, peer communication, and consumption to online service use) are positively related to political participation. Contrary to common wisdom, this article shows that the young online consumer is also politically active.

Keywords: Internet; political engagement; youth; consumerism

Digital Renaissance: Young Consumer and Citizen?

By
CLAES H. DE VREESE

The term *renaissance man* suggests an individual who has multiple skills and qualities, who knows a bit about a lot, and who can cover a whole spectrum of activities. Based on extant research, this is not the first term that comes to mind when thinking about young persons and their political engagement. Despite the focus on the enabling and empowering qualities of the Internet, many studies of young people and the Internet have not provided empirical evidence in support of an improved or revived civic youth culture online. This article addresses the question of how Internet use among young persons relates to their civic and political engagement and participation. The

Claes H. de Vreese (www.claesdevreese.com) is a professor and chair of political communication and director of the Amsterdam School of Communications Research (ASCoR) at the University of Amsterdam. He has published on media and campaign effects, electoral behavior, comparative journalism, EU referendums, and public opinion in journals such as Communication Research, European Journal of Political Research, EU Politics, West European Politics, *and* Political Communication.

DOI: 10.1177/0002716206298521

study investigates different uses of the Internet and proposes different forms of online civic and political participation. It shows that most Internet activities such as online communication, services use, and consumer behavior are positively related to different dimensions of civic and political participation.

Political participation among youth is a well-established field of research (and issue of concern). Research in the past has explored the relationship between media use and political participation (e.g., Shah, Kwak, and Holbert 2001), and today's media environment has if anything increased the relevance of looking at information and media use patterns to understand variation in political engagement. The media use among young people has been described by Rideout, Roberts, and Foehr (2005, 60), commenting on U.S. eight- to eighteen-year-olds, as follows: "Without question, this generation truly is the media generation, devoting more than a quarter of each day to media. As media devices become increasingly portable, and as they spread even further through young people's environments—from their schools, to their cars, to their pockets (e.g., cell phones with TV, audio, print, video gaming, and online capabilities)—media messages will become an even more ubiquitous presence in an already media-saturated world. Anything that takes up this much space in young people's lives deserves our full attention."

The young online consumer is also politically active.

The centrality of media (in the widest sense of the word) is a starting point for this study. However, to better understand the relationship between media use and civic and political engagement, the notions of civic and political engagement are in need of further consideration.

Civic and political engagement: Broadening the scope

General wisdom suggests that youth civic and political engagement is in decline and that extensive media use (in particular conceptualized as time spent with the media) facilitates this decline (e.g., Putnam 1995). However, some studies have suggested that the "decline" in interest and engagement among youth has more to do with negative or critical attitudes and ideas vis-à-vis politics (e.g., Henn, Weinstein, and Wring 2002) rather than a decline in interest. Yet other researchers have pointed to the limited conceptualization of political engagement in most research (Norris 2003). Dunleavy (1996) emphasized that "mainstream political behavior research has been criticized for its lack of engagement with political involvement in community-based or protest movements, and its unchanging reliance on institutional measures of participation." The focus has been on traditional politics, defined as "party politics, interest in government and voting" (Livingstone, Bober, and Helsper 2005, 288). A plea for widening the conceptualization of political and civic engagement finds resonance in several places (Barnhurst 1998; Dahlgren 2000; de Vreese 2006), and the Internet accentuates the need to investigate less traditional forms of engagement and participation.

The Internet offers a vast opportunity to be politically engaged: searching for information, at your discretion, from your preferred source, at your preferred time, and in your preferred mode. The Internet thus, in principle, increases the opportunities for individuals to be part of civic and political discussion and for becoming informed (Dahlgren 2000). The Internet provides particular potential for young people who are often politically engaged at local levels and in untraditional forms of participation (Delli Carpini 2000; O'Toole et al. 2003). The alternative forms of political participation taking place via the Internet can also be considered political engagement. After all, participation in both an election meeting and an online forum express political engagement (Livingstone, Bober, and Helsper 2005; Scheufele and Nisbet 2002). Digital modes of political participation include forums, polls, discussion groups, or organizing a Web site on a civic or political issue. One can also think of traditional participation in an electronic mode, such as downloading PDF files of election programs or sending an e-mail to an elected officer or the media.

Internet use: Opening the box

Previous research has focused mostly on the potential negative consequences of Internet use for political engagement and participation. However, some of this evidence has been questioned (Kraut et al. 1998; Nie and Erbring 2002), and later studies have shown both negative and positive effects (Bargh and McKenna 2004; Katz and Rice 2002; Shah et al. 2005). Indeed, for example, Kraut et al (2002) revised their original negative hypothesis (Kraut et al. 1998). In later studies, it has also been argued that differentiation is needed in the measures of use of the Internet and in the discussion of possible effects. Shah et al. (2005) emphasized that if different use is observed, different effects should be expected. It is indeed not so much the time spent online, but rather what is done online that matters (Shah et al. 2005; Shah, McLeod, and Yoon 2001; Schönbach, de Waal, and Lauf 2005). Nonetheless, most studies have been limited in the range of online activities that have been considered; some have tended to take a rather isolationist view of the Internet (rather than considering it in the context of other media); and finally, most studies have focused on particular forms of political engagement and participation.

Expectations

Based on the considerations outlined above, this article tests a number of expectations. First, we expect that (Hypothesis 1) news consumption (in traditional and online media) is positively related to political engagement and participation (see also Shah, McLeod, and Yoon 2001). Based on findings suggesting that some young people tend to act as active Internet "inter-actors" (Livingstone, Bober, and Helsper 2005) and multitaskers, we next expect (Hypothesis 2) that online activity in general is positively related to online political participation. Third, we expect that (Hypothesis 3) interactive online communication is positively related to political engagement and participation. Finally, we expect, given the centrality of the Internet for young persons, that (Hypothesis 4) the importance of the Internet exceeds the explanatory value of "traditional media use" for understanding variation in political engagement and participation.

Method

To test the proposed relationships between differentiated measures of youth Internet use and different dimensions of civic and political engagement, a survey was conducted among Dutch youth. Ten thousand respondents in the age group sixteen to twenty-four were drawn from the TAPPS database and invited to fill in an online survey. Of these, 2,849 respondents started filling in the survey and 2,404 completed it (M age = 19.2 years, SD = 2.29), resulting in a 24 percent response rate. This is an acceptable result for an online survey among this age group (Cook, Heath, and Thompson 2000). It was essential to collect new data for this research project, as existing data sets do not contain the necessary combination of variables. We chose an online survey design given our key interest in different uses of the Internet and their relation to different dimensions of civic and political engagement. We aimed not to make inferences about individuals who are online and offline but to be able to differentiate between different types of online behavior. This choice should also be seen in light of the very high degree of Internet penetration (80+ percent) in the Netherlands.

The survey was administered by the ComLab at the Amsterdam School of Communications Research (ASCoR) at the University of Amsterdam in February 2006. The average completion time was 9 minutes and 38 seconds. The survey contained detailed media use questions, questions about civic and political engagement, and a number of (social-demographic) background variables.

In this article, the key dependent measures pertain to *political participation*. We focus here on digital, online forms of participation. Digital participation was tapped using a battery of items measuring the frequency with which respondents participated in online political activities. A factor analysis (principal component analysis [PCA] with Varimax extraction) yielded two distinguishable factors, one labeled *digital passive participation* and one labeled *digital active participation*. The two factors (eigenvalues 3.82 and 1.07) explained 42 and 12 percent of the variance, respectively. Two scales were formed. Digital passive participation (M = 2.89, SD = 0.89) was measured using three items. All items asked respondents to indicate (on a 5-point scale ranging from *never* to *very frequently*) how often they in relation to political issues (1) visit Web sites of their local community,

(2) visit Web sites of the government and public administration, and (3) visit Web sites with political content. The items form an internally consistent scale with alpha = .77. Digital active participation (M = 3.05, SD = 0.88) was also measured using three items. Again, all items asked respondents to indicate (on a 5-point scale ranging from *never* to *very frequently*) how often they in relation to political issues (1) react online to a message or article on the Internet, (2) sign an online petition, and (3) participate in online polls. The three items form an acceptable scale of digital active participation, with alpha = .59.

The key *independent* variables relate to media use. Media use can be tapped in different ways (Chaffee 1986; Prior 2005). When investigating media effects, the construction of media exposure and attention variables should be dependent on the features of the actual media content (see Slater [2004] for this argument and de Vreese and Boomgaarden [2006] for an example and discussion). In this study, we distinguish between newspaper reading, different types of television viewing, and different types of Internet use. In addition, we tap *reading time* (newspapers, with a separate measure of reading free dailies), *viewing time* (television), and *surfing time* (Internet).

For *newspaper use*, a self-reported measure taps the frequency of reading different newspapers. For each title, respondents indicated how often they read the title, ranging from *never, 1-2 days a week, 3-4 days a week,* to *5-7 days a week.* A combined measure of newspaper reading (standardized to range from 1 to 5) was constructed (M = 3.69, SD = 1.15). For *television use*, we asked respondents to indicate how often they watched different channels ranging from *never, 1-2 days a week, 3-4 days a week,* to *5-7 days a week.* A factor analysis yielded two distinct factors of viewing behavior (eigenvalue 3.98 and 1.85) explaining 31 and 14 percent of the variance, respectively. The two factors represent public channels viewing (M = 1.83, SD = 0.73, alpha = .78) and commercial channel viewing (M = 2.41, SD = 0.66, alpha = .78).

Since a main purpose of the study was to differentiate between types of Internet use, we included a list of Internet activities. A factor analysis yielded four distinguishable factors (eigenvalues 2.91, 1.99, 1.37, 1.10; explained variance 18 percent, 12 percent, 9 percent and 7 percent, totaling 46 percent). The first is a three-item measure of *Internet news use* (visiting newspaper sites, following news blogs, reading showbiz news) (M = 2.05, SD = 0.83, alpha = .59). The second is a three-item measure of *Internet services use* (e-banking, job searching, house searching) (M = 2.39, SD = 0.68, alpha = .65). The third is a two-item measure of *Internet entertainment use* (entertainment downloading, music listening) (M = 3.59, SD = 1.11, alpha = .69). The fourth is a measure of using the Internet to keep up to date about *club or associations activities* (M = 2.46, SD = 1.31). We finally included measures for the frequency of different types of Internet communication (measured on a 5-point scale): e-mailing (M = 4.25, SD = 0.77), social networking (chatting, online communities) (M = 3.33, SD = 0.98), and forum participation (M = 2.29, SD = 1.24). These types of Internet and communication use bear some resemblance with Norris and Jones's (1998) distinction between researchers (news users), home consumers (services), political expressives (forum use), and party animals (entertainment use).

Finally, we included a number of control variables. Given the homogeneity of the respondents in terms of age, we discarded this factor ($M = 19.2$ years, $SD = 2.29$). Key controls are gender (60 percent female) and educational level (measured on a 4-point scale of educational level, $M = 1.76$, $SD = 0.85$). Following Prior (2005), we also included a measure of *relative entertainment preference* (REP) (measures as entertainment viewing)/(entertainment viewing + news viewing). Respondents could choose, in five rounds, between two programs (entertainment versus news/current affairs). REP was recoded to range from 0 to 1 with higher values expressing a relative entertainment preference ($M = .73$, $SD = .24$). We expect that in an abundant media choice situation, an intrinsic preference for entertainment products above news and current affairs is negatively related to political engagement and participation. We also included a control for *political engagement*, which was measured using three items (5-point Likert scales). The items (1: To me it is important to follow political discussions; 2: It is important for society that as many people as possible follow political discussions; 3: Politics is interesting) form a reliable scale (alpha = .79) ($M = 1.92$, $SD = 0.76$).

Results

In the investigation of how media use relates to political participation among young people, we see (Table 1) that (following hypothesis 1) news consumption in both traditional and online media is positively related to political participation. However, the relationships between traditional media use (newspapers and television) are weak and, except for public television viewing in the case of traditional digital participation, all below the threshold of significance. Online news use is positively and significantly related to both forms of online participation. Hypothesis 1 is therefore partially supported.

Looking at the variety of online activities, we find that use of online services (such as e-banking), keeping updated with clubs and associations, as well as consumption of entertainment products, including music downloading, are all significantly related to our dependent variables. All relationships are positive, except between music and entertainment consumption and digital passive participation. Hypothesis 2, which predicted these positive relationships, is therefore largely confirmed. Similarly, we can confirm hypothesis 3, which suggested that interactive online communication is positively related to political participation. Finally, as expected (hypothesis 4), the explanatory value of Internet use exceeds the explanatory value of "traditional media use" for understanding variation in political engagement and participation. The Internet block of variables accounts for 15 percent (passive) and 26 percent (active) of explained variation, while the traditional media use variables account for 14 percent (passive) and 5 percent (active) of the variation (this finding is not reported in Table 1).

We find no effects of our sociodemographic controls (gender and education). We find an expected negative relationship between relative entertainment preference

TABLE 1
DIGITAL PASSIVE AND ACTIVE PARTICIPATION:
THE POSITIVE RELATIONS BETWEEN CONSUMPTION AND POLITICS

	Digital Passive Participation		Digital Active Participation	
	Beta	SE	Beta	SE
Controls				
Gender (female)	−.03	.03	−.01	−.03
Education	.00	.01	−.01	.01
Print media				
Reading time (newspaper)	.00	.01	−.02	.01
Reading time free (newspaper)	.00	.01	.02	.01
Newspaper reading	−.01	.01	−.01	.02
Television				
Viewing time TV	.01	.01	.02	.01
Public viewing	.11°°°	.02	.02	.02
Commercial viewing	−.01	.02	.04	.03
Relative entertainment preference (REP)	−.14°°°	.06	−.08°°°	.06
Internet				
Surfing time	.00	.00	−.02	.01
News	.20°°°	.02	.19°°°	.02
Services	.20°°°	.02	.04°	.02
Music/entertainment	−.05°	.01	.06°°°	.01
Club	.04°	.01	.05°°	.01
E-mail	.07°°°	.02	.04°	.02
Online networking	−.01	.01	.04°	.01
Forum	.06°°°	.01	.37°°°	.01
Political engagement	.26°°°	.01	.12°°°	.02
N	2,404		2,404	
R^2	.38		.33	

NOTE: Entries are standardized beta coefficients and standard errors.
°$p < .05$. °°$p < .01$. °°°$p < .001$.

and participation and a positive relationship between political engagement and digital forms of online participation.

Discussion

This article set out to investigate the relationship between Internet use among young people and their "political consumption" and political participation. The article emphasizes that Internet use has to be understood in more detail. First, we found that use of news and current affairs media, both offline and online, is generally positively related to online political engagement and participation for young people but that online news use is a stronger predictor for online partici- pation. The study also shows that it is not the time spent online (or with another medium) that matters but rather the activities that are undertaken (see Shah et al. [2005] for corroborating evidence). The study moved beyond the established positive effects of news use and also included online communication, use of dig- ital services, and being part of online networks and communities. These activities were all found to be positively related to political participation. The study thus supports Putnam's (1995) idea that social networks are positively related to polit- ical participation, though the networks alluded to by Putnam were more likely to be offline. Our findings corroborate the observation that social networks matter, but very importantly point out that *online* social networking and interactivity with others is also good for political participation.

It is not the time spent online . . . that matters but rather the activities that are undertaken.

The study found robust positive relationships between diverse uses of the Internet, including services and consumption, and various measures of engage- ment and participation. We applied a broad notion of political participation and identified in particular digital forms of online participation. Online communica- tion and activities were found to be more important for digital forms of political participation. In essence, it suggests that among young people, communicating online and making use of online services correlate strongly, significantly, and robustly with online political participation (such as, for example, taking part in online polls, online petitions, e-mail letters to the editor, etc). This suggests that a specific kind of "digital citizenship" is observable. These findings run somewhat counter to the typology suggested by Livingstone, Bober, and Helsper (2005), who found that civic-minded young persons was a distinct category, while our findings show that civic-mindedness, digital political participation, consumption, and online social networking can go hand in hand.

The study has a number of caveats. While it is positive that we were able to include differentiated measures of Internet use and differentiated measures of polit- ical participation to study the consumption of politics in an appropriate context, the survey is obviously limited in its cross-sectional nature to only speculate about the causal direction of the relationships observed. Also, our focus on online young citizens (and our use of an online survey instrument) has advantages, but it also makes us cautious in the interpretations. Our "nonfindings" of newspaper impact on participation could be influenced by our sample, in which readership might be less prominent than in a nononline sample. These reservations notwithstanding, we have taken a step forward toward understanding young persons' media use and its relationship with political engagement and participation. The contours of a renaissance young person who can be both an online consumer *and* a citizen are visible.

The contours of a renaissance young person who can be both an online consumer and *citizen are visible.*

References

Bargh, J. A., and K. Y. A. McKenna. 2004. The Internet and social life. *Annual Review of Psychology* 55:573-90.

Barnhurst, K. 1998. Politics in the fine meshes: Young citizens, power and media. *Media, Culture & Society* 20:201-18.

Chaffee, S. H. 1986. Measurement and effects of attention to media news. *Human Communication Research* 13 (1): 76-107.

Cook, C., F. Heath, and R. L. Thompson. 2000. A meta-analysis of response rates in Web- or Internet-based surveys. *Educational and Psychological Measurement* 60 (6): 821-36.

Dahlgren, P. 2000. The Internet and the democratization of civic culture. *Political Communication* 17:335-40.

Delli Carpini, M. X. 2000. Gen.com: Youth, civic engagement, and the new information environment. *Political Communication* 17:341-49.

de Vreese, C. H. 2006. *10 observations about the past, present, and future of political communication.* Inaugural lecture delivered at the University of Amsterdam, Chair in Political Communication. Amsterdam: Amsterdam University Press.

de Vreese, C. H., and H. Boomgaarden. 2006. How content moderates the effects of television news on political knowledge and engagement. *Acta Politica. International Journal of Political Science* 41: 317-41.

Dunleavy, P. 1996. Political behavior: Institutional and experiential approaches. In *A new handbook of political science*, ed. R. Goodin and H.-D. Klingemann. Oxford: Oxford University Press.

Henn, M., M. Weinstein, and D. Wring. 2002. A generation apart? Youth and political participation in Britain. *British Journal of Politics and International Relations* 4 (2): 167-92.

Katz, J. E., and R. E. Rice. 2002. Project syntopia: Social consequences of Internet. *IT & Society* 1 (1): 166-79.

Kraut, R., S. Kiesler, B. Boneva, J. Cummings, V. Helgeson, and A. Crawford. 2002. Internet paradox revisited. *Journal of Social Issues* 58 (1): 49-74.

Kraut, R., M. Patterson, V. Lundmark, S. Kiesler, T. Mukopadhyay, and W. Scherlis. 1998. Internet paradox: A social technology that reduces social involvement and psychological well-being? *American Psychologist* 53:1017-31.

Livingstone, S., M. Bober, and E. J. Helsper. 2005. Active participation or just more information? Young people's take-up of opportunities to act and interact on the Internet. *Information, Communication & Society* 8 (3): 287-314.

Nie, N. H., and L. Erbring. 2002. Internet and mass media: A preliminary report. *IT & Society* 1 (2): 134-41.

Norris, P. 2003. Young people & political activism: From the politics of loyalties to the politics of choice? Rapport voor het Council of Europe Symposium: "Young people and democratic institutions: From disillusionment to participation," November, in Straatsburg, Germany.

Norris, P., and P. Jones. 1998. Virtual democracy. *Harvard International Journal of Press/Politics* 3 (2): 1–4.

O'Toole, T., M. Lister, D. Marsh, J. Jones, and A. McDonagh. 2003. Tuning out or left out? Participation and nonparticipation among young people. *Contemporary Politics* 9 (1): 45-61.

Prior, M. 2005. News vs. entertainment: How increasing media choice widens gaps in political knowledge and turnout. *American Journal of Political Science* 49 (3): 577-92.

Putnam, R. D. 1995. Tuning in, tuning out: The strange disappearance of social capital in America. *PS: Political Science and Politics* 28:664-83.

Rideout, V., D. F. Roberts, and U. G. Foehr. 2005. *Generation M: Media in the lives of 8-18 year-olds.* Washington DC: Kaiser Family Foundation.

Scheufele, D. A., and M. C. Nisbet. 2002. Being a citizen online: New opportunities and dead ends. *Harvard International Journal of Press/Politics* 7 (3): 55-75.

Schönbach, K., E. de Waal, and E. Lauf. 2005. Online newspapers: A substitute or complement for print newspapers and other information channels. *Communications* 30 (1): 55-72.

Shah, D. V., J. Cho, W. P. Eveland Jr., and N. Kwak. 2005. Information and expression in a digital age: Modeling Internet effects on civic participation. *Communication Research* 32 (5): 531-65.

Shah, D. V., N. Kwak, and R. L. Holbert. 2001. "Connecting" and "disconnecting" with civic life: Patterns of Internet use and the production of social capital. *Political Communication* 18 (2): 141-62.

Shah, D. V., J. M. McLeod, and S. Yoon. 2001. Communication, context, and community: An exploration of print, broadcast and Internet influences. *Communication Research* 28 (4): 464-506.

Slater, Michael D. 2004. Operationalizing and analyzing exposure: The foundation of media effects research. *Journalism and Mass Communication Quarterly* 81 (1): 168-83.

Political Consumerism: How Communication and Consumption Orientations Drive "Lifestyle Politics"

By
DHAVAN V. SHAH,
DOUGLAS M. McLEOD,
EUNKYUNG KIM,
SUN YOUNG LEE,
MELISSA R. GOTLIEB,
SHIRLEY S. HO,
and
HILDE BREIVIK

Historians and cultural theorists have long asserted that a desire to express political concerns often guides consumer behavior, yet such political consumerism has received limited attention from social scientists. Here, the authors explore the relationship of political consumerism with dispositional factors, communication variables, and consumption orientations using data collected from a panel survey conducted in the United States between February 2002 and July 2005. The authors test a theorized model using both cross-sectional and auto-regressive panel analyses. The static and change models reveal that conventional and online news use encourage political consumerism indirectly through their influence on political talk and environmental concerns. However, media use may also have some suppressive effects by reducing the desire to protect others from harmful messages. Results demonstrate how communication practices and consumption orientations work together to influence political consumerism beyond previously delineated factors. Implications for declines in political and civic participation and youth socialization are discussed.

Keywords: antisweatshop; boycott; buycott; fair trade; lifestyle politics; political consumerism; socially conscious consumption

The intersection of markets and politics has a long history. As Breen (2004) convincingly argued, consumer politics shaped the American Revolution and laid the groundwork for nationhood. The colonists, who differed in many respects, shared an identity as aggrieved consumers of British goods. It was through their behavior as consumers that the colonists developed their most innovative and potent form of political action: boycotts (Schudson 2007 [this volume]).

The act of boycotting remains a powerful form of political engagement, though it is now seen as part of a much broader array of consumer behaviors that are shaped by a desire to express and support political and ethical perspectives. Labeled *political consumerism* by some (Stolle, Hooghe, and Micheletti 2005) and *socially*

DOI: 10.1177/0002716206298714

conscious consumption by others (Anderson and Cunningham 1972; Keum et al. 2004), it is puzzling that, considering their historical and contemporary relevance, these behaviors have been so rarely subjected to social science inquiry.

This is particularly surprising if one recognizes that the politics of consumption is central to a large number of modern social movements, including but not limited to World Trade Organization protests, fair-trade advocacy, antisweatshop

Dhavan V. Shah is Maier-Bascom Professor in the School of Journalism and Mass Communication and the Department of Political Science at the University of Wisconsin–Madison. His recent research focuses on (1) the capacity of interpersonal and mass communication, particularly the Internet, to encourage engagement in civic life and (2) the influence of news framing on social judgment. He recently received the Krieghbaum Under-40 Award for early career contributions to the field.

Douglas M. McLeod is a professor in the School of Journalism and Mass Communication at the University of Wisconsin–Madison, where he conducts three interrelated lines of inquiry: (1) social conflicts and the media; (2) media content, public opinion, and knowledge; and (3) advertising and consumer culture. He recently coedited The Evolution of Key Mass Communication Concepts.

Eunkyung Kim is a doctoral student in the School of Journalism and Mass Communication at the University of Wisconsin–Madison. Her research interests include (1) the impact of interpersonal discussion and media use on information processing and political behavior, (2) the processes underlying opinion formation about science and politics, and (3) quantitative research methods.

Sun Young Lee is a doctoral candidate in the School of Journalism and Mass Communication at the University of Wisconsin–Madison. Her research focuses on health communication, socially responsible consumer behavior, and communication research methods. Specific interests include the effects of emotion, cognition, and risk perceptions on social and health-related issues.

Melissa R. Gotlieb is a doctoral student in the School of Journalism and Mass Communication at the University of Wisconsin–Madison. Her research focuses on understanding (1) media effects on perceptions, attitudes, and behavior from both a social cognitive and semiotic perspective and (2) the role of individual differences and predispositions in fostering a more active and critical consumption of media.

Shirley S. Ho is a doctoral student in the School of Journalism and Mass Communication at the University of Wisconsin–Madison. Her research focuses on the social impact of communication technologies, the influence of media on public opinion about science- and health-related issues, and the impact of media on participatory and consumption behavior.

Hilde Breivik is a master's student in the School of Journalism and Mass Communication at the University of Wisconsin–Madison. Her interests center on the intersection of politics and consumerism. She is the co-author of the paper "Representation in Transition: Media Portrayal of the UN in the Context of the War in Iraq," presented at the International Communication Association in 2004.

NOTE: The authors, who all contributed equally to this manuscript, thank DDB-Chicago for access to the Life Style Study, and Marty Horn and Chris Callahan, in particular, for sharing study details. Major support for the panel study reported in this article was provided through grants from the Russell Sage Foundation, Carnegie Corporation of New York, Pew Charitable Trusts, Center for Information & Research On Civic Learning & Engagement (CIRCLE), Rockefeller Brother Fund, and Damm Fund of the Journal Foundation. Conclusions in this article are those of the authors and do not necessarily reflect the views of DDB-Chicago or the funding sources.

activism, and the antiapartheid movement (Bennett and Lagos 2007 [this volume]; Micheletti and Stolle 2007 [this volume]). More important, perhaps, is the introduction of the agendas of these social movements into the daily practices of ordinary citizens. Such political consumerism deserves special attention because it involves a large cross-section of the citizenry and has come to structure a wide range of consumer decisions.

Defined as the act of selecting among products and producers based on social, political, or ethical considerations, political consumerism may provide people with an alternative mode to engage with public issues outside of conventional political and civic behaviors such as voting or volunteering (Bennett and Entman 2000). Consumers who engage in such behaviors seek to hold companies and governments responsible for the manner in which products are produced, as well as for the nature of social and environmental consequences of this production. In the process, they challenge narrow definitions of political participation.

In this article, we explore individual differences and change over time in levels of political consumerism as a function of dispositional factors, communication variables, and consumption orientations. To do so, we use data collected from a three-wave panel survey conducted in the United States between February 2002 and July 2005. A number of the variables we consider, such as conventional and online news consumption and political talk, have proven to be consistent predictors of conventional forms of participation. We do this to examine whether models of communication and participation can be extended to political consumerism, yet we also consider how orientations toward consumption may mediate the effect of communication on political consumerism in an effort to further specify the antecedents of this phenomenon.

Political consumerism and lifestyle politics

By using the market as a venue to express political and moral concerns, political consumerism is a manifestation of what Bennett (1998) has termed "lifestyle politics." It reflects the broader tendency to see political meaning in recreational experiences, entertainment choices, fashion decisions, and other personal happenings. As Sapiro (2000, 4) explained, political consumerism can be readily adopted because it involves the "use of repertoires or familiar languages of action and interaction" (see also Frank 1994; Traugott 1995). As "politics by other means," it reflects a movement away from institutional and formal modes of engagement. Instead, it is grounded in the belief that day-to-day action might be a more effective way to achieve political ends by using the market to influence public policy (Sapiro 2000).

Past research indicates that women, young people, and more educated individuals are particularly likely to make consumption decisions based on political and ethical considerations. Political consumerism has been linked to factors known to explain political participation such as religiosity, partisanship, and government trust, but it is also associated with postmaterialism and a sense of moral obligation, orientations more closely tied with "lifestyle politics" (Bennett 1998; Inglehart 1997; Stolle, Hooghe, and Micheletti 2005). Notably, political consumers' low regard for the political establishment may indicate a general skepticism of institutionalized power and authority (Zijderveld 2000). Rather than relying on governmental institutions, these consumers have decided to take on this responsibility themselves through their economic behaviors (Beck 1997; Shapiro and Hacker-Cordon 1999).

As "politics by other means," [political consumerism] reflects a movement away from institutional and formal modes of engagement.

Theses associations and what they indicate about the politicization of the day-to-day suggest how political consumerism "blurs the distinction between the public and the private realms" (Stolle, Hooghe, and Micheletti 2005, 254). Indeed, political consumerism speaks to the fact that for many people civic engagement only makes sense when it is organized around their personal values (Shah, Domke, and Wackman 1996). People might prefer participating in informal, lifestyle-based mobilization as a way to avoid traditional politics (Eliasoph 1998; Putnam 2002). They see the link between personal consumption and the politics of "environmentalism, labor rights, human rights, and sustainable development" (Micheletti 2003, 2). Research finds that media use, particularly news consumption, plays an important role in predicting such socially conscious consumption (Holt 2000; Keum et al. 2004). If institutional forms of political participation are any indication, news consumption works through political talk to define concerns and help forge the connection between these issues and action.

Communication, participation, and environmentalism

A particularly relevant theoretical framework for understanding how communication factors may encourage political consumerism is the O-S-O-R perspective, originally suggested by Markus and Zajonc (1985). The first O in this model represents "the set of structural, cultural, cognitive, and motivational characteristics the audience brings to the reception situation that affect the impact of messages (S)," whereas the second O represents "what is likely to happen between the reception of messages and the subsequent response (R)" (McLeod, Kosicki, and McLeod 1994, 146-47). In sum, the O-S-O-R model provides a lens for explaining the causal ordering of relationships among structural sociodemographic factors, individual predispositions, messages obtained from media, and attitudinal and behavioral outcomes.

This perspective emphasizes that the effects of mass media on participatory behaviors are typically not direct but operate indirectly through factors such as political talk and procivic attitudes. These insights have been summarized as a *communication mediation model* predicting participation, with political talk as an intervening variable (Sotirovic and McLeod 2001). Shah et al. (2005) found that the effect of both traditional and online news media use on civic participation is mediated by political talk among citizens. These findings illustrate the role news plays in prompting political talk and the implications of talk for political action.

Although most past research employing this model has focused on conventional models of civic and political participation (Shah et al. 2005; Sotirovic and McLeod 2001), a wider range of prosocial behaviors has been theorized. Of particular relevance for this study, the O-S-O-R framework has been used to study the relationship between media use and individual expression of environmental concerns (Holbert, Kwak, and Shah 2003). This is not true of most prior efforts to connect mass communication use to proenvironmental attitudes, which have generally relied on direct effects models of agenda setting (Atwater, Salwen, and Anderson 1985), news framing (Karlberg 1997), or cultivation (Shanahan, Morgan, and Stenbjerre 1997). These studies have generally offered a pessimistic or inconclusive view of media influence on environmental action.

These studies share the view that people mainly "learn about environmental issues through the news, rather than by direct experience" (Karlberg 1997, 22), understanding environmental threats such as global warming and pollution through secondhand media accounts (Shanahan, Morgan, and Stenbjerre 1997). In line with this, Atwater, Salwen, and Anderson (1985) provided evidence that news media heighten concern about the environment. Other work has observed a relationship between TV viewing and environmental concern, but it did not find that concern influenced environmental action (Shanahan, Morgan, and Stenbjerre 1997).

By contrast, Holbert, Kwak, and Shah (2003), who adopted an O-S-O-R framework, found that media can have a positive influence on proenvironmental behavior among individuals who consume factual media content. Individuals who express environmental concern tend to consume public affairs programming and nature documentaries at higher levels, with this viewing, in turn, positively predicting efforts to engage in proenvironmental behaviors such as recycling and making a special effort to purchase products that are energy efficient. The authors theorized that environmentally concerned individuals are perhaps motivated to seek out and attend to relevant information provided by the media and that the consumption of such information mediates the relationship between concern and actual behavior. However, they acknowledged that their reliance on cross-sectional data limits their claims concerning the causal order among these variables.

Consumption orientations and political consumerism

Indeed, a sizeable body of research in the fields of political science, sociology, psychology, and marketing provides evidence of a direct association between environmental concern and environmentally friendly behavior (Bamberg 2003; Blake 2001; Mainieri et al. 1997; Roberts and Bacon 1997). This relationship tends to be concentrated among those who are politically interested and civically engaged (Keum et al. 2004; Guerin, Crete, and Mercier 2001). Thus, it is likely that environmental concern is spurred by news use and correlated with other socially conscious consumption behaviors.

The impact of environmental concern on socially conscious behavior may include buying a product that is benign toward the environment, purchasing recyclable or recycled packaging, boycotting companies that are seen as harmful to the environment or society, or favoring companies and brands that support shared values. According to Kempton (1993), when public concern is high on an environmental issue, consumer actions are far more common than political actions. Corroborating evidence for this relationship is found by Minton and Rose (1997), who observed that the more concerned individuals are about the environment, the more likely they are to seek or purchase environmentally friendly products.

However, environmental concern may not be the only consumption orientation that is shaped by media exposure and that influences political consumerism. Of particular interest is the concept of advertising paternalism, the belief that certain types of commercial messages should be limited to protect sensitive populations from the perceived harm that they pose. Originally examined in the context of impersonal influence research (McLeod, Eveland, and Nathanson 1997), the "practice of treating or governing others in a parental manner, sometimes limiting others' rights with a benign intention" (Chia, Lu, and McLeod 2004, 115), has its roots in exposure to objectionable media content. Studies have found that paternalism is linked to the third-person perception, where people believe that others are more vulnerable to undesirable media content than themselves, which in turn drives the desire to censor the content deemed harmful, such as pornography, TV violence, and rap music (McLeod, Eveland, and Nathanson 1997; Rojas, Shah, and Faber 1996).

When placed in context, advertising paternalism can therefore be seen as a manifestation of an individual's desire to restrict commercial messages and content perceived as harmful to others. A sensitivity to messages thought to be damaging to vulnerable populations, such as children, or containing unacceptable depictions, such as overly sexualized imagery, may reflect a deeper belief that the companies that engage in such targeting and messaging deserve economic countermeasures such as boycotts. Thus, we speculate that ad paternalism may encourage political consumption, as consumers express their concern about social issues and promote the protection of groups by avoiding certain products and patronizing others.

Theorized Model

These insights regarding the range of factors that might contribute to political consumerism can be summarized in the following model (Figure 1). This model begins with demographics and predispositions (O_1), the background factors that likely structure all of the subsequent factors in the model. This block includes a range of factors previously found to influence differences in political consumerism, as well as predictors of communication practices and consumption orientations. The second block contains information-seeking variables via mass media (S), specifically, conventional and online news consumption. These stimuli are expected to influence the amount of political discussion and the degree of environmental concern, as found by much past research, as well as advertising paternalism (i.e., protectionist attitudes regarding commercial messages deemed harmful). These outcome orientations are then expected to most directly influence political consumerism, explaining both individual differences and change over time. Notably, consistent with models of communication mediation, we expect the effects of information-seeking variables in this dynamic to be indirect on political consumerism.

Method

To test this model, we use panel survey data conducted in February 2002, November 2004, and July 2005. February 2002 data were collected by Synovate, a commercial survey research firm, for DDB-Chicago's annual mail survey, the "Life Style Study." The Life Style Study relies on a stratified quota sampling technique to recruit respondents. Although this method differs from probability sampling procedures, it produces highly comparable data (see Putnam 2000). For details on this procedure, see Shah et al. (2005).

Of the 5,000 mail surveys distributed, 3,580 usable responses were received, which represents a response rate of 71.6 percent against the mailout for the February 2002 survey. For the November 2004 survey, we developed a custom questionnaire and recontacted the individuals who completed the February 2002 survey. Due to some panel erosion in the two years since the original survey, 2,450 questionnaires were mailed. We received 1,484 completed responses, for a panel retention rate of 41.4 percent and a response rate against the mailout of 60.1 percent. For the July 2005 recontact, another questionnaire was developed. Again, individuals who completed the prior survey were recontacted. Due to panel erosion, 1,446 questionnaires were mailed to November 2004 respondents. With 1,080 completed responses, the panel retention rate was 72.7 percent with a response rate against the mailout of 74.7 percent.

Measures

The criterion variable of *political consumerism* was operationalized as an index of three indicators measured on a 6-point agree-disagree scale: (1) "I will not buy a product from a company whose values I do not share," (2) "I have boycotted products or companies in the past," and (3) "I make a special effort to buy from companies that support charitable causes" (first recontact: $M = 3.95$, $SD = 1.22$, alpha = .60; second recontact: $M = 3.99$, $SD = 1.20$, alpha = .63).

FIGURE 1
O-S-O-R MODEL OF POLITICAL CONSUMERISM

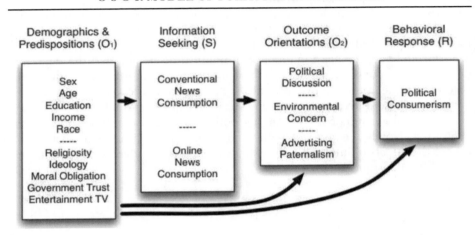

Demographic variables were measured in the baseline survey. Respondents' *age* was measured as a continuous variable (M = 47.46 years, SD = 15.72), and *gender* was a dichotomous variable (56.40 percent female). *Education* was assessed using an 18-point nonlinear scale ranging from "attended elementary school" to "attended grad school" (M = 14.04, SD = 2.29). *Total household income* was assessed on a 13-point nonlinear scale ranging from $5,000 to $117,500 ($M$ = $50,120, SD = $33,785). *Ethnicity* was measured as a dichotomous variable with white coded as 0 and nonwhite coded as 1 (10.40 percent nonwhite).

Predispositions including ideology, religiosity, and entertainment television viewing were also measured in the baseline survey. Moral obligation and trust in government were measured in the first recontact. *Ideology* was measured using five categories ranging from *very conservative* (coded 1) to *very liberal* (coded 5) (M = 2.70, SD = 0.97). *Religiosity* was measured using a composite index of three 6-point agree-disagree items: (1) "Religion is an important part of my life," (2) "It's important to me to find spiritual fulfillment," and (3) "I believe in God" (M = 4.72, SD = 1.27, alpha = .81). *Moral obligation* was measured by indexing two 6-point agree-disagree items: (1) "I have an obligation to help others in need" and (2) "It is important to me to reach out to others who need help" (M = 4.62, SD = 1.06, r = .68). *Trust in government* was an index of two 6-point agree-disagree items: (1) "An honest man cannot get elected to high office" and (2) "Elected officials don't tell us what they really think" (M = 3.09, SD = 1.28, r = .55). Habitual entertainment TV viewing was measured by summing viewership of twenty-three hour-long and twenty half-hour shows (weighted by .50) (M = 4.90, SD = 3.60, alpha = .78).

Next, conventional news consumption, online news consumption, political talk, environmental concern, and advertising paternalism were created to tap communication practices and consumption orientations. All of these variables, with the exception of advertising paternalism, were measured in the first and second recontact studies. In both studies, conventional news consumption was created by averaging across standardized measures of exposure and attention to newspapers and television news (first recontact: $M = 0.001$, $SD = 0.77$, alpha = .92; second recontact: $M = 0.003$, $SD = 0.78$, alpha = .87). Likewise, online news consumption was created by standardizing and averaging measures of exposure and attention (first recontact: $M = 0.005$, $SD = 0.92$, alpha = .93; second recontact: $M = 0.01$, $SD = 1.16$, alpha = .64).

We measured *political talk* by using a composite index of six items in which respondents were asked to indicate how much they talked about politics with (1) "friends," (2) "family," (3) "coworkers," (4) "ethnic minorities," (5) "people who disagree with me," and (6) "people who agree with me" on an 8-point frequency scale (first recontact: $M = 3.64$, $SD = 1.71$, alpha = .89; second recontact: $M = 2.75$, $SD = 1.68$, alpha = .92). *Environmental concern* was created by averaging responses to the following 6-point agree-disagree items: (1) "I would be willing to accept a lower standard of living to conserve energy," (2) "I'm very concerned about global warming," and (3) I "contributed to an environmental or conservation organization" (first recontact: $M = 2.72$, $SD = 0.90$, alpha = .45; second recontact: $M = 2.87$, $SD = 0.93$, alpha = .43). *Advertising paternalism* was an index containing the following 6-point agree-disagree items: (1) "Advertising for beer and wine should be taken off TV," (2) "Advertising directed to children should be taken off television," and (3) "TV commercials place too much emphasis on sex" (baseline: $M = 3.76$, $SD = 1.16$, alpha = .57; second recontact: $M = 4.01$, $SD = 1.23$, alpha = .69).

Analytic strategy

To examine the effects of communication practices and consumption orientations on political consumerism, we employed two different analytic strategies: (1) a cross-sectional model, which relates individual differences in these indicators based solely on data from the first recontact survey; and (2) an auto-regressive model, which relates aggregate change estimates generated by lagging baseline or first recontact variables on their second recontact counterparts.

Each approach has unique advantages and disadvantages (Finkel 1995). The cross-sectional model does not take advantage of the panel design; nonetheless, we include it here for three reasons: (1) it retains a larger and more representative sample; (2) it serves as a baseline against which we compare the auto-regressive model; and (3) it allows us to connect this research to previous scholarship that has mainly relied on cross-sectional analyses.

In the auto-regressive model, each T_2 measure is regressed on its corresponding T_1 measure, with the T_1 measure retained as a common variance component. The shared variance between T_1 and T_2 measures represents temporal stability and effectively controls for prior levels of the variable, making the auto-regressive component interpretable as relating change among outcomes in a synchronous model. This approach aims to explain variance among endogenous T_2 variables while accounting for stability in these variables over time.

Whether modeling the cross-sectional relationships or relating change over time, we employed a series of path analyses using ordinary least squares (OLS) regression to test the mediating role of the outcome orientations (political talk, environmental concern, and advertising paternalism) for the effects of information seeking on political consumerism. To do this, we first used the demographic, predispositional, and information-seeking variables to predict the outcome orientations before including these orientations in the models predicting the behavioral responses of political consumerism. This was done to observe the nature of the relationships among news consumption and the factors subsequent in our model.

Results

The cross-sectional model

We used the OLS regression model to test the outcome variables of political talk, environmental concern, and then political consumerism. Because there was no measure of advertising paternalism in the first recontact survey, that variable was not included in the cross-sectional analysis. The predictor variables were entered simultaneously but are presented in blocks according to their assumed causal order in the O-S-O-R framework.

Both conventional and online news consumption . . . were substantial predictors of political talk.

Predicting political talk. The regression model predicting political talk performed well, accounting for a total of 26.5 percent of the variance (see Table 1). Demographic and predispositional factors (O_1) accounted for 12.0 percent of the variance in political talk. Among these predictors, age, gender, income, education, ideology, and moral obligation remained significant in the final model. Those who were more educated ($\beta = .09$, $p < .001$), had higher incomes ($\beta = .12$, $p < .001$), were more liberal ($\beta = .08$, $p < .001$), and held stronger moral obligations ($\beta = .08$, $p < .01$) were more likely to participate in political talk; while those who were female ($\beta = -.07$, $p < .05$) or older ($\beta = -.13$, $p < .001$) were less likely to engage in political talk. Both conventional and online news consumption (S) were substantial predictors of political talk, accounting for 14.5 percent of incremental variance. Both conventional ($\beta = .36$, $p < .001$) and online news consumption ($\beta = .11$, $p < .001$) were positively related to political talk.

TABLE 1
CROSS-SECTIONAL MODELS OF POLITICAL TALK,
ENVIRONMENTAL CONCERN, AND POLITICAL CONSUMERISM

	Political Talk	Environmental Concern	Political Consumerism
Demographics			
Gender (female)	−.07°	.04	.03
Age	−.13°°°	.13°°°	.06°
Education	.09°°°	−.02	.08°°
Income	.12°°°	−.08°°	.01
Race (nonwhite)	−.02	−.03	−.07°
Predispositions (O_1)			
Religiosity	.05	−.09°°	.03
Ideology	.08°°°	.15°°°	−.04
Moral obligation	.08°°	.25°°°	.20°°°
Trust in government	−.02	−.08°°	−.03
Entertainment TV	.04	.03	−.02
News use (S)			
Conventional news use	.36°°°	.07°	.03
Online news use	.11°°°	−.01	.05
Orientations (O_2)			
Political talk	—	—	.11°°°
Environmental concern	—	—	.13°°°
Total R^2 (percentage)	26.5	12.6	13.2

NOTE: Cell entries are final standardized regression coefficients.
°$p < .05$. °°$p < .01$. °°°$p < .001$.

Predicting environmental concern. A total of 12.6 percent of the variance in environmental concern was accounted for by the variables in the model. Demographics and predispositions (O_1) accounted for 12.0 percent of the variance in environmental concern. Among the sociodemographic variables, age, income, religion, ideology, moral obligation, and trust in government remained significant in the final model. The older ($\beta = .13, p < .001$) and the more liberal ($\beta = .15, p < .001$) respondents showed higher levels of environmental concern, while those with higher incomes ($\beta = −.08, p < .01$) and those who were more religious ($\beta = −.09, p < .01$) were less likely to express environmental concern. Moral obligation ($\beta = .25, p < .001$) was positively related to environmental concern, while trust in government ($\beta = −.08, p < .01$) was negatively related to environmental concern, supportive of an antiestablishment morality. Consumption of news (S) also predicted environmental concern, accounting for an additional 0.6 percent of the variance, most explained by conventional news use ($\beta = .07, p < .05$).

Predicting political consumerism. A total of 13.2 percent of the variance in political consumerism was accounted for by the variables in the model. Demographics and predispositions accounted for 9.8 percent of the variance.

Among the demographic factors, age, race, and education remained significant in the final model. The older ($\beta = .06$, $p < .05$) and more educated ($\beta = .08$, $p < .01$) respondents were more likely to take part in political consumerism, while non-whites ($\beta = -.07$, $p < .05$) were less likely. Among the predispositions, only moral obligation ($\beta = .20$, $p < .001$) was related to political consumerism, reinforcing the view that personal values and a sense of altruism underlie certain forms of political consumerism.

Conventional and online news consumption accounted for a significant 1.2 percent of the incremental variance in political consumerism, yet neither of these news consumption indicators was significantly related to political consumerism in the final model. Political talk and environmental concern, both of which were directly predicted by news consumption, accounted for an additional 2.3 percent of the variance in political consumerism. Political talk ($\beta = .11$, $p < .001$) and environmental concern ($\beta = .13$, $p < .001$) were positively related to political consumerism. This finding suggests that the effect of news consumption on political consumerism is mediated through political talk and environmental concern.

Change model

In addition to the cross-sectional analysis, we also examined how change in news media consumption, political talk, environmental concern, and advertising paternalism directly or indirectly affects political consumerism. To examine this, we employed the following strategy: after accounting for the demographics and predispositions, stability and change estimates for the antecedent variables were regressed on changes in the mediating variables, after which stability and change in these antecedent and mediating variables were regressed on the criterion variable. Specifically, for each model, (1) a "stability factor" representing the value of the dependent variable at T_1 was first entered into the equation to account for variance in this variable at T_2 that could be explained by its own prior value, (2) time-invariant variables such as demographics and predispositions were entered, and (3) stability and change in key variables were included to explain the outcome orientations and behaviors. To do so, we included the value of these variables from T_1—essentially a stability estimate—and difference in these variables between T_1 and T_2—an auto-regressive change estimate (see Cohen et al. 2002, 570-71). Using this approach, four synchronous change models were generated and tested with the panel data against political talk, environmental concern, advertising paternalism, and, ultimately, political consumerism to further specify the relationships between variables.

Predicting political talk. We first predicted change in political talk (see Table 2). All variables were entered simultaneously, accounting for 37.7 percent of the variance in the dependent variable. The stability factor representing the value of the dependent variable at T_1 revealed considerable consistency in political talk ($\beta = .42$, $p < .001$). In contrast to the cross-sectional model, only gender ($\beta = -.08$, $p < .01$) remained a significant demographic predictor, while none of the predispositions

TABLE 2
CHANGE MODELS OF POLITICAL TALK, ENVIRONMENTAL CONCERN, AND ADVERTISING PATERNALISM

	Δ Political Talk	Δ Environmental Concern	Δ Advertising Paternalism
Stability factor	.42°°°	.51°°°	.52°°°
Demographics			
Gender (female)	−.08°°	.07°	.00
Age	.01	.05	.12°°°
Education	−.03	.01	−.01
Income	.04	−.06	−.04
Race (nonwhite)	.05	.01	−.03
Predispositions (O_1)			
Religiosity	−.02	−.01	.05
Ideology (liberal)	.02	.03	−.07°°
Moral obligation	.04	.11°°°	.08°°
Trust in government	.02	−.03	−.06°
Entertainment TV	.03	−.02	−.10°°°
News use (S T_1)			
Conventional news	.15°°°	−.02	.01
Web news	.05	.02	.03
Δ News use (Δ S)			
Δ Conventional news	.14°°°	.00	−.06°
Δ Web news	.14°°°	.06°	.03
Total R^2 (percentage)	37.7°°°	33.8°°°	39.9°°°

NOTE: Cell entries are final standardized regression coefficients.
°$p < .05$. °°$p < .01$. °°°$p < .001$.

achieved statistical significance. Overall, the results show that only 1.2 percent of the variance in political talk at T_2 can be explained by demographics and predispositions. The stability estimates, operationalized using media use measured from the first recontact survey, accounted for 1.4 percent of change in political talk, with only conventional news consumption achieving statistical significance ($\beta = .15, p < .001$). In contrast, change in media use between T_1 and T_2 (conventional and online news use) accounted for an additional 4.7 percent of change in political talk during this period. Change in both conventional and online news use were found to be significant predictors ($\beta = .14, p < .001$, and $\beta = .14, p < .001$, respectively).

Predicting environmental concern. We next predicted environmental concern at T_2 (see Table 2). Again, all variables were entered simultaneously, explaining 33.8 percent of the variance in the dependent variable. The stability factor of the dependent variable at T_1 revealed considerable constancy in environmental concern ($\beta = .51, p < .001$). Among the demographic factors, only gender was a significant predictor of change in environmental concern between T_1 and T_2 ($\beta = .07, p < .05$).

Moral obligation also predicted change in environmental concern ($\beta = .11, p < .001$). Among the media variables, only the change estimate in Web news consumption ($\beta = .06, p < .05$) was a significant predictor of change in environmental concern.

Predicting advertising paternalism. The availability of the measures of advertising paternalism in the July 2005 data allowed us to add it as a factor in our broader analysis. Again, all predictors were entered simultaneously, explaining 39.9 percent of the variance in the dependent variable. The stability factor yielded a strong relationship ($\beta = .52, p < .001$), indicating considerable overtime consistency in this attitude. Among the demographics, only age was a significant predictor ($\beta = .12, p < .001$). A much wider range of predispositions contributed to change in this attitude: liberal ideology ($\beta = -.07, p < .01$), moral obligation ($\beta = .08, p < .01$), government trust ($\beta = -.06, p < .05$), and habitual entertainment TV viewing ($\beta = -.10, p < .001$). Only change in conventional news media use was a significant predictor among the information-seeking variables, though this variable yielded a negative relationship with change in advertising paternalism ($\beta = -.06, p < .05$). In combination with entertainment TV viewing, these results suggest that conventional media use, especially entertainment television use, reduces advertising paternalism.

Predicting political consumerism. Our final model attempted to explain change in political consumerism (see Table 3). This model accounted for a total of 36.9 percent of the variance in the criterion variable. The stability factor performed as expected, yielding a strong positive relationship ($\beta = .50, p < .001$). None of the demographic variables remained significant predictors of change in political consumerism. Among the predispositional variables, only religiosity ($\beta = .09, p < .01$) was a positive predictor of the unexplained variance in political consumerism at T_2. The media use variables, which helped explain individual differences and over-time change in the three outcome orientations thought to encourage political consumerism, were not statistically significant predictors.

The outcome orientations, however, were significant predictors, consistent with the cross-sectional model and with the communication mediation framework. In addition to the stability estimate for advertising paternalism ($\beta = .06, p < .05$), the change estimates for environmental concern ($\beta = .07, p < .05$) and advertising paternalism ($\beta = .11, p < .001$) were significant predictors of change in political consumerism. Change in political talk was also positively related to the criterion variables, though this relationship did not achieve significance.

Discussion

Historians and cultural theorists have long asserted that consumer behavior is guided by a desire to express political concerns and social preferences, yet social scientists have only begun to explore the factors that contribute to political consumerism. This research observes direct and mediated relationships with

TABLE 3
CHANGE MODEL OF POLITICAL CONSUMERISM

	Δ Political Consumerism
Stability factor	.50°°°
Demographics	
Gender (female)	−.05
Age	−.02
Education	.02
Income	.01
Race (nonwhite)	−.03
Predispositions (O_1)	
Religiosity	.09°°
Ideology (liberal)	.02
Moral obligation	.03
Trust in government	.02
Entertainment TV	.00
News Use $(S\ T_1)$ and Orientations $(O_2\ T_1)$	
Conventional news use	.06
Web news use	.00
Political talk	.02
Environmental concern	.04
Advertising paternalism	.06°
Δ Media use (Δ S)	
Δ Conventional news	.01
Δ Web news	.02
Δ Orientations $(\Delta\ O_2)$	
Δ Political talk	.06
Δ Environmental concern	.07°
Δ Advertising paternalism	.11°°°
Total R^2 (percentage)	36.9°°°

NOTE: Cell entries are final standardized regression coefficients.
°$p < .05$. °°$p < .01$. °°°$p < .001$.

dispositional factors, communication variables, and consumption orientations, confirming some of what is known about this practice while adding substantially to our understanding of the factors that drive "lifestyle politics." The consistency seen across both static and change models, tested using cross-sectional and panel data, respectively, largely confirms our theoretical model of mediated effects of information-seeking variables on this economic form of political behavior. Both sets of models reveal that conventional and online news use encourage political consumerism indirectly through their influence on political talk and environmental concerns. However, media use may also have some suppressive effects by reducing the desire to protect others from harmful messages (i.e., advertising paternalism).

These results demonstrate how communication practices and consumption orientations work together to influence political consumerism beyond previously delineated factors. In particular, information seeking through conventional and online news sources appears to encourage orientations toward politics and society, namely, greater frequency of political talk and more pronounced concern about the environment. These two factors, in turn, encourage political consumerism, along with the sizable effects of advertising paternalism. The relationship between media consumption and advertising paternalism observed in the synchronous change models somewhat complicates this dynamic, with habitual entertainment television viewing and conventional news use both decreasing advertising paternalism and indirectly suppressing political consumerism. Thus, media use may both encourage and discourage political consumerism through its indirect effects on political talk and consumption orientations.

[C]ommunication practices and consumption orientations work together to influence political consumerism.

The results provide general support for the O-S-O-R framework that structures our analysis. For the most part, the results are consistent across cross-sectional and change models, with many of these models accounting for a large proportion of variance in political talk, environmental concern, advertising paternalism, and political consumerism. Notably, the role of predispositions is comparatively powerful in cross-sectional models but does much less to explain change. This lends support to the view that these predispositions help to set basic levels of attitudes and behaviors but do little to explain change. We suspect that predispositions may even suppress change, which would make the explanatory power of the other variables in our model more impressive. In fact, we found that over-time variation is explained by synchronous change in causally proximate communication practices and consumption orientations.

These findings have important implications for research on the intersection of consumer and civic culture. Consumer-citizens, who exercise their political values and concerns through their consumption patterns, view the economic realm as an efficient and meaningful sphere in which to advance their deeper moral and social concerns. This may reflect anti-institutionalism, as Stolle, Hooghe, and Micheletti (2005) asserted, though we find little evidence of that here. Instead, we find political consumerism to be a more dynamic behavioral response to contemporary information and the orientations that are a consequence of exposure to news. This underscores the importance of communication factors in political consumerism and "lifestyle politics."

Consumer-citizens, who exercise their political values and concerns through their consumption patterns, view the economic realm as an efficient and meaningful sphere in which to advance their deeper moral and social concerns.

The politics of consumption seems to occupy an increasingly central place in the daily activities of ordinary citizens, becoming an essential element in many people's political repertoires. The decision to drive an extra two blocks to a BP gas station, a company that has received some praise for its environmental practices, rather than frequenting an Exxon-Mobil outlet, a corporation that has received much lower marks from activists, politicizes a day-to-day activity and reflects an orientation to "vote with one's pocketbook" rather than only at the polling place. Moreover, political consumption may be a more expedient way of expressing dissatisfaction than protesting in the streets, especially since companies are increasingly responsive to such efforts. As such, this form of political action, whether buying fair-trade products, avoiding sweatshop clothing, or boycotting nations, is a viable and meaningful alternative to conventional modes of participation, and it merits further study by social scientists.

References

Anderson, W. T., Jr., and W. H. Cunningham. 1972. The socially conscious consumer. *Journal of Marketing* 36:23-31.

Atwater, T., M. B. Salwen, and R. B. Anderson. 1985. Media agenda-setting with environmental issues. *Journalism Quarterly* 62:393-97.

Bamberg, S. 2003. How does environmental concern influence specific environmentally related behaviors? A new answer to an old question. *Journal of Environmental Psychology* 23:21-32.

Beck, U. 1997. *The reinvention of politics: Rethinking modernity in the global social order.* Oxford, UK: Polity.

Bennett, W. L. 1998. The uncivic culture: Communication, identity, and the rise of lifestyle politics. *PS: Political Science and Politics* 31 (4): 741-61.

Bennett, W. L., and R. M. Entman, eds. 2000. *Mediated politics: Communication in the future of democracy.* New York: Cambridge University Press.

Bennett, W. L., and T. Lagos. 2007. Logo logic: The ups and downs of branded political communication. *Annals of the American Academy of Political and Social Science* 611:193-206.

Blake, D. E. 2001. Contextual effects on environmental attitudes and behavior. *Environment and Behavior* 33 (5): 708-25.

Breen, T. H. 2004. *The marketplace of revolution: How consumer politics shaped American independence.* New York: Oxford University Press.

Chia, S.C., K. Lu, and D. M. McLeod. 2004. Sex, lies and video compact disc: A case study on third-person perception and motivations for censorship. *Communication Research* 31:109-30.

Cohen, J., P. Cohen, S. G. West, and L. S. Aiken. 2002. *Applied multiple regression/correlation analysis for the behavioral science*, 3rd ed. Mahwah, NJ: Lawrence Erlbaum.

Eliasoph, N. 1998. *Avoiding politics.* Cambridge: Cambridge University Press.

Finkel, S. E. 1995. *Causal analysis with panel data.* Thousand Oaks, CA: Sage

Frank, D. 1994. *Purchasing power: Consumer organizing, gender, and the Seattle labor movement, 1919-1929.* New York: Cambridge University Press.

Guerin, D., J. Crete, and J. Mercier. 2001. A multilevel analysis of the determinants of recycling behavior in the European countries. *Social Science Research* 30 (2): 195-218.

Holbert, R. L., N. Kwak, and D. V. Shah. 2003. Environmental concern, patterns of television viewing, and pro-environmental behaviors: Integrating models of media consumption and effects. *Journal of Broadcasting & Electronic Media* 47:177-96.

Holt, D. B. 2000. Postmodern markets. In *Do Americans shop too much?* ed. J. Schor. Boston: Beacon.

Inglehart, R. 1997. *Modernization and post-modernization: Cultural, economic and political change in 43 societies.* Princeton, NJ: Princeton University Press.

Karlberg, M. 1997. News and conflict: How adversarial news frames limit public understanding of environmental issues. *Alternatives Journal* 23:22-27.

Kempton, W. 1993. Will public environmental concern lead to action on global warming? *Annual Review of Energy Environment* 18:217-45.

Keum, H., N. Devanathan, S. Deshpande, M. R. Nelson, and D. V. Shah. 2004. The citizen-consumer: Media effects at the intersection of consumer and civic culture. *Political Communication* 21 (3): 369-91.

Mainieri, T., E. G. Barnett, T. R. Valdero, J. B. Unipan, and S. Oskamp. 1997. Green buying: The influence of environmental concern on consumer behavior. *Journal of Social Psychology* 137 (2): 189-204.

Markus, H., and R. B. Zajonc. 1985. The cognitive perspective in social psychology. In *The handbook of social psychology*, 3rd ed., ed. G. Lindzey and E. Aronson. New York: Random House.

McLeod, D. M., W. P. Eveland Jr., and A. I. Nathanson. 1997. Support for censorship of violent and misogynic rap lyrics: An analysis of the third-person effect. *Communication Research* 24:154-74.

McLeod, J. M., G. M. Kosicki, and D. M. McLeod. 1994. The expanding boundaries of political communication effects. In *Media effects: Advances in theory and research*, ed. J. Bryant and D. Zillmann. Hillsdale, NJ: Lawrence Erlbaum.

Micheletti, M. 2003. *Political virtue and shopping: Individuals, consumerism, and collective action.* New York: Palgrave.

Micheletti, M., and D. Stolle. 2007. Mobilizing consumers to take responsibility for global social justice. *Annals of the American Academy of Political and Social Science* 611:157-75.

Minton, A. P., and R. L. Rose. 1997. The effects of environmental concern on environmentally friendly consumer behavior: An exploratory study. *Journal of Business Research* 40 (1): 37-48.

Putnam, R. D. 2000. *Bowling alone: The collapse and revival of American community.* New York: Simon & Schuster.

———. 2002. *Democracies in flux.* Oxford: Oxford University Press.

Roberts, J. A., and D. R. Bacon. 1997. Exploring the subtle relationships between environmental concern and ecologically conscious consumer behavior. *Journal of Business Research* 40 (1): 79-89.

Rojas, H., D. V. Shah, and R. J. Faber. 1996. For the good of others: Censorship and the third-person effect. *International Journal of Public Opinion Research* 8 (2): 163-86.

Sapiro, V. 2000. Economic activity as political activity. Paper presented to the annual meeting of the American Political Science Association, Washington, DC.

Schudson, M. 2007. Citizens, consumers, and the good society. *Annals of the American Academy of Political and Social Science* 611:236-49.

Shah, D. V., J. Cho, W. P. Eveland Jr., and N. Kwak. 2005. Information and expression in a digital age: Modeling Internet effects on civic participation. *Communication Research* 32: 531-65.

Shah, D. V., D. Domke, and D. B. Wackman. 1996. To thine own self be true: Values, framing and voter decision-making strategies. *Communication Research* 23 (5): 509-60.

Shanahan, J., M. Morgan, and M. Stenbjerre. 1997. Green or brown? Television and the cultivation of environmental concern. *Journal of Broadcasting & Electronic Media* 41:305-23.

Shapiro, I., and C. Hacker-Cordon. 1999. *Democracy's edges*. Cambridge: Cambridge University Press.

Sotirovic, M., and J. M. McLeod. 2001. Values, communication behavior, and political participation. *Political Communication* 18:273-300.

Stolle, D., M. Hooghe, and M. Micheletti. 2005. Politics in the supermarket: Political consumerism as a form of political participation. *International Political Science Review* 26 (3): 245-69.

Traugott, M., ed. 1995. *Repertoires and cycles of collective action*. Durham, NC: Duke University Press.

Zijderveld, A. C. 2000. *The institutionalist imperative*. Amsterdam: Amsterdam University Press.

Citizens, Consumers, and the Good Society

Advocating a "postmoralist" position in the analysis of consumer culture, this article holds that it is a mistake to identify political action with public-spirited motives and consumer behavior with self-interested motives. Both political behavior and consumer behavior can be either public-spirited or self-interested. Consumer choices can be expressly political and public-spirited, and styles of consumer behavior can enlist and enshrine values that serve democracy, from going to coffee-houses in eighteenth-century London to eating at McDonald's in twenty-first-century Beijing. Political behavior, meanwhile, may be a particular kind of consumer behavior, and political practice often turns out not to be public-spirited but egocentric and grasping. The article concludes with some suggestions for making political activity more like the experience of consumer choice, that is, more like a situation in which people can take their own preferences seriously because there is a reasonable prospect that they will ultimately matter.

Keywords: citizens; civic virtue; consumers; elections; McDonald's; politics; postmoralism

By
MICHAEL SCHUDSON

In 2004, historian Daniel Horowitz published *The Anxieties of Affluence*, a book that examines critics of American consumer culture from 1939 to 1979. In a brief epilogue, Horowitz takes the story into the twenty-first century. He includes a long footnote on a set of thinkers he calls "postmoralist," in which camp he counts me. He observes that postmoralists, beginning with anthropologists in the 1980s, notably Mary Douglas and Baron Isherwood, do not necessarily

Michael Schudson is a distinguished professor of communication at the University of California, San Diego, as well as a professor of communication in the Graduate School of Journalism, Columbia University. He is the recipient of a Guggenheim Fellowship, a MacArthur Foundation Fellowship, and a residency at the Center for Advanced Study in the Behavioral Sciences, Palo Alto, California. He has coedited two books and authored six, the latter including Discovering the News *(1978),* Advertising, the Uneasy Persuasion *(1984),* The Good Citizen *(1998), and* The Sociology of News *(2003).*

DOI: 10.1177/0002716207299195

celebrate consumer culture but seek to "understand people's longings for afflu-ence as inevitable and genuine." Postmoralists see consumer culture in a way "appreciative yet analytic" (p. 256).

I accept Horowitz's characterization of my work as postmoralist in this "appre-ciative yet analytic" vein. I think a lot of criticism of consumer culture has been moralistic, judgmental, intolerant, condescending, and, perhaps worse, muddled. The revisionist thinkers from anthropology and cultural studies of the 1980s and after, although sometimes in their zeal lurching to the side of celebration, have provided a useful corrective. Having said that, there is still something about con-sumerism that does not sit right with me. Consider how you would like to be remembered on your gravestone. Beloved parent. Cherished spouse. Devoted friend. Something like "citizen of the world" would be nice, too, or simply "citi-zen," would it not? Compare that to "he shopped till he dropped" or "a consumer of exquisite taste" or "she could always find it wholesale." These do not have quite the same ring to them. If being a "good citizen" as we often define it is not neces-sarily a sign of inner virtue—which is what I am about to argue—and if consump-tion is sometimes a route to admirable civic participation, a view I shall endorse, why is the label "citizen" a term of praise and the label "consumer" is not?

The position I am arguing against is well known. We have a long tradition of distinguished intellectuals, artists, and politicians who attack consumer culture and see it as inferior in every way—except its popularity with the unwashed masses—to political engagement. Adlai Stevenson, a case in point, complained that the effort to merchandise candidates like cornflakes in presidential cam-paigns was "the ultimate indignity to the democratic process" (quoted in Westbrook 1983, 156). Marketers may romanticize consumers, but social critics are unlikely to. British scholar Philip Elliot in 1982 expressed what was and remains the left-liberal consensus. He wrote that we faced "a continuation of the shift away from involving people in society as political citizens of nation states toward involving them as consumption units in a corporate world. The conse-quence of this for the culture is a continuation of the erosion of what Habermas called the public sphere or C. Wright Mills the community of publics" (p. 244).

The basic assumption of this line of criticism is that buying in the marketplace is an inferior form of human activity compared to voting at the polling place or otherwise exercising citizenship. Although no particular thinker has provided us the key text on this, the assumption pervades many texts and authors from John Dewey to John Kenneth Galbraith to Vance Packard to Christopher Lasch, from Adlai Stevenson to Jimmy Carter to George W. Bush's first inaugural address, and many others. The inferiority of consumer behavior seems to be either that con-suming is self-centered whereas political behavior is public-regarding or public-oriented, or that consuming, whatever its motives, distracts people from their civic obligations. Either consumption is in itself unvirtuous because it seeks the individual's own pleasures, or its displacement of political activity has unfortunate consequences for the social good.

It is high time to put both of these notions in the trash rather than the recycling bin. Measuring the virtue of "the citizen" against the virtue of "the consumer" should be recognized as a ridiculous exercise on its face since nearly all of us, with the possible exceptions of Mother Teresa, Mahatma Gandhi, and Ralph Nader, are and necessarily must be consumers as well as citizens. There are important distinctions between ordinary consumer behavior and ordinary civic behavior, but they are not invidious distinctions.

As for the argument that consumerism distracts us from civic duties, this has been forthrightly stated many times. To take one example, consider John Dewey writing in 1927: "Man is a consuming and sportive animal as well as a political one. . . . [T]he movie, radio, cheap reading matter and motor car with all they stand for have come to stay. That they did not originate in deliberate desire to divert attention from political interests does not lessen their effectiveness in that direction. The political elements in the constitution of the human being, those having to do with citizenship, are crowded to one side" (p. 139). With all due respect to a great thinker, this is largely nonsense. The starting point for analysis should not be that activities of consuming and activities of politics are equally appealing and that people would pursue politics were it not for the glitter and glamour of consuming. The starting point should be that politics is time-consuming, alternately boring and scary, often contentious, often remote from the present and the concrete, and often makes people feel ineffectual, not empowered. Politics raises difficult and complex matters that make one feel stupid. No one needed to invent pet rocks and sport utility vehicles (SUVs) and iPods, cosmetics and movies and casinos, to distract people from something they were not attracted to in the first place.

Of course, some consumption may be distracting. Perhaps some people put off jury duty so they can attend a rock concert, although more often they put off jury duty to deal with the obligations of work and family. Some forms of consumption clearly weaken political life. Cigarette consumption kills citizens, particularly older citizens who are more inclined to vote than young people; alcohol consumption destroys families. But tobacco also is or was a social, sharing, sociable activity; alcohol use is also frequently sociable, and in American political life the saloon was a central institution of American democracy for more than a century.

So there is reason to be wary of the tradition of moralizing about consumption. It offers a narrow and misleading view of consumer behavior as well as an absurdly romanticized view of civic behavior. True, some of us who do not own Hummers imagine buying a Hummer to be an act of conspicuous disregard of everyone and everything except oneself. But there are not many purchases of this sort. Quite a number of conscientious citizens who would not dream of buying a Hummer have spent far more than the price of a Hummer on two other items— a house and private higher education for one or more children. Is such lavish spending to be judged moral? One might claim, for instance, that the Harvards and Columbias and Amhersts of the world should not receive our approbation or financial support. The money they cost and the competition to get into them is a realm of consumer activity and anxiety that distracts people from the higher life of politics. But that view is unlikely to win many adherents, most of whom see their investment in their children's education, public or private, as an act of love and a vote for a brighter future.

As this may suggest, a great deal of consumer behavior is anything but selfish. It is a form of gift-giving. An interesting study of what material objects people value among their possessions found that 40 percent of the objects mentioned had been received as gifts or had been inherited—this included 65 percent of the jewelry mentioned, 73 percent of the clocks, 76 percent of the silverware, 89 percent of the stuffed animals, and 65 percent of the house plants (Rochberg-Halton 1979). Some of the material goods that critics might judge the most frivolous are goods most often given or received as gifts—Macy's sells a quarter of its annual supply of cosmetics in December. In the Christmas season, department stores sell more than 40 percent of their toys, 28 percent of their candy, 20 percent of tobacco and liquor (Schudson 1984, 138).

[A] great deal of consumer behavior is anything but selfish. It is a form of gift-giving.

So, postmoralist? Yes. There are reasons to believe that the contrast between consumer and citizen is neither as flattering to political choice nor as favorable to a strong civic life as those who uphold the distinction imagine. There are five reasons to complicate the consumer/citizen contrast. First, sometimes consumer choices are political in even the most elevated understandings of the term, that is, choices made not to maximize individual utility but to weigh social value or the public good in a calculus along with individual utility.

Second, consumer behavior is more than just the moment of choosing; it is a complex set of activities, some of which enable, enact, and engender democratic values. When looking at the larger array of consumer behavior, some of it clearly promotes a democratic culture, as I hope to demonstrate.

Third, sometimes political choices are—and have long been—consumer-like in the narrow and morally dubious sense, that is, self-centered, intended to maximize individual or group (class, ethnic, racial, or religious) utility rather than to consider the public good.

Fourth, sometimes political behavior in a democracy is not a morally elevating education in democratic values. Often politics is primarily about winning and losing. It is about ego and the personal utility invested in winning and losing, not about finding a path to the public good. In other words, political action can be as self-serving as consumer behavior at its most self-centered.

Finally, consumer and civic behavior and styles are in flux. The difference between them is in flux. Critics in 2006 should not be trapped with models of citizenship or consumption that are a half century or more out of date.

Consumer Choice Can Be Political[1]

This is the easiest point to make. If you have ever boycotted grapes to support the United Farm Workers union or decided to drive a hybrid car to help conserve the earth's resources, if you have ever "bought green," or paid extra to purchase "fair trade" coffee, you know perfectly well that consumer decisions can be political. Sometimes, these individual choices at the point of purchase are planned ahead and direct you to some stores rather than others; patronage at these stores—the health foods store, for instance—may lead you to informal associations that are not as random or nonpolitical as those you would have at the neighborhood market.

To add some symbolic weight to this point, historian T. H. Breen (2004) has argued that consumer choice was a critical element in the American Revolution. The boycott of British goods was a key tactic for involving the general public in a fight for independence. Issues of political theory that agitated some of the colonial leaders did not agitate anybody else. A revolution could not be mounted unless it had some popular support, and what brought along that popular support was the experience of ordinary people joining up in the nonimportation movement that began with the Stamp Act in 1765. In the nonimportation effort, citizens signed their names to a publicly circulated and posted list, testifying to their commitment not to purchase imported British goods. This public affirmation of the boycott brought ordinary people, women as well as men, into the public realm as never before. By the time of the Boston Tea Party, British goods had "invited colonists to think radical new thoughts about empire. British manufactures came to symbolize dependence and repression" (p. 299). History would repeat itself. What the American colonists learned in the 1760s, Mahatma Gandhi would reinvent as the central tactic of the Indian independence movement in the 1920s and 1930s.

Lizabeth Cohen (1990) made a related point. She argued persuasively in *Making a New Deal* that even when consumption is not intended to be political, it may have important consequences that are politicizing rather than distracting. Cohen argued that one reason the CIO was so successful in its organizing efforts in the 1930s is that workers once separated into ethnically and racially separate communities gradually in the 1920s came together as participants in mainstream commercial culture. "Workers in the 1930s were more likely to share a cultural world, to see the same movies and newsreels in the same chain theaters, shop for the same items in the same chain stores, and listen to the same radio shows on network radio, a situation very different from that of 1919 when workers lived in isolated cultural communities" (p. 325). Mass culture—particularly network radio—helped make industrial workers more cosmopolitan. Far from depoliticizing them, it gave them resources to reach out to one another and "enabled them to mount more effective political action" (p. 357). Far from distracting, consumption can create the conditions for political action and mobilization.

Consumerism Can Enlist and Enshrine
Values that Serve Democracy

In contrasting consumers and citizens, neither consuming nor being an active citizen can be or should be reduced to occasions when the individual makes choices among alternatives. In both consumer behavior and civic action, individuals enact social rituals that instruct them and others in a set of expectations and values. These expectations and values either enhance democracy or endanger it; it all depends on what kind of consumer behavior or civic action we are talking about.

Studies of fast-food restaurants in Asia have been illuminating in showing that what matters at McDonald's is not whether one selects a Big Mac or a chicken sandwich but the egalitarian ambience of the setting. In contrast to traditional restaurant-going behavior in urban China, going to McDonald's or KFC empowers the young over the old and women over men. In conventional, formal restaurants, "men usually order the food for their female companions and control the conversation. In contrast . . . at a McDonald's everyone can make his or her own choices and, because smoking and alcohol are prohibited, men dominate less of the conversation" (Yan 2000, 217; see also Yan 1997). Fast food also equalizes relations between restaurant employees and clients—both stand when the clients are placing their orders. The smiles and friendliness of the carefully trained staff "give customers the impression that no matter who you are you will be treated with equal warmth and friendliness." Accordingly, anthropologist Yunxiang Yan (2000) wrote, many people patronize McDonald's "to experience a moment of equality" (p. 214). Customers also learn, often from observing foreigners in the restaurants, to clear their own tables. In the old Maoist China, Yan wrote, organized, public sociality was guided by the state and focused on mass rallies. In post-Maoist China, there is a new form of public sociality that "celebrates individuality and private desires in unofficial social and spatial contexts" (p. 224).

One may resist identifying McDonald's in Beijing today as the equivalent of the coffeehouses of London or Paris that cultivated the emerging and revolutionary public sphere that Habermas writes about, but why? The story Habermas tells is another vitally important instance of the democratic political value of consumer behavior. In both cases, London and Paris in the late eighteenth century and Beijing in the late twentieth century, private people come together safely in public, commercial spaces to talk and to socialize around food and drink. Many of the Chinese customers at McDonald's Yan (2000) interviewed did not particularly care for the food. Nor were they attracted to the speed with which they could complete a meal; McDonald's proved to be a place they could linger over a meal in a clean, brightly lit, friendly, and egalitarian atmosphere. McDonald's will not turn China into a democracy, but it is perfectly apt to recognize it as a small Trojan horse inside the gates of autocratic party rule.

What this example suggests, more broadly, is that some manners and modes of consuming have more affinity with democratic cultural presuppositions than others. Everyone has had the uncomfortable experience of walking into a snooty retail establishment for clothing or jewelry or a restaurant meal where the staff make one instantly uncomfortable. If you do not know what you are looking for, if you are all too obviously unfamiliar with the merchandise and unaccustomed to shopping in a high-priced establishment, you are quickly made to feel that you are socially presumptuous even to have walked in the door. Department stores and self-service-style stores empower the browser, the newcomer, the immigrant, whether from another country or another neighborhood. Cohen's (1990) work indicates that as common places to shop supplanted ethnic neighborhood shopping sites, this had politically mobilizing consequences for the Chicago working classes of the 1920s and 1930s. The relationship of consuming to democracy is not a constant but a variable; consuming may or may not be a detriment to civic life. It all depends on what kind of consuming under what kinds of conditions.

The relationship of consuming to democracy is not a constant but a variable; consuming may or may not be a detriment to civic life.

Political Behavior, in Terms of Its Moral Framework, May Be a Particular Kind of Consumer Behavior

Voters often look at political candidates in terms of what benefits the candidates will be likely to provide them or what costs they might inflict on them through raising taxes. Voters are not mechanically pocketbook voters, but "It's the economy, stupid" is a plausible first approximation of voters' moods and preferences. "A chicken in every pot" was not a slogan intended to appeal to voters' public-spirited instincts. Nor was "the full dinner pail"; nor was "no new taxes." Politicians have accepted that when voters go to the polls, one of the important things they do is a kind of price comparison shopping.

As with the citizens of eighteenth-century Boston who did not read Montesquieu but did drink tea, matters close to home for reasons close to home bring people into the political arena. This is not to say that voters are simply selfish or self-interested. It is only to say that self-interest is frequently politically motivating and mobilizing. It can be educative. It can be transformative. True, some people are more interested in clearing mine fields halfway around the world than in going to the meeting down the street to insist on a traffic light at the corner where their children cross to school. But this is not a contrast between public-minded and self-centered. The more self-centered act—going to the meeting about the traffic light—is also the one likely to require a more substantial personal sacrifice (attending a boring meeting rather than writing a check) and to put more at risk (because of the discomfort of conflict and confrontation).

The question, again, is not about individual virtue. It is in part about the opportunity structure and the costs of action. Is political or civic action relatively accessible and convenient or not? Politics cannot always be convenient, but there are many cases where making it more convenient and more accessible will make it more popular. Efforts to make voting more accessible or to make jury service more a matter of serving on a jury than of sitting around all day at the courthouse waiting to be called are well worth undertaking.

Curiously, liberal critics of consumer culture often urge voters to act more like consumers, not less. I have in mind people who believe that if only the broad middle-class and working-class voters knew what was good for them economically, they would realize that Republican promises to lower taxes would be harmful to them. Yes, they would save a few hundred dollars in taxes, but the public schools they depend on would have fewer teachers, the school nurse would be let go, the art program would die. There would be charges for garbage collection that government once provided free. The bus fare would increase, and the frequency of buses would decline. The lines at the social security office or the motor vehicles department would be longer with the number of employees reduced. Public library hours would be cut. After-school care or before-school child care for working parents would close. Why, liberals wonder, can people not read the bookkeeping on the wall and vote their pocketbooks?

This view recognizes that politics is often bound to questions of self-interest. Undergirding its hope that people of modest means will come to recognize how useful government services are to them is a question of justice, of fairness. The activist liberals want ordinary people to vote their interests, in an informed way, even though the activists themselves may be seeking to serve others more than they want to serve themselves. They—the activists—by invoking a sense of justice are treating politics with the public-spirited ethos we connect with citizenship, but they are urging others to treat politics as a form of self-interested consumption.

Political Practice Is Often
Not Virtuous or Public-Spirited

Historian Gordon Wood (2006) made a strong case that James Madison's disappointment with the government under the Articles of Confederation had less to do with the weakness of the confederation than with the venality of the state legislatures. The plan of a Constitution Madison originally proposed would have allowed the new national government to veto any and all state laws. He found the legislators in his own state of Virginia to be driven by parochial interests, their debates to be marked by "crudeness and tedious discussion," and the results of their lawmaking to be "unjust" (pp. 148-49, 157).

But perhaps this is just politicians whose political views are particular rather than public-spirited; are citizen-activists made of finer stuff? Sometimes they are. But it takes no imagination for us to recognize that the White Citizens Councils were volunteer social organizations just as the National Association for the Advancement of Colored People was. There are surely difficult issues concerning the justice and injustice of U.S. immigration policies today, but active anti-immigration groups are evidently driven by fear and by racism, not by public spirit or perhaps, more generously, by a public spirit that draws narrowly the circle of who is to count as part of "the public." It is not sensible to judge the moral quality of political action by noting that George Wallace, David Dukes, and Strom Thurmond were all politically active. One should not judge the worth of political idealism by the actions of a political ideologue like Timothy McVeigh. But neither is it sensible to imagine Rosa Parks as a typical representative of political activity.

The motives of political actors are ordinarily mixed. Political motivation is about the narcissistic pleasure of winning, of being in the public eye, of dispensing favors, of ironing out a compromise others were unable to achieve, the thrill of seizing the moment or seeing the opportunity to untie a political knot that stymied others, the pulse-quickening excitement of competition and of victory. One hopes this is not the whole story of politics, but that is a part of it. From James Madison, offended by the demagogic Patrick Henry and eager to best him, to Karl Rove, politics is a mixed bag of ideals, interests, and the sheer motivating energy of doing battle.

Citizen and Consumer Behavior Have Changed

Making political choice less consumer-like is a task democracies undertake at their peril. I make this claim with a glance back to the Progressive Era political reforms between 1890 and 1920. Reformers of that day were not crusading against consumerism but against a mindlessness or thoughtlessness in political life, a mindlessness or thoughtlessness that political parties organized and exploited for their own ends. American political life in the late nineteenth century, for white males, was more participatory and more enthusiastic than at any other point in our history, with election turnouts routinely in the 70 to 80 percent range. Vast numbers of people participated in election campaigns in torchlight processions, brass band concerts, parades, picnics, pole raisings, and other activities that shocked visitors to our shores. When Jules Verne's (1872/1962) fictional hero, Phileas Fogg, arrives in San Francisco, he is literally swept up in an election rally, a rally that turns into a brawl. Barely escaping, Fogg later asks someone what all the commotion was about—just a political meeting, he is told. For "the election of a general-in-chief, no doubt?" Fogg asked. "No, sir; of a justice of the peace" (p. 180).

This political hoopla is just what the Progressives sought to phase out. They wanted electoral campaigns focused on issues, not on the military-like recruitment of knee-jerk partisans. They urged secret ballots, rather than the standard public distribution of party-printed tickets that voters placed in the ballot box in return for a convivial reward at the party's favorite saloon. They fought for primary elections to remove from party hacks the power to choose candidates. They sponsored laws for initiatives and referenda to place complex legislative matters directly before the voters, providing a new check on the power of party-controlled legislatures. What they accomplished with these reforms was to reduce voter turnout from more than 70 percent in the 1880s and 1890s to less than 50 percent by the 1920s. This sharp decline was no doubt a product of many forces, but these included what we might think of as the de-branding or unbranding of politicians, forcing individual voters to read the package ingredients rather than just the party logo on the package. The reformers pressed individuals to rely on information and not on personal influence and social pressure. They protected the individual conscience at the expense of separating the act of voting from the fraternity it had once expressed.

These reforms brought a kind of Protestant reformation to American politics, removing the idols and the incense from the political church, offering a politics cleansed of the souvenirs, the sensuous experience, and the small everyday rewards that once enhanced political life. No more Election Day hooliganism, or at least a lot less, no more festivity, no more emotionalism and soccer-team-style loyalties. The new voter should be motivated by ideas and ideals and information, not by social pressure or the social pleasure of a free drink and an extra dollar (Schudson 1998, 144-87).

The reformers of the day self-servingly, but not without cause, contrasted honest politics with corruption. The nineteenth-century politics they opposed was one of emotional, partisan manipulation and mobilization that had more to do with feelings of fellowship and teamwork and rivalry, and the good feeling engendered by alcohol, than it did with considerations of policy or the public good. The new politics may have led to superficiality in presenting candidates to the public and may have been the avenue that would one day lead high-minded leaders to complain of being marketed like breakfast cereal, but the old politics was no closer to the sort of "rational-critical" public discussion that political philosophers think should be the heart of democracy.

Political choices and consumer choices are not just the same, but we will not enhance the value of public affairs by positing the moral weakness of consuming as if any of us could, or would want to, do without it. Better, I think, to find strategic opportunity in consuming to enlarge the points of entry to political life. Better, also, to underline the political dimensions of our private, consuming world with cases in point. I would love to see someone write, for instance, about the politics of the morning bathroom ritual—what political choices and public investments have made possible clean running water in sink and shower and toilet? What regulation of the licensing of plumbers, of housing inspections, of water filtration, of waste disposal, of fluoridation, of the ingredient labeling on the toothpaste or the trustworthiness of the claims on the shampoo bottle that no animals were used in testing—not to mention that the bathroom light turned on reliably? In a day when even Democrats will not talk about raising taxes, is this in part because the political infrastructure of our everyday consumer lives has become invisible to us? There are ways for the consumer and the citizen in each of us to meet.

[W]e will not enhance the value of public affairs by positing the moral weakness of consuming as if any of us could, or would want to, do without it.

Could we make our political actions more satisfying in ways that our consumer behavior already often is? That is, could we make politics a domain where we feel more empowered and more satisfied in the act itself? I think the answer is yes. Most people find jury service fascinating; almost everybody finds sitting around the jury pool room for half a day an imposition. Politics can be and should be enjoyable. Everybody knows that you get better attendance at colloquia or lectures or committee meetings if you offer lunch. Is there anything wrong with offering lunch? Why not offer lunch at the voting booth? Too expensive? Maybe. Why not offer a lottery ticket to each voter? A quixotic Arizona reformer got such a proposal on the ballot in November 2006 and was attacked in op-ed pages across the country by pundits who are still living in the Progressive Era of the 1890s. His proposition went down to an inglorious defeat by a margin of two to one. Why? I am not convinced voters made the right call on this. Why not bring out the Boy Scouts and the Girl Scouts on Election Day? Why are they not selling cookies or singing songs at the polling places? Why is the arts community not engaged in enhancing aesthetically the act of voting, whether with posters or with glee clubs? We do not need to restore the corner tavern to increase voter turnout, but there is no reason to keep Election Day sterile. We should not be mental captives of the political purity crusades of the late nineteenth century.

People can feel as powerless at a town meeting as at a polling station. Romanticizing the small group is an error. But moderated small groups, with norms and rules about participation to both protect and encourage minorities or shy persons, can be worked out. The Constitutional Convention in 1787 operated by a rule that no one could speak twice to an issue unless all who wanted to had spoken once. I suspect attendance at public meetings would quickly grow if only people were assured that rules of this sort would be strictly enforced.

The distinction between citizen and consumer remains a stand-in for the difference between the self-centered and the public-spirited. But this is misleading. Both consumer choices and political choices can be public-spirited or not; both consumer behavior and political behavior can be egalitarian and tolerant and respectful of others, or not. There are differences between the modal act of consuming and the modal act of political engagement. But it is not that in consuming one looks out only for oneself. It is only that in the ordinary act of consuming, the circle of people one thinks about tends to be small; in the ordinary act of politics, the circle of people one *should* be thinking about should extend to the boundary of whatever polity one is acting in—if not further! Consuming feels good not only because it may provide material pleasures but because it is enacted largely within a comfortable social circle. Politics feels tense and dangerous, even under relatively peaceful circumstances because it is performed in the midst of and because of significant conflict with others.

Citizenship differs from consumerism because it is more likely to involve the question of fairness in the distribution of resources. Consumerism may involve guilt over having too many resources compared to starving children somewhere or disappointment at having too few resources relative to family and friends—but it does not pose a question of collective decision making about just distribution. It raises questions of individual conscience and questions of prudence.

Citizenship differs from consumerism because it is more likely to involve the question of fairness in the distribution of resources.

Part of what distinguishes those questions from questions one might ask at the voting booth or in deciding whether to attend a public meeting about a traffic light is that the consumer decision is either entirely up to you or up to you and a small number of people you know well. You can be sure your vote either is the only one that counts or one of the two that counts in a marriage or one of a few that counts when a group of friends orders dinner together at a Chinese restaurant. In choosing to attend the community meeting or in voting at the polls, most people can be confident their voices will matter little and that their contribution to the ultimate decision will be vanishingly small. This is what makes the political act selfless compared to the consuming act—not that the person who takes it is a better human being, not that the person who takes it has more lofty and public-spirited goals, but that the person acting in politics chooses to do something where the outcome is uncertain and control over the outcome is minimal. What is in it for me? Almost nothing: just the satisfaction of expressing oneself, occasionally the larger satisfaction of working with a group or a kind of team to achieve a desired end, sometimes the satisfaction of winning, and maybe—but this is rare—the pleasure of experiencing power in persuading others of one's position, of turning the tide in a public discussion. This is most likely in the smallest democracies—a faculty meeting; a book club; a block association; or a committee at school, work, or church.

The strange result of this line of thinking is that the various efforts both practical and utopian to keep democracy small are ways to make the experience of politics more like the experience of consumer choice, that is, more like situations in which one is obliged to take one's own preferences seriously because they are likely or certain to matter. People frequently enjoy the act of shopping. Yes, they also enjoy cooking and eating the steak, wearing and showing off the new tie—but they also enjoy shopping for these goods. They do so, I would suggest, because shopping is empowering. It does not make shoppers sovereign of all they survey—for most of us, the caviar really is beyond our means. But it enables one to make choices that make a difference to ourselves and our families. We can feel gratification in the very act of choosing and purchasing. Nineteenth-century Americans felt something like that on Election Day, and they deserve credit for having invented a politics where that could happen. We need to think harder about these matters and determine what really the political act and the consuming act are, and what variety of things they are or have been in different times and places and civic circumstances. We need to move from moralism and complaint to analysis and action where the necessary and often enjoyable acts of consuming are appreciated—but where the political structure that makes those acts possible is made visible.

Note

1. Parts of the following sections also appeared verbatim in Michael Schudson, "The Troubling Equivalence of Citizen and Consumer," *Annals of the American Academy of Political and Social Science* 608 (November 2006): 193-204.

References

Breen, T. H. 2004. *The marketplace of revolution: How consumer politics shaped American independence*. New York: Oxford University Press.

Cohen, Lizabeth. 1990. *Making a new deal: Industrial workers in Chicago, 1919-1939*. New York: Cambridge University Press.

Dewey, John. 1927. *The public and its problems*. New York: Henry Holt.

Elliot, Philip. 1982. Intellectuals, the "information society" and the disappearance of the public sphere. *Media, Culture and Society* 4:243-53.

Horowitz, Daniel. 2004. *The anxieties of affluence: Critiques of American consumer culture, 1939-1979*. Amherst: University of Massachusetts Press.

Rochberg-Halton, Eugene. 1979. Cultural signs and urban adaptation: The meaning of cherished household possessions. Ph.D. diss., University of Chicago.

Schudson, Michael. 1984. *Advertising, the uneasy persuasion*. New York: Basic Books.

———. 1998. *The good citizen: A history of American civic life*. New York: Free Press.

Verne, Jules. 1872/1962. *Around the world in 80 days*. New York: Heritage Press.

Westbrook, Robert B. 1983. Politics as consumption: Managing the modern American election. In *The culture of consumption: Critical essays in American history, 1880-1980*, ed. Richard Wightman Fox and T. J. Jackson Lears. New York: Pantheon.

Wood, Gordon. 2006. *Revolutionary characters*. New York: Penguin.

Yan, Yunxiang. 1997. McDonald's in Beijing: The localization of Americana. In *Golden arches east*, ed. James L. Watson. Stanford, CA: Stanford University Press.

———. 2000. Of hamburger and social space: Consuming McDonald's in Beijing. In *The consumer revolution in urban China*, ed. Deborah S. Davis. Berkeley: University of California Press.

QUICK READ SYNOPSIS

The Politics of Consumption/
The Consumption of Politics

Special Editors: DHAVAN V. SHAH
LEWIS FRIEDLAND
DOUGLAS M. McLEOD
University of Wisconsin–Madison

and

MICHELLE R. NELSON
University of Illinois at Urbana-Champaign

Volume 611, May 2007

Prepared by Herb Fayer, Jerry Lee Foundation

DOI: 10.1177/0002716207301853

In Defense of Consumer Critique: Revisiting the Consumption Debates of the Twentieth Century

Juliet B. Schor, Boston College

Background	Research contributions have enormously enhanced scholars' understandings of the emergence and growth of consumer society regarding

- how consumers experience their consumption activities and goods, subcultures, consumer agency, and meanings;
- the role of consumption in the constitution of social inequalities such as gender, race, and class;
- the connections between consumption, nationalism, and empire; and
- the nature of retailing, spatial dimensions of consumption, and many more dimensions of consumption.

NOTE: This article considers three major traditions of consumer critique: Veblenian accounts of status-seeking, the Frankfurt School, and Galbraith and the economic approach to consumer demand. The article argues that the flaws of these models are not necessarily fatal, and especially that the ongoing debate about producer versus consumer sovereignty should be revisited in light of the changing political power of transnational corporations.

Veblen   The core of the Veblen approach is a hierarchical social structure driven by
                      a competitive status competition in which position is determined by wealth.
                      • Publicly visible consumption is the mechanism by which wealth is vali-
                        dated in the competition, or "game."
                      • The need to commit real resources eliminates pretenders and provides a
                        readily assessable status claim.
                      • The emphasis on visibility also signals that this is a model of alternatives to
                        private consumption (such as public consumption, savings, and leisure time).
                      • The critics of Veblen have rightly identified key shortcomings and limita-
                        tions of both his theory and status models more generally.
                          ◦ The universe of goods is far more complex than the model suggests,
                            and the informational demands on consumers to keep up with the array
                            of goods are substantial and increasing.
                          ◦ However, the Internet has made information cheap and accessible.
                            There may be an increasing preoccupation with consumption because
                            the informational demands are so high.

Adorno and   Within the humanities, the Frankfurt School has been the most influential of
Horkheimer   the consumer critiques: In their classic article, Adorno and Horkheimer
                      (1944) outlined a pessimistic view of the "culture industries."
                      • Consumers are trapped in a circle of manipulation and retroactive need.
                      • Life outside the factory (the sphere of leisure) is an "afterlife," structured
                        by a dehumanized workplace.
                      • Art loses its revolutionary potential, instead acting like a drug that lulls the
                        worker into passivity outside the factory, and makes it possible for him
                        (this is a very male vision) to return the next day to his mindless work.
                      • The critics see this as a so-called "totalized" and functionalist vision with-
                        out contradiction or possibility for resistance and that it is elitist in its den-
                        igration of popular culture.

Galbraith   Galbraith's *The Affluent Society* was the most influential popular discussion
                      of consumption in the post-WWII era.
                      • It makes three major claims about consumption:
                          ◦ that producers create consumer desire,
                          ◦ that the consumption–well-being link is weak, and
                          ◦ that the structural pressures to increase private consumption drive out
                            public goods.
                      • Like the Frankfurt School, Galbraith has been criticized for viewing con-
                        sumers as passive and manipulated, and he has been attacked as a hyp-
                        ocrite and an elitist, a charge leveled at many consumer critics.

Conclusion   So where does the discussion of market sovereignty leave us?
                      • Are we closer to the new wisdom that consumers rule, either through
                        their considerable power to reject products they do not like, or through
                        their growing role in the production of cultural innovation and ultimately
                        not only products but marketing messages as well?
                      • Or is the growing corporate power that is widely acknowledged in other
                        spheres, such as the state and the university, also relevant in consumer
                        markets, in ways that are not identical to what Galbraith argued, but
                        closely related?

- Having succeeded spectacularly well in ensuring growing demand for goods, perhaps the transnational companies that dominate consumer markets have redirected their attention to consolidating control over the environment in which they operate.
  - This growing power has been accompanied by the dominance of an ideology that posits the reverse—that the consumer is king and the corporation is at his or her mercy.
- Finally, the argument in this article is not that a return to the critical traditions of the early twentieth century is a sufficient basis for articulating a compelling challenge to contemporary consumer culture.
  - But it is a necessary first step to recovering a tradition of engaged, critical scholarship at the macro level.
  - From here the task is to construct a truly twenty-first-century approach: a new, critical paradigm that engages the ways in which consumption has grown and has radically transformed notions of individuality, community, and social relations.

Capital, Consumption, Communication, and Citizenship: The Social Positioning of Taste and Civic Culture in the United States

Lewis Friedland, Dhavan V. Shah, Nam-Jin Lee,
Mark A. Rademacher, Lucy Atkinson, and Thomas Hove,
University of Wisconsin–Madison

Background

Pierre Bourdieu's *Distinction* (1979/1984) has earned wide influence for its path-breaking and elaborate analysis of the economy of cultural goods: the social conditions for their production, consumption, and valuation.

- Bourdieu's great innovation was to connect the production, consumption, and valuation of cultural capital with the social practices of establishing hierarchies, maintaining distances, and legitimating differences between dominant and dominated groups.
- Since taste plays such an important part in these social practices, its logic needs to be examined sociologically and placed within a history of struggles between the dominant and the dominated.
- *Distinction* outlines a complex program for a science of cultural consumption. In pursuing this program, Bourdieu's goal was to demystify and expose the social misrecognitions that the Kantian tradition of aesthetic judgment helped rationalize.

The United States

In this article, the authors take Bourdieu's concept of the field of consumption and apply it to the United States in 2000.

- The United States in 2000 differs not only in its class and cultural structure; it also lies at the other side of a historical shift in which consumption is less clearly the outcome of the intersection of class and culture but rather actively shapes it.

- Consumption of television, radio, magazines, newspapers, and the Internet has become an increasingly important marker of cultural consumption in this context.
- The authors generated correspondence maps of the social positioning of taste in the United States with the goal of exploring the social stratification of taste culture and integrating media consumption and civic practices into this investigation of the U.S. context.

Examination of Four Quadrants

To fully understand how occupation, media use, consumption, and civic and social practices define and situate distinct lifestyles in this social space, the authors examine each of four quadrants.

- *Quadrant 1: High volume of capital-communal orientation:* This first quadrant is inhabited by middle- and upper-income, well-educated individuals with patterns of cultural consumption that correspond to an emphasis on cultural capital.
- *Quadrant 2: Low volume of capital-communal orientation:* These are somewhat older, less affluent, and less educated individuals; at the bottom of this quadrant are individuals who did not graduate from high school and who earn less than $10,000.
- *Quadrant 3: High volume of capital-individual orientation:* Individuals who possess a relatively high volume of capital, but in contrast with the first quadrant, their composition of capital is more economic than cultural.
- *Quadrant 4: Low volume of capital-individual orientation:* Individuals with relatively lower volumes of capital, though they still emphasize the economic over the cultural.

Mapping Goals

The preliminary mapping of the field of consumption in the United States has two primary goals:

- first, to compare the results with the general structure of the field of consumption found by Bourdieu;
- second, to understand whether the dual axes of volume and composition of capital remain determinant or whether some other principles may be at work in structuring the U.S. field.

Discussion

Moving to the comparison with Bourdieu's analysis of the field of cultural consumption in 1960s France, the upper left quadrants in both *Distinction* and the author's analysis appear similar in some respects.

- The U.S. quadrant may be dominated by a larger class of professionals and knowledge workers shaped by legal and financial services and other highly educated fractions of the upper middle classes.
- There is a clear split between high-income members of this grouping, who appear to be higher cultural consumers, and a lower group that is among the most civically and politically active.
- There may be a shift to a principle of stratification defined by volume of capital and media use. The middlebrow in America confounds the presence of "high" culture.
- America in 2000 and beyond is a more age-segregated society, and much of this segregation is a direct principle of lifestyle segmentation.
- The use of various newspapers, television programs, radio formats, and magazines were particularly relevant in marking individuals' social position,

distinguishing them from others in the social space, while also providing aspirational reference points for consuming.
- Television consumption, especially of escapist fare such as sitcoms and reality shows, tends to cluster along the bottom half of the social space, whereas newspaper and magazine consumption tends to distinguish between those with higher and lower volumes of capital.
- There is a correspondence between civic behavior, political ideology, and the social positioning of taste cultures within the U.S. context.

Representing Citizens and Consumers in Media and Communications Regulation

Sonia Livingstone, London School of Economics and Political Science; and Peter Lunt, Brunel University

Background

This article considers the consequences for citizens and consumers of the changing regulatory regime in Western democracies, from "command-and-control" government to discursive, multistakeholder governance, focusing on the case of media and communications regulation in the United Kingdom.
- The authors show how the terms *consumer* and, especially, *citizen*, are variously used to promote stakeholder interests, not always to the benefit of the citizen.
- The new-style regulation moves away from the previous hierarchical, "command-and-control" regime.
- It claims to democratize power by dispersing and devolving the role of the state, establishing accountable and transparent administration, and engaging multiple stakeholders in the process of governance.
- Regulation must make unified and strategic decisions for the whole market that reflect economic, technical, and social policy trends and balance the needs of the market with those of an "empowered" public.

Communications Act

In a lively debate over media and communications regulation, two distinct terms emerged as the discursive solution, *citizen* and *consumer*, supposedly resolving ambiguities in the plethora of "listeners," "viewers," "users," and "customers," of the legacy regime.
- Yet once the Communications Act was passed in 2003, this solution began to unravel, with boundary disputes demanding remedial action of various kinds on the part of the regulator and civil society.
- It was proposed that the consumer interest should be understood in relation to economic goals while the citizen interest inheres in cultural goals, and that these in turn map onto the domain of telecommunications networks and services, on one hand, and broadcast content, on the other.
- Consumers are understood as individuals while citizens have collective status.

NOTE: "It's a very tricky question. Because some issues are obviously consumer issues and some issues are obviously citizen issues but at the end of the day we're talking about people" (Helen Normoyle, director of market research, Office of Communications). "The risk is if you have just the language of citizens then you end up with a load of nebulous and quite high level public interest-type objectives rather than actually seeing if people are getting the best deal in this market" (Allan Williams, senior policy advisor for communication at Which? [formerly the Consumers' Association]).

- It is much easier to regulate consumer issues, which are basically economic issues, than citizenship issues involving social, cultural, democratic issues, which are more difficult to quantify and measure.

Public's Perspective

Sixteen focus groups were carried out to see how the public envisions the role of regulation in their lives.

- They are neither apathetic and disengaged nor actively engaged and responsive to regulatory initiatives or consultations.
- Rather, they expressed strongly felt but contrary views that, though aware of the contradictions, they seemed unable to resolve.
- Alternative stories emerged of consumer failures, unprotected consumers, dangerous situations, and exploited individuals.
- Although the discussions covered many issues, those that directly influence people's health, work, finances, or family generated more attention than media and communications issues.
- In short, the public struggles to speak as a collective, being torn between its self-image as agentic and as vulnerable.

Access to Information and Communication Resources

Most academics concerned with the relation between the media and politics agree that access to information and communication resources are fundamental to informed citizenship and a prerequisite for democratic participation.

- Many worry that neoliberal economics and neoconservative politics have altered the balance of power in media and communications to the detriment of citizens.
- Murdock and Golding (1989) focused on the distribution of communicative resources—notably, access to information and communication content and technologies, maximum diversity in content production, and mechanisms for feedback and to enable participation.
- Hamelink (2003) argued that governments and civil society bodies must guarantee the conditions for freedom of expression, universality of access, diverse sources of information, diversity of ownership, and plurality of representation.

Conclusion

Access to, and the content of, the press, television, Internet, and so on should be evaluated, therefore, not in terms of what contents or services they provide but in terms of the possibilities they afford or impede.

- The citizen interest, in other words, lies in determining what real choices are open to them in seeking to meet their needs, in a particular information and communication environment.
- McChesney (2003) has been spearheading a media reform movement that supports such interventions as developing community radio and television, applying antimonopoly laws to the media, establishing formal study to determine fair media ownership regulations, reinvigorating public service broadcasting, and so forth.

Consumers and the State since the Second World War

Matthew Hilton, University of Birmingham

Background

This article analyzes the development of, and compares the differences in, the various consumer protection regimes since World War II.

- It points to processes of convergence in consumer politics across the globe that saw the development of consumer political thinking in the Soviet bloc and the development of supranational protection regimes at the European level.
- In more recent decades, the politics of consumer society based upon access and the collective has been eclipsed with a politics that emphasizes choice and the individual.
- Such a change represents a profound shift in the relations between consumers, citizens, and governments. The significance of the 1950s as a key moment in consumer politics was the growth in interest in affluence as well as necessity.

NOTE: Elected politicians promised shoppers a better life just around the corner, state officials developed informative labeling schemes, business developed quality certification marks, and the cooperatives continued their campaigns against the abuses of the marketplace by trusts and cartels.

Government

Twentieth-century governments have maintained a complex set of relationships with consumer organizations.

- Many consumer groups have been nurtured by public finances and incorporated within, or emerged from, the institutions of the state.
- What is clear is that consumer protection had become a state project.
- Defending the consumer-citizen and working to protect his or her standard of living, while offering rewards in the future, became a typical populist manifesto of politicians of all persuasions.
- As affluence arrived, governments around the world attempted to develop regimes of consumer protection to provide consumers with the confidence to enter and participate in the market.
- Specific legislative remedies to market abuses were backed up with the creation of entire bureaucracies for protecting the consumer.

Consumer Citizenship

Gunnar Trumbull has argued that there have been three broad models of consumer citizenship:

- an economic model of citizenship has regarded consumers as partners in the economy,
- consumers have been given the right to participate in forums dealing with overall structural issues, and
- a model of political citizenship emphasizes the rights of consumers and recognizes their roles as sociopolitical actors.

The United States

In the late 1960s, a regulatory framework emerged in the United States that was often far more rigorous than that achieved in European economies.

- The primacy of the market cannot be denied, nor the faith held in it as a solver of consumer problems.
- The individual consumer is also a rights-based citizen.
- Regulatory agencies such as the Federal Trade Commission and the Federal Energy Administration were strengthened and new consumer protection agencies came into existence.

NOTE: Consumer protection has become an international phenomenon from which states learn from one another and adopt measures that take best practices from different contexts.

Europe

The European Union has had a tremendous impact on national consumer protection regimes, ensuring that the differences between countries such as France and Germany have been blurred.

- It has also meant that in states where consumer protection was weak or underdeveloped, such as Greece, Spain, Italy, and Portugal, a ready-made model for consumer protection has been provided.
- Increasingly, that model of consumer protection has been dictated by the wider goal of market reform, ensuring an emphasis on choice, competition, and ever-expanding markets.

Conclusion

Consumer activists have often liked to argue that their heyday was in the 1960s and 1970s; if they have declined as a political and social force thereafter, it is due to their having achieved many of their own goals.

- Compared to the fledgling technocratic age of the 1950s, commodities no longer break down as soon as they are taken home.
- Guarantees and standard contracts ensure that forms of redress are available to dissatisfied customers.
- Advertisements might well continue to exaggerate, but there are restrictions on overtly false claims.
- Sources of information are available to shoppers other than those provided by the manufacturer or retailer.
- Most dramatically, the danger of death and injury from negligently assembled products has declined.

NOTE: Yet in all the measures that have been successfully implemented, there has also been a narrowing of the vision of consumer protection. Protection became unevenly distributed: those who can afford to choose alternatives can bear the costs of deceptive practices, and can simply live to spend another day, have their own protection mechanisms. But for the poor and disadvantaged, access to such protection is less readily available, and their participation in consumer society comes at a struggle and a cost.

Buying into Downtown Revival:
The Centrality of Retail to Postwar Urban
Renewal in American Cities

Lizabeth Cohen, Harvard University

Background

This article argues that the link between consumption and civic engagement has an important local, not just national, history and that retailers' involvement in the downtown urban renewal of American cities in the post-WWII era offers a particularly fruitful avenue of investigation.

- The article focuses on New Haven, Connecticut, and Boston, where Edward J. Logue served both cities as development chief from 1954 to 1967.
- His record over these fourteen years offers a revealing case of how consumption and civic culture intersected at the local level.
  - In both cases, department stores were deemed essential to the viability of the central business district.
  - That priority limited the success of downtown revitalization, given the department store sector's suburban orientation and steady economic concentration from the 1960s on.
- As locally based urban planners and policy makers struggled to make downtowns appealing, economic decision making in corporate boardrooms, far out of their control, was undermining their efforts.

Department Stores

The case of department stores' involvement in the enormous effort by American cities to revitalize themselves demonstrates that the link between consumption and civic engagement has an important local history as well.

- In New Haven and Boston, downtown department store owners and executives played central roles in urban renewal efforts, while their stores became important sites for redevelopment projects.
- Once the lifeblood of downtown development, after World War II the number of downtown stores steadily declined, their share of metropolitan shoppers and their dollars likewise shrinking.
- Still strongly identified with their home cities, department stores clamored for help sustaining downtown retail.
  - They called for thousands more off-street parking spaces, new roadways, improvements in mass transportation, slum clearance of "gray belt" neighborhoods bordering retail cores, and updated shopping environments that resembled the new modern malls beginning to appear in suburban rings.
  - They also complained of high real estate taxes.

Conclusions

What can we learn from the tale of downtown urban renewal in New Haven and Boston, where in both cases department stores were viewed as the solution to downtown's ills?

- Department stores' insistence on suburban-style store designs often undermined the uniqueness of the urban experience and encouraged the construction of enormous, self-contained, superblock projects that were rarely adaptable to other purposes should the need arise.

- The cases of downtown New Haven and Boston testify to the importance of preserving a mix of commerce and a diversity of consumers to protect cities from falling victim to the internal restructuring of any one commercial sector or the shifting loyalties of any particular group of consumers.
- There is also a deeper lesson to draw about the way governments and corporations have been entwined in shaping the urban built environment.
  - Enormous amounts of federal, state, and local dollars all went toward buttressing old, and creating new, infrastructure to support downtown commerce.
  - This huge public investment, however, did not keep the tax code from favoring new suburban mall construction or major retailers from ultimately reneging on that partnership by abandoning downtown stores.

NOTE: The advocates of urban renewal may have miscalculated what was possible in reviving downtowns, but we might rightfully ask what obligation these retail corporations had, and still have, to the urban citizens whose tax dollars have underwritten their postwar development.

Should Consumer Citizens Escape the Market?

Eric J. Arnould, University of Arizona

Background Postmodern consumers' ability to act for themselves comes through recognition that one is "a participant in an ongoing, never ending process of construction that includes a multiplicity of moments where things (most importantly as symbols) are consumed, produced, signified, represented, allocated, distributed, and circulated" (Firat and Venkatesh 1995, 250).
- The above stresses consumers' proactive behaviors in contrast with the passive consumers of late modern social theory.
- Cyberspace may offer yet more freedom of action if one believes that in cyberspace the consumer is freed from constraints that hamper freedom of action in the sociophysical world.

Consumer The ideas referred to above may improperly suggest that "consumers have
Agency free reign in the play of signs to piece together a collage of meanings that express the [individual's] desired symbolic statements" (Murray 2002, 428).
- Unfortunately, the agency construct encounters some fundamental conceptual problems.
  - First, the notion of agency attributes some form of innate capacity, ability, or intention to actors and their action.
  - Second, it is impossible to separate empirically autonomous, or "free," from "determined" behaviors.
- In the end, consumer agency is a folk model. In other words, if people act agentically, they are agentic (Fuchs 2001). This model also universalizes a Western version of actorhood and evokes ethnocentric notions of freedom, constraint, and transcendence of constraint via choice.

Consumers There is a sociological cottage industry devoted to the proposition that consumers cannot escape their degraded condition as pawns in a marketing power game.

- This work unintentionally distorts the lived experience of consumer culture because of the use of analytic methods that generally rely either on no data or on aggregate data, which leads to a confusion of causes with effects.
- Another problem with the portrayal of consumers in much of the critical sociology of consumption is an implicit class bias concerning "popular culture."

The Market   Market capitalism is often attacked as the primary contemporary source of all kinds of social pathology.

- These attacks fix advertising, brands, commercial electronic media, marketing research, and marketing formula squarely in their sights.
- It is claimed that consumer conformity, loss of autonomy, falsity, materialism, kitsch, ecological collapse, routinization, global poverty, addiction, and obesity flow from the expanding reach of the market.
- We should recognize that late market capitalism democratizes the space of consumption, but at the cost of a growing gap between rich and poor and exacerbation of the effects of economic externalities such as pollution and resource depletion.
- But alienation and social pathology really emerge only when people are unable to perceive the means of self-creation through consumption, or because objective conditions prevent self-creation, not from the engagement with markets or consumption objects.
- And it is easy to identify all kinds of market-mediated social and political activism. Consumers act through market-mediated forms because there are no templates for action and interpretation located in some utopian elsewhere from where they might act.

Commercial Media   Active participation in contemporary commercial media plays a complex social and potentially liberatory political role, and is thus at odds with the sociology of marketing and consumption supportive of the dupe theory.

- Critical sociologists also recognize the importance of discriminating markets as an idealization of neoliberals and as social and political forms whose effects and purposes are susceptible to influence through discourses and practices in which state, corporation, national, and global regulatory bodies as well as citizen activists play a governance role, if often unequal ones.

A Carnivalesque Approach to the Politics of Consumption (or) Grotesque Realism and the Analytics of the Excretory Economy

Craig J. Thompson, University of Wisconsin–Madison

Background   This article addresses the moral critique of consumption as a profligate pursuit, driven by status emulation, leading to indolence, insipidness, and invidious comparison.

- The key assumption is that personal well-being, family life, aesthetic virtues, natural resources, and the inhabitability of the planet are all being sacrificed on the altar of status-chasing consumerism.

The
carnivalesque

The carnivalesque body is equally copulative and excretory, salacious and scatological, vibrant and on the way to becoming decomposing humus.

- The carnivalesque de-centers subjectivity and directs attention toward the web of transpersonal and ecological interconnections that sustain an indissoluble cycle of degeneration and regeneration.
- Bakhtin's (1965/1984) portrayal of the carnivalesque is structured by two dimensions: transgressive resistance and grotesque realism.
  - The transgressive dimension has been embraced as an emancipatory practice through which consumers can elude and defy the ideological imperatives, conformist mandates, and materialistic inducements of the capitalist marketplace.
- In contrast, writings on the politics of consumption have studiously ignored the implications of grotesque realism and the degrading project of critically situating socioeconomic relationships of power, and their ennobling rationalizations, in the excretory economy.
- Bridging this chasm between the politics of consumption and the reeking reality of corporate capitalism's shit requires that critical theorists abandon moralistic preoccupations with consumers' well-being, their existential states, their creative defiance, or slack-jawed submissions to the interruptions of the marketplace.

NOTE: The author's overriding agenda is to assert the generative power of this latter dimension for developing realpolitik critiques of commercial culture and mobilizing consumer citizens to take transformative actions.

The Analytics
of the Excretory
Economy

The theoretical and realpolitik differences that distinguish the politics of consumption, in its moral/therapeutic form, and an analytics of the excretory economy, can be demonstrated through a comparison of two parallel critiques of commercial culture, one that is unabashedly spermatic in moral tenor and the other that digs into the excretory muck: George Ritzer's (1993) *The McDonaldization of Society* and Eric Schlosser's (2002) *Fast Food Nation*.

- Much like proposals for downshifting and voluntary simplicity, Ritzer's action strategies seek to place some (therapeutic) boundaries on the corporate colonization of everyday life, but they do not challenge the underlying structural conditions that make these encroachments possible and problematic.
- An action-oriented insight that academics can glean from Schlosser is the importance and realpolitik value of investigating a defined market system within commercial culture, rather than making sweeping generalizations that presuppose the operation of a singularly dominant ideology.

The Press

The institutional erasure of investigative journalism—which can shine a critical light on all the shit that corporate power brokers would just as soon remain out of public view—is a major structural impediment to consumer citizenship and democratic dialogue.

- If the "fourth estate" is suffering from investigative constipation, being unable to move muckraking exposés past the colonic blockages of ideology, economics, and institutional disincentives, then some roles for academics are to
  - leverage their skills and cultural authority to bring institutional power structures to light,

Q
R
S

- critically interrogate the network of relationships and alliances through which they operate, and
- identify their institutional contradictions and susceptibilities to various kinds of change strategies.
- By transgressing conventional boundaries between academics and activism, critically minded researchers can facilitate grassroots political action and empower consumer citizens with realpolitik knowledge for collectively redressing specific failings, excesses, abuses, and exploitations of a given market system.

Why Not Share Rather Than Own?

Russell Belk, York University

Background

The focus in this article is on shared consumption.
- Rather than distinguishing what is *mine* and *yours*, sharing defines something as *ours*.
- In addition to sharing tangibles, we may also share abstract things like knowledge, responsibility, or power.
- Individuals, groups, and even nations can share.
  - Production units may share in producing something through profit sharing, employee-owned corporations, stock share ownership, and other joint ownership of the means of production.
  - But the emphasis here is on shared consumption.

Commodity Transactions

In economic theory, commodity transactions are balanced with no lingering indebtedness and no residual feelings of friendship.
- Each partner need never see the other again.
- Many forms of business exchange involve embedded relationships and are better characterized as gift exchanges than commodity exchanges.
- But neither commodity exchange or gift giving are the same as sharing.

Sharing Issues

A recent hotbed of sharing activity and discussions involves the Internet. Sharing with others online includes open-source code writing, Internet bulletin boards, chat rooms, and so on.
- Some see such sharing as a new age of altruism brought about by the magic of cyberspace; others suggest that such acts are largely egoistic.
- The Internet revolution is also fostering a new age of expanding intellectual property rights that threatens to replace the altruism of sharing with the egoism of commoditization.
- Issues arise in sharing human organs and personal information: at issue is what can or cannot be shared and under what conditions.

Sharing Process

Sharing, like ownership, is an interpersonal process, sanctioned and prescribed by culture.
- Sharing can reduce envy and create feelings of community, or it can create dependency and foster feelings of resentment and inferiority.
- When someone shares with us, we can see their action as a sincere effort to please us or as insincere and designed to pacify and placate us.

Sharing *Impediments*	There are some impediments to sharing. • If ownership allows sharing, feelings of possessiveness and attachment toward the things we own or possess discourage sharing. • Another factor that inhibits sharing is materialism, defined as the importance a person attaches to possessions. • Another impediment to sharing is the perception that resources are scarce, and if we share we may miss something we might have enjoyed.
Sharing *Intangibles*	There are some incentives to sharing intangibles. • In academia, we are satisfied with the fame or reputation that may result from sharing knowledge and ideas with people we may inspire, even though we may also enjoy indirect economic benefits. • We can share or give away some things without losing them—a song, a joke, a story, our bodies, things we put up on the Web. • The Internet is leading to a global community of sharing, communicating, and giving, with a free flow of information providing equality of access. • There is the effect of feeling a part of a community of kindred spirits. • The joint possession of certain goods can also convey status and power by demonstrating the group's command of scarce resources.
Sharing *Tangibles*	There are also some incentives to sharing tangibles. • There may be the sense of paying back for one's prior good fortune. • There is also genuine altruism and helping others to nourish a self-image that we are generous and helpful. • A further incentive for sharing tangible things is an extension of the keeping-while-giving motivation identified with nontangible things. • It can make not only economic sense but also "leverage" our lifestyle when we share things we would otherwise all have to purchase. • Another incentive to share tangibles is when our extended sense of self embraces other people outside of our immediate family.
Conclusion	As we have replaced social security with financial security, trust in money and things have supplanted trust in people, and economic capital has become more important than social capital. • Individual bank accounts and credit cards are growing as joint accounts and cards decline. • Ironically, we are becoming more likely to share our deepest secrets, insights, information, and loyalties with someone whom we know only by an online pseudonym than we are with our partners or family. • Materialism, possessive individualism, and the conviction that self-identity must be developed by extension into possessions are all factors that inhibit sharing. • Still there are some reasons to hope; possessions and individual ownership can be a burden, many resources are scarce, and the "virtual corporation" shows that ownership is not always best.

Q
R
S

Downshifting Consumer = Upshifting Citizen?
An Examination of a Local Freecycle Community

Michelle R. Nelson, University of Illinois at Urbana-Champaign;
Mark A. Rademacher, University of Wisconsin–Madison;
and Hye-Jin Paek, University of Georgia

Q R S

Background

Critics suggest that contemporary consumer culture creates overworked and overshopped consumers who no longer engage in civic life.

- This research examines those who reject the "work and spend" cycle by examining these downshifting attitudes among members of freecycle.org, a grassroots "gift economy" community.
- Results of an online survey show that downshifting consumers are less materialistic and brand-conscious. They also civically engage through boycotts and buycotts and online political participation.
- The authors contend that alternative forms of consumption might be a new form of civic engagement.

NOTE: The purpose of this study is to investigate whether people who simplify their lives or downshift their work and/or consumption behaviors then "upshift" or increase their civic life.

Downshifters

In response to hyperconsumption and the stress, overtime, and psychological expense that may accompany it, a growing number of people (estimated at 19 percent of the U.S. population [Schor 1998]) are simplifying their lifestyle.

- The above are "downshifters," people who voluntarily choose to work less and/or consume less. They want more time and less stress.
- As a result of reduced incomes or a less materialistic life, downshifters often try to repair, reuse, share, and make goods rather than buy them.
- Downshifters may focus on civic reengagement—they have more time in their lives and use it to help the community or society.
- Downshifters are primarily white consumers with middle- to upper-middle-class incomes from Western, affluent countries.

Consumer Culture

Critics have argued that the increased availability of consumer goods partnered with increased disposable income has resulted in hedonistic, individualistic consumers.

- Instead of using consumption to achieve social equality and other collective social goals, these consumers are viewed as seeking personal satisfaction through goods at the expense of democracy.
- In a recent critique of consumer culture, Schor (1998) cited statistics that show increased work hours, credit card balances, and stress levels and decreased household savings and quality-of-life indicators such as time spent with family and happiness.
  - In addition, scholars have argued that contemporary American culture is witnessing the decline of civic-mindedness.

NOTE: The ultimate response to the decline thesis is that civic engagement now includes a wider range of activities—debating and seeking political information online and political consumption (e.g., boycotts and buycotts).

| *freecycle.org* | Among the downshifters, freecycle.org members are an interesting case because their practice in reusing consumer goods is characteristic of voluntary simplicity. |

- Some shop at secondhand stores or flea markets for fun, while others are doing so out of economic and material necessity.
- The motivations for freecycle membership were fairly balanced between self-oriented motivations and environmental reasons.
- Unlike consumers, who view consumption objects as a reflection of self or as a means of maintaining social hierarchies, consumers seeking to truly engage in de-cluttering must be able to dispose of goods and de-couple notions of "identity" from goods.
- The findings also support the assertion made by Elgin (2000) that those who engage in work and consumption downshifting are also likely to express their personal values and political orientation through consumer activism such as boycotts and buycotts.

Internet Use:
Consumption
and Civic
Society

The Internet, as a new public sphere, may provide opportunity for people to engage in socially responsible consumption, such as the reuse and recycling witnessed among the freecycle community, and to engage civically in Web and geographic communities.

- Spending time online should not be viewed as automatically detrimental to civic life.
- Instead of asking how much time people spend online (i.e., time displacement), it is more beneficial to ask *what* are they doing online.

Conclusion

Overall, the findings of this study imply that the critique of consumption eroding civic life is too simplistic to truly capture the nuanced roles of consumption and civic life in contemporary society.

- As the case of freecycle illustrates, individuals brought together around consumption acts can have a positive relationship with both consumption and civic life.
- The ultimate effect of alternative consumption communities like freecycle on consumer or civic culture, however, is yet to be realized.
- By engaging in alternative forms of consumption while simultaneously holding antimaterialist and anti-brand-conscious values, by engaging in political consumption, and by participating in civic life, downshifters may ultimately serve as "moral agents" (Shi 1985) who, through their behavior, challenge the consumer culture from within.

Mobilizing Consumers to Take Responsibility for Global Social Justice

Michele Micheletti, Karlstad University; and Dietlind Stolle, McGill University

Background

This article studies the antisweatshop movement's involvement in global social justice responsibility-taking. The study shows that the movement actors view the role of consumers in four different ways:

- support group for other causes,
- critical mass of shoppers,
- agent of corporate change, and
- ontological force for societal change.

Government Inaction

Government inaction on global social justice responsibility is of central interest in political science.
- Existing political institutions charged with caring for the world are not proving that they can successfully take on global problems.
- Even if good laws are in place, governments in developing countries for different reasons may not have the capability or willingness to prosecute transnational garment corporations for wrongdoings.

Garment Industry

In weakly regulated settings as in global garment manufacturing, corporate conduct frequently creates social injustice and environmental problems.
- Corporate conduct has been shown to be harmful but not necessarily illegal and, therefore, not really solvable through law.
- These developments show the difficulty in applying conventional responsibility models because their logic of accountability assumes
  - a governmental regulatory framework, and
  - an intimate link between problem cause and problem solving that allows government and citizens to bring wrongdoers to court and be sanctioned and forced to right their wrongs.

Overcoming Weaknesses

Weaknesses in the conventional responsibility model and disappointment with the World Trade Organization's (WTO's) policy on free trade have led the antisweatshop movement to developing new ways to fill the responsibility vacuum created by government and corporate inaction.
- Movement actors may use public law and prod governments to enact better laws.
- For the antisweatshop movement, the most important strategy is to target global capitalism and logo corporations.

Antisweatshop Cause

Old and new civil society teamed up in the antisweatshop cause. The movement globally includes more than one hundred organizations.
- Noteworthy is the less common cooperation between unions and consumers, as illustrated by
  - the UNITE! (Union of Needle, Industrial, and Technical Employees) and the National Consumers League's Stop Sweatshop campaign that reached out to more than 50 million, and
  - the coalition of the AFL-CIO, UNITE!, and students that led to the founding of United Students Against Sweatshops (USAS).
- The need to develop innovative tactics and solutions for global social responsibility-taking is giving new life to social justice-oriented old civil society, which has been out of touch with younger generations.

Consumer Role

What unites the heterogeneous organizations into a movement is their agreement that the common goal is improved workers' rights in the global garment industry where consumers can play key roles.

- For unions, consumers are supporters that help them to solve sweatshop problems through increased unionization.
- International humanitarian organizations and USAS (United Students against Sweatshops) want to use consumer practice to promote the development of a market for sweat-free goods and indirectly influence corporate practice.
  - Critical mass shopping is an important step toward a more equitable world—mobilized consumers can "use their purchasing power to tilt the balance, however slightly, in favour of the poor" (Oxfam International 2006).
- New consumer thinking about consumption can shift present power alliances, shake up governments, and force corporations to change.

Sports   Targeting big sports is increasingly important for the movement.
- Millions of people follow these high-media-profile events, which anti-sweatshop actors use to play on the virtues of fair play and fair competition associated with sports and which make sportswear companies easy targets.

Effectiveness   Measuring effectiveness is very difficult when activism, as in the present case, is (1) controversial and understudied; (2) not solely collectively organized; (3) not delimited to one target, issue, and time frame; and (4) focused on corporations that, unlike many governments, are not required to reveal important information for scholarly assessments.
- The critics are right when they say that high visibility and recognition of sweatshop problems and even a mobilized consumer do not automatically lead to corporate change.
- However, ongoing research finds that corporations are developing more antisweatshop-friendly policies and practices as a consequence of movement pressure.

Conclusion   To succeed, the movement must continue to mobilize consumers as supporters, as critical shopping mass, as a spearhead force of corporate change, and as ontological agents of deeper structural societal change.

Political Brands and Consumer Citizens: The Rebranding of Tony Blair

Margaret Scammell, London School of Economics and Political Science

Background   This article describes how and why branding is used in politics, focusing in particular on the rebranding of Tony Blair in 2005.
- It argues that branding is the new form of political marketing.
- Branding is now the hallmark of marketed parties and candidates.
- It is a demonstration that we are moving from mass media model to a consumer model of political communication.

Branding   The peculiar property of the brand, as distinct from the product, is that it is
                      not under the sole authorship of the owner companies.
                      • Ultimately, the brand is "only as good as the grapevine says it is."
                      • The customer or voter contribution is known as brand equity.

Brand Research   The task of brand research lies in discovering how differentiators operate in
                      consumers' perceptions and in finding patterns of differentiation.
                      • While brand differentiators emerge from multiple and diverse experi-
                        ences and psychological associations, they often work at a low level of con-
                        sumer attention.
                      • The skill of brand research is to make explicit that which is normally unex-
                        pressed and to convert it into a prioritized order that can assist brand
                        development and promotion.

Rebranding   Reconnecting Tony Blair with disaffected voters prior to the 2005 election
Tony Blair   offers a sharp illustration of the centrality of brand thinking in politics.
                      • Charles Travail, branding consultant and cofounder of Promise consul-
                        tancy, argued that Labour was a "premium brand"—a high-cost, high-service
                        product that, precisely because it raised consumer expectations to high
                        levels, was vulnerable to credibility problems.
                        • It was decided a new perspective was needed on the New Labour brand.
                        • Promise summarized the emotional experiences of Blair under three
                          broad headings: "you've left me," "you've become too big for your
                          boots," and "you need to reflect on what you've done and change."
                      • Women's anger towards Blair stemmed from perceptions of Blair's patron-
                        izing tone and self-justificatory response to criticism.
                      • Promise suggested the rebranding of New Labour as "progressive real-
                        ists": passionate, friendly, and inclusive for the benefit of all.
                        • It needed to show strength in depth by promoting a greater range of
                          spokespeople.
                        • It needed to emphasize through public services ("this brand is about
                          we, not *me*") and communications that it was "in touch."

Political   Branding as a concept and research method has both particular and general
Branding Value   value for campaigners as demonstrated in the Blair "reconnection strategy."
                      • The general thrust of Promise's recommendations was to demonstrate
                        that the party was still in touch and listening.
                      • New Labour needed to change tack and reestablish "Tough Tony" as the
                        listening, caring, in-touch leader that target voters thought he was when
                        they first elected him.
                      • The crucial added value of branding is that it provides a conceptual struc-
                        ture to link advertising insight into all aspects of the brand, positioning,
                        development, and promotion, and unlike advertising, it is not wedded to
                        a particular form of communication.

                      NOTE: The permanent (continuous) campaign focuses on the instruments
                      of media politics; the brand concept uncovers the underlying strategic con-
                      cerns of efforts to maintain voter loyalty through communication designed to
                      provide reassurance, clear differentiation from rivals, consistency of values,
                      and emotional connection with voters' values and visions of the good life.

*Consumer
Communication
Model*

Below are a few preliminary conclusions of the consequences of consumer
politics:

- The mass-media-dominated, agenda-setting, advertising-driven model of
  political campaigning, while far from dead, is in decline.
- Political brand equity has shallow roots and is easily buffeted. This is a
  striking difference from commercial branding where much of the effort is
  directed at retaining the loyalty of existing customers.

NOTE: Branding is not easily categorized as a force for either good or ill. It
does not, any more than any other marketing technique in politics, supply
single-route solutions. Its research results, like any other, must be interpreted and negotiated by the relevant political actors. Its application, as for
any commercial brand, will be shaped by consideration of the environment,
the structural, social, and cultural factors which affect people's choices.

Logo Logic: The Ups and Downs of
Branded Communication

W. Lance Bennett and Taso Lagos, University of Washington

Background

Attacking corporate brands is not in itself a new thing for activists.

- Labor unions have long promoted boycotts and "buycotts" to use consumers to discipline the labor policies of companies.
- NGOs and activist groups have also used campaigns to get corporations
  such as Nestle to stop offending practices.
- Activists are learning to tap into personal identification with brands and to
  recognize the importance of lifestyles as the organizers of personal meaning in everyday life—using the often negative publicity about the brand to
  develop political relationships with corporations.

*New Ways to
Connect with
Issues*

Citizens in postindustrial societies are detaching from parties and group-based
memberships and finding new ways to connect more directly with issues that
impact how they live their personal lives.

- If Starbucks coffee can be associated with the destruction of bird habitat,
  consumers can be brought to the issue in ways that avoid conventional
  political action, yet express personal values.
- A sustained public challenge to an otherwise strong lifestyle brand may
  produce a response from the company.
- The brand is the key because, increasingly, what is being sold by corporations is less the product than the brand image.

*Digital
Communication*

The advance of digital communication technologies enables activists, at a low
cost, to "Be the Media," as the slogan for Indymedia puts it.

- Branded messages cross diverse social networks more easily than conven-
  tional political content.
- The viral transmission, network-jumping, and media boundary-crossing of
  Jonah Peretti's famous Nike sweatshop culture jam has become legendary.
- In many cases, branded messages may be picked up as humor, consumer
  news, or business stories about troubled companies.

- Similarly, hard-to-sell messages about labor conditions in foreign factories become easier to deliver when simplified and paired with a brand that already travels far and wide (e.g., Nike-sweatshop).

Behavior
Change

The ultimate goal of much of this communication is to use consumer power to pressure companies and industries to change their behaviors.
- Getting companies to mouth the words of social responsibility is one thing, but evaluating their actual practices is something else.
- Even when companies cooperate, activists must find resources to conduct effective monitoring and certification of compliance.
- In short, there is a long chain of political relationships between getting the attention of consumers and using that attention to develop effective industry standards and certification systems that work.

Problems

Despite encouraging developments in industries from food, to fashion, to forest products, there are also problems inherent in using logo campaigns to leverage nongovernmental regulatory schemes.
- Logo campaigns may also send mixed messages due to lack of coordination among different organizations.
- The lack of (governance) mechanisms may result in the proliferation of different and sometimes competing standards systems.
- Where this makes for confusing signals to consumers, the chain of communication power driving these systems may be broken.

Conclusion

While branding communication may help messages travel, do those messages actually raise consumer awareness about the politics beyond the brands?
- On the plus side, the growth of certification systems seems clear—the steady growth of Fair Trade sales is an example.
- The story becomes a bit less clear when we consider the diversity of certification systems and issue frames that may end up confusing the very consumers whose continuing demand is so important to the effectiveness and growth of the process itself.
- In the absence of institutional support, the viability of many systems depends on finding the resources to pay for the monitoring and certification of corporate compliance, and to expand markets for certified goods so that companies may eventually self-regulate on grounds that it is simply good for business.
- The grand dilemma is that logo campaigns and culture jamming may win public attention and success at some levels, but many other links in the process must be joined to create a successful system for producing "clean" clothes or "just" coffee.

Digital Renaissance: Young Consumer and Citizen?

Claes H. de Vreese, University of Amsterdam

Background

This article explores the relationship between Internet use among young people, their political consumption, and their political participation.
- The study widens the notion of online civic and political engagement and includes measures of active and passive forms of participation.

- The research results demonstrate the importance of the Internet for political activities for young people.
- They also show that most online activities (ranging from news use, peer communication, and consumption to online service use) are positively related to political participation. It is shown that the young online consumer is also politically active.

The Internet The Internet offers a vast opportunity to be politically engaged: searching for information, at your discretion, from your preferred source, at your preferred time, and in your preferred mode.

- The Internet thus increases the opportunities for individuals to be part of civic and political discussion and for becoming informed.
- The Internet provides potential for youths who are often politically engaged at local levels and in untraditional forms of participation.
- Digital modes of political participation include forums, polls, discussion groups, or organizing a Web site on a civic or political issue.

NOTE: Based on findings suggesting that some young people tend to act as active Internet "inter-actors" and multitaskers, we expect that online activity, in general, is positively related to online political participation.

Results In the investigation of how media use relates to political participation among young people, we see the following:

- News consumption in both traditional and online media is positively related to political participation.
- Use of online services (such as e-banking), keeping updated with clubs and associations, as well as consumption of entertainment products, are all significantly related to our dependent variables.
- We can confirm that interactive online communication is positively related to political participation.
- As expected, the explanatory value of Internet use exceeds the explanatory value of "traditional media use" for understanding variation in political engagement and participation.

Discussion This article set out to investigate the relationship between Internet use among young people and their "political consumption" and political participation.

- First, it found that use of news and current affairs media, both offline and online, is generally positively related to online political engagement and participation for young people but that online news use is a stronger predictor for online participation.
- The study also shows that it is not the time spent online (or with another medium) that matters but rather the activities undertaken.
- Online communication, use of digital services, and being part of online networks and communities were all found to be positively related to political participation.
- Our findings corroborate the observation that social networks matter but very importantly point out that *online* social networking and interactivity with others is also good for political participation.
- The study found robust positive relationships between diverse uses of the Internet, including services and consumption, and various measures of engagement and participation.

Q
R
S

- Among young people, communicating online and making use of online services correlate strongly, significantly, and robustly with online political participation (such as, for example, taking part in online polls, online petitions, email letters to the editor, etc.).
- All of this suggests that a specific kind of "digital citizenship" is observable. Civic-mindedness, digital political participation, consumption, and online social networking can go hand in hand.

Political Consumerism: How Communication and Consumption Orientations Drive "Lifestyle Politics"

Dhavan V. Shah, Douglas M. McLeod, Eunkyung Kim,
Sun Young Lee, Melissa Gotlieb, Shirley S. Ho, and Hilde Breivik,
University of Wisconsin–Madison

Background

In this article, research results demonstrate how communication practices and consumption orientations work together to influence political consumerism beyond previously delineated factors.

- Boycotting is part of a broad array of behaviors that are shaped by a desire to express and support political and ethical perspectives.
- The politics of consumption is central to a large number of modern social movements, including but not limited to World Trade Organization (WTO) protests, fair-trade advocacy, and antisweatshop activism.
- Such political consumerism deserves special attention because it involves a much larger cross-section of the citizenry and has come to structure a wide range of consumer decisions.

Political Consumerism

Political consumerism may provide people with an alternative mode to engage with public issues outside of conventional political and civic behaviors such as voting or volunteering.

- Consumers seek to hold companies and governments responsible for the manner in which products are produced, as well as for the nature of social and environmental consequences of this production.
- They expand narrow definitions of political participation.
- Political consumerism has been linked to factors known to explain political participation such as religiosity, partisanship, and government trust, but it is also associated with postmaterialism and a sense of moral obligation (i.e., lifestyle politics).

Mass Media Effects

The effects of mass media on participatory behaviors are typically not only direct but operate through factors such as political talk and procivic attitudes.

- The effect of both traditional and online news media use on civic participation is mediated by political talk among citizens.

- The research findings illustrate the role news plays in prompting political talk and the implications of talk for political action.

Discussion   Historians and cultural theorists have long asserted that consumer behavior is an expression of political concerns and social preferences—social scientists have only begun to explore the factors that contribute to political consumerism.

- This research observes direct and mediated relationships with dispositional factors, communication variables, and consumption orientations—confirming some of what is known about this practice while adding substantially to our understanding of the factors that drive "lifestyle politics."
- The consistency seen across both static and change models largely confirms the theoretical model of mediated effects of information seeking variables on this economic form of political behavior.
- However, media use may also have some suppressive effects by reducing the desire to protect others from harmful messages.
- These results demonstrate how communication practices and consumption orientations work together to influence political consumerism beyond previously delineated factors.
  - In particular, information seeking through conventional and online news sources appears to encourage orientations toward politics and society—namely, greater frequency of political talk and more pronounced concern about the environment.
  - These two factors, in turn, encourage political consumerism, along with the sizable effects of advertising paternalism.
- The relationship between media consumption and advertising paternalism complicates this dynamic, with habitual entertainment television viewing and conventional news use both decreasing ad paternalism and indirectly suppressing political consumerism.

NOTE: Thus, media use may both encourage and discourage political consumerism through indirect effects on political talk and consumption orientations.

Conclusion   These findings have important implications for research on the intersection of consumer and civic culture.

- Consumer-citizens view the economic realm as a meaningful, day-to-day manner in which to advance their deeper concerns.
- This may reflect anti-institutionalism, as Stolle and colleagues (2005) asserted, though the authors find little evidence of that here. Instead, they find political consumerism to be a more dynamic behavioral response to contemporary information and the orientations that are a consequence of exposure to news.
  - This underscores the importance of communication factors in political consumerism and "lifestyle politics."
- Moreover, political consumption may be a more expedient way of expressing dissatisfaction than protesting in the streets, especially since companies are increasingly responsive to such efforts.

Q
R
S

Citizens, Consumers, and the Good Society

Michael Schudson, University of California, San Diego

Background

There is reason to be wary of the tradition of moralizing about consumption—it offers a narrow and misleading view of consumer behavior as well as an absurdly romanticized view of civic behavior.

- A great deal of consumer behavior is anything but selfish. Rather, it is a form of gift-giving.
- There are reasons to believe that the contrast between consumer and citizen is neither as flattering to political choice nor as favorable to a strong civic life as those who uphold the distinction may imagine.
- Five reasons complicate the consumer/citizen contrast:
  - First, sometimes consumer choices are political in even the most elevated understandings of the term.
  - Second, consumer behavior is more than just the moment of choosing; it is a complex set of activities, some of which enable, enact, and engender democratic values.
  - Third, sometimes political choices are, and have long been, consumer-like, that is, self-centered, intended to maximize individual or group (class, ethnic, racial, or religious) utility rather than to consider the public good.
  - Fourth, sometimes political behavior in a democracy is not a morally elevating education in democratic values.
  - Finally, consumer and civic behavior and styles are in flux—critics in 2006 should not be trapped with models of citizenship or consumption that are out of date.

Consumer Choice Can Be Political

Consumer choice being political is the easiest point to make based on thinking about boycotted grapes to support the United Farm Workers union, or deciding to drive a hybrid car to help conserve the earth's resources.

- Even when consumption is not intended to be political, it may have important consequences that are politicizing rather than distracting.
- Far from being distracting, consumption can create the conditions for political action and mobilization.

Consumerism Can Serve Democracy

In both consumer behavior and civic action, individuals enact social rituals that instruct them and others in a set of expectations and values.

- These expectations and values either enhance democracy or endanger it; it all depends on what kind of consumer behavior or civic action we are talking about.
  - Private people come together safely in public, commercial spaces to talk and to socialize around food and drink.
  - McDonald's will not turn China into a democracy, but it is perfectly apt to recognize it as a small Trojan horse.

Political Behavior

Political behavior, in terms of its moral framework, may be a particular kind of consumer behavior.

- Voters often look at political candidates in terms of benefits and costs they might inflict on them through raising taxes.

- This is not to say that voters are simply selfish or self-interested—however, self-interest is frequently politically motivating and mobilizing.
- The activist liberals want ordinary people to vote their interests, in an informed way, even though the activists themselves may be seeking to serve others more than they want to serve themselves.

Political
Practice

Political practice is often not virtuous or public-spirited.
- The motives of political actors are ordinarily mixed: political motivation is about the narcissistic pleasure of winning, of being in the public eye, of dispensing favors, of ironing out a compromise others were unable to achieve, the thrill of seizing the moment or seeing the opportunity to untie a political knot that stymied others, the pulse-quickening excitement of competition and of victory.

Different
Behaviors

The distinction between citizen and consumer remains a stand-in for the difference between the self-centered and the public-spirited.
- The above can be misleading—both consumer choices and political choices can be public-spirited or not, respectful of others or not.
- In the ordinary act of politics, the circle of people one *should* be thinking about should extend to the boundary of whatever polity one is acting in— if not further.
  - Politics feels tense and dangerous because it is performed in the midst of, and because of significant conflict with others.
- Consuming feels good not only because it may provide material pleasures but because it is enacted within a comfortable social circle.

NOTE: We need to determine what the political act and the consuming act really are, and what variety of things they are or have been in different times and places and civic circumstances.

UBIQUITOUS MEDIA:

ASIAN TRANSFORMATIONS
Culture in Process.

UMAT 2007

IIIS Tokyo University/*Theory, Culture & Society*
25th Anniversary Conference
Tokyo University 13–16 July 2007

Today media are increasingly ubiquitous: they become increasingly embedded in material objects and environments, bodies and clothing. Media mobility means greater connectivity but also great surveillance.

To theorize about today's world, we need to theorize media. Media deal in material images, but also symbols and the transcendental. They are ubiquitous in art, religion and our use of language.

We need to address the question of the relationship of media practices to politics: the power of transnational media, intellectual property rights, openness of access and the generation of informed publics.

The shifting global geopolitics raises the question of 'ubiquitous Asia:' new trans-Asian culture industries, social movements and activism.

Plenary Speakers

Rem Koolhaas OMA
Rotterdam

Mark Hansen University of Chicago
Katherine Hayles UCLA

Ken Sakamura Tokyo University
Barbara Stafford University of Chicago

Friedrich Kittler Humboldt University
Akira Asada (Kyoto University)

Bernard Stiegler Centre Pompidou, Paris

Call for Papers

Paper and round table submissions as well as offers to organise additional sessions welcome

Please contact **info@u-mat.org and visit http://www.u-mat.org/**

Theory
Culture &
Society

東京大学大学院情報学環
Interfaculty Initiative in Information Studies
The University of Tokyo